THE ART of TIME TRAVEL

THE ART OF TIME TRAVEL

PETER MCKINSTRY

THE *DOCTOR WHO* ART AND DESIGN OF PETER MCKINSTRY

BBC
BOOKS

CONTENTS

FOREWORD

Oh, this book really is time travel!

It took me back 20 years. Before Peter Mckinstry arrived, the art department for Series 1 was stuffed into an old catering college. Still with a faint smell of cabbage and beans. It was directly opposite BBC Llandaff, and you'd risk crossing a motorway to get there. Then you'd enter a room, and I mean a room singular, which was... well, the opposite of the TARDIS. Smaller on the inside. Designers jam-packed into a tiny space. Drawings pinned and overlapping on every wall. It was a bristling, inky chaos, like the inside of an artist's mind (Peter will agree, a terrifying place to be).

But the joy of it! Artwork summoning monsters and planets and sonics into life. I'd sit in there for as long as I could, sometimes unable to believe that we were really making this show. Until Ed Thomas, my wonderful mate, the big, beaming Welsh boss of all these imaginations, would say 'Get out, lazybones, we're busy!'

Peter arrived as we expanded into the second year, and it was wonderful, getting to know him: his mind, his designs, his ideas. Turning these pages brought jolts of memory. Mainly, the horror of the BT connection in my Cardiff flat, which meant a drawing would take half an hour to download! And there are things in this book that I'd forgotten, first-draft ideas which never made it to the screen – look, there was once a Torchwood Cross! The Coral City of Malcassairo was a genuine loss. The Shadow

Proclamation Hangar, damn it, we had such plans for that! (In fact, I drew the Inside of the Hangar, look, here it is, no wonder we could never afford it.)

And there are things in here I never knew. The Sontarans had pips? Lieutenant, Commander, General, really? Wait a minute, Peter, I have notes!

I knew Peter was a great artist, but I didn't realise until now that he's such a great writer. The best part about this wonderful book is how personal Peter makes it. Because you know full well, Faithful Reader, that *Doctor Who* isn't just some TV show. It's woven into our lives, it's our mums and dads and childhoods, it's our hopes and dreams, and some of us were lucky enough to have those dreams come true. For Peter, it led him to the love of his life (that's Chris, not the Torchwood magnaclamp). And when the complete history of this show is written, nothing will be more important than that.

I love this book as much as I loved those days we spent working together. The laughs, the intensity, the hours, the deadlines, the budgets, the losses. The absolute triumph.

Thank you, Peter. I stand by what I said, all those years ago. You are brilliant.

Russell T Davies

12 May 2025 (still sitting at the same desk, but with a better connection!)

INTRODUCTION: INTO THE TARDIS

There's an art to time travel. And no, you don't need a TARDIS for it.

You just need an old photo, a well-worn memory... maybe a dodgy haircut or two. It's amazing how it all comes flooding back: recalling key moments can unlock lots of others, proving that the events from years ago aren't truly lost. If we're lucky, they stay with us.

I can still picture clearly the day in late summer of 2005 when I left my job, packed up my life, handed the keys back to my landlord, and climbed into a taxi bound for the train station. The driver took one look at my luggage bursting at the seams and said, 'Big day is it? Where you off to then?'

'Wales,' I replied. 'I'm going to work on *Doctor Who*.'

He glanced at me in the rearview mirror, his eyes wide with surprise. 'You're joking! I love that show!'

'Me too!' I said, and off we went. That was it – my first step into a whole new chapter, off on the adventure of a lifetime.

SKETCHING THE FUTURE

My first memories of watching *Doctor Who* as a child weren't unusual – I'd been one of those kids who hid their eyes in gleeful terror every time the monsters showed up on telly. Not behind the sofa, mind you; I had my special red cushion that I'd peek over, then duck back under when it got too terrifying. *Doctor Who* was the absolute highlight of my Saturday nights – the Daleks, the Mandrels, all of it! The earliest terrifying, thrilling moment of childhood fear that's burned into my memory is from *Destiny of the Daleks* in September 1979: the Daleks crashing through a wall screaming 'Do not move! Do not move!' as they cornered Romana.

The show was unmissable, appointment viewing, a vital part of the evening schedules that I'd be waiting all week for. I also loved *Star Trek, Batman* and anything else that sparked my imagination with images and ideas.

Some kids would run about pretending to be Daleks – '*Ex-ter-min-ate!*' – but my response was to draw them. After every episode, there I was, at the dining table, drawing my heart out. I can still feel the wood texture of the dining table and the softness of the tablecloth under the paper I was drawing on, my legs swinging beneath me, trying to capture the magic I'd seen while it was still fresh in my mind.

Like all kids, I loved to draw. But to me it wasn't just a pastime; it was also an escape. Although we lived in a quiet village, our house was a madly busy place thanks to my six sisters. So, I used to find a quiet corner somewhere and occupied myself by reading comics and drawing.

And a cricket jumper just like Peter Davison's Doctor. I wore both with pride, as if I had pieces of the *Doctor Who* world wrapped around me.

In my room I'd sit drawing at my wooden flip-top school desk, which sloped just like the TARDIS console. I scratched the shapes of TARDIS controls into its surface with a compass, colouring them in with felt tips. I even stuck paper-plates to the Anaglypta wood-chip wallpaper in my bedroom, pretending they were the TARDIS roundels. Mum had a permanent 'what now?' expression every time she walked past.

My dad helped me to hone my illustrative skills. He was a telephone engineer by day and a superhero artist by night! Barely had he come through the door before there I was, tugging at his sleeve, begging him to draw Batman or Superman.

I'd sit by his side and watch, confused at first by the marks he was making, watching as the apparently random lines slowly became characters, like magic, coming to life before my eyes. Then he'd set me to work: 'Now it's your turn, go draw them like I showed you.' I did so, and it was his constant encouragement that spurred me to improve.

Dad was my first art teacher, and the one who taught me the most. I remember him explaining light and shade and how to transform a flat drawing into something with depth. That lesson stayed with me, and when I later repeated it in a school essay, I was asked to read it aloud to the class.

My mum was also creative, whenever she had the time. I'd come home from school to find her painting still lifes, but her specialty was knitting. She'd knit for everyone, family and friends, and when my turn came round, there was only one thing I wanted – a multicoloured scarf, like the one worn by Tom Baker's Doctor. She made it for me, bless her.

Doctor Who wasn't just a TV show, it offered year-round treats. Every Christmas, there was a new *Doctor Who* annual. My favourite parts were the behind-the-scenes stuff – the bits they don't show you on telly! And every week, there was the trusty *Doctor Who Weekly*, packed with stories and photos. Every day, I'd be in the newsagent's going, 'Is it in yet? Is it in yet?' Days early! In the end, they took pity and promised to set one aside for me each week, right along with my *2000 AD*.

I ended up with a stack of issues. I'd often sit and flip through the pages, marvelling at photos from stories shown before I was even born, featuring Doctors I'd never seen on screen! One afternoon, armed with scissors, I cut out the pin-ups and pinned them to my bedroom walls. I'd ruined some comics but now I had Ogrons and Cybermen and so many others staring down at me!

My favourite comic book artist was Dave Gibbons – still is! He drew loads of *Doctor Who Weekly* and *2000 AD* strips, and I would spend hours at my desk trying to copy his style. Much

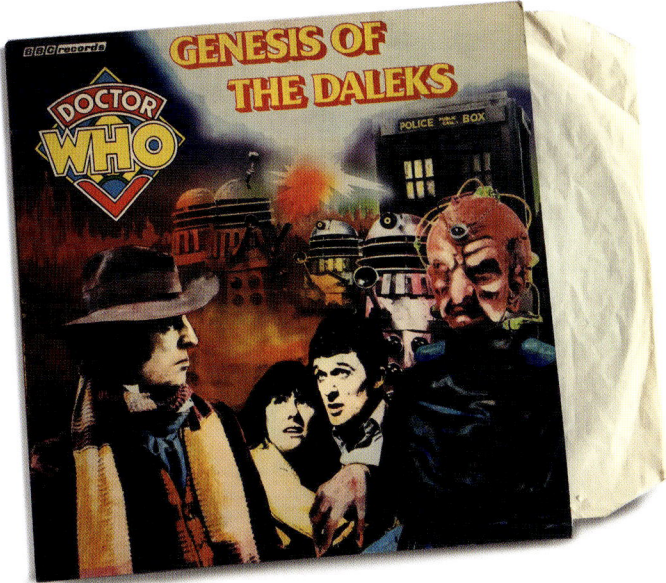

later, I managed to get my hands on a few original Gibbons *Doctor Who* comic pages. They're still hanging in my studio now, framed and magnificent, prized possessions that to this day make me feel like a fanboy whenever I look at them.

Then there were the toys! Like the TARDIS Tuner – nothing more than a radio that also made weird noises, but you couldn't tell me that! I also loved the Denys Fisher TARDIS with the magic spinning compartment inside that made action figures 'disappear'. My Fourth Doctor action figure would team up with Batman in my Batmobile, while Leela rode shotgun in Action Man's jeep.

There were talking Daleks from Palitoy in red and grey. I still have a scar on my wrist from the time I tried to find out (once and for all!) what was inside one. I don't know if you've ever tried to cut open a plastic Dalek with scissors, but it didn't work; I ended up jabbing them into my wrist. That scar is my very own Dalek battle wound, and a permanent reminder of Dalek superiority.

FROM BEHIND THE CUSHION TO BEHIND THE SCENES

These memories aren't just snippets of nostalgia; they're the building blocks of who I am today, part of my DNA. They all came flooding back when I was on that long train ride to Wales, off to join the *Doctor Who* art department.

What followed was a five-year voyage across the universe that changed me, professionally and personally. It set me on a path that would lead to my designing for other iconic projects like *Harry Potter*, *Game of Thrones* and *Star Wars*, and it introduced me to the city of Cardiff. I felt at home there straight away, and it's where I met my civil partner, Chris.

This book is a collection of the work I did as a concept designer during those years, alongside many of the illustration assignments I took on during and after. But it's more than just a portfolio. It's a statement of gratitude – for the adventure, for the opportunities, and for the people I worked with along the way.

I've included loads of sketches and concept pieces I've only recently rediscovered, plus email exchanges with the one and only Russell T Davies. Showrunner, head writer and executive producer, Russell's the creative legend behind the return of *Doctor Who*, and let me tell you, the man's got an eye for design – he was an artist before he was a writer, and his visual sense of story matches the strength of his scripting.

We discussed design choices and explored different options to bring the concepts to life before they hit the screen, tweaking things till we got them just right. Now, I've worked on all sorts of other film and TV projects since then, but that direct line of creative dialogue with the top man? Unheard of! I'll always be grateful to Russell for that, I really will.

A production like *Doctor Who* is a massive, complex affair, with teams of talented people working together under the showrunner's direction to bring the show to life. On any typical day, scenes were being shot on at least one set while others were being designed. At the same time, locations were being scouted, costumes fitted, visual effects developed,

music composed, rushes scrutinised... And then the next script would arrive, and the whole process would begin again.

While all this went on around me, I drew and drew. Spaceships and monsters, gadgets and sets, in all scales and sizes from a hundred different time periods. And through all of it, I never forgot the little kid I used to be – the one who'd sit with his pencil and pad, capturing the Doctor's latest adventure as best he could.

Often in the *Doctor Who* art department, there'd be visitors passing through: executives, competition winners or cast and crew showing their children what goes on behind the scenes. They'd be given a tour of the whole studio and would eventually arrive at my desk, where they'd stop to take in all the drawings and design printouts awaiting approval. Many of them would sit beside me for a while, and I'd show them a little of what I was working on.

I want to share with you a similar experience, but in much more depth. It's a look at the making of the show from my perspective, and an insight into the creative process that went on in my corner of the art department.

I've laid everything out for you chronologically, season by season, just as I worked on them. But like a journey in the TARDIS, expect a few time jumps! Between the main chapters, you'll find thematic collections of images from other *Doctor Who* projects I've been involved with. This is the first time all these works have been brought together in a single volume, and they're accompanied by a running commentary from my perspective.

As I was preparing this book, looking through all the old sketches and emails and everything, it really hit me. Creativity and imagination; they're like a personal time machine, aren't they? They can take you anywhere. I hope you enjoy coming along for the ride... after all, the TARDIS is much bigger on the inside. There's room for all of us.

PART 1 | SERIES 2

LAND OF DRAGONS AND DALEKS

When I began work on *Doctor Who*, on 12 August 2005, Series 1 had already aired and been a huge success. It had swiftly become essential family viewing, delighting fans of the original show while hooking a younger generation of viewers too.

I'd watched those first 13 episodes avidly. The adventures were imaginative and playful, dramatic and exciting, and for all the wonderful fantasy they felt grounded in the real world.

As Series 1 aired, I was working for Rare, the videogame developer, producing concept art for a game I'd been involved with for a couple of years. As I watched *Doctor Who* each week I'd think, 'That's what I want to be working on. That's where I should be.'

Then – plot twist! – the game I'd given two years of my life to got canned. There was just one silver lining: I'd built up a solid portfolio of concept art in the process. So, I decided to send my folio to BBC Wales speculatively, just in case there was any interest. It felt such a long shot; I didn't really expect a response. But a couple of weeks later, my phone rang and I found myself talking to Jonathan Allison, *Doctor Who*'s Art Department Production Manager. 'We received your work folio,' he informed me in a very well-spoken and upbeat voice. 'Would you be interested at all in doing some work on the next series of *Doctor Who*?' I was so stunned that it took me a couple of seconds to say, 'Yes!'

As a result of the first series's popularity, the art department I walked into was on a high; a tight-knit group of seven with a real sense of camaraderie.

Production Designer Edward Thomas was the captain steering this ship through wild waters. The production designer is responsible for shaping the whole look and visual tone of the show, overseeing the visual identity and feel of the entire series. This includes all the sets, props, and environments that bring the show's worlds to life – from alien planets and futuristic cities to accurately detailed period sets. Ed collaborated closely with the showrunner, Russell T Davies, and also involved directors, writers, and other departments to ensure the visual elements aligned with each episode's tone and themes. Given that each *Doctor Who* story is set in a different place and time, you can appreciate what a mammoth task this was.

As I joined, production on Series 2 was already underway, and filming for the episode *New Earth* was wrapping up. Unlike at Rare, the art department wasn't in a fancy building – Q2 was a standard looking office facility, which also housed a large empty space that had been turned into the shooting stage for the production of Series 1. It may have seemed unremarkable from the outside, but inside it was buzzing with energy. From the main entrance, the art department was straight upstairs in a large, brightly lit open-plan room.

At one end, Ed had his desk, piled high with paperwork, set models, and scripts. His right-hand men – Supervising Art Director, Stephen Nicholas; Assistant Supervising Art Director, James North and Production Manager, Jonathan Allison – were stationed next to him.

In the opposite corner was 'Drawing Club' – a nickname coined fondly by Construction Manager, Matthew Hywel-Davies – where myself and my fellow concept artist, Matt Savage, sat beavering away. Matt had done many of the concept designs for Series 1, including the iconic bronze revamp of the Daleks. I quickly learned that while Ed steered the art department with a firm hand on the wheel, he encouraged creative input from all his staff. The best idea always won, no matter who came up with it, and it was an environment rich with creativity and collaboration.

The centre of the room was dominated by a huge plan chest, where all the working drawings were stored. The surface of this was always in creative disarray, as it so often doubled as an impromptu meeting table where set models were reviewed, concepts discussed, problems ironed out and tea was drunk. On the other side of the plan chest was an old sofa that reminded me of the one from *The Royle Family*, usually buried under art supplies and old models.

In the far corner of the art department was a door that led out onto a long flight of metal stairs. This was the route down to the large open space where all the sets were built. At the foot of the stairs was the standing set of the TARDIS control room. (Standing sets remain in place on the studio floor because they are needed throughout the entire run of the production. The TARDIS featured in almost every episode, so while other sets for individual stories were built, filmed on, then torn down and replaced, the TARDIS interior was always standing.) Stepping onto that set for the first time through the Police Box doors really was like climbing through the TV into another world. The fact that one side of the set was wide open for cameras and lights made it even more fascinating. This was where imagination met reality, as the team took the writers' words and realised them as pure entertainment.

The first thing that struck me was the urgency of everything that was going on. This wasn't like working on a game where the release date is some distant point years in the future. Here, the clock was always ticking. Sets were being built for scenes soon to be filmed, and everyone worked to tight deadlines. The filming schedule was a fast-moving train, and the art department was frantically laying down the tracks just ahead of it.

Yet somehow, to me, it just felt like home. I instantly understood my place in this creative machine, and everything just *clicked*.

After spending the morning of my first day meeting everyone, setting up my equipment, and exploring the studio with Matt, Ed handed me a stack of scripts: early drafts for the yet-to-be-filmed Series 2 stories. This was a *very* exciting first look at episodes that wouldn't air until the following year. Tasked with doing a Design Breakdown – that is, making a note of all the design elements in the script that would need to be realised – I flopped down on the well-worn sofa and began to read. I kept a calm professional exterior, but inside, I was definitely geeking out.

It was the start of a thrilling, challenging, and incredibly rewarding journey.

WHAT IS CONCEPT ART?

I can't stress enough how vital Russell T Davies' role was as showrunner and head writer. He brought *Doctor Who* back from the dead, and without his brilliant words on the page, we'd have had nothing to draw! He was the one setting the stage for all of us.

Concept art and design brings descriptions from the script pages into their initial visual form. These images are then discussed, tweaked, and eventually approved, resulting in a final 'locked' design that represents a defined vision. Copies of this design are handed out to all departments – set builders, prop makers, visual effects and so on – so everyone's on the same page.

THE GIRL IN THE FIREPLACE

SS *MADAME DE POMPADOUR* SPACESHIP

At the top of the script pile, next in production order, was *The Girl in the Fireplace* by Steven Moffat. During my first read-through I listed all the elements that would require a concept design for approval. On page three, I found a passage that made my eyes light up:

A BEAUTIFUL STARSCAPE. OVER THIS, THE WORDS: "3000 YEARS LATER…" This time we don't pan down, we pan up – to see the underside of a spaceship hanging above us.

I quickly jotted this down in my sketchbook and continued reading. This spaceship, the SS *Madame de Pompadour*, was the subject of my first *Doctor Who* concept design. There was

no actual description of the ship, which was an early indication of how much freedom I'd often get to generate designs.

I began sketching my first ideas and an interesting shape began to emerge: a massive industrial cargo hauler, built for heavy-duty tasks in deep space. Its most distinctive feature was the large wedge-shaped sections at both the front and rear. I kept drawing into the evening, just excited to be designing a spaceship for *Doctor Who*.

After sleeping on it and rereading the script, I reflected on the way the narrative was set in two distinct worlds – the spaceship in the future and Madame de Pompadour's home in

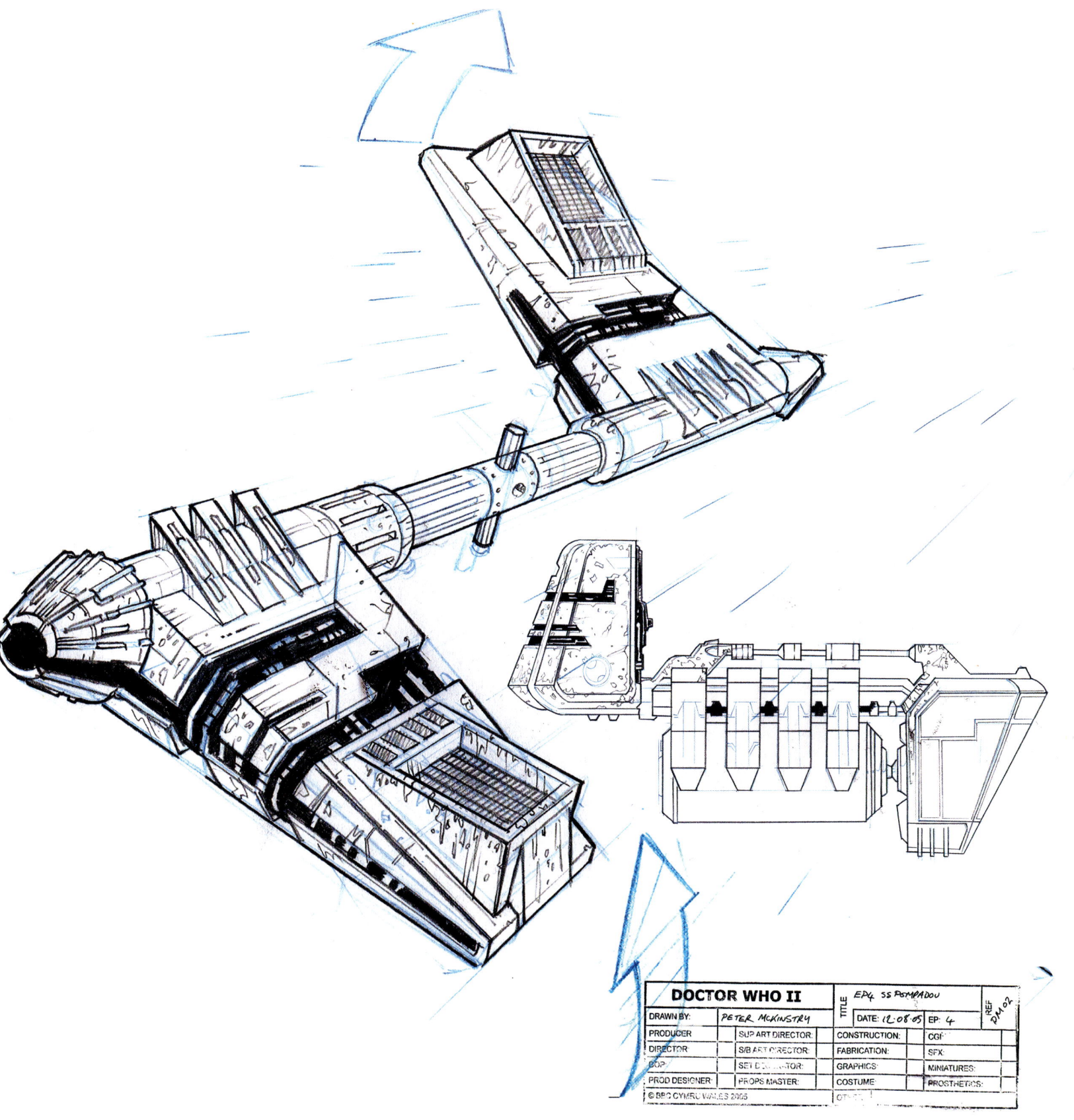

DOCTOR WHO II

DRAWN BY: PETER MCKINSTRY

TITLE: EP4 SS POMPADOU

DATE: 12·08·05   EP: 4

REF: DM02

PRODUCER	SUP ART DIRECTOR	CONSTRUCTION	CGI
DIRECTOR	S/B ART DIRECTOR	FABRICATION	SFX
DOP	SET DECORATOR	GRAPHICS	MINIATURES
PROD DESIGNER	PROPS MASTER	COSTUME	PROSTHETICS

© BBC CYMRU WALES 2005

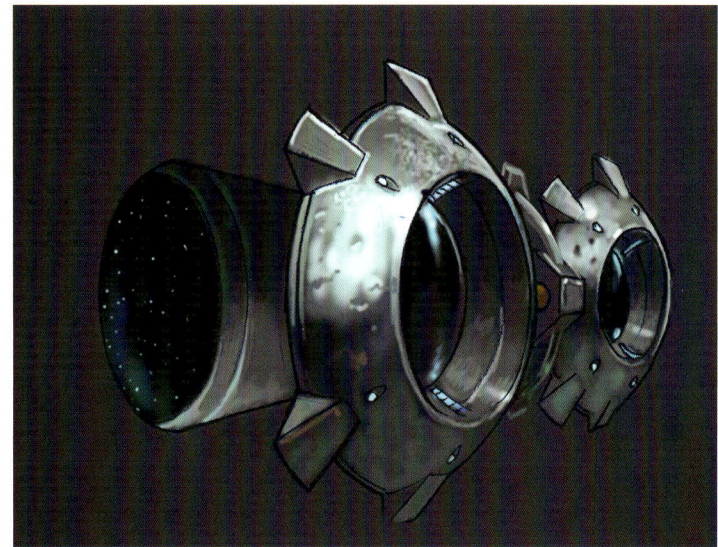

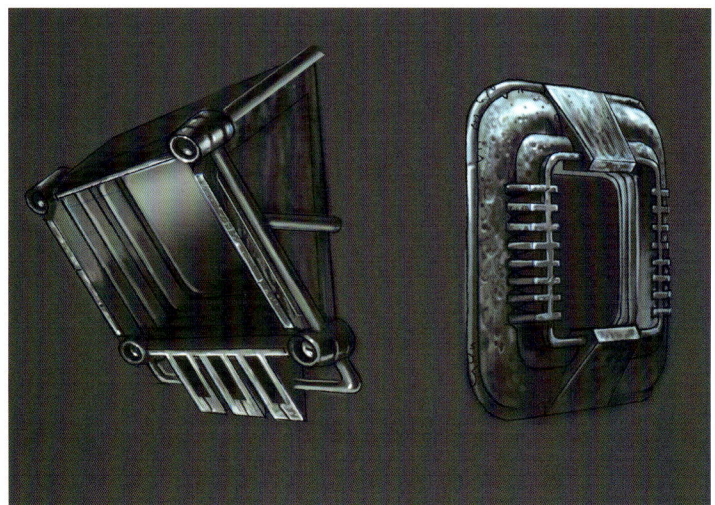

the past. This sparked a new idea, and I began playing with the placement of the wedge shapes, flipping one upside down.

That was my lightbulb moment. I started drawing a new version of the ship, the design of which would subtly mirror the structure of the story. The vessel's two opposing wedge shapes, each positioned at either end of a central spine, now wound in opposite directions, reflecting the duality of a narrative set in two different worlds. The winding movement also tied into the Clockwork Droids, which, as automated robots, were part of the ship's maintenance crew. While the ship's technology wasn't literally clockwork, it made sense for its design to evoke that winding, mechanical motion.

This approach pleased Ed, and when he presented it to Russell, it was approved as the final design. Straight away, I'd learned the importance of being able to work with a design brief as short as 'a spaceship' and come up with an original, distinctive design that also helped to tell the story.

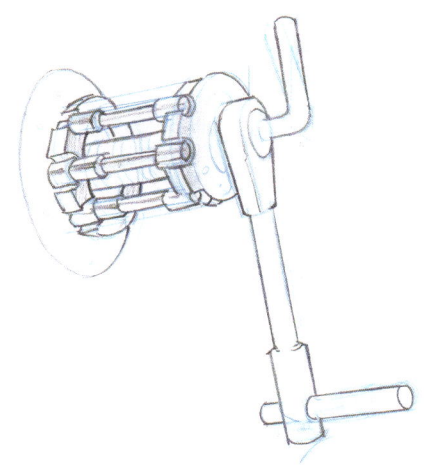

THE EYE CAM

The script vividly described the surveillance cameras on board the SS *Madame de Pompadour*:

A wall-mounted security camera buzzes to life, springs up, and looks around. It's mounted on a snake of cable and thrashes about, more like a living thing than a machine... bulging out where a lens should be, there is what appears to be a real human eye...

I set to work. My initial sketches leaned toward the grotesque, and I vividly remember the response to my first version: 'Very nice... but untransmittable!'

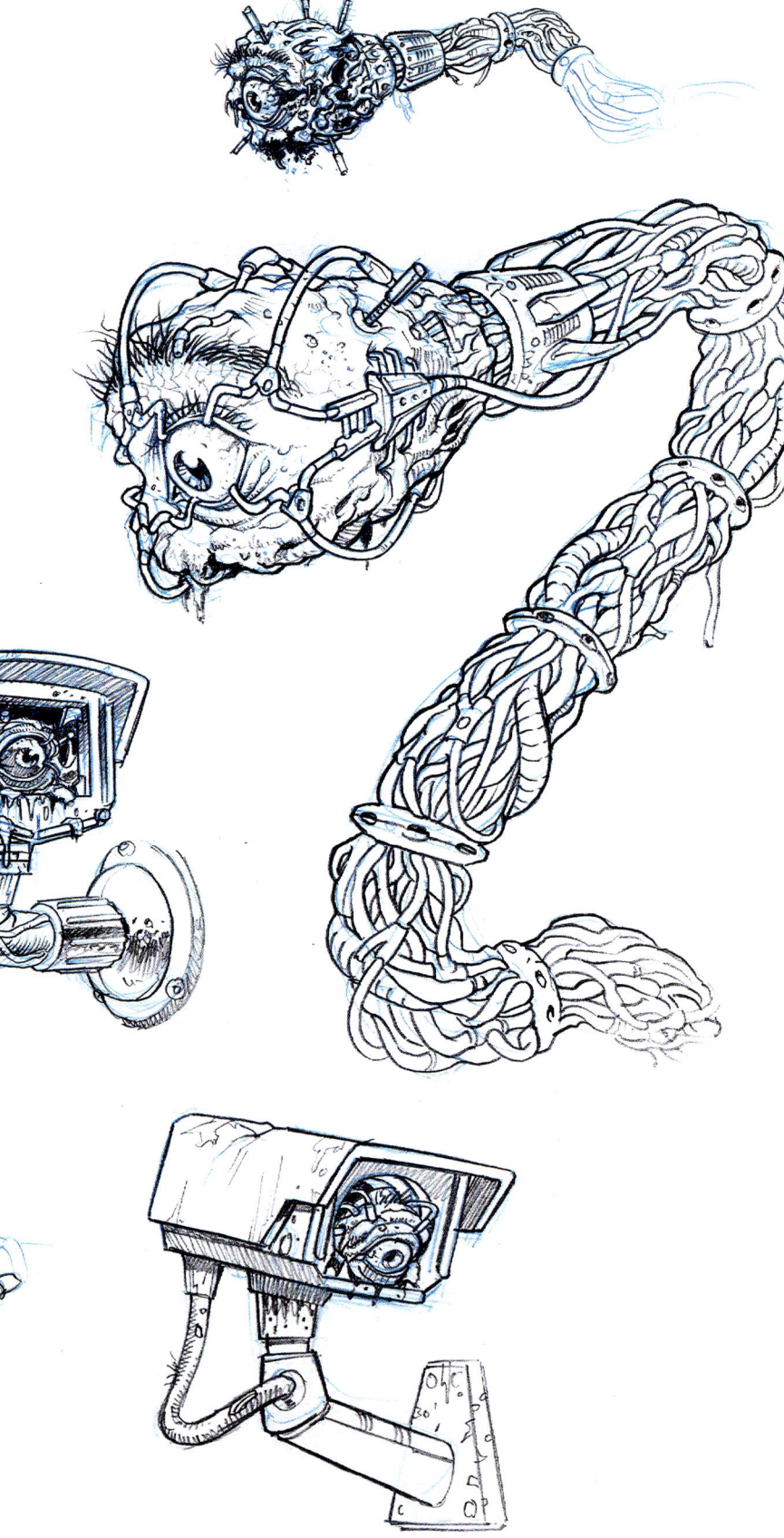

EARDUCT INCLUDED!

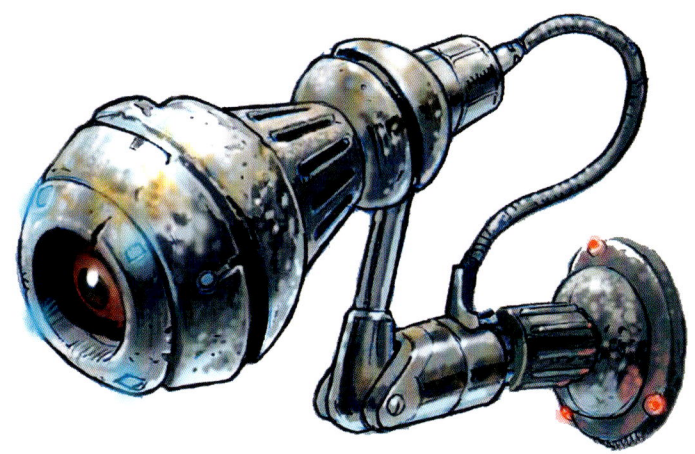

Standard surveillance mode

This feedback led to a more streamlined design. I sketched something reminiscent of the cone shape of a standard desk lamp, removing the more gruesome elements to leave just a single eyeball nestled inside a sleek, sci-fi casing. This design was approved by Russell (Ed forwarded me his response – 'Beeeauuuuutiful!') and the design was stamped as LOCKED, meaning it was ready to be turned into an actual prop.

About a week later, prop maker Mark Cordory arrived in the art department with the newly crafted Eye Cam prop, completely faithful to my design. I held it carefully by the 'metallic' rod that connected the main section to the base and made eye contact with the eyeball. And that's when the prop snapped in two!

'Just as well I made copies!' Mark quipped. It was a valuable lesson: even though props may look robust, they're often incredibly delicate!

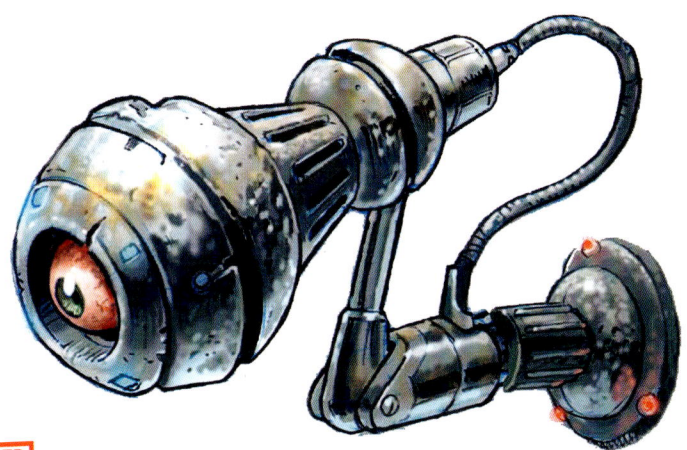

Alert mode

LOCKED
7.09.05

DOCTOR WHO II		TITLE EYE-CAM	REF PM
DRAWN BY: PETER MCKINSTRY		DATE 17.08.05 EP. 4	11
PRODUCER:	SUP ART DIRECTOR:	CONSTRUCTION:	CGI:
DIRECTOR:	S/B ART DIRECTOR:	FABRICATION:	SFX:
DOP:	SET DECORATOR:	GRAPHICS:	MINIATURES:
PROD DESIGNER:	PROPS MASTER:	COSTUME:	PROSTHETICS:
© BBC CYMRU WALES 2005		OTHER:	

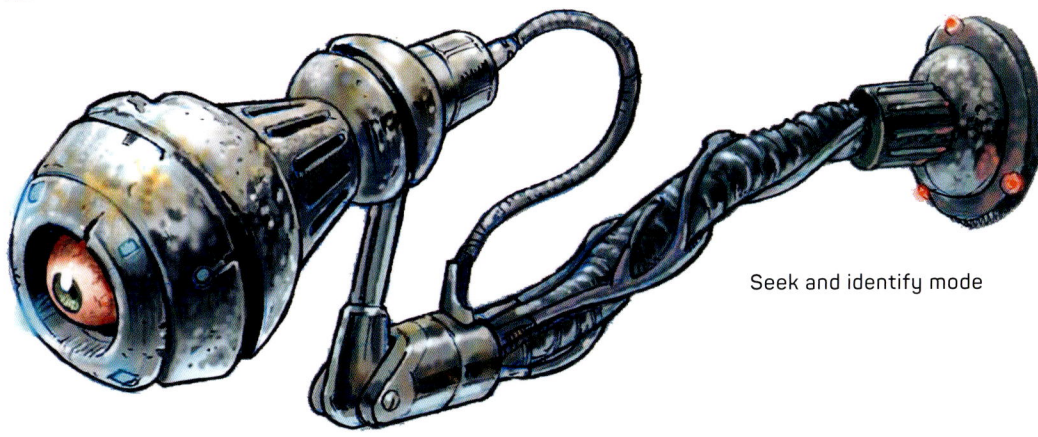

Seek and identify mode

THE HEART OF THE SHIP

The next piece of concept design was guided by the following script passage:

ROSE's POV. Gleaming tech machinery surrounds her— flashing lights, glass rods, wires—a mass of futuristic equipment. In the middle, encased in glass and crudely wired to the rest of the tech, is something eerily familiar: a human organ.

The Clockwork Droids had harvested a literal human heart to power the ship, as a grim part of their warped logic of repair. When designing this element, I decided to place the heart at a slight distance within the machinery, rather than having it immediately visible upon opening the hatch. It's a 'less is more' effect – we see the heart, but it's small on-screen, leaving much to the imagination. This also adds depth to the ship, creating the illusion that the ship's bulkheads house layers of hidden workings and machinery.

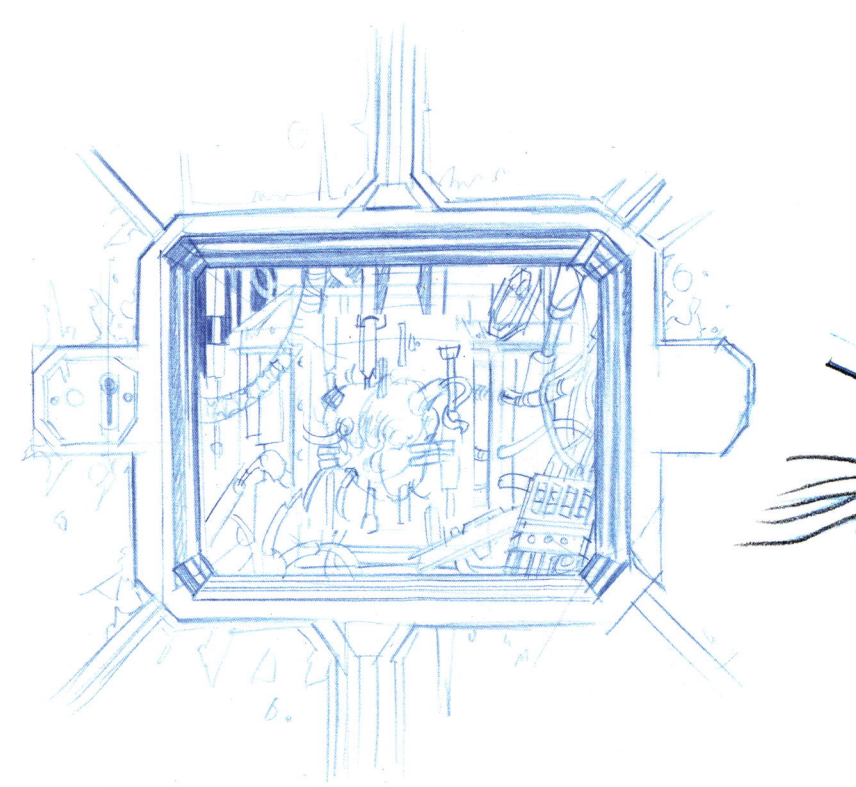

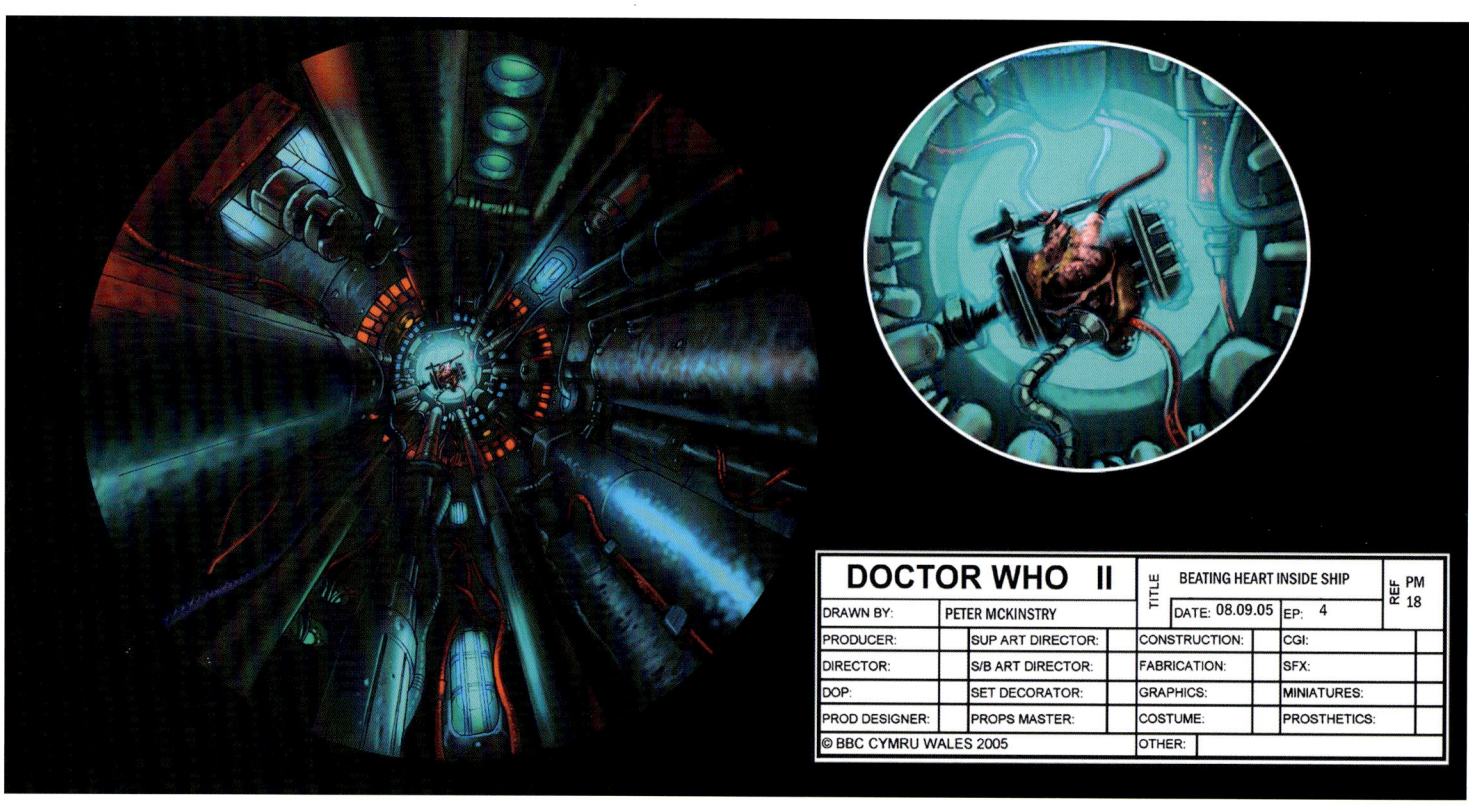

DOCTOR WHO II		TITLE	BEATING HEART INSIDE SHIP		REF	PM 18
DRAWN BY:	PETER MCKINSTRY		DATE: 08.09.05	EP: 4		
PRODUCER:		SUP ART DIRECTOR:	CONSTRUCTION:	CGI:		
DIRECTOR:		S/B ART DIRECTOR:	FABRICATION:	SFX:		
DOP:		SET DECORATOR:	GRAPHICS:	MINIATURES:		
PROD DESIGNER:		PROPS MASTER:	COSTUME:	PROSTHETICS:		
© BBC CYMRU WALES 2005			OTHER:			

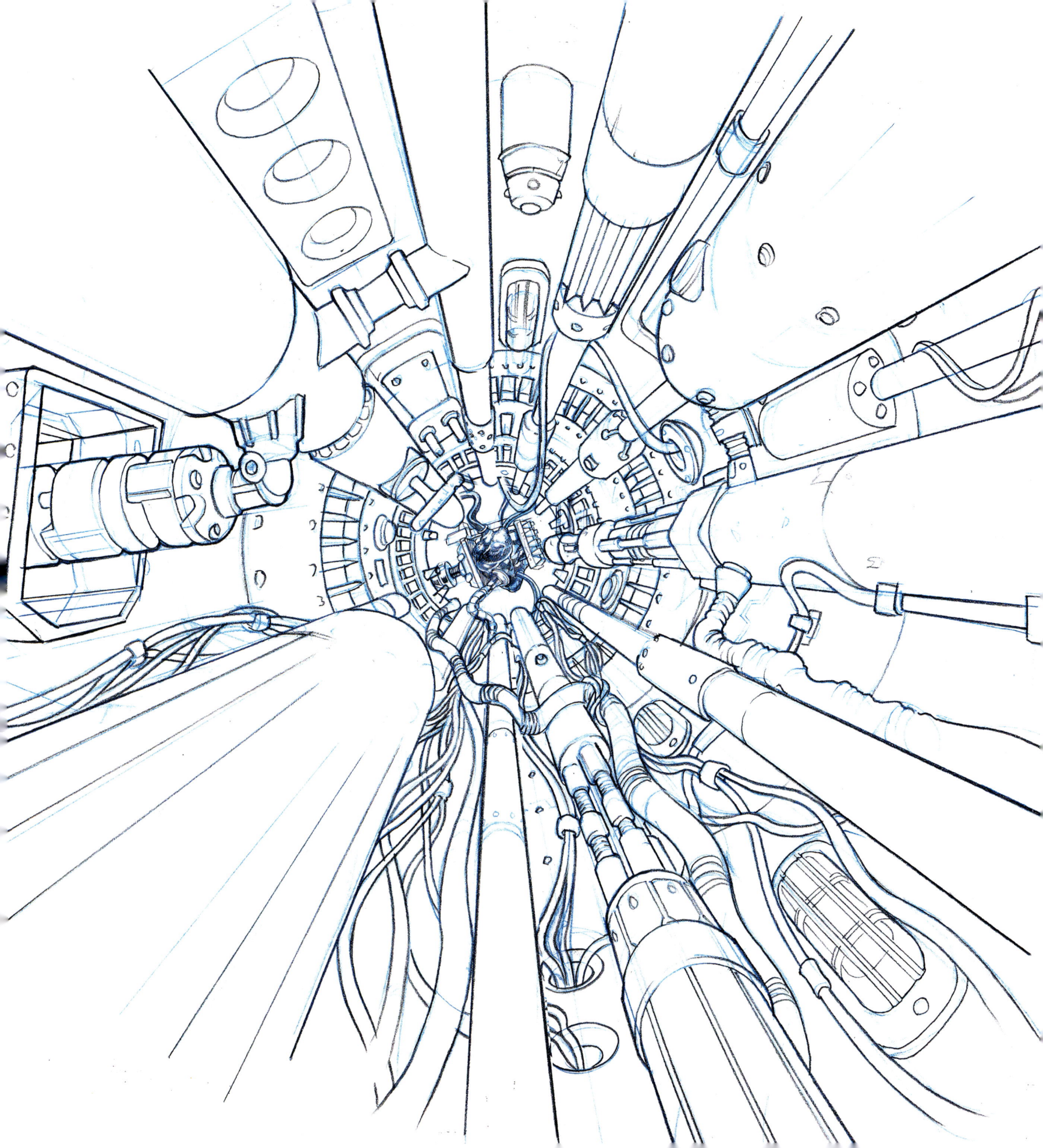

MED BEDS

CLOSE ON ROSE.
Unconscious, stirring... Wider
angle: she is fastened to
a sloping table by loops of
metal round her limbs.

When we see these beds
aboard the SS *Madame de
Pompadour*, they are being
used by the Clockwork
Droids to restrain Rose.
I designed them to be
consistent with the overall
aesthetic of the ship, so
they feature both metallic
surfaces and soft, glowing
lights. I added three
rectangular blocks to the
design, a simple design motif
to match the ship's exterior.

Once the design was
locked and the beds were
constructed, they had to be
locked away until needed
– too many people took
advantage of them to relax
between takes!

DOCTOR WHO II

SLOPING TABLES

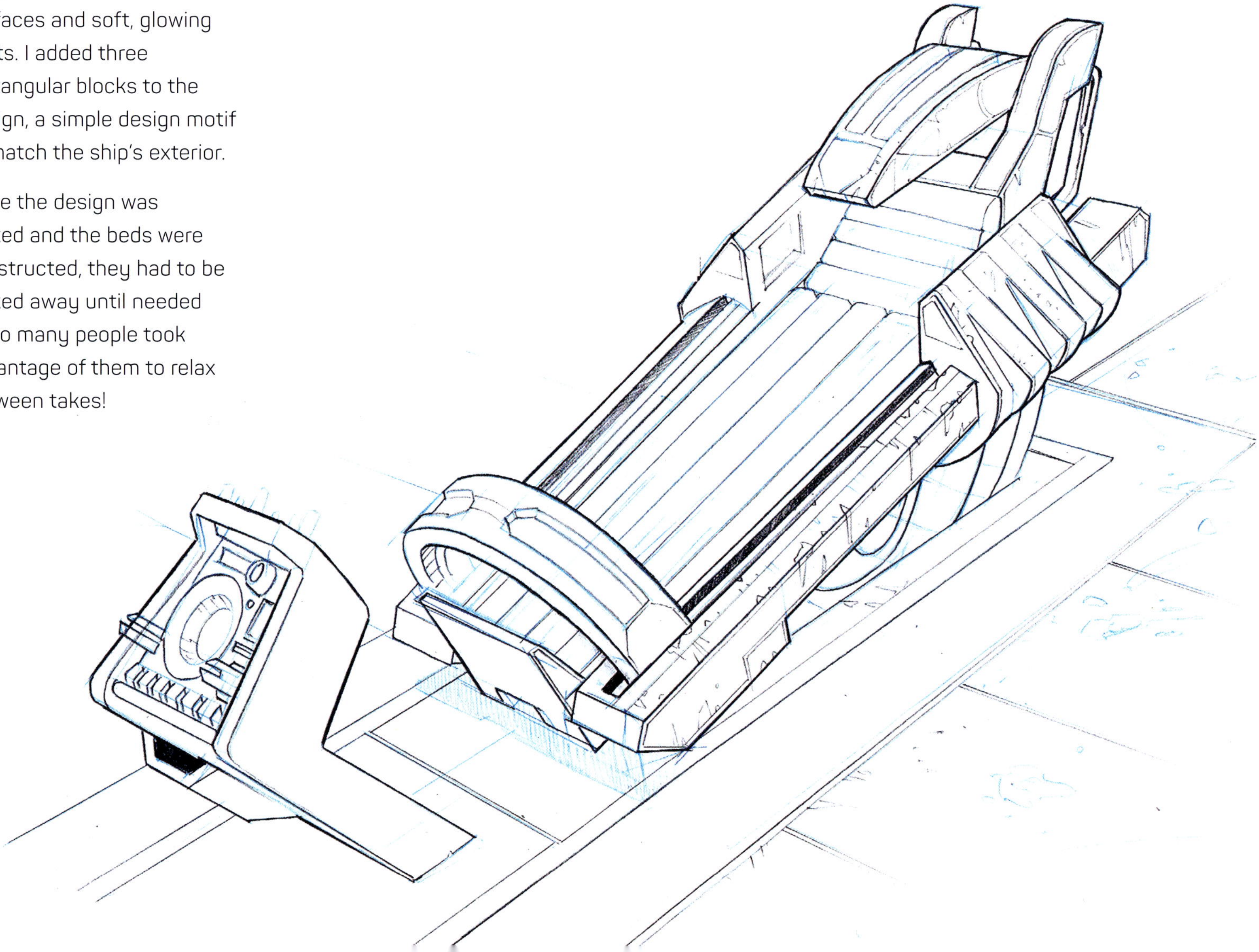

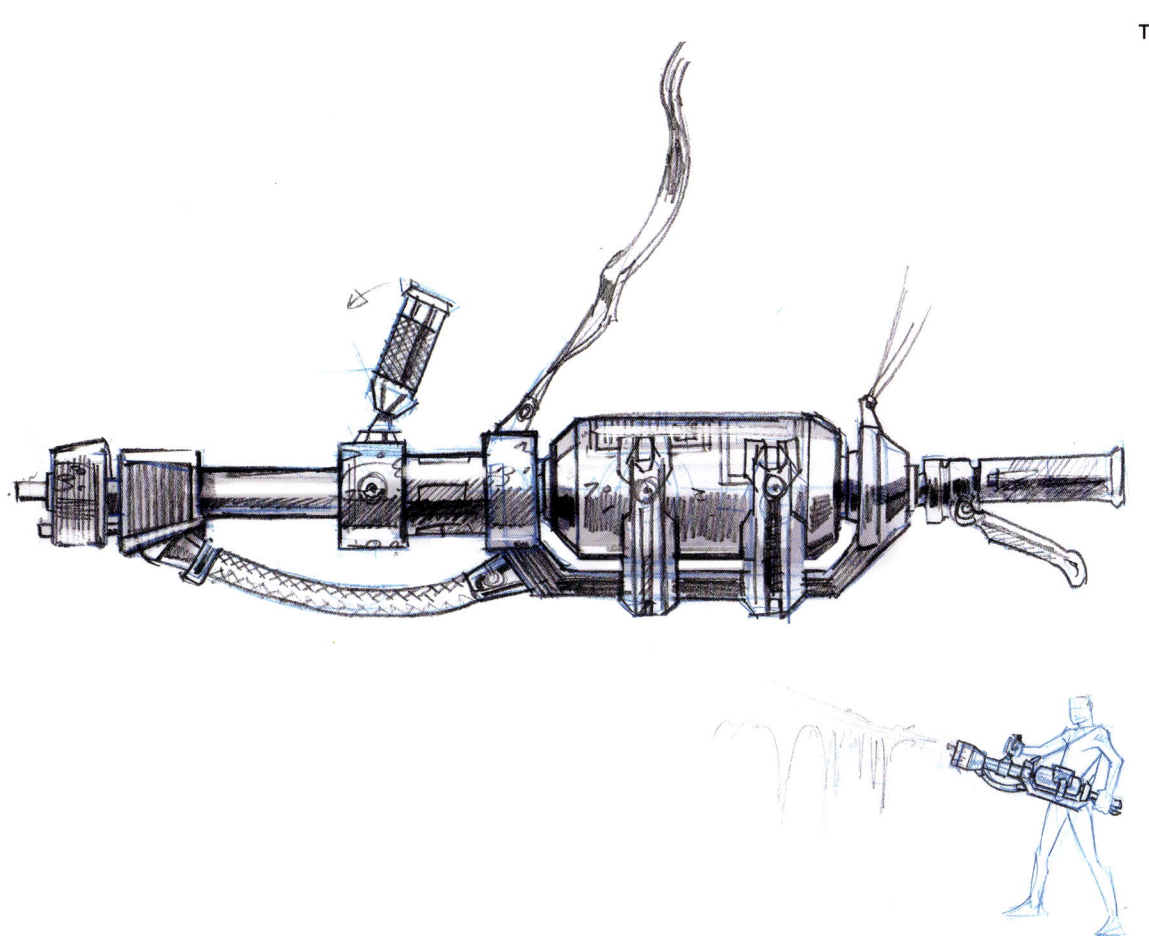

ICE GUN

The Ice Gun was a prop weapon that would need to incorporate a working fire extinguisher and be strong enough to withstand being thrown about by the actors.

When the Ice Gun props arrived, they were both functional and robust. I fear Billie Piper may have struggled with the weight of hers a little, thanks to the built-in extinguisher. Still, it added to the overall impact and gave the scene a nice, action-packed edge.

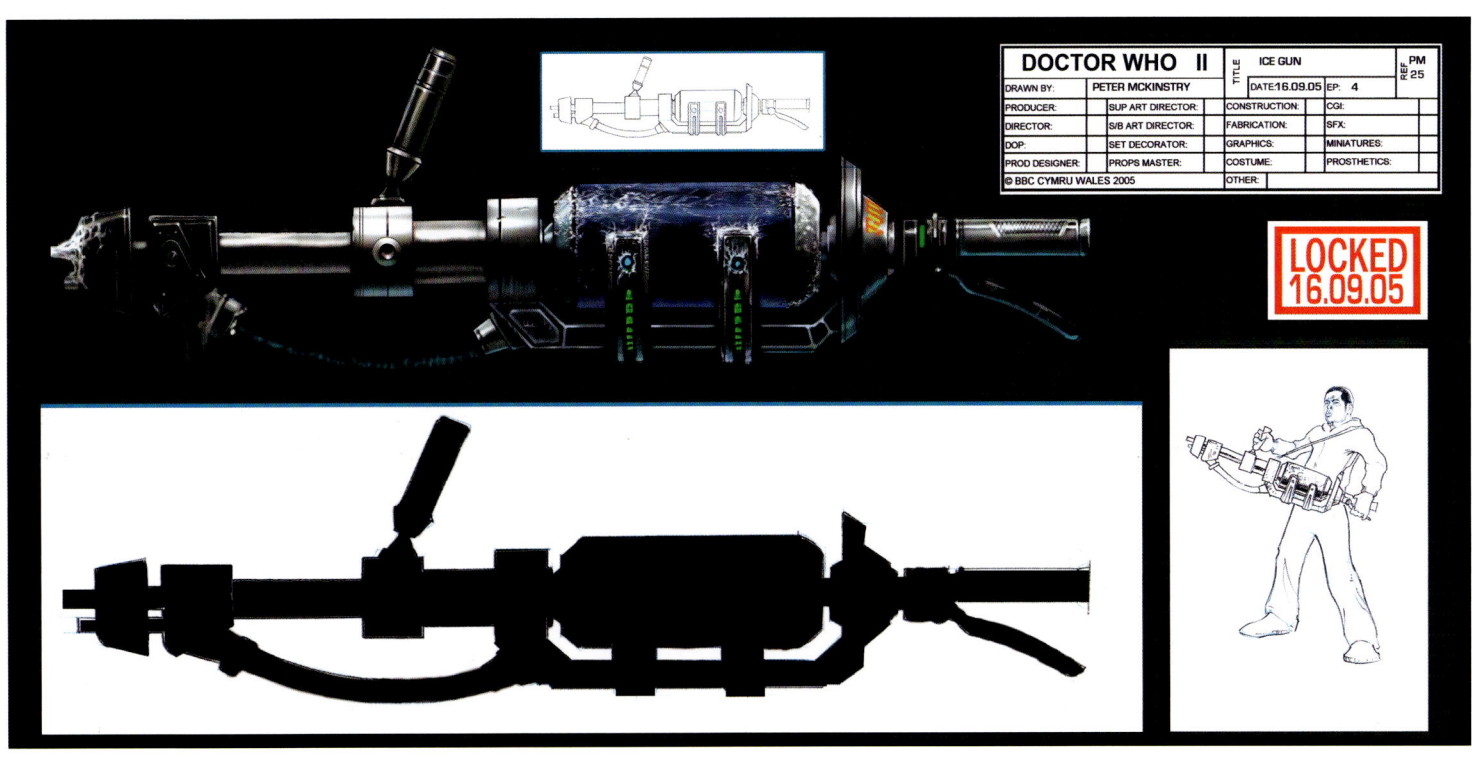

DOCTOR WHO II		TITLE	ICE GUN			REF PM 25
DRAWN BY:	PETER MCKINSTRY		DATE 16.09.05	EP: 4		
PRODUCER:	SUP ART DIRECTOR:	CONSTRUCTION:		CGI:		
DIRECTOR:	S/B ART DIRECTOR:	FABRICATION:		SFX:		
DOP:	SET DECORATOR:	GRAPHICS:		MINIATURES:		
PROD DESIGNER:	PROPS MASTER:	COSTUME:		PROSTHETICS:		
© BBC CYMRU WALES 2005		OTHER:				

LOCKED
16.09.05

TOOTH AND CLAW

THE TELESCOPE

To this day, the massive telescope that forms the heart of the story remains one of the largest things, scale-wise, that I've ever designed and had built. It was so grand in scale that CGI would have to be incorporated to fully bring it to life.

The script describes it as:

A huge, brass beast – handmade, very Heath Robinson – about 40 feet long, standing on a wrought iron metal-grille-circular-platform, with big metal wheels at its side, like hand-turned clockwork cogs, to adjust the angle.

The original sketch started as just a large telescope, but I felt it needed something extra to create a sense of intrigue and impact. So, I added a large decorative crescent moon; this addition brought a sense of mystery and conveyed the lunar link with the werewolf creature at the heart of the plot.

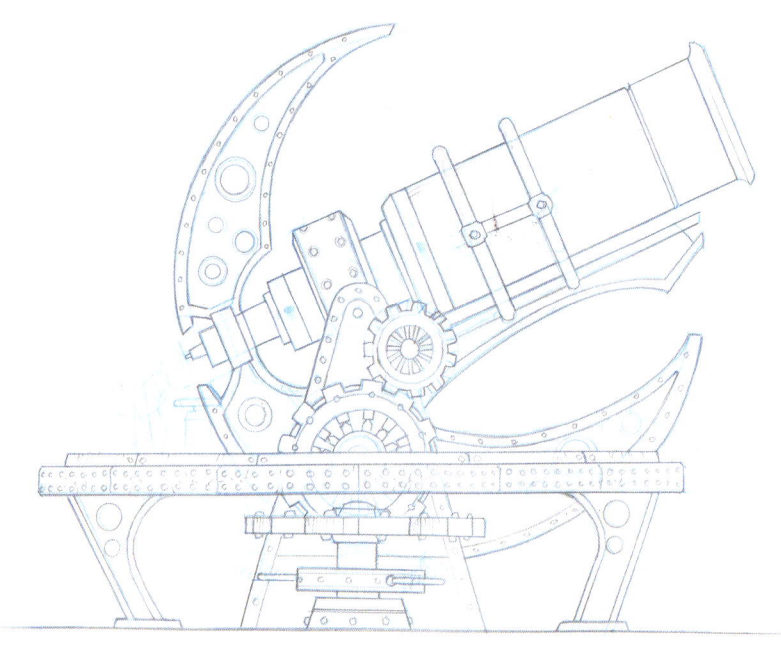

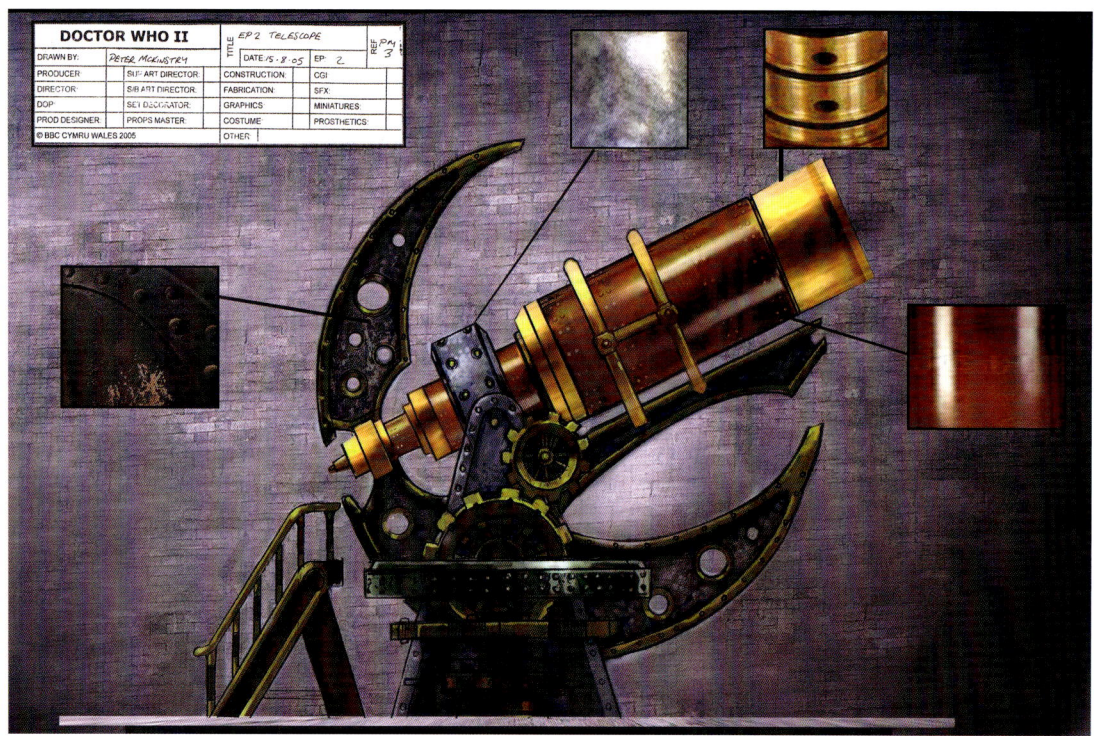

DOCTOR WHO II		TITLE	TELESCOPE		REF PM 16
DRAWN BY:	PETER MCKINSTRY		DATE: 7.9.05	EP: 2	
PRODUCER:	SUP ART DIRECTOR:	CONSTRUCTION:		CGI:	
DIRECTOR:	S/B ART DIRECTOR:	FABRICATION:		SFX:	
DOP:	SET DECORATOR:	GRAPHICS:		MINIATURES:	
PROD DESIGNER:	PROPS MASTER:	COSTUME:		PROSTHETICS:	
© BBC CYMRU WALES 2005		OTHER:			

LOCKED 08.09.05

When the true nature of the telescope was revealed at the episode's climax – that it was actually a light-focusing chamber designed to defeat the werewolf – there was a sense of the creator's intent coming full circle, visually connecting the entire narrative.

Watching my design be transformed into such a massive prop within the space of a couple of weeks was very exciting, and gave me a good indication of how the process would work going forward.

DOCTOR WHO II		TITLE	TURNING WHEEL		REF PM 29
DRAWN BY:	PETER MCKINSTRY		DATE 22.09.05	EP: 2	
PRODUCER:	SUP ART DIRECTOR:	CONSTRUCTION:		CGI:	
DIRECTOR:	S/B ART DIRECTOR:	FABRICATION:		SFX:	
DOP:	SET DECORATOR:	GRAPHICS:		MINIATURES:	
PROD DESIGNER:	PROPS MASTER:	COSTUME:		PROSTHETICS:	
© BBC CYMRU WALES 2005		OTHER:			

RISE OF THE CYBERMEN / THE AGE OF STEEL

THE CYBERMAN

Series 1 had successfully reintroduced the Daleks, creating a more solid, riveted bronze version that still retained the essence of Raymond Cusick's classic design from 1963.

For Series 2, the big returning monster was the Cybermen. It was a huge secret, and the producers were desperate to keep it under wraps until the episodes aired. What I didn't know then was that I would soon find myself wearing a Cyberman suit, for shooting both this story and the season finale, *Doomsday*!

Both Matt and I were excited to dive into concepting Cyberman designs. They are iconic villains and proved just as much fun to design as they are to watch on-screen.

I didn't want the Cybermen to look like robots instead of what they truly are: humans who have replaced limbs and organs in an attempt to make themselves superior. As a result, my own Cyberman designs leaned more into the body-horror aspect – perhaps more suited to a post-watershed show than family viewing! At the same time, there was a long list of other concepts that needed to be done anyway, so I got on with those.

Ed ultimately favoured a design by Alex Fort, a matte painter working at The Mill. Alex had created some very striking designs with an art deco influence, which dovetailed with what Ed had in mind for the overall aesthetic of the episodes. Alex's designs were then developed further by Millennium FX, who were responsible for fabricating the costumes.

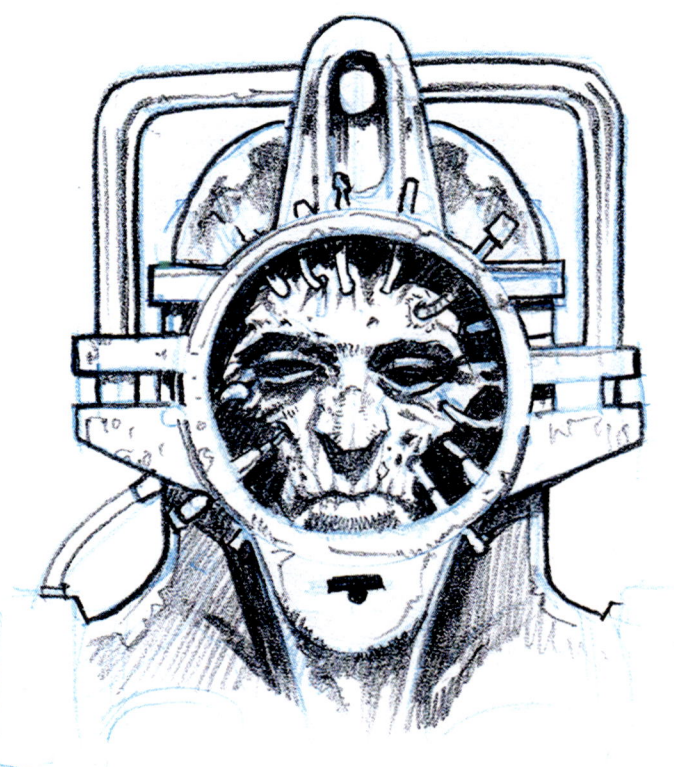

CYBERMAN IN THE RAIN

This illustration was for the BBC Books title *A History of the Universe in 100 Objects* by James Goss and Steve Tribe. It was commissioned as a full page, moody, dramatic portrait. And I've stood in the rain in a Cyberman costume — so I know what it's like!

BECOMING A CYBERMAN

One day in early December 2005, *The Age of Steel*'s Second Assistant Director, Steffan Morris, burst into the art department. He looked frantic – one of the Cyberman actors had gone home sick, and a replacement was desperately needed, someone slim enough to fit into the suit.

Steffan pointed at me: 'You'll do, Peter, come on!' Before I knew it, I was being marched down to the huge lorry parked outside, which Millennium FX personnel were using to dress the supporting artists in their Cyber-suits.

Getting into costume was an ordeal. Prosthetic Technicians Jon 'Ginge' Moore and Charlie Bluett worked at speed like an F1 pit crew, strapping, fastening and securing each piece of Cyber-armour with practised efficiency. First came the all-over flight suit – snug, warm, and already a bit stifling. Then, piece by piece, they strapped on the moulded fibreglass sections – chest plate, upper and lower arms, legs – until my body was fully encased. The tricky bit was getting into the helmet. It came in two halves, front and back, which were screwed together tightly around my head. *Uncomfortably* tightly, actually – like having my skull in a vice.

That first night, they took me and my cyber colleagues straight to location to film a short scene in an alleyway. Then, on 10 December, I got called back for something much bigger – spending a day shooting battle scenes for *Doomsday*. Cardiff Bay was transformed into a war zone. A whole group of us, suited up as Cybermen, stomped through the streets and then lifted our arms to fire at imaginary Daleks in the sky.

It was surreal. I was actually *in Doctor Who*. And it was such fun! I felt unbelievably lucky to be there, part of something so iconic. But when the day wrapped, and they finally unscrewed my helmet? *What a relief!*

CYBUS AIRSHIP

Designing the Cybus airship, I began with a very traditional shape and then developed a range of shapes and configurations for the additional structures seen on the exterior like the control bridge, antenna and so on.

Subject: Cybus Zeppelin Concept
Sent: Thursday, September 29, 2005 10:50 AM
To: Russell T Davies
From: Peter Mckinstry

Hi Russell,

Pete Mckinstry, new concept artist in the art department here!

Here's a version of the Cybus Industries zeppelin, plenty of our art deco nods and winks, see what you think.
The transmitter dish is scripted as deploying from the rear of the zep, what about switching it to the front?
I think visually it might be more effective, what are your thoughts?

Thanks,
Pete

Sent: Thursday, September 29, 2005 11:09 AM
To: Peter Mckinstry
From: Russell T Davies

Absolutely brilliant. And hello, Pete!

I think the transmitter would be good at the front – though check with Ed that it would fit his designs of the Int. Zeppelin sets.
Also – and this might be a texturing note for t'Mill – but it's nice if things aren't too glossy and spick-and-span. Not too sci-fi, in other words. This parallel world isn't too far from ours. So it might be good to tone down the silver, make sure it's more steel, and a bit lived in rather than super-clean.

But hooray, marvellous stuff.
R x

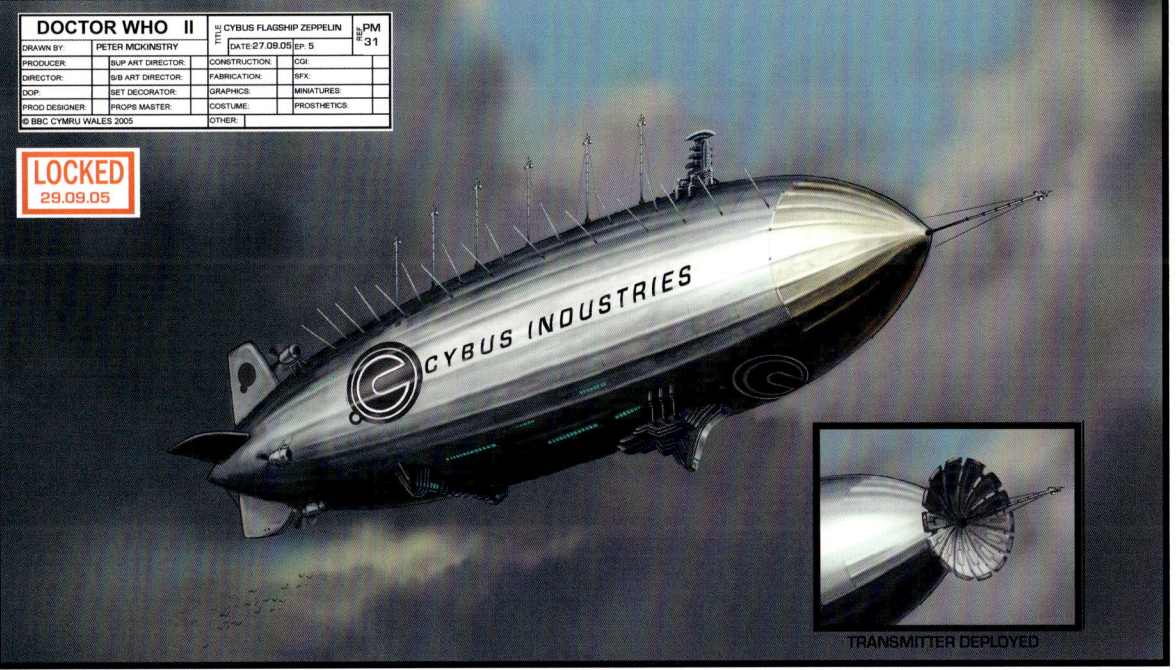

DOCTOR WHO II — CYBUS FLAGSHIP ZEPPELIN — DATE:27.09.05 EP: 5 — PM 31
DRAWN BY: PETER MCKINSTRY
PRODUCER: — SUP ART DIRECTOR: — CONSTRUCTION: — CGI:
DIRECTOR: — S/B ART DIRECTOR: — FABRICATION: — SFX:
DOP: — SET DECORATOR: — GRAPHICS: — MINIATURES:
PROD DESIGNER: — PROPS MASTER: — COSTUME: — PROSTHETICS:
© BBC CYMRU WALES 2005 — OTHER:

LOCKED 29.09.05

CYBUS INDUSTRIES

TRANSMITTER DEPLOYED

AIRSHIP LIFT

At an early stage of scripting, characters boarded the airship by lift, as this image illustrates from ground level. This was printed as a *Big Issue* cover for use in the episode as a background detail, but the scenes were cut before shooting and the lift was no longer needed.

THE TARDIS DIAMOND

The TARDIS diamond, essentially a small power cell, needed to look intriguing and cool. Since it would be seen up close in the Doctor's hand, every detail had to be just right.

I took inspiration from certain shapes in the TARDIS console design, blending the organic feel with technical elements that implied functionality – a suitably Gallifreyan power source.

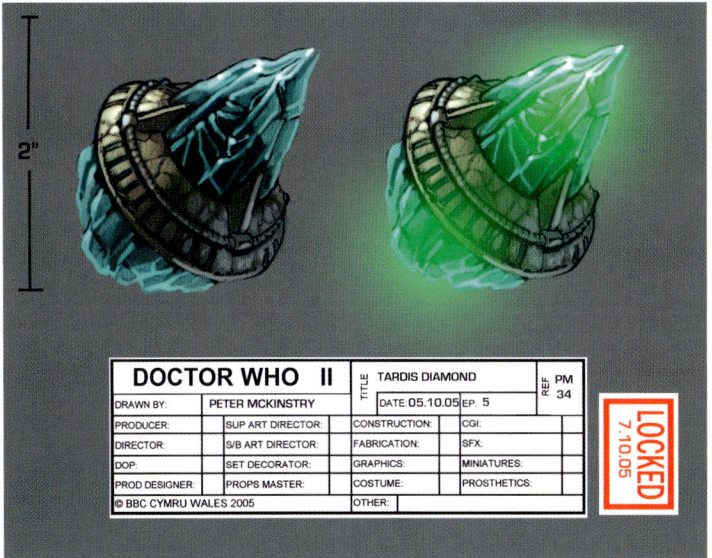

2"

DOCTOR WHO II		TITLE	TARDIS DIAMOND		REF	PM 34
DRAWN BY:	PETER MCKINSTRY		DATE: 05.10.05	EP: 5		
PRODUCER:	SUP ART DIRECTOR:	CONSTRUCTION:		CGI:		
DIRECTOR:	S/B ART DIRECTOR:	FABRICATION:		SFX:		
DOP:	SET DECORATOR:	GRAPHICS:		MINIATURES:		
PROD DESIGNER:	PROPS MASTER:	COSTUME:		PROSTHETICS:		
© BBC CYMRU WALES 2005		OTHER:				

LOCKED 7.10.05

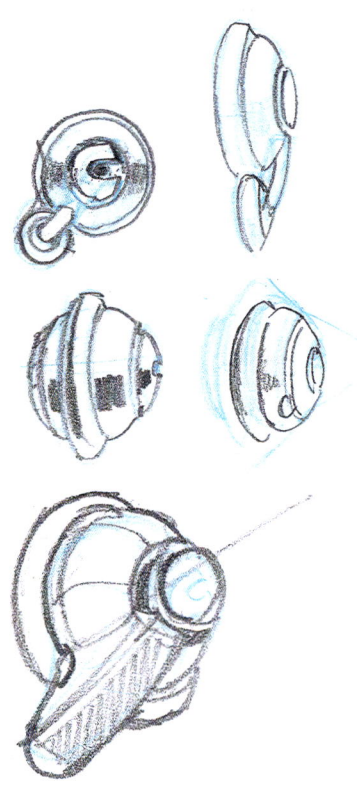

EARPODS

The design for the Cybus Industries earpods was sleek and modern, resembling the then-new earbud headphones. While the finished props did feature the metallic finish, the repurposed hearing aids that the props were made from meant they stood out more prominently from the actors' ears than originally intended.

JAKE'S SCANNER

This scanner was used by Jake Simmonds, one of the freedom fighters in this parallel world. I wanted to give the hand-prop a bit of life, so I incorporated some moving parts – a simple mechanism with small cylinders (I imagined them as signal-locaters) that swung down on either side when activated by the user. Prop makers Mark Cordory and Penny Howarth came through again with a great prop that was very similar to the locked design.

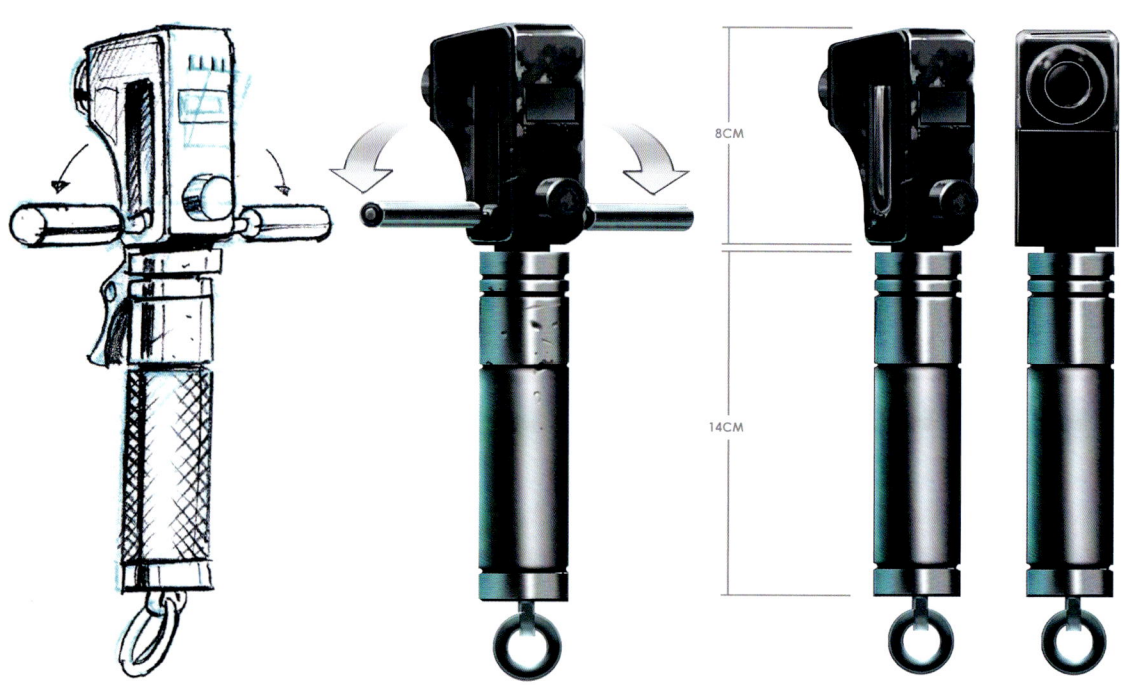

8CM

14CM

PREACHER LOGO

The Resistance movement fighting against John Lumic and his Cybermen, known as the Preachers, needed a symbol that could serve as a bold, graffiti-like calling card. Their mark had to be something they could spray-paint in visible places, helping their legend grow among the oppressed population. After some thought, a solution emerged that felt both fitting and meaningful: the Preachers' 'P' insignia would be a defaced version of the Cybus Corporation's 'C' logo, echoing the simplicity of the iconic anarchy 'A' symbol from our world.

the Preachers logo is
a deface version of the
Cybus logo.
the Preachers have flipped it
and put a line through it
to form the 'P' shape

MR CRANE'S DASHBOARD TERMINAL

The script showed John Lumic's deputy, Mr Crane, communicating with his master from the cabin of his transport. This prop was designed and approved pretty quickly – indeed, it was locked in its sketch form. I added the small mirror at the top of the unit so we could see Crane's reaction when Lumic orders him to gather more candidates for cyber-conversion. As Crane himself would say, 'Ain't technology wonderful!'

LUMIC'S CHAIR

My first design for Lumic's life-support chair was big and bold with small visual nods to classic series Cyberman motifs. I wanted to give it a larger-than-life presence that would fit the villainous character of John Lumic. But while it looks good on paper, it would have been expensive to realise and, on-screen, may have looked a bit 'too much'.

I created a second design, based around the boardroom chairs that we already had. Adapting one of these would be more cost-effective than constructing something entirely new.

Russell liked the design, noting 'maybe the more pipes and tubes, the better, cos when it gets attacked, we want Mr Crane to rip out as many tubes as possible'.

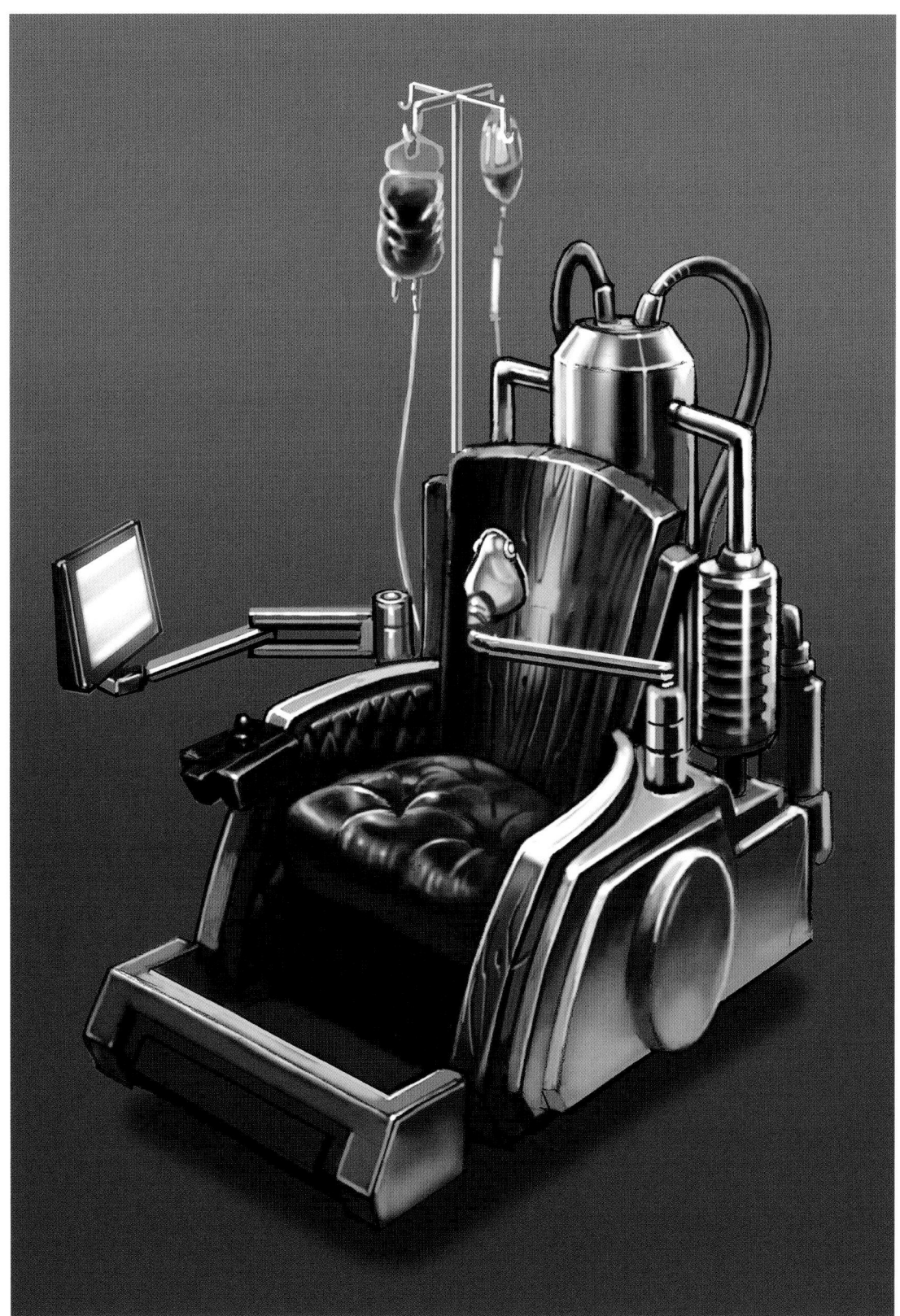

THE IDIOT'S LANTERN

STREET

In an early draft of this episode, the TARDIS materialised in a World War II bomb site between two terraced houses. I loved the idea – it was such a striking visual – and immediately sketched this concept. The influence of comic artist Dave Gibbons on my work is perhaps clearest here.

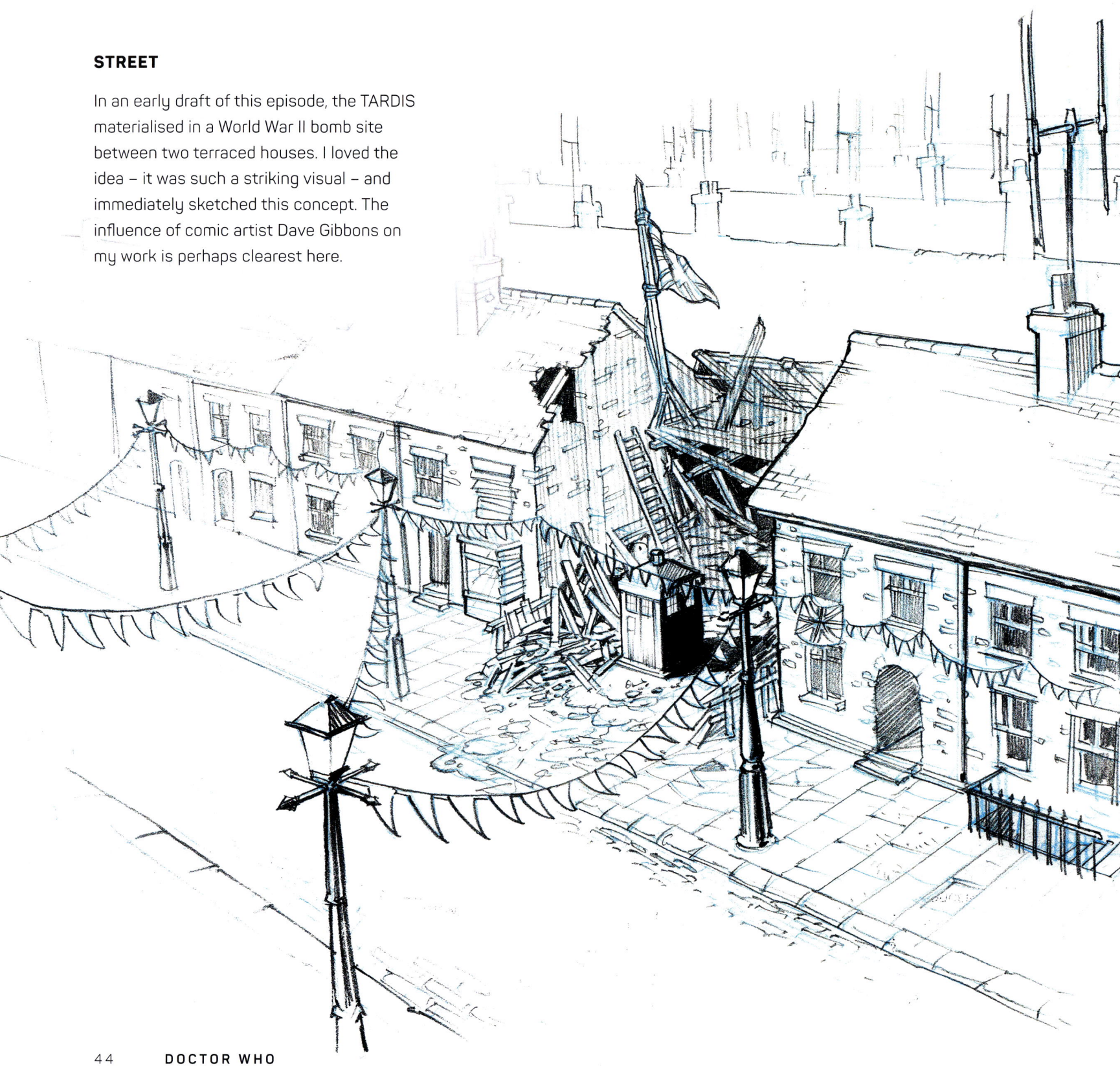

THE IMPOSSIBLE PLANET / THE SATAN PIT

MOONBASE AND CRATER VIEWS

Designing a moon base facility – not a bad way to earn a living! This is a good example of my sketching process; while I'm drawing my first idea, another option (or three or four) will occur to me, so I'll get them all down on paper as fast as I can. The best one, I thought, placed the base inside the protective ring of a crater; this would be a logical place to make camp in such a hostile environment.

Subject: *The Impossible Planet*
Sent: Wednesday, March 2, 2005 11:24 AM
To: Russell T Davies
From: Peter Mckinstry

Hello Russell,

Please find attached our visual of said planet. At first we were going really extreme, with whole chunks of the planet missing, but it seems to work better if we keep it fairly intact, detailing the surface with these huge, layered canyons, plains and gorges.

Please bear in mind this visual is focusing on the planet itself (the graphics dept need to know how it should look for the hologram images they're producing). The background detail, size and orientation of the black hole is for atmosphere only.

Thoughts and feelings appreciated as usual!

Pete

Sent: Wednesday, March 2, 2005 1:01 PM
To: Peter Mckinstry
From: Russell T Davies

That's brilliant, love it. The more craggy and forbidding we can make it, the better.

Funnily enough, cos we had to cut back on CGI, we're never going to see the planet hanging in space, as a 'real' shot, as it were – we're *only* going to see it as graphics on the computer screens and within the holograms. So, it's in our interest to make the graphics representation of the planet as gorgeous and detailed as possible!

R x

900m

900m

CORRIDOR AND DOOR

These concept images depict the interior of Sanctuary 6 Base. They're based on Set Designer Al Roberts' brilliant card models, which laid the groundwork for the overall look of the base. Al's design gave the space a heavy industrial feel, grounding the sci-fi environment in a way that felt believable and authentic. The attention to detail in his designs created a setting that felt functional and lived-in, giving the impression that this beat-up facility had been inhabited for years.

DOCTOR WHO II		MOONBASE DOOR (MODEL BY AL ROBERTS)		REF 111 4 PM
	TITLE	DATE: 10.02.06	EP: 8/9	
DRAWN BY:	PETER MCKINSTRY	CONSTRUCTION:	CGI:	
PRODUCER:		FABRICATION:	SFX:	
DIRECTOR:	SUP ART DIRECTOR:			
DOP:	S/B ART DIRECTOR:	GRAPHICS:	MINIATURES:	
	SET DECORATOR:	COSTUME:	PROSTHETICS:	
PROD DESIGNER:	PROPS MASTER:	OTHER:		
© BBC CYMRU WALES 2005				

SEAL / JARS AND PLINTHS

For these designs I created motifs intended to convey the culture of the ancient, mysterious race that imprisoned the Beast in his tomb. The seal was the first piece I developed, and I imagined it as a kind of warning – something like 'Here Be Dragons.'

My initial designs featured runic markings, but I also incorporated shapes that echoed the layout of the Sanctuary Base when viewed from above. This was a subtle suggestion that the events unfolding might have been preordained, adding to the mythological tone of the story.

Russell preferred the top left design, just as Ed did, but added, 'I'd just make it more... curvy. More occult, more *Buffy*. It's very straight-line-scientific at the moment; just needs to be more arcane.'

This feedback led to a more refined design that felt like it belonged to an ancient, ritualistic culture, and also laid the groundwork for much of the Beast's alphabet. The amphora jars and the plinths they rest on incorporate graphics that match the symbols on the seal, creating a consistent visual language throughout the two episodes.

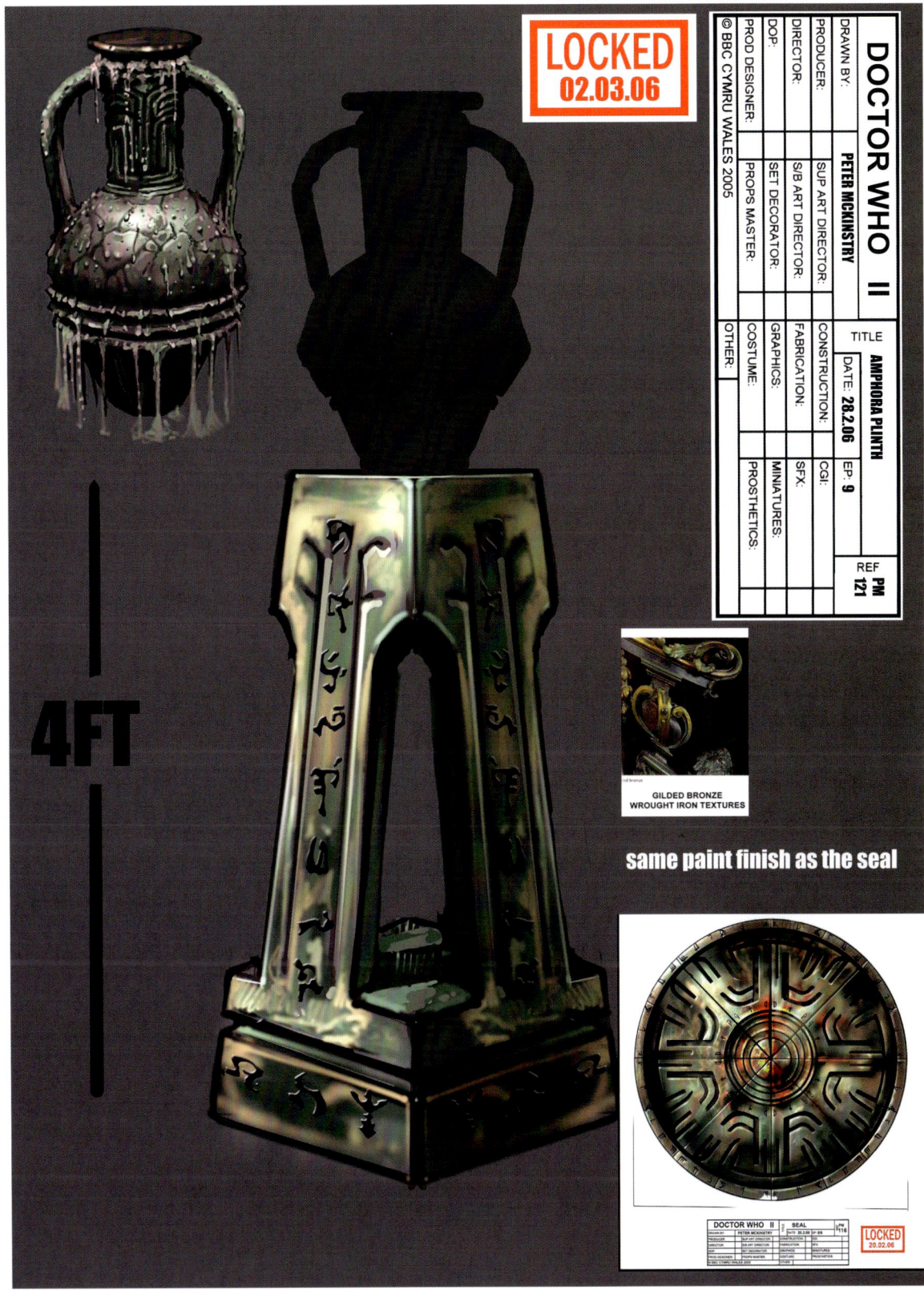

4FT

LOCKED
02.03.06

DOCTOR WHO II

DRAWN BY: **PETER MCKINSTRY**

PRODUCER: | SUP ART DIRECTOR:
DIRECTOR: | S/B ART DIRECTOR:
DOP: | SET DECORATOR:
PROD DESIGNER: | PROPS MASTER:

TITLE **AMPHORA PLINTH**

OTHER: | COSTUME: | GRAPHICS: | CONSTRUCTION:
| | MINIATURES: | FABRICATION:
| PROSTHETICS: | SFX: | CGI:

DATE: 28.2.06 | EP: 9

REF **PM 121**

© BBC CYMRU WALES 2005

GILDED BRONZE
WROUGHT IRON TEXTURES

same paint finish as the seal

DOCTOR WHO II | SEAL | PM 116
LOCKED 20.02.06

ALIEN TEXT, SET GRAFFITI

Developing an alien language was a fun creative challenge. My starting point was the Rorschach test, where inkblot shapes are said to hold hidden meanings, which I thought meshed nicely with the notion of the Beast's demonic influence. My revision included sharp shapes, hooks, and spikes, which created a more menacing, otherworldly feel.

This 'Beast's alphabet' would appear primarily on the face of a character possessed by the Beast. Knowing that transfers would be used to achieve this, I made sure each character was thick and strong, avoiding any delicate details that might break during the process. This also ensured the symbols would be clear and impactful on camera.

Before shooting began, I was instructed to go down to the Sanctuary Base set and hand-draw the symbols onto various surfaces. I also had to spray-paint the large 'WELCOME TO HELL' message on the wall, a slightly tense moment. I knew that if I messed it up the wall would have to be repainted and left to dry, then resprayed before shooting could begin. No time for any of that, I had to get it right first time!

DOCTOR WHO II		TITLE	ALIEN TEXT		REF	PM
DRAWN BY:	PETER MCKINSTRY	DATE: 22.2.06	EP: 8/9			118
PRODUCER:	SUP ART DIRECTOR:	CONSTRUCTION:		CGI:		
DIRECTOR:	S/B ART DIRECTOR:	FABRICATION:		SFX:		
DOP:	SET DECORATOR:	GRAPHICS:		MINIATURES:		
PROD DESIGNER:	PROPS MASTER:	COSTUME:		PROSTHETICS:		
© BBC CYMRU WALES 2005		OTHER:				

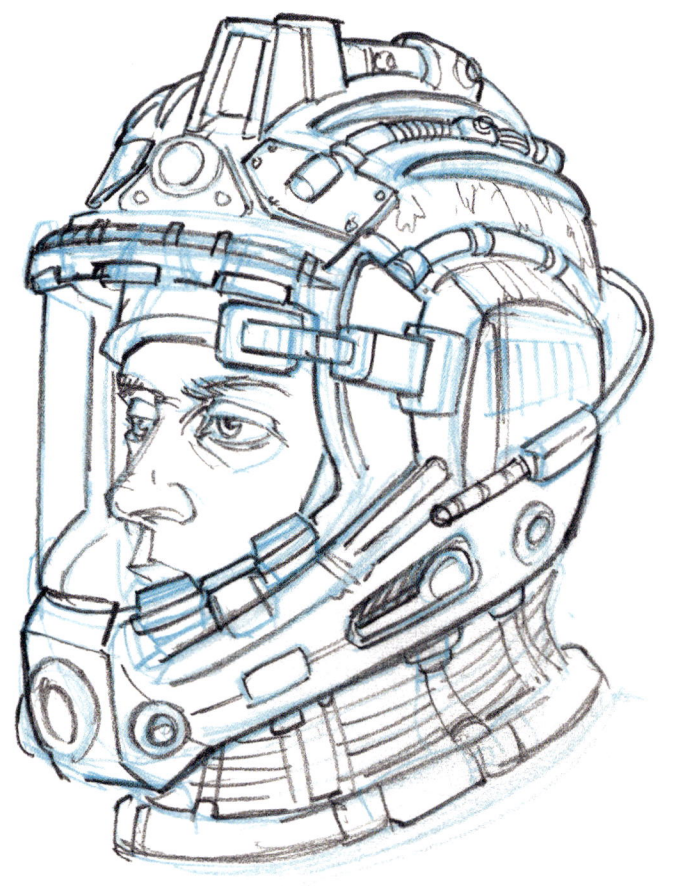

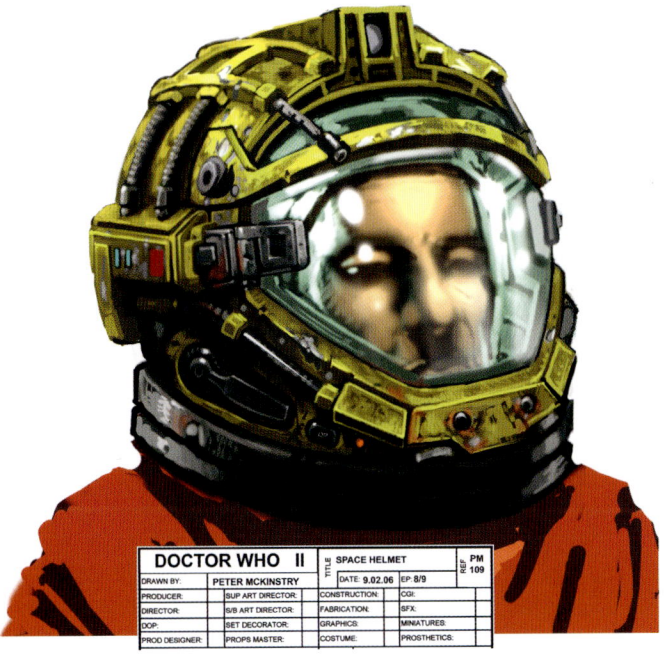

DOCTOR WHO II		TITLE	SPACE HELMET		REF	PM 109
DRAWN BY:	PETER MCKINSTRY		DATE: 9.02.06	EP: 8/9		
PRODUCER:	SUP ART DIRECTOR:		CONSTRUCTION:	CGI:		
DIRECTOR:	S/B ART DIRECTOR:		FABRICATION:	SFX:		
DOP:	SET DECORATOR:		GRAPHICS:	MINIATURES:		
PROD DESIGNER:	PROPS MASTER:		COSTUME:	PROSTHETICS:		

HELMET

This helmet went on to appear in later episodes, including *Hide*, *Kill the Moon*, *The Girl Who Died*, and *Listen*. We had a welding helmet in the props department, which I used as the basis for the design. When a prop is based on a pre-existing object, it's far easier to add things on than to take them off.

I presented two versions to Russell, and while preferring the one on the right, he noted: 'Because the suits themselves are very simple and straightforward, I'm worried that the suit and the helmet will look like they've come from two different sources. Can we see what it looks like if we lose a lot of the panelling and ridges and bumps and buttons and things?'

A new concept was created based on those notes, and the final space helmet design was approved – ready to begin its long career on-screen!

OOD TRANSLATION SPHERES

Scripted as simple white balls that light up whenever the Ood speak, and which each Ood must carry, the Ood spheres' simplicity marked them out from my other prop designs. I asked Russell if he had any specific notes and he confirmed: 'Basically, simple. Something kids can draw. Not a complicated gadgety-thing.'

Based on this feedback, I created very minimal designs, but I added a subtle metallic pattern to give some visual interest – and to help hide the seam where the two halves of the sphere opened, allowing access to the lightbulb mechanism inside.

OOD SKETCHES

After completing my design breakdown for these episodes, I realised that in all the work I'd done so far for Series 2, I hadn't had the chance to dive into any alien creature designs. So, I spent a short time excitedly sketching ideas for the look of the Ood. Their design had in fact already been developed expertly and brilliantly by Millennium FX, so while my digital sketches weren't needed, they demonstrated my enthusiasm for creature and alien design, showing that I was keen to contribute in this area as well.

DOCTOR WHO II		TITLE	OOD 1 FULL LENGTH	REF	PM 98
DRAWN BY:	PETER MCKINSTRY		DATE: 24.1.06 EP: 8		
PRODUCER:	SUP ART DIRECTOR:	CONSTRUCTION:	CGI:		
DIRECTOR:	S/B DIRECTOR:	FABRICATION:	SFX:		
DOP:	SET DECORATOR:	GRAPHICS:	MINIATURES:		
PROD DESIGNER:	PROPS MASTER:	COSTUME:	PROSTHETICS:		
© BBC CYMRU WALES 2005		OTHER:			

BOLT GUN

The Bolt Gun design was approved almost immediately after I sketched it. The annotations on the drawing reflect my thought process as I developed it – a piece of battered Sanctuary Base equipment that balanced the line between functional sci-fi hardware and a visually striking gun design. This is the weapon Rose uses to send the Beast back to hell, and so the primary consideration was to make Rose look as heroic as possible holding it in that crucial moment.

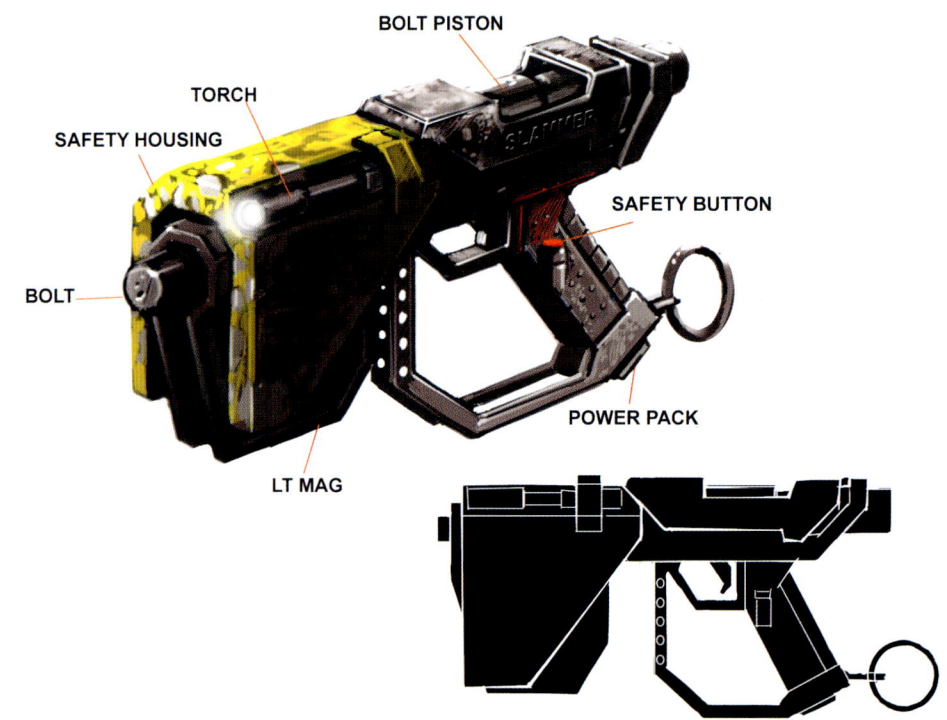

BOLT PISTON

TORCH

SAFETY HOUSING

SAFETY BUTTON

BOLT

POWER PACK

LT MAG

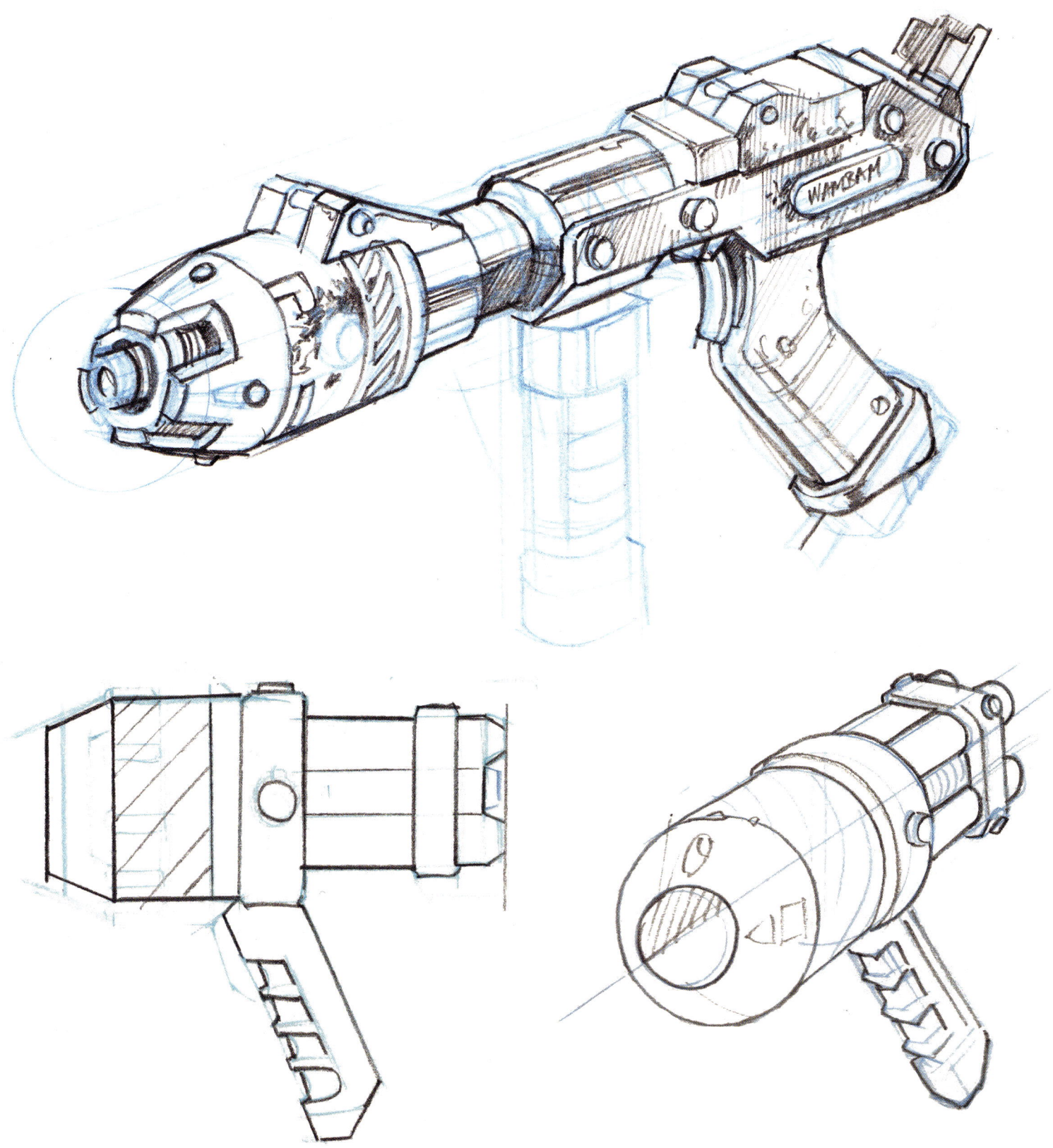

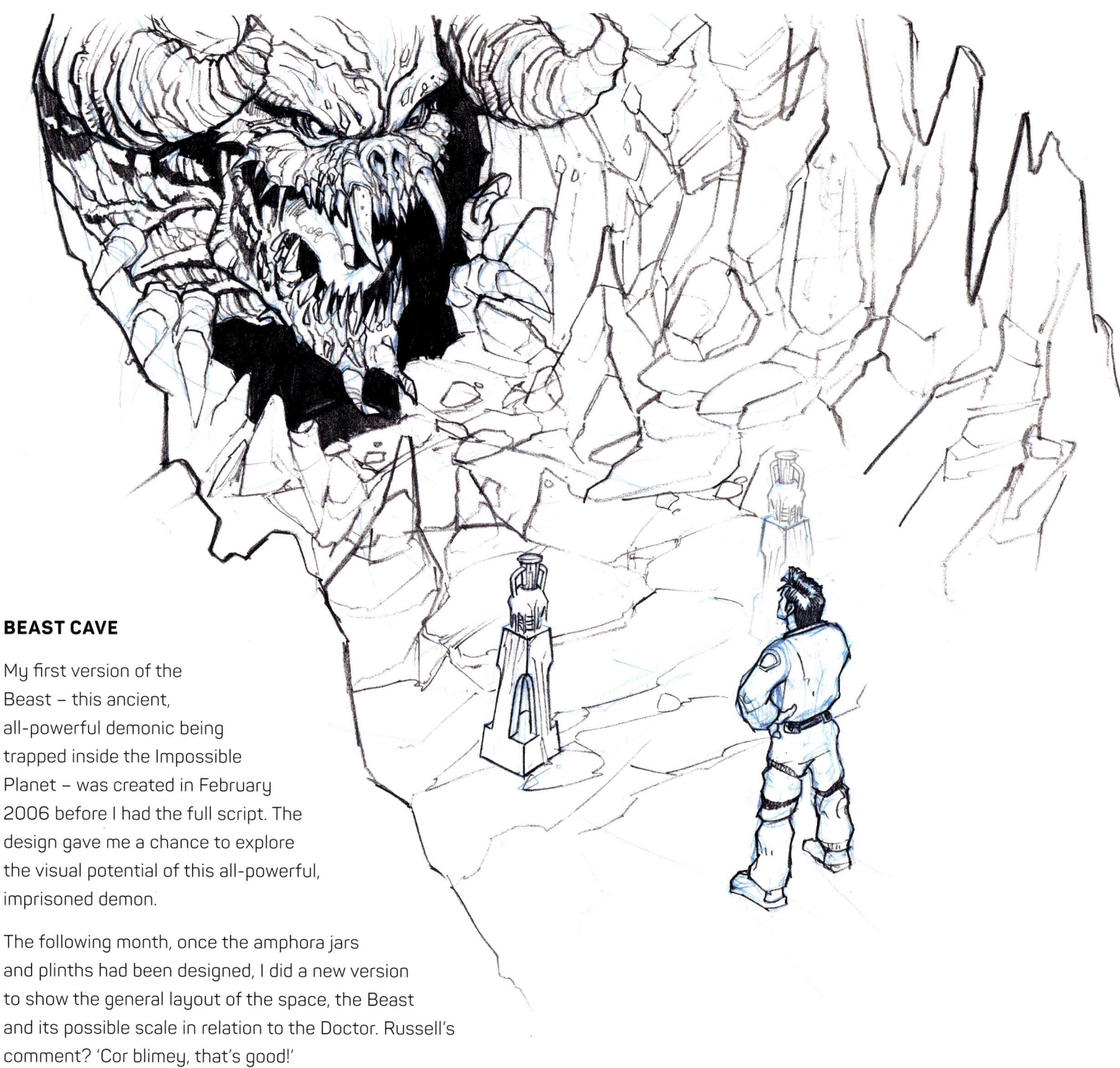

BEAST CAVE

My first version of the Beast – this ancient, all-powerful demonic being trapped inside the Impossible Planet – was created in February 2006 before I had the full script. The design gave me a chance to explore the visual potential of this all-powerful, imprisoned demon.

The following month, once the amphora jars and plinths had been designed, I did a new version to show the general layout of the space, the Beast and its possible scale in relation to the Doctor. Russell's comment? 'Cor blimey, that's good!'

DEEP CAVE

I created these images to explore what the deep space inside the planet might look like. This is the location of the seal – the locked door behind which the Beast is held captive. I was interested in the possible scale of such a place, but also wanted to show remnants of an ancient civilisation – adding layers of authenticity and history to the environment.

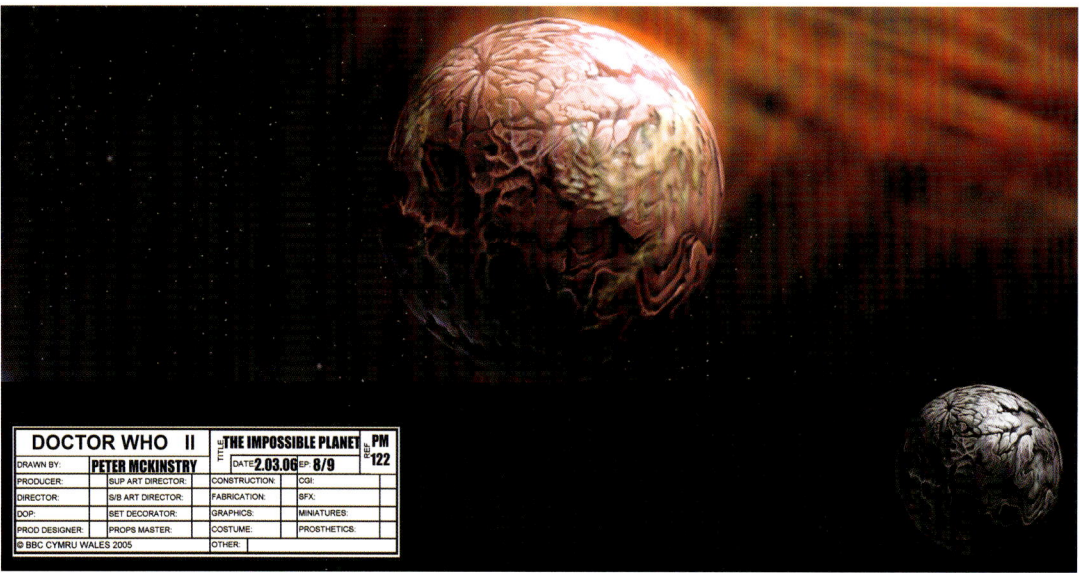

DOCTOR WHO	II		THE IMPOSSIBLE PLANET	PM
		TITLE		REF 122
DRAWN BY:	PETER MCKINSTRY	DATE 2.03.06	EP: 8/9	
PRODUCER:	SUP ART DIRECTOR:	CONSTRUCTION:	CGI:	
DIRECTOR:	S/B ART DIRECTOR:	FABRICATION:	SFX:	
DOP:	SET DECORATOR:	GRAPHICS:	MINIATURES:	
PROD DESIGNER:	PROPS MASTER:	COSTUME:	PROSTHETICS:	
© BBC CYMRU WALES 2005		OTHER:		

DOCTOR WHO II
DRAWN BY: PETER MCKINSTRY
TITLE: SUBTERANEAN CAVERN
DATE: 2.02.06 EP: 8/9
REF PM 104
PRODUCER: SUP ART DIRECTOR: CONSTRUCTION: CGI:
DIRECTOR: S/B ART DIRECTOR: FABRICATION: SFX:
DOP: SET DECORATOR: GRAPHICS: MINIATURES:
PROD DESIGNER: PROPS MASTER: COSTUME:
OTHER: PROSTHETICS:
© BBC CYMRU WALES 2005

DOCTOR WHO II
DRAWN BY: PETER MCKINSTRY
TITLE: SUBTERANEAN CAVERN
DATE: 6.02.06 EP: 8/9
REF PM 106
PRODUCER: SUP ART DIRECTOR: CONSTRUCTION: CGI:
DIRECTOR: S/B ART DIRECTOR: FABRICATION: SFX:
DOP: SET DECORATOR: GRAPHICS: MINIATURES:
PROD DESIGNER: PROPS MASTER: COSTUME: PROSTHETICS:
OTHER:
© BBC CYMRU WALES 2005

DOCTOR WHO II
DRAWN BY: PETER MCKINSTRY
TITLE: SUBTERANEAN CAVERN
DATE: 3.02.06 EP: 8/9
REF PM 105
PRODUCER: SUP ART DIRECTOR: CONSTRUCTION: CGI:
DIRECTOR: S/B ART DIRECTOR: FABRICATION: SFX:
DOP: SET DECORATOR: GRAPHICS: MINIATURES:
PROD DESIGNER: PROPS MASTER: COSTUME: PROSTHETICS:
© BBC CYMRU WALES 2005 OTHER:

CAVE PAINTING

Next, I needed to create the cave painting that the Doctor would discover just before his confrontation with the Beast. The painting needed to evoke a primitive, cave-art style while being visually clear on camera as it depicted how the Beast was imprisoned, including important symbols like the seal and the amphora jars. The Doctor refers back to this painting while piecing together the Beast's backstory during their encounter.

The scenic painter, who would transfer my design onto the actual cave wall, had only a limited surface area to work with, and so I had to ensure the image conveyed all the necessary information within a small space. I sent the initial design to Russell, joking that I had gotten 'in touch with my inner caveman' to capture the right feel for the artwork.

Russell's feedback was insightful and practical, as ever. I simplified the design to improve clarity and add focus to the narrative details. When I sent the revised version back, I got Russell's reply: 'Ug! (Which is caveman for "perfect", as you well know.)'

SANCTUARY BASE – CUTAWAY

This illustration of the central hub of the Sanctuary Base was done for GE Fabbri's *Doctor Who: The DVD Files* magazine.

LOVE AND MONSTERS

VICTOR'S CANE

This brilliantly bonkers episode introduced Victor Kennedy, AKA the Abzorbaloff, who had an aversion to touching. Victor was never without his cane, which was secretly a device for wielding control over his absorbed victims. In the end, the cane is snapped and his power is lost.

Focusing on the 'no touching' idea, I imagined the head of the cane as a pair of clasped hands that open when the cane is broken. *This will never work*, I thought, but still I sent the idea off to Russell. And on 9 March 2006 he responded, 'That cane is MAGNIFICENT. Hooray!'

Again, the prop makers did us proud – the cane even gets its own close-up moment at the climax of the episode when the hands open, releasing the Abzorbaloff's energy.

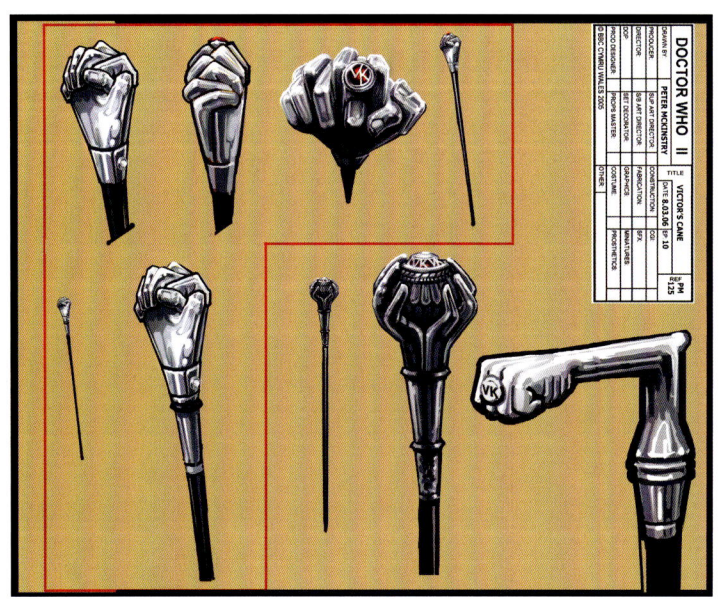

TARDIS HIEROGLYPH

Occasionally, I'd be asked to take a pre-existing image and
subtly alter it to include a new element. One particularly
fun example was when I had to incorporate a pictogram of
the TARDIS into a line of Egyptian hieroglyphs. This piece
actually made it on-screen in the episode as part of Bridget's
slideshow, showcasing instances of the TARDIS appearing
throughout history.

SCULPTURES

In the episode, the character Bliss expresses her feelings for the Doctor through the medium of sculpture. It reminded me of my art school days and some of the stuff I'd see there. Fun though they were to do, I knew my early versions were too comedic and so came up with a further version which felt a bit more real.

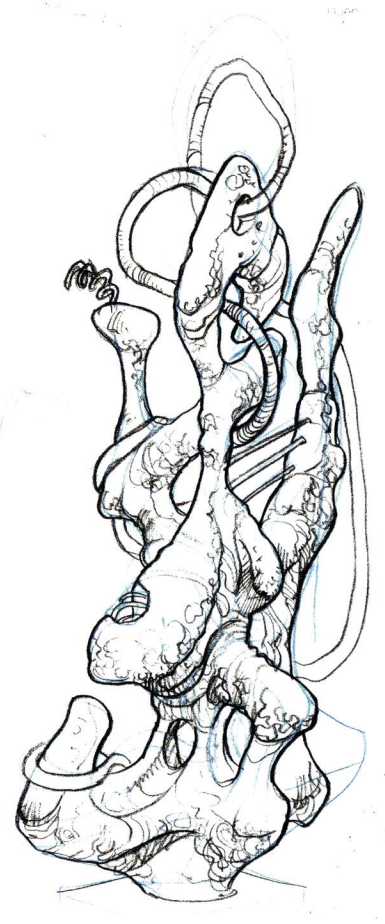

FEAR HER

PODS AND MOTHER

These concepts for how the Isolus Mother should look were another welcome opportunity to get out my pencils in Drawing Club! There's something about organic natural forms (even alien ones!) that seem to lend themselves to working in graphite.

The story also required a design for the Isolus pod, which – unlike the Mother, who was realised through CGI – would involve a physical prop build. I went for a dark polished glass look, with grey 'gull egg' markings. A resin was injected into the pod to give it an internal environment which the wizards at The Mill then enhanced for the glowing effect at the episode's climax.

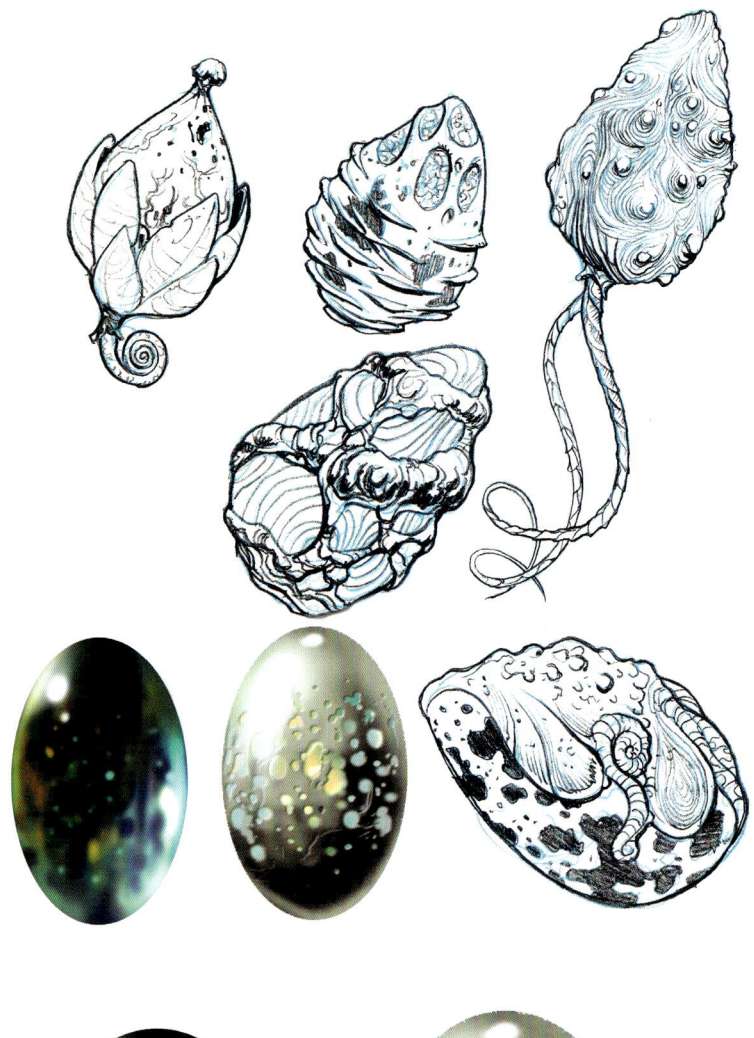

DOCTOR WHO II		TITLE	ISOLUS POD		REF	PM 87
DRAWN BY:	PETER MCKINSTRY		DATE: 9.1.06	EP: 11		
PRODUCER:	SUP ART DIRECTOR:	CONSTRUCTION:		CGI:		
DIRECTOR:	S/B ART DIRECTOR:	FABRICATION:		SFX:		
DOP:	SET DECORATOR:	GRAPHICS:		MINIATURES:		
PROD DESIGNER:	PROPS MASTER:	COSTUME:		PROSTHETICS:		
© BBC CYMRU WALES 2005		OTHER:				

DOCTOR WHO II		TITLE	ISOLUS FLOWER		REF	PM 85
DRAWN BY:	PETER MCKINSTRY	DATE: 9.1.06		EP: 11		
PRODUCER:	SUP ART DIRECTOR:	CONSTRUCTION:		CGI:		
DIRECTOR:	S/B ART DIRECTOR:	FABRICATION:		SFX:		
DOP:	SET DECORATOR:	GRAPHICS:		MINIATURES:		
PROD DESIGNER	PROPS MASTER:	COSTUME:		PROSTHETICS:		
© BBC CYMRU WALES 2005		OTHER:				

ARMY OF GHOSTS / DOOMSDAY

TORCHWOOD LOGO

I brainstormed several different ideas for the official Torchwood logo. The one that was successful – the capital T made up of hexagonal shapes – was the strongest visually. The hexagons represent the different 'cells' of the Torchwood Institute active in other parts of the country, and are also a visual nod to the cellular structure of diamonds. This works as a neat callback to the Koh-i-Noor diamond, which was a key plot element in *Tooth and Claw* – the episode where Queen Victoria founded Torchwood.

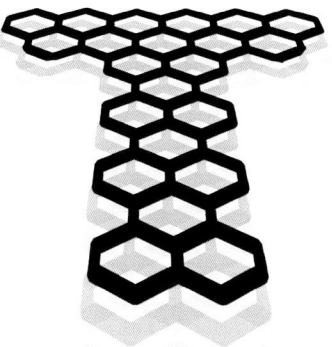

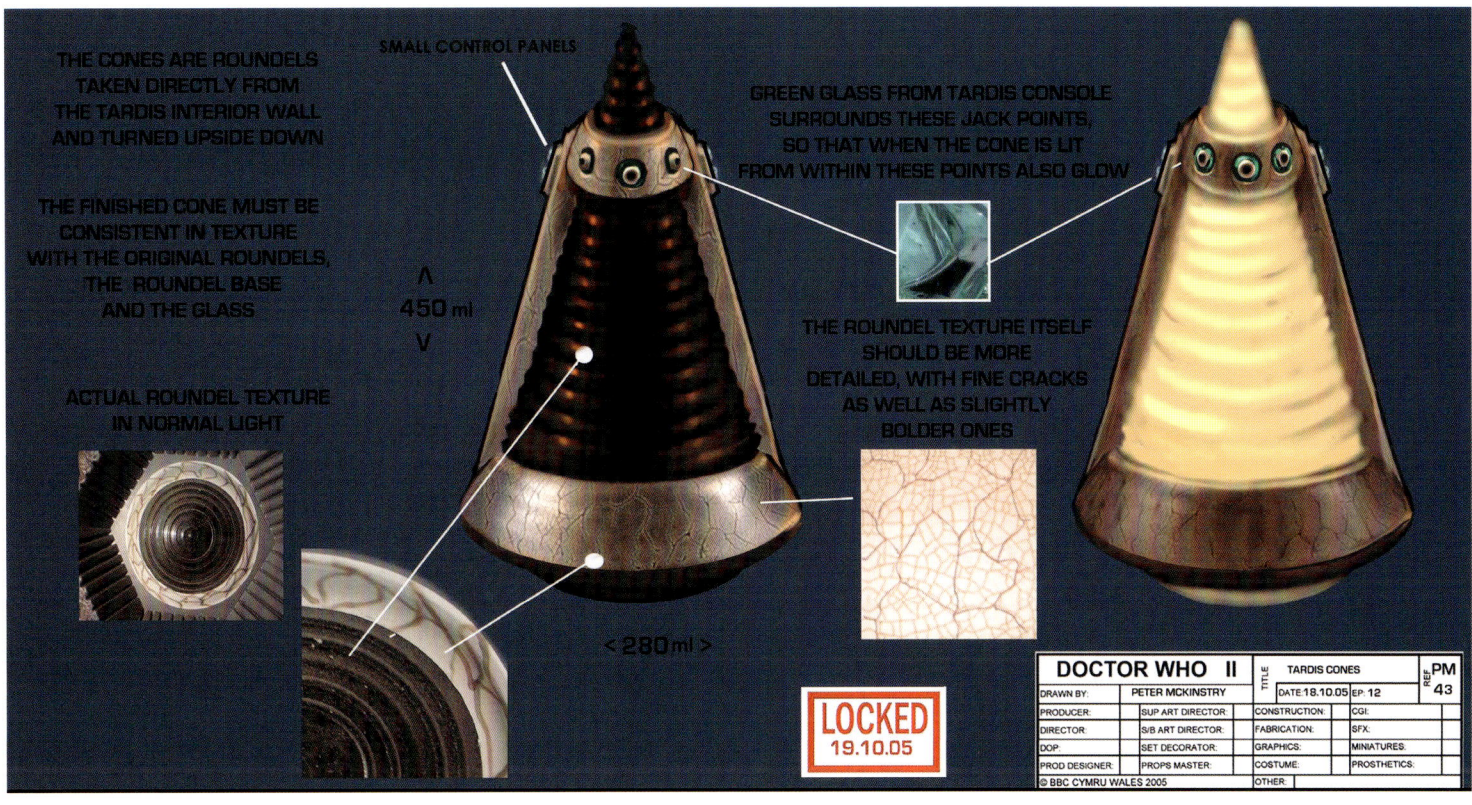

THE CONES ARE ROUNDELS TAKEN DIRECTLY FROM THE TARDIS INTERIOR WALL AND TURNED UPSIDE DOWN

THE FINISHED CONE MUST BE CONSISTENT IN TEXTURE WITH THE ORIGINAL ROUNDELS, THE ROUNDEL BASE AND THE GLASS

ACTUAL ROUNDEL TEXTURE IN NORMAL LIGHT

SMALL CONTROL PANELS

GREEN GLASS FROM TARDIS CONSOLE SURROUNDS THESE JACK POINTS, SO THAT WHEN THE CONE IS LIT FROM WITHIN THESE POINTS ALSO GLOW

THE ROUNDEL TEXTURE ITSELF SHOULD BE MORE DETAILED, WITH FINE CRACKS AS WELL AS SLIGHTLY BOLDER ONES

Λ 450 ml V

< 280 ml >

LOCKED 19.10.05

DOCTOR WHO II			TARDIS CONES		REF PM 43
DRAWN BY:	PETER MCKINSTRY	TITLE	DATE:18.10.05	EP: 12	
PRODUCER:	SUP ART DIRECTOR:	CONSTRUCTION:		CGI:	
DIRECTOR:	S/B ART DIRECTOR:	FABRICATION:		SFX:	
DOP:	SET DECORATOR:	GRAPHICS:		MINIATURES:	
PROD DESIGNER:	PROPS MASTER:	COSTUME:		PROSTHETICS:	
© BBC CYMRU WALES 2005		OTHER:			

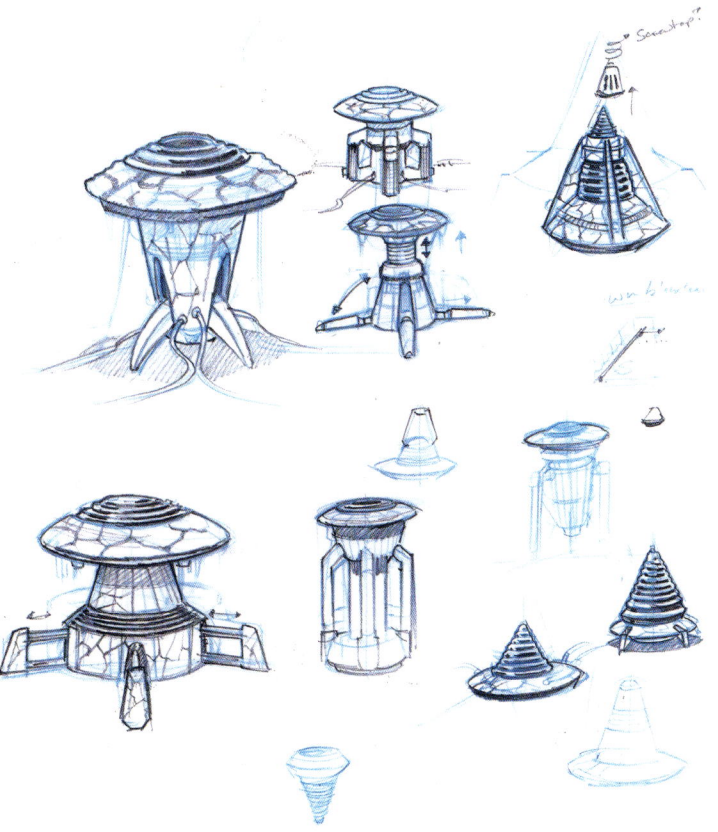

TARDIS CONES AND BOX

Russell's script called for two-foot-high cones that the Doctor produces from inside the TARDIS to triangulate the source of the titular ghosts. Since they were scripted as TARDIS technology, I suggested using the TARDIS roundels as the foundation for the cone.

In the classic series, the roundels were sometimes removed to reveal bits of circuitry and wiring. Here was an opportunity to make our new TARDIS roundels more intriguing; they aren't just flat little portholes but are, in fact, important parts of the TARDIS technology that can be reconfigured with other tech in order to function in different ways.

VOID DISC

The Void Discs allow Jake and his fellow freedom-fighters to travel back and forth between the parallel worlds. In what they can and cannot do, they're hugely important to the plot of the story. I got to work and sent my initial ideas to Russell. He felt they looked too much like buckles and needed to be a more pivotal part of the overall design. They also needed to be put on and taken off in the briefest of moments if the practical demands of the script were to be met.

I developed further designs but Russell felt they were still too integrated. 'I think we should go for something really, really simple and bold,' he told me, 'even if it's the Fisher-Price of dimensional teleports!'

Subject: Void Disc
Sent: Wednesday, November 9, 2005 6:26 PM
To: Russell T Davies
From: Peter Mckinstry

Hello Russell,

Please have a look at the attached file and see what you think, I've kept it quite rough till we arrive at a general design we can lock down.

Thanks again

Pete

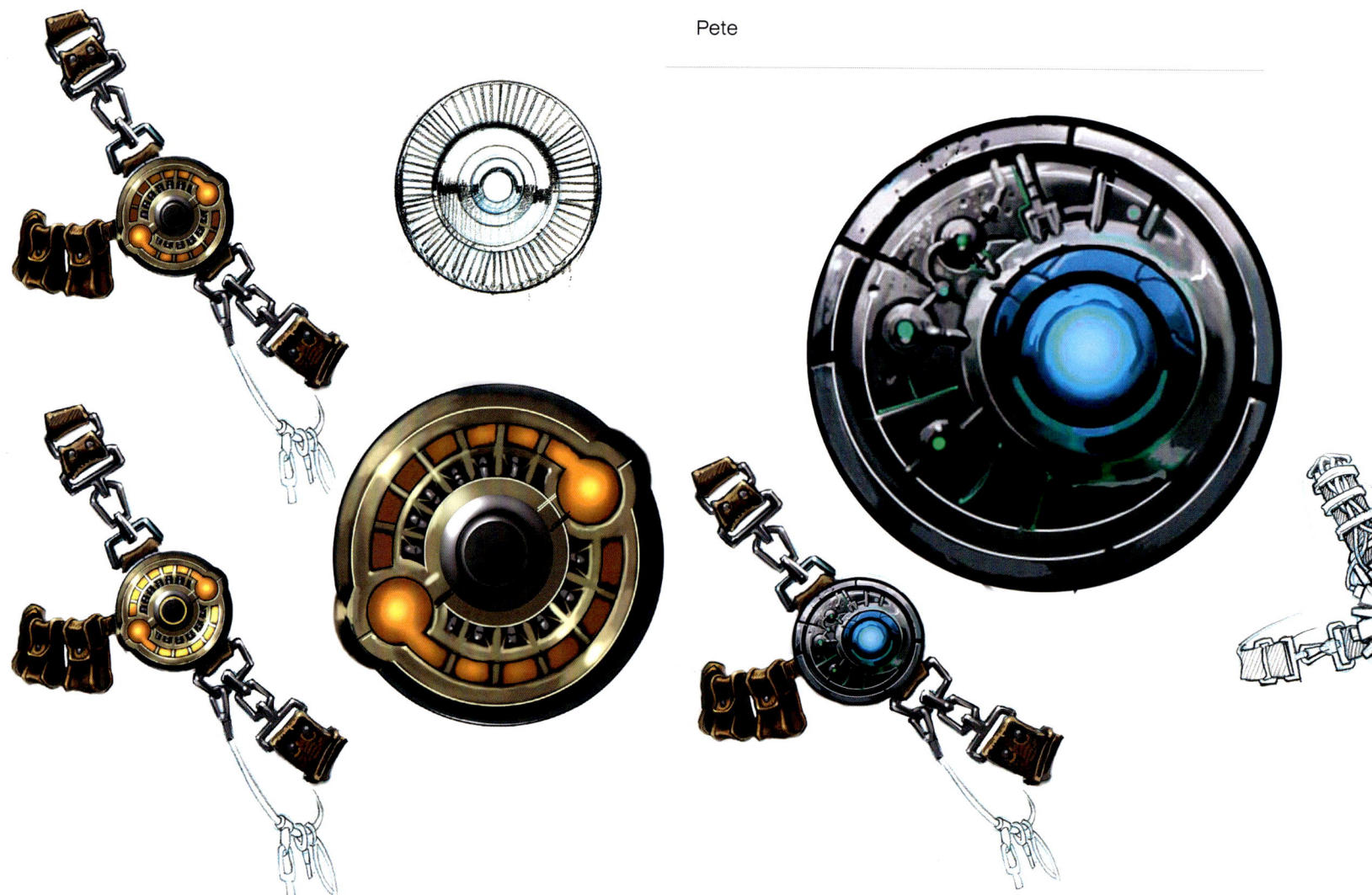

Sent: Wednesday, November 9, 2005 6:42 PM

To: Peter Mckinstry

From: Russell T Davies

Oh that's LOVELY! I hope they don't offend you by being so bold, but really, that so works. Gorgeous.

Since there's got to be a big, central button to be pressed, then I like the bottom left. Though I also like top right. I like the yellow, we've had a few red/green/blue lights, but yellow feels new. And the chain attachment on the yellow looks thin enough to be broken, when Pete rips them off. So the button-effect of bottom left, with the yellow and chain and simplicity of top right. In fact, if the central circle of top right can actually act as a button, then top right it is! If that makes sense!

Rx

DOCTOR WHO II			TITLE TROOPERS' VOID DISC		REF PM 65
DRAWN BY:	PETER MCKINSTRY		DATE: 9.11.05	EP: 13	
PRODUCER:		SUP ART DIRECTOR:	CONSTRUCTION:	CGI:	
DIRECTOR:		S/B ART DIRECTOR:	FABRICATION:	SFX:	
DOP:		SET DECORATOR:	GRAPHICS:	MINIATURES:	
PROD DESIGNER:		PROPS MASTER:	COSTUME:	PROSTHETICS:	
© BBC CYMRU WALES 2005			OTHER:		

← 7cm →

10cm

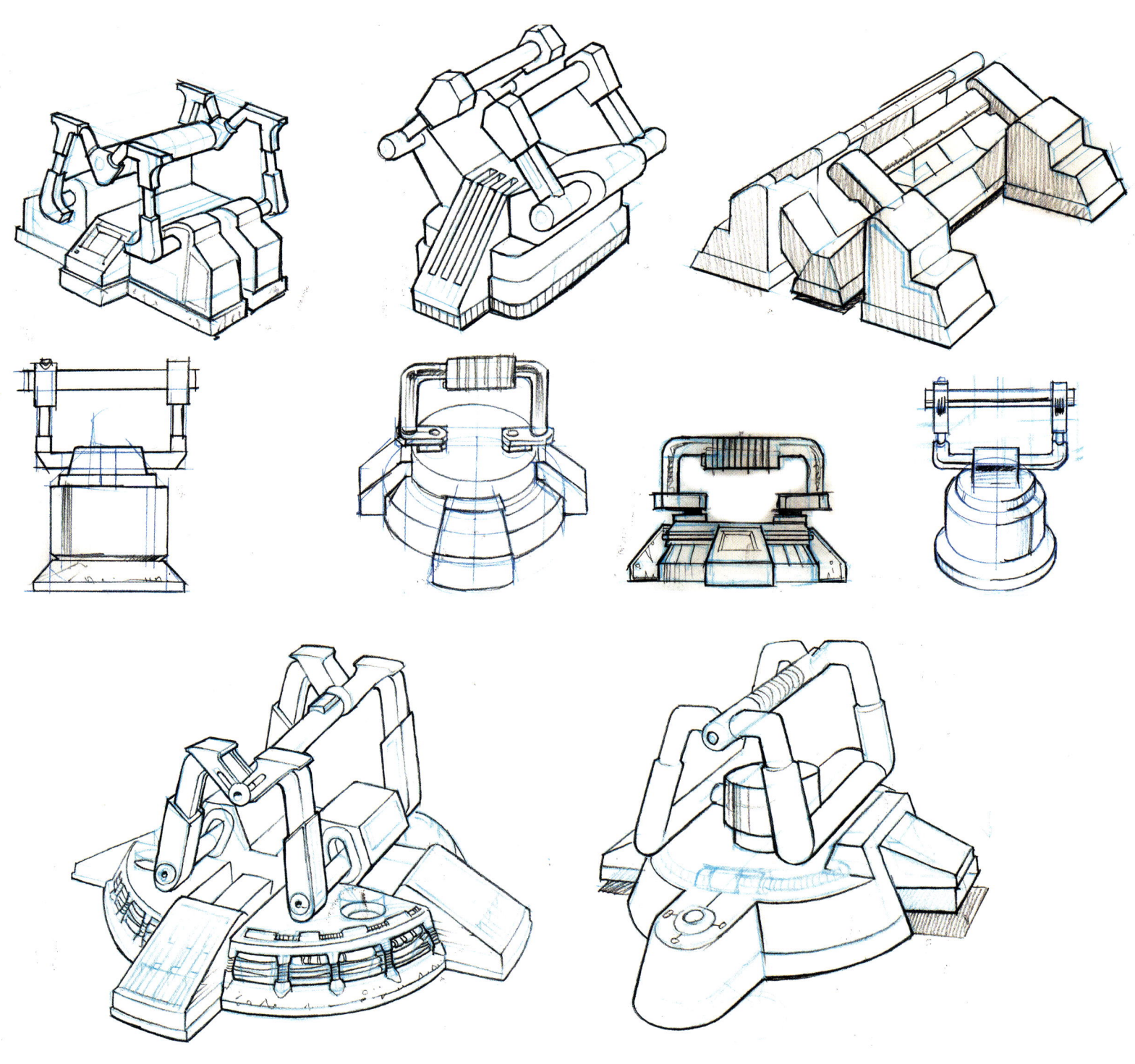

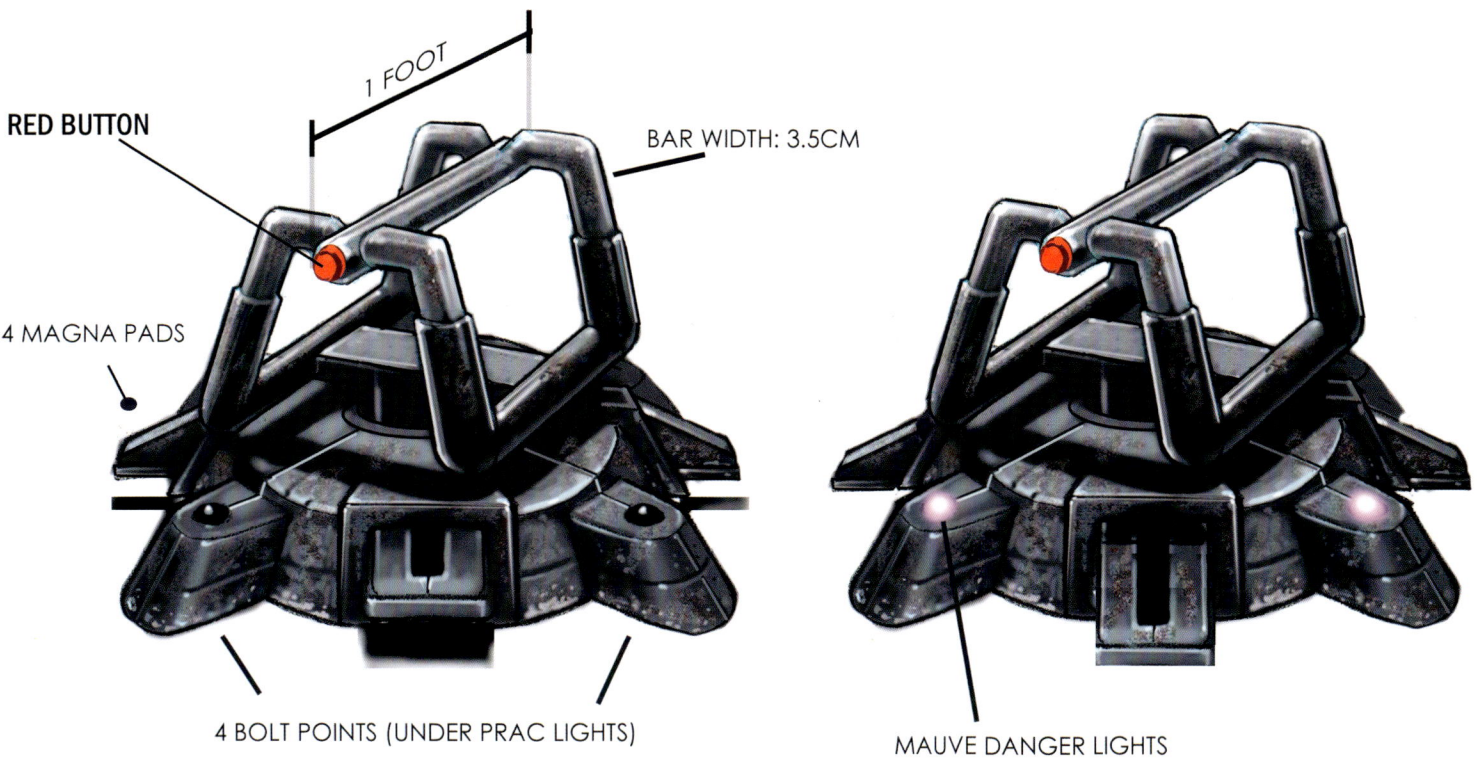

RED BUTTON

1 FOOT

BAR WIDTH: 3.5CM

4 MAGNA PADS

4 BOLT POINTS (UNDER PRAC LIGHTS)

MAUVE DANGER LIGHTS

THE MAGNACLAMPS

The magnaclamps play a big role in the finale of Series 2, *Doomsday*. These futuristic devices can magnetise or clamp onto any surface – perfect to hold on to when a powerful vortex is pulling everyone into a parallel world!

The final design was locked and sent to be fabricated. Their huge size gave them a substantial presence, just as I had envisioned: a piece of technology that felt powerful and functional within the context of the story.

MAGNACLAMP ACTION

'OFF' STATE:
MAGNA PADS RETRACTED

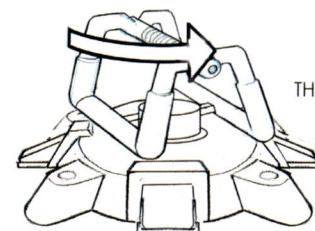

'ON' STATE:
AS THE HANDLE IS TWISTED ROUND THE MAGNA PADS CLAMP DOWN INTO PLACE, PRACS LIGHTS ARE LIT.

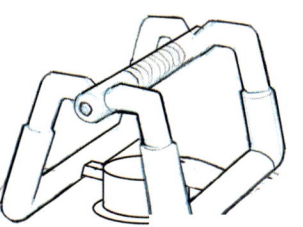

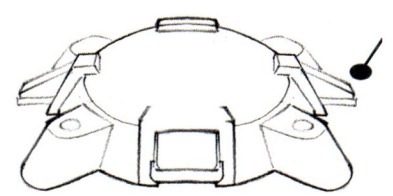

THE GENESIS ARK

This illustration of the Genesis Ark – a dimensionally transcendental Time Lord prison ship to house Daleks, designed by Matt Savage – was produced for the BBC Books title *A History of the Universe in 100 Objects* by James Goss and Steve Tribe.

LOOKING BACK ON SERIES 2

By the time *Doctor Who*'s second run of 13 episodes wrapped up in March 2006, I'd been working almost non-stop since August 2005 – an intense but unbelievably fun experience!

Beyond the work itself – which I loved – there had been some surreal moments along the way. I had met the Doctor himself when David Tennant dropped by the art department to say hello, held the door open for Queen Victoria (Pauline Collins in full costume) and discussed the Cybermen with their creator John Lumic (Roger Lloyd Pack). I'd watched scenes being shot on various sets, recorded an episode commentary with Russell. I'd even spent a few days suited up as a Cyberman and filmed stomping around Cardiff Bay.

Instead of winding down, I was eager to keep the momentum going. Luckily, any concerns I had about needing to find other work after the production ended were quickly dismissed. Russell and Julie Gardner had conceived a spin-off series that would brilliantly expand the *Doctor Who* franchise for adult viewers – *Torchwood*. This fresh and exciting project would keep us busy and creative until work on Series 3 of *Doctor Who* kicked off...

POLICE PUBLIC CALL BOX

POLICE TELEPHONE
FREE
FOR USE OF
PUBLIC
ADVICE & ASSISTANCE
OBTAINABLE IMMEDIATELY
OFFICER & CARS
RESPOND TO CALLS
PULL TO OPEN

Phil Collinson
Producer, Dr Who
invites you to the wrap party for

DOCTOR·WHO

Time:
Friday 31 March 2006
8pm to 4am

Venue:
No. 10 Club, 10-11 Mill Lane, Cardiff CF10 1FL

RSVP

This is a personal invitation and is not transferable
Please bring this invitation with you
ADMITS ONE

TIME JUMP: THE DOCTOR RETURNS

Our first jump in time gathers a selection of my illustrations relating to the Doctor's return in Series 1...

SLITHEEN SPACESHIP – CUTAWAY

The 2005 episodes *Aliens of London* and *World War Three* introduced the family Slitheen – aliens from the planet Raxacoricofallapatorius. This cutaway illustration of their spaceship shows the so-called Space Pig at the controls. The unlucky swine was genetically altered by the Slitheen as part of their plan to put Earth on worldwide alien alert, paving the way for global catastrophe.

(Source: *Doctor Who: The DVD Files* magazine, GE Fabbri)

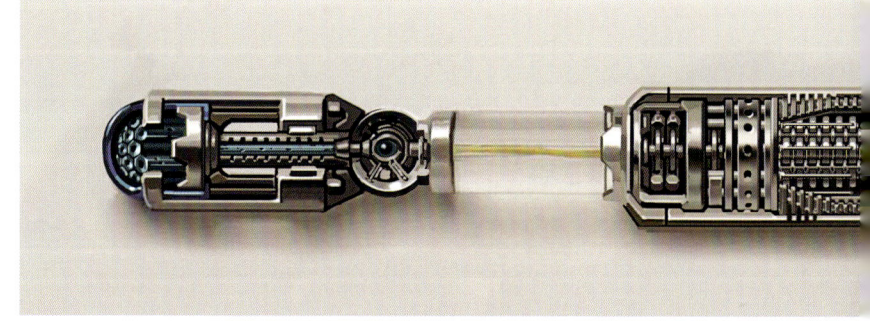

PRIMARY EMITTER CLUSTER

CENTRAL EMITTER CHANNEL

NINTH AND TENTH DOCTORS' SONIC SCREWDRIVER – CUTAWAY

This version of the sonic first appeared in *Rose*, the new series's debut episode. This cutaway illustration gave me the opportunity to delve into its inner workings in detail.

(Source: *Doctor Who: The Visual Dictionary*, Dorling Kindersley)

WAVE PRISM
surrounded by micro stabiliser fields

ANECHOIC CHAMBER

RESONATOR CAGE

FUNCTION DRUMS

THERMAL INSULATION CASING

ACOUSTIC ACCELERATORS

CHARGING CELLS

COOLING CELLS

BRACING COIL

SECONDARY EMITTER CLUSTER

CHULA WARSHIP – CUTAWAY

In the 2005 episodes *The Empty Child* and *The Doctor Dances*, we were introduced to Time Agent Captain Jack Harkness and his stolen spacecraft – a Chula Warship. This illustration was an absolute blast to produce. I loved all the intricate details, mirroring the interior space we see in the episodes, including the cockpit and the sleeping bunk.

(Source: *Doctor Who: The DVD Files* magazine, GE Fabbri)

SQUARENESS GUN – CUTAWAY

The inner workings of the Squareness Gun, a sonic blaster that was introduced in the 2005 episode *The Empty Child*.

(Source: *Doctor Who: The DVD Files* magazine, GE Fabbri)

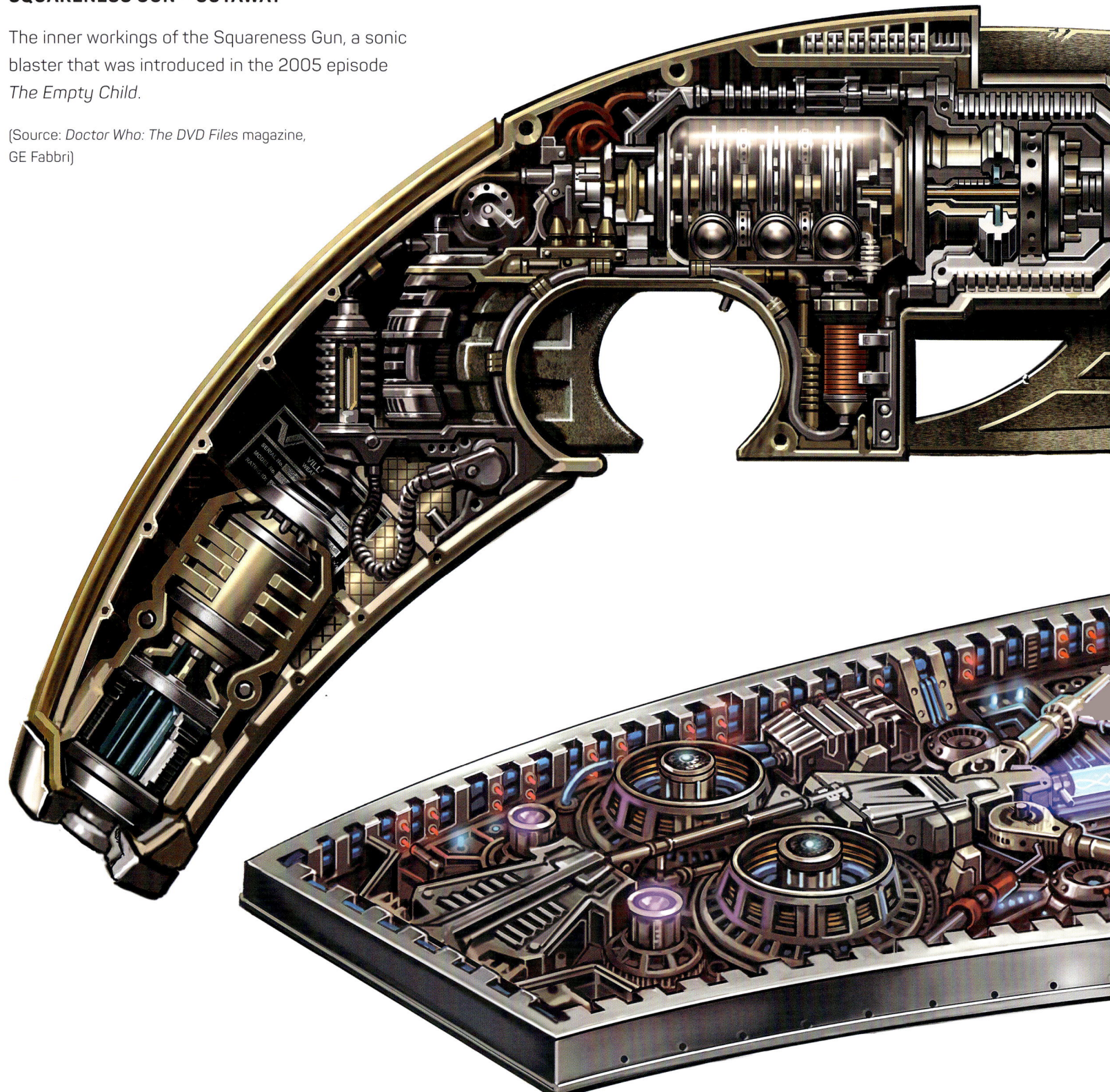

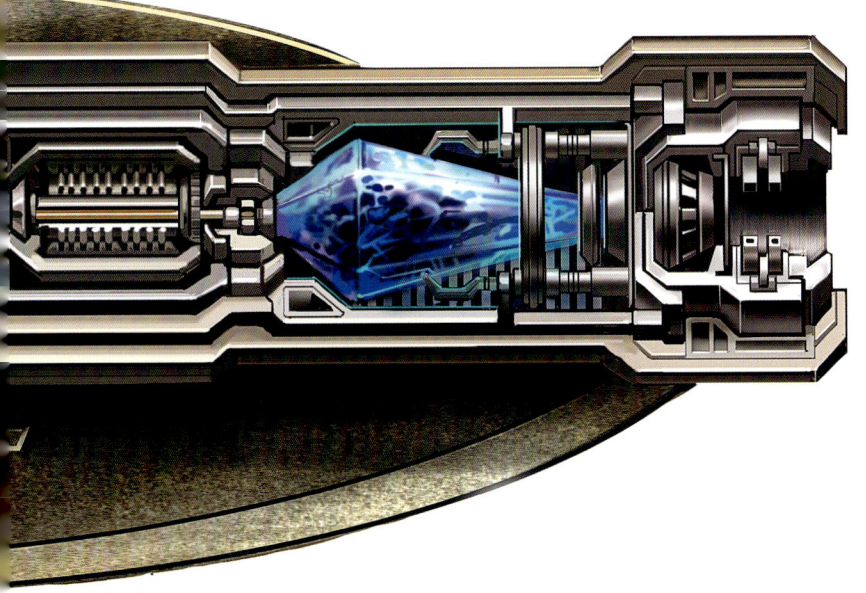

TRIBOPHYSICAL WAVEFORM MACRO-KINETIC EXTRAPOLATOR – CUTAWAY

Featured in the 2005 story *Boom Town*, the Extrapolator was designed to transport a Slitheen across the stars. It harnessed a wave of energy to propel its user through space, functioning both as a vehicle and an energy shield. The illustration reveals the complex energy systems of this unique piece of technology.

(Source: *Doctor Who: The DVD Files* magazine, GE Fabbri)

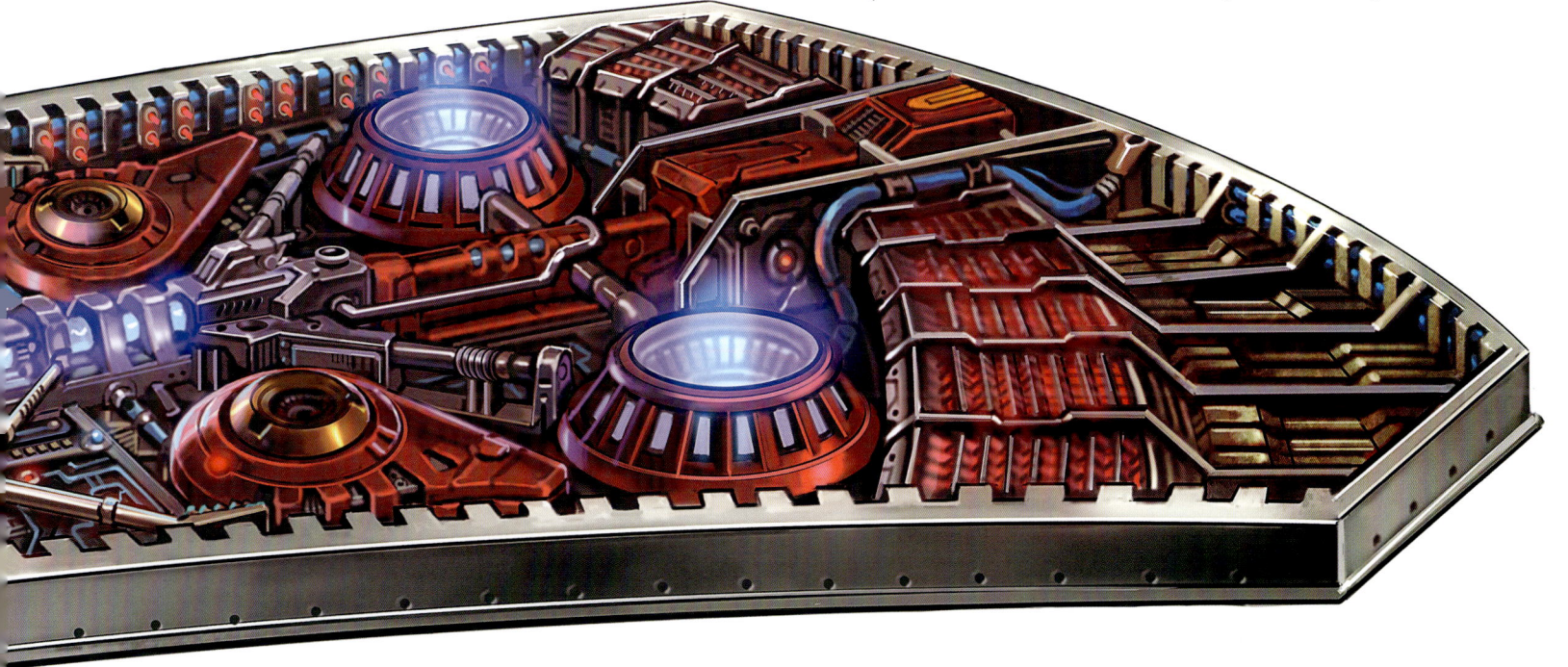

TORCHWOOD SERIES 1

TALES FROM THE RIFT

A selection of concept art and designs for Series 1 of *Torchwood* (2006-7).

THE TORCHWOOD MORGUE AND EARLY DEVELOPMENT CONCEPTS FOR THE TORCHWOOD HUB FOR *EVERYTHING CHANGES*.

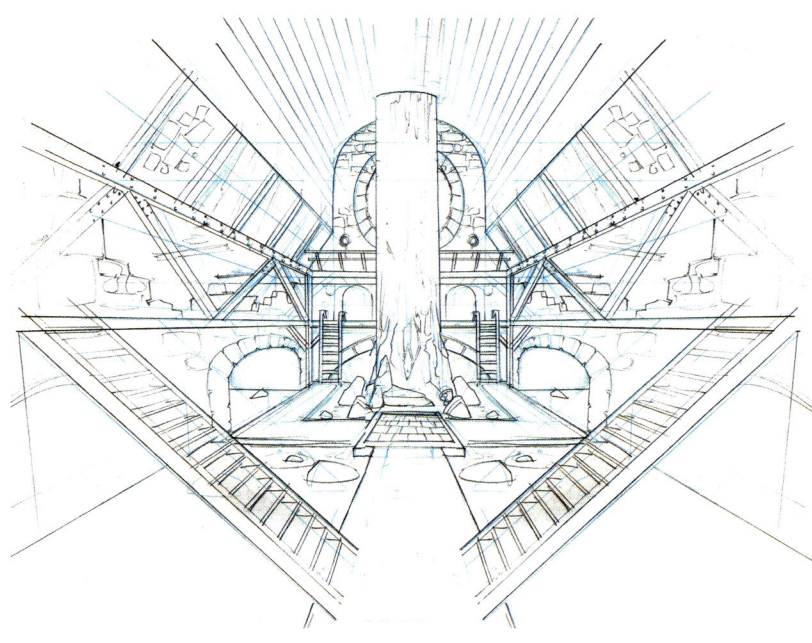

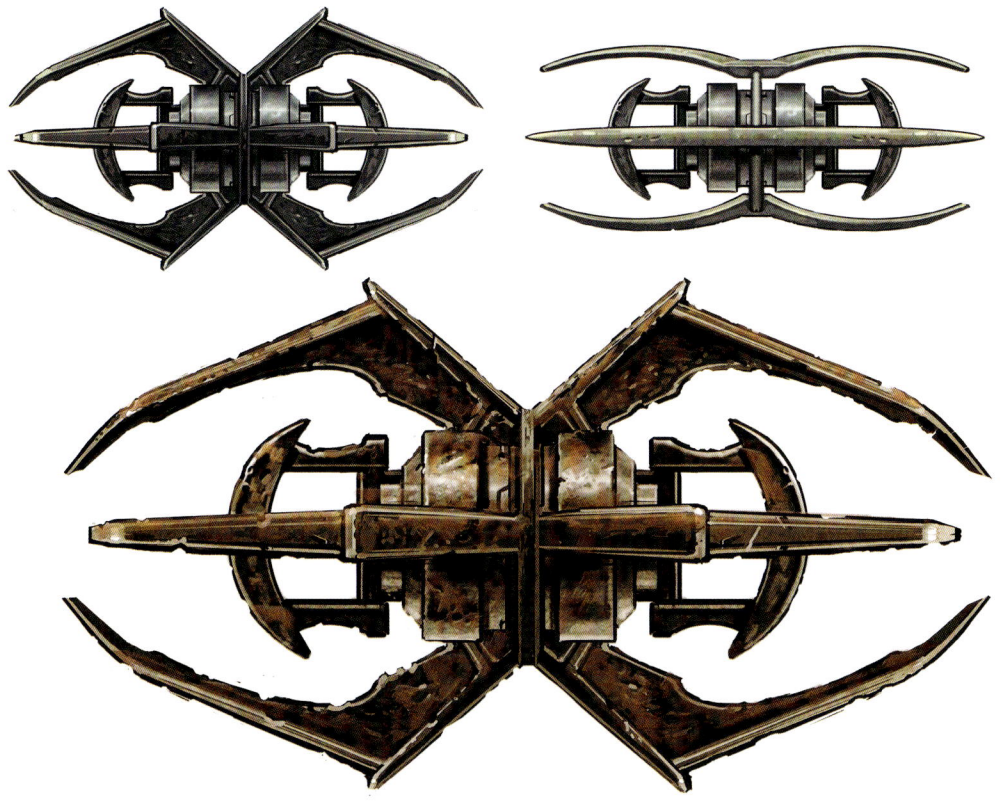

DESIGN DEVELOPMENT FOR THE ALIEN TRANSPORTER PROP FROM *GREEKS BEARING GIFTS*.

DEVELOPMENT CONCEPTS FOR THE TORCHWOOD LIFT.

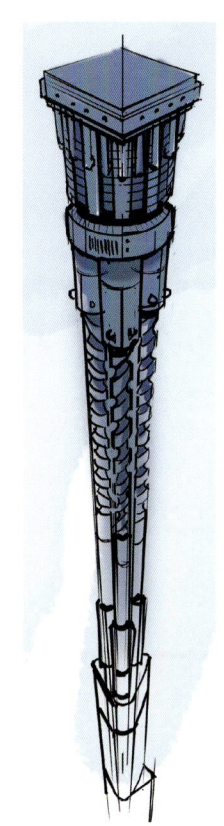

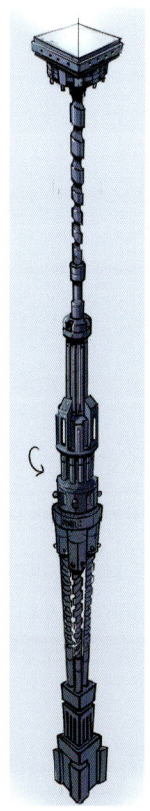

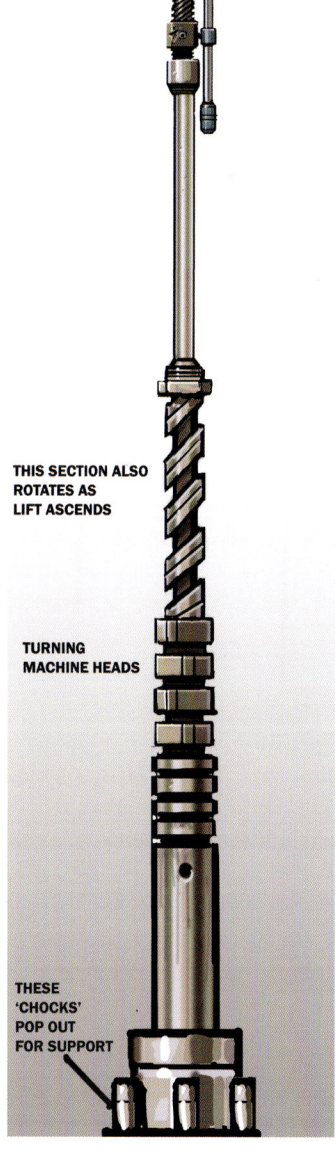

THIS SECTION ALSO ROTATES AS LIFT ASCENDS

TURNING MACHINE HEADS

THESE 'CHOCKS' POP OUT FOR SUPPORT

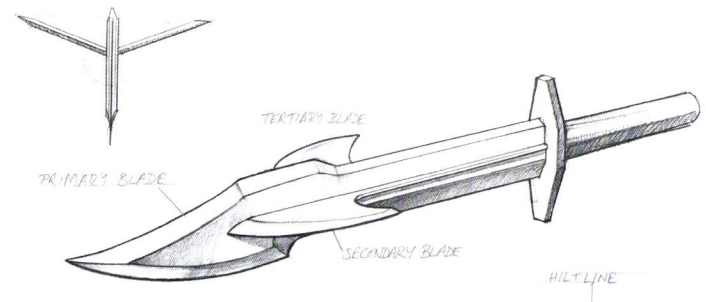

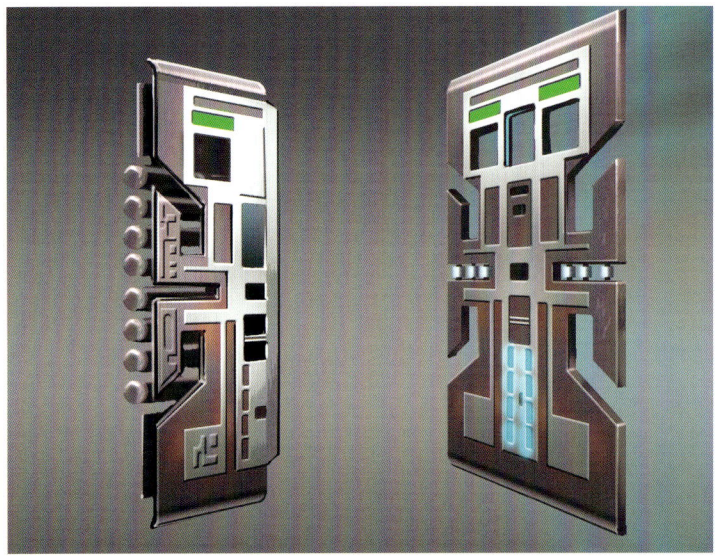

THE LIFE KNIFE (POLICE DRAWING) FROM *EVERYTHING CHANGES.*

THE GREEN MAN PUB SIGN.

COPY DEVICE PROP DESIGN.

PLAGUE WARD CONCEPT FROM *END OF DAYS.*

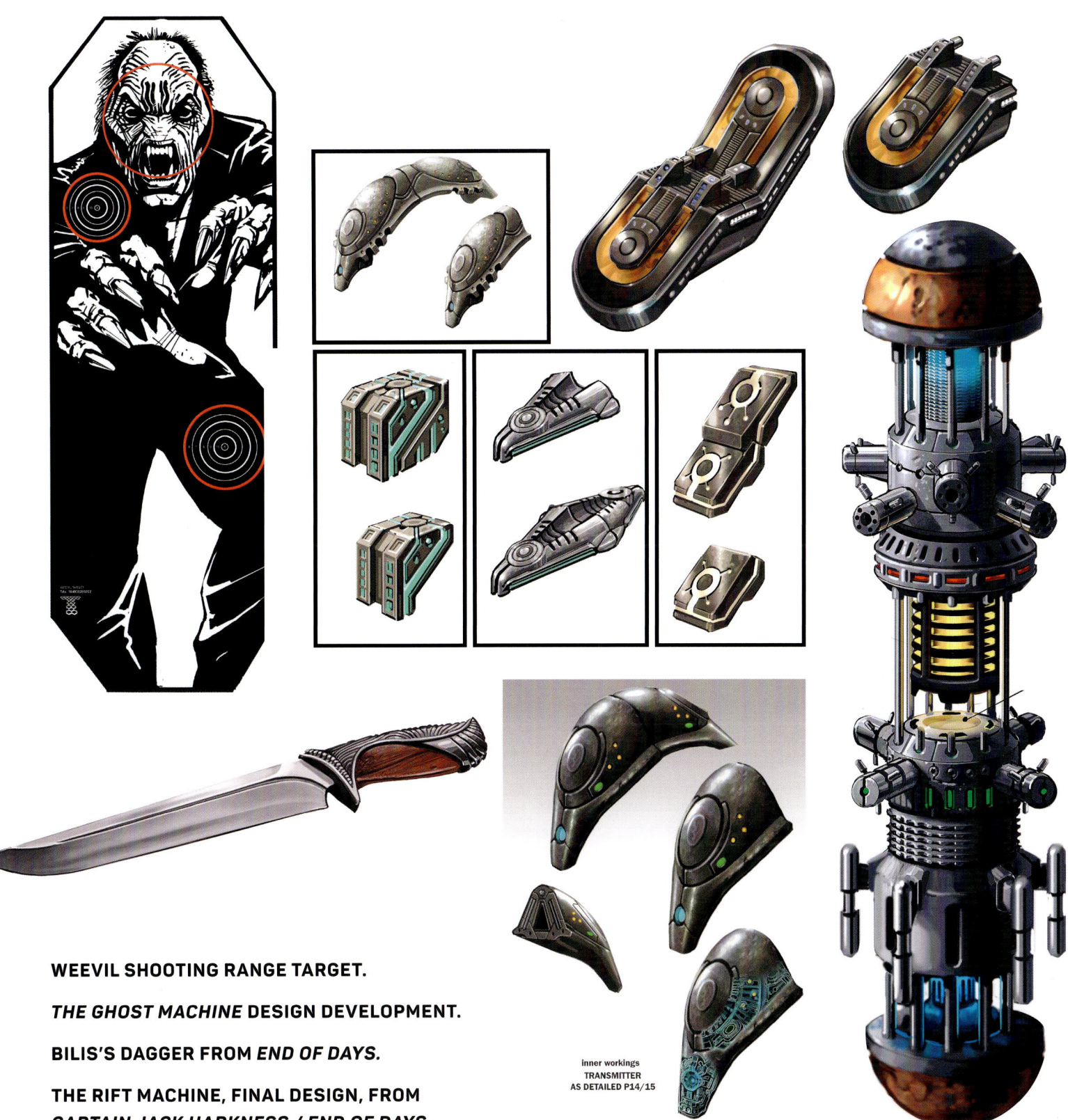

inner workings
TRANSMITTER
AS DETAILED P14/15

WEEVIL SHOOTING RANGE TARGET.

THE GHOST MACHINE DESIGN DEVELOPMENT.

BILIS'S DAGGER FROM *END OF DAYS*.

THE RIFT MACHINE, FINAL DESIGN, FROM
CAPTAIN JACK HARKNESS / END OF DAYS.

DALEKS OVER TOWER BRIDGE (PREVIOUS PAGE)

I really enjoyed this chance to do a big, cinematic *War of the Worlds* style painting of the Daleks wreaking havoc over London!

(Source: *Doctor Who: The Secret Lives of Monsters* by Justin Richards, BBC Books)

GLASS DALEK

The Glass Dalek, a gruesome synthesis of organic horror and cold machine, stands as one of the most unsettling creations in *Revelation of the Daleks* (1985).

(Source: *Doctor Who: A History of the Universe in 100 Objects* by James Goss and Steve Tribe, BBC Books)

**CLASSIC SERIES
DALEK – CUTAWAY**

This was my chance to contribute to a long tradition of 'Dalek Cutaway' artworks that have appeared over the years.

(Source: *Doctor Who: The DVD Files* magazine, GE Fabbri)

DAVROS

It was good to draw Davros as he appeared in his brutal debut, *Genesis of the Daleks* (1975).

(Source: *Doctor Who: A History of the Universe in 100 Objects* by James Goss and Steve Tribe, BBC Books)

DEFENCE DRONE DALEK – CUTAWAY

With its modern, militarised appearance, the Defence Drone Dalek from *Revolution of the Daleks* (2021) really grabbed my attention. I like the idea of a Dalek repurposed for modern security duties while remaining unmistakably 'Dalek'.

(Source: *Doctor Who: The Gold Archive* by Mike Tucker and Steve Cole, BBC Books)

DALEK SHUTTLE – CUTAWAY

For its on-screen appearance in *Remembrance of the Daleks* (1988), this modular ship was built as an impressive full-scale prop. For this cutaway I made some minor interior modifications to give the Dalek flight crew a little more elbow (or should that be plunger?) room.

(Source: *Doctor Who: The DVD Files* magazine, GE Fabbri)

THE SPECIAL WEAPONS DALEK

Possibly the coolest Dalek to appear in *Doctor Who*'s classic series, the Special Weapons Dalek (like the shuttle, from 1988's *Remembrance of the Daleks*) was an absolute gift to illustrate. I was so fond of this relentless war machine that I used it as the basis for one of my Supreme Dalek designs.

(Source: *Doctor Who: A History of the Universe in 100 Objects* by James Goss and Steve Tribe, BBC Books)

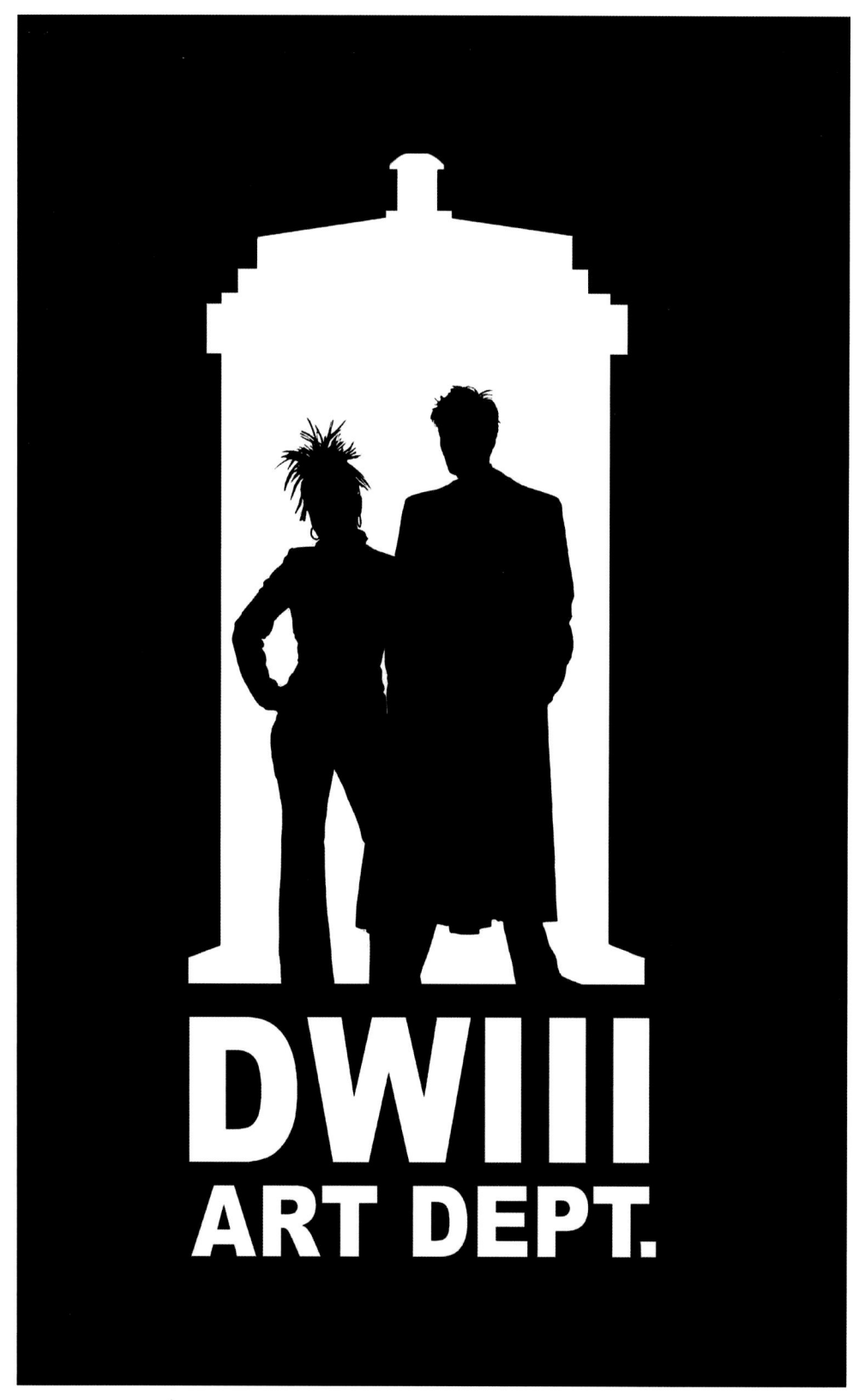

The logo I created for the Series 3 art department crew T-shirt.

PART 2 | SERIES 3

ALL ABOARD AT UPPERBOAT

Series 3 of *Doctor Who* felt like a fresh beginning, largely because the entire team had relocated. We'd left behind Q2 and moved to new premises at Upper Boat Studios – a former seatbelt factory turned into a bustling television studio complex. Spanning 86,000 square feet, it housed everything from prop and construction workshops to video editing suites, six sound stages and the entire art department.

Nestled on an industrial estate near Treforest, the studio took its name from the nearby village. A welcome highlight of the new set-up was the Blue Box Café, a TARDIS-blue cafeteria where cast and crew could unwind and grab a bite to eat throughout the day. The café's atmosphere was always unpredictable – sometimes it was calm and quiet while other times I'd walk in to find cast members belting out show tunes or entertaining the crew with stories and jokes.

One of my favourite memories was heading into the Blue Box for a tea one grey afternoon to find the Doctor himself, David Tennant, all alone and whirling round in his iconic long coat loudly singing along to the Scissor Sisters' 'I Don't Feel Like Dancin' ' as it played on the café radio.

I was by now fully immersed in my work on *Doctor Who*, but I didn't know that I was about to start a new chapter in my personal life. Cardiff, which had already felt like home during Series 2, was about to shape my future in ways I hadn't anticipated...

THE RUNAWAY BRIDE

THE WEBSTAR

The Webstar, the vessel belonging to the Empress of the Racnoss, was my first design for Series 3 and Russell and I discussed it at length over email. He loved the mixture of the pointed star design and organic layered webbing and commented that 'by the end of the script, the Web Star will be filling the sky over London like a proper Christmas star, except evil'. So while how the ship functions isn't important to the plot, I did push the pointed arms of the star back slightly to imply forward movement and give it a dynamic feel.

This story-driven design gave the ship a striking silhouette from afar, while up close it suggested the darker, more sinister nature of the Racnoss. It made the vessel both beautiful and ominous in that signature *Doctor Who* way, balancing fantasy with just enough sci-fi to make it feel part of this universe.

WEBSTAR INTERIOR

My first image portrayed how the shot might look with the camera looking over the shoulder of the Empress as she's watching the Doctor on her screens. This space was then expanded with new visuals showing the interior more fully.

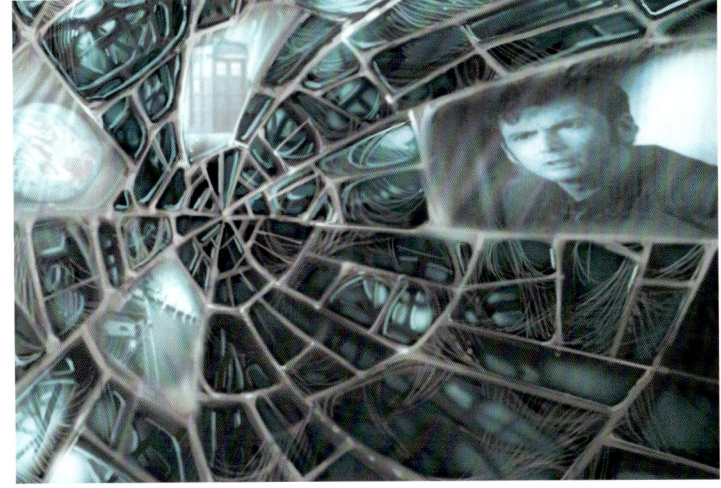

Subject: Web Star Interior
Sent: Monday, June 19, 2006 6:57 PM
To: Russell T Davies
From: Peter Mckinstry

Hello

Attached are designs for the Web Star interior. The first image shows the general interior, where the layered structure echoes the ships exterior. In the centre is the Empress's cocoon, the focal point where she spends her time... doing Empress type things... the second image is of the Empress's cockpit. This is the practical set which houses the 4 projected screens.

Please let us know your thoughts,

Thanks

Pete

Sent: Monday, June 19, 2006 9:51 PM
To: Peter Mckinstry
From: Russell T Davies

Brilliant, beautiful stuff! Thank you.

Director Euros Lynn wanted to see a wider shot of the space to get a better understanding of the scale of the Empress within it, and to think about further possible shot set ups.

R x

Sent: Wednesday, June 21, 2006 1:45 PM
To: Russell T Davies
From: Peter Mckinstry

Hello

Attached are two new images based on Euros' feedback. The Empress is now in the larger open area. Let us know if this works better.

Thanks!

Pete

Sent: Wednesday, June 21, 2006 11:22 PM
To: Peter Mckinstry
From: Russell T Davies

That is amazing, how brilliant. Beautiful work! Thank you!

As Euros says, she's hidden in her lair at the beginning, as she is in your INTERIOR, just legs a-poking. Though if we can use the SIDE-ELEVATION later, at the end... well, that would be lovely, but it depends on our shot allocations.

Many thanks,

R x

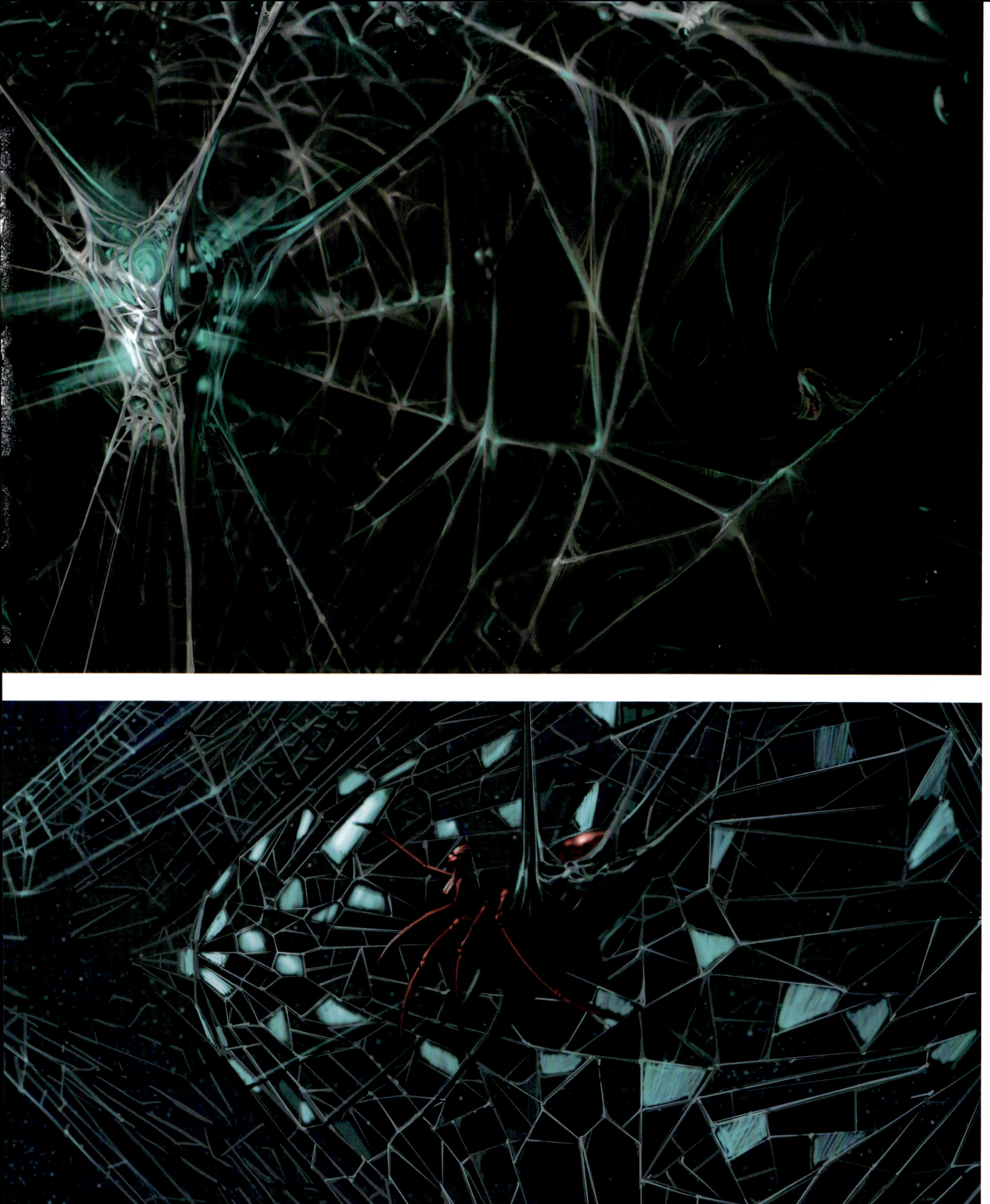

THE EMPRESS OF THE RACNOSS

Russell's script for *The Runaway Bride* portrayed the Empress as a figure of intergalactic royalty – imposing, otherworldly and powerful. I was eager to start capturing some ideas for the upcoming Tone Meeting, where these early sketches would help kick off discussions on how best to bring the Empress to life – whether through prosthetics, practical effects or CGI. Given the sheer scale of her character and the complexity of the special effects required, it was crucial to start these conversations early so that the Empress not only aligned with Russell's ambitious vision but also looked spectacular on screen.

As I developed the design, I wanted to explore her royal status in a way that felt unique to the Racnoss. I added a cobweb-like veil and a webbed tiara, complete with jewel-like spider eyes that would blink with the aid of CGI. It gave her a certain Miss Havisham quality, playing off the bridal theme in the episode while emphasising her sinister, ancient grandeur. Her on-screen appearance would ultimately be more alien, but this version makes her less of a monster, balancing her otherworldly menace with an eerie, decayed elegance.

Russell's reaction was: 'Cor blimey, that's beautiful. She's beautiful. I could almost fancy her. Almost.'

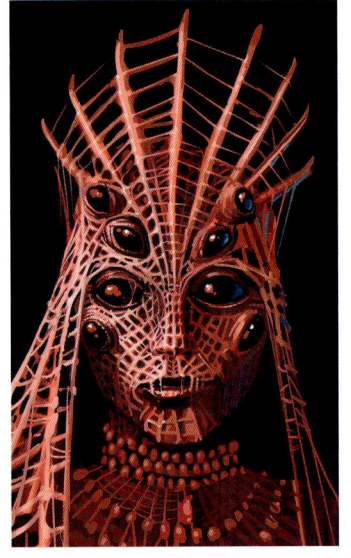

DONNA AND LANCE WEBBED UP

This concept was done to show how Donna and Lance might look while they're all webbed up, attached to the roof of the Empress's underground lair.

HUON TUBES

The Huon Tubes were essential for the particle extrusion process used by Torchwood to manufacture Huon particles, and so needed to feel industrial and high-tech.

In these designs, you can see the initial concept sketches, which lay out the structure and flow of the pipe systems. I also included a version where I painted the pipes into a location photo, to give a sense of how they would integrate into the real-world set. This approach helped ensure that the pipes would feel like a natural part of the environment, while still conveying the futuristic technology central to the story.

Subject: Huon Pipes
Sent: Thursday, June 15, 2006 3:18 PM
To: Russell T Davies
From: Peter Mckinstry

Hi Russell,

Attached is a visual of the Huon pipe system. The phials can be seen at the base of the central tube.

Let me know what you think.

Thanks,

Pete

Sent: Thursday, June 15, 2006 3:37 PM
To: Peter Mckinstry
From: Russell T Davies

Absolutely gorgeous! Cor, that's one of your best yet. Thank you!

R x

ACTUAL LOCATION   TWO ARMED HUON EXTRUSION CHAMBER   THREE ARMED HUON EXTRUSION CHAMBER

SANTA MASK

The Santa masks in *The Runaway Bride* were a fresh take on those used in *The Christmas Invasion*. Since the masks would be seen repeatedly in close-up this time around, they needed a more finished look. For inspiration, I thought back to some of the moulded plastic wall decorations that were popular in the seventies and early eighties. Those decorations had a kitschy yet slightly eerie quality, which I wanted to channel into this updated version.

As a fun extra, this mask design was made available over the festive season for fans to print out and turn into their own Santa masks at home.

BANKNOTES

Talk about something unexpectedly taking on a life of its own! These banknotes were originally created for a scene where the Doctor sonics a cash machine, causing a flurry of notes to fly out. The notes needed to look believable on screen, but clearly fake when examined up close, so no one would mistake them for actual currency.

I came up with the idea of replacing the usual portraits with one of David Tennant as the Tenth Doctor (on a £10 note, fittingly!). It was then suggested I include a portrait of our producer, Phil Collinson, on another note. I really enjoyed getting into the details – designing the intricate geometric patterns, selecting the fonts, and creating something that felt right for this quirky moment.

For David's note, I added the motto from his debut episode *The Christmas Invasion*: '*No second chances – I'm that sort of man.*' Phil's note featured a classic Fourth Doctor line from the story *Robot*: '*There's no point in being grown-up if you can't be childish sometimes.*' Banknotes usually have a signature – often the Chief Cashier, so I took the opportunity to put my own signature on them, but as the less lofty position of 'Chief Numpty'.

These custom notes quickly became quite popular among the crew. Since we printed plenty, anyone who wanted a few could grab some as souvenirs. I was later astonished when, in 2009, I was contacted by one of the curators from the British Museum's Department of Coins and Medals. They informed me that the banknotes would be going on display in Room 68 – a surreal and unexpected honour for a prop I thought would only exist in a fleeting moment on screen!

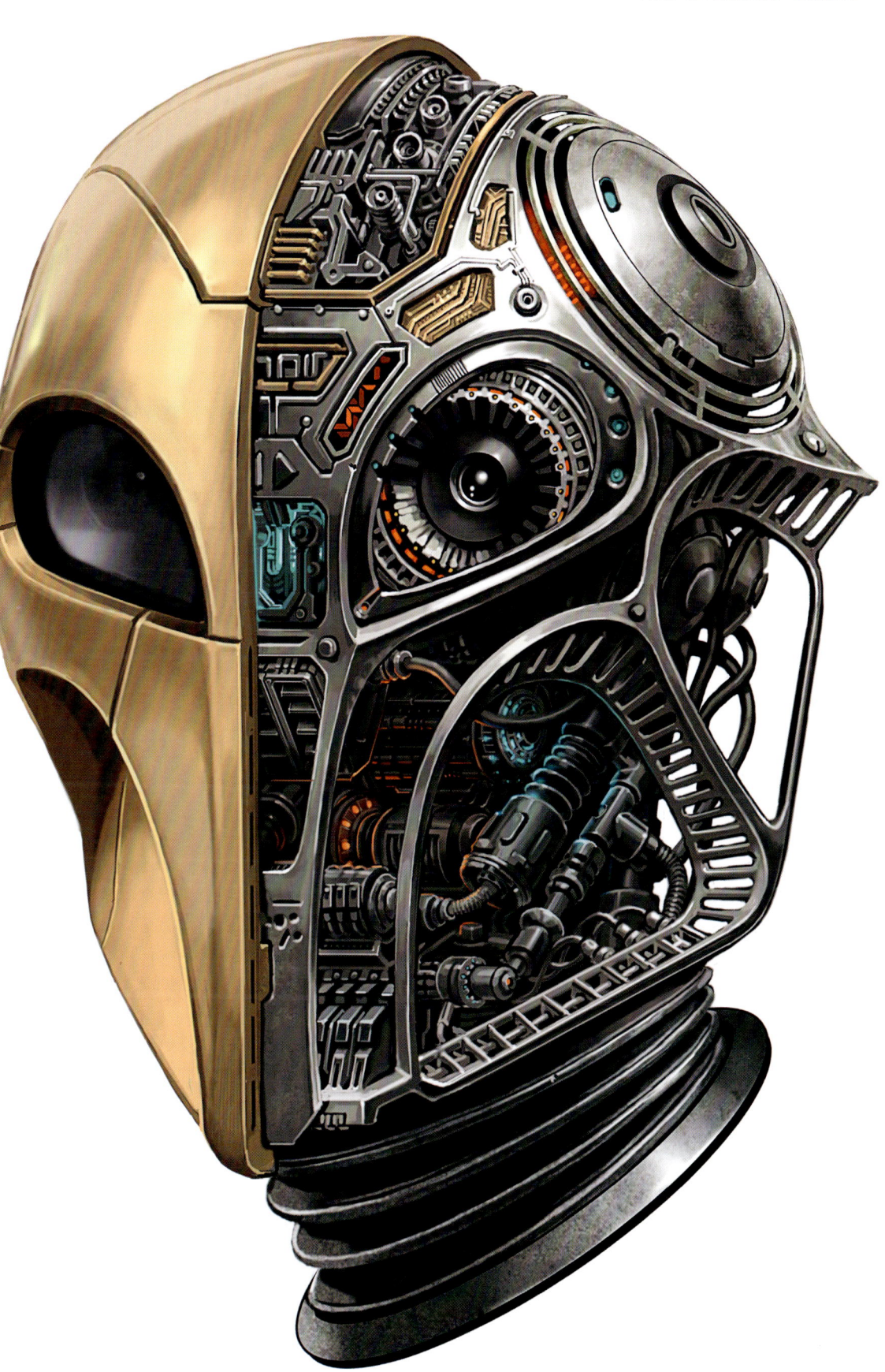

ROBOFORM – CUTAWAY

Originally produced for the *Doctor Who: The DVD Files* magazine from GE Fabbri, this cutaway illustration unmasks a Roboform – one of the robots hiding their true form beneath the sinister Santa masks. It's another fully digital painting. I really enjoyed getting into the detail of this one... and like to think the sideways glance suggests they're not *all* bad!

SMITH AND JONES

JUDOON GUNS

Catherine Samuels, production buyer on 41 episodes of *Doctor Who*, was another friendly face in the art department. For this episode, Cath had brought in a selection of toy guns to serve as the basis for the Judoon's weapons. These particular toys had been chosen because of their horn-shaped hand grips, which tied in perfectly with the overall look of the Judoon. I took some photos of the toys and painted over them, illustrating how we could build upon the base design to create the distinct, futuristic weapons for the Judoon.

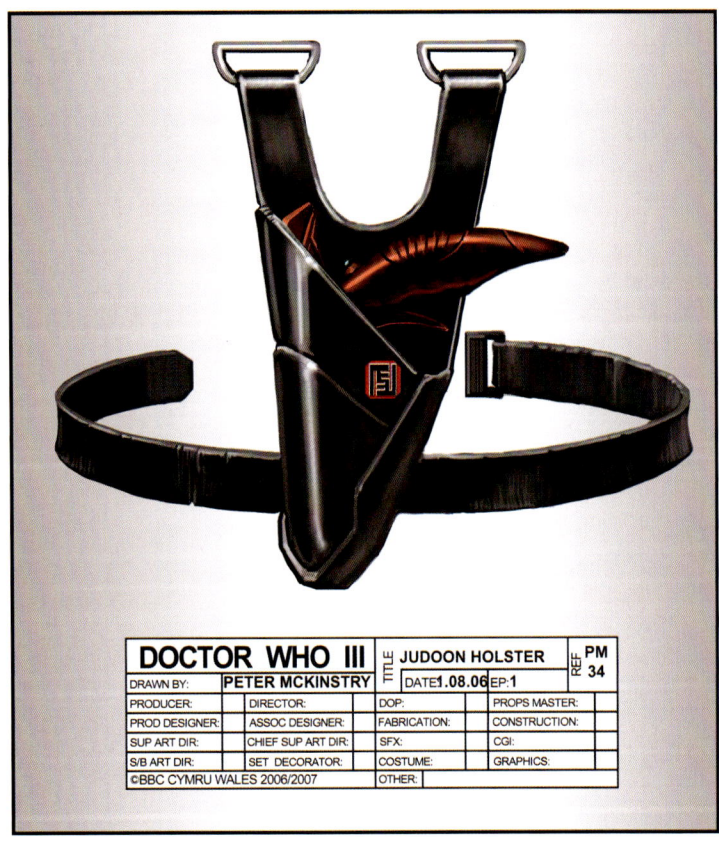

DOCTOR WHO III						JUDOON HOLSTER		REF	PM
				TITLE					34
DRAWN BY:	PETER MCKINSTRY				DATE 1.08.06	EP:1			
PRODUCER:		DIRECTOR:		DOP:			PROPS MASTER:		
PROD DESIGNER:		ASSOC DESIGNER:		FABRICATION:			CONSTRUCTION:		
SUP ART DIR:		CHIEF SUP ART DIR:		SFX:			CGI:		
S/B ART DIR:		SET DECORATOR:		COSTUME:			GRAPHICS:		
©BBC CYMRU WALES 2006/2007				OTHER:					

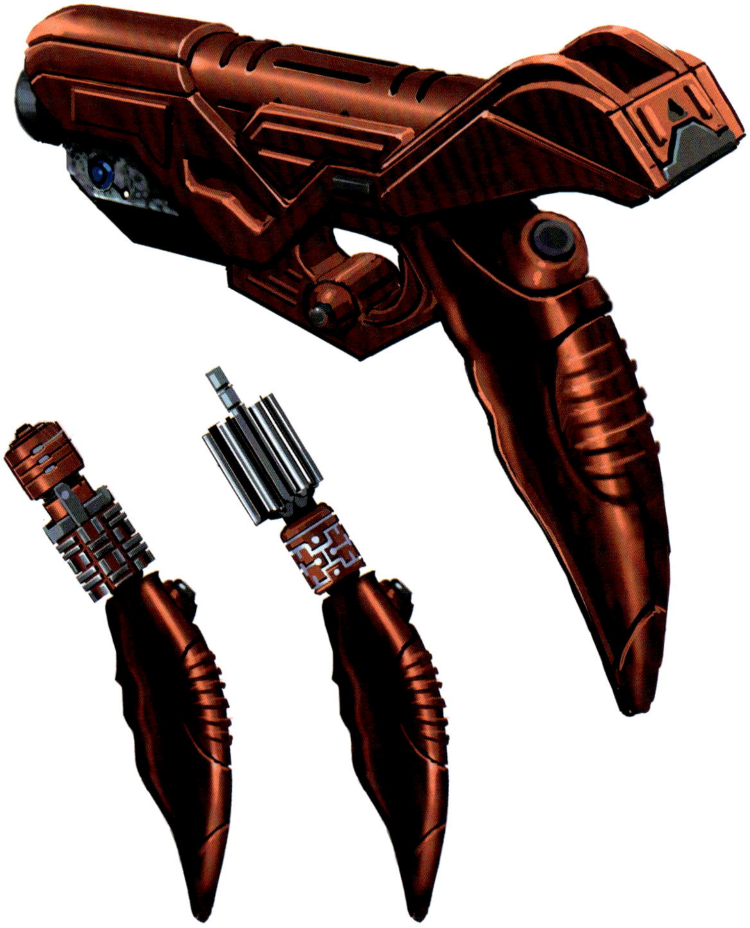

JUDOON ALPHABET

When designing the Judoon alphabet, I was conscious of making it distinct from the alien text seen in *The Impossible Planet* and *The Satan Pit*. After gathering a range of visual references, I settled on a bold, blocky design, focusing on straight lines and sharp corners. This gave the Judoon alphabet a militaristic, no-nonsense feel, perfectly matching their nature.

Subject: Judoon Language
Sent: Tuesday, August 1, 2006 8:38 AM
To: Russell T Davies
From: Peter Mckinstry

Hello,

Time for the Judoon language. It's based loosely on a particular symbol from the Adrinka language of West Africa. It reflects the Judoon characteristics – it's bold, strong and has visual elements seen in the other Judoon paraphernalia.

The first image shows all the different symbols. The idea is that the top and bottom of each block symbol is different, and it's how you place these ends opposite each other which forms the words/phrases etc. At the bottom is the symbol for the Judoon themselves, which if you are happy with, we can put on the gun and the chest. The second image shows the compensation form itself.

Thanks,

Pete

Sent: Tuesday, August 1, 2006 9:11 AM
To: Peter Mckinstry
From: Russell T Davies

Love it! Brilliant.

You speak Judoon!

R x

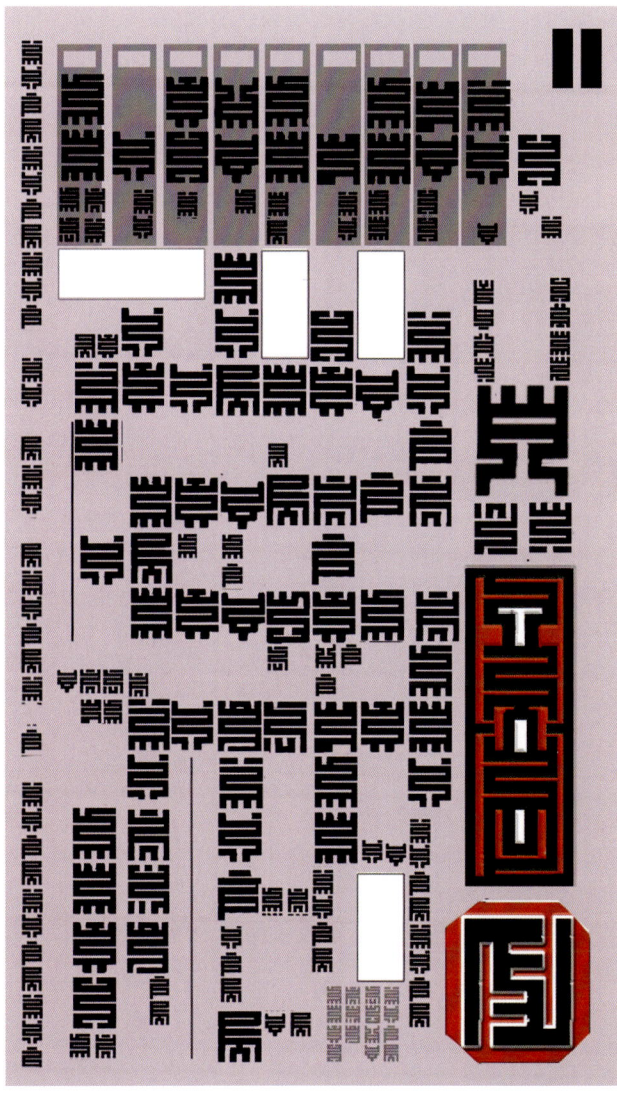

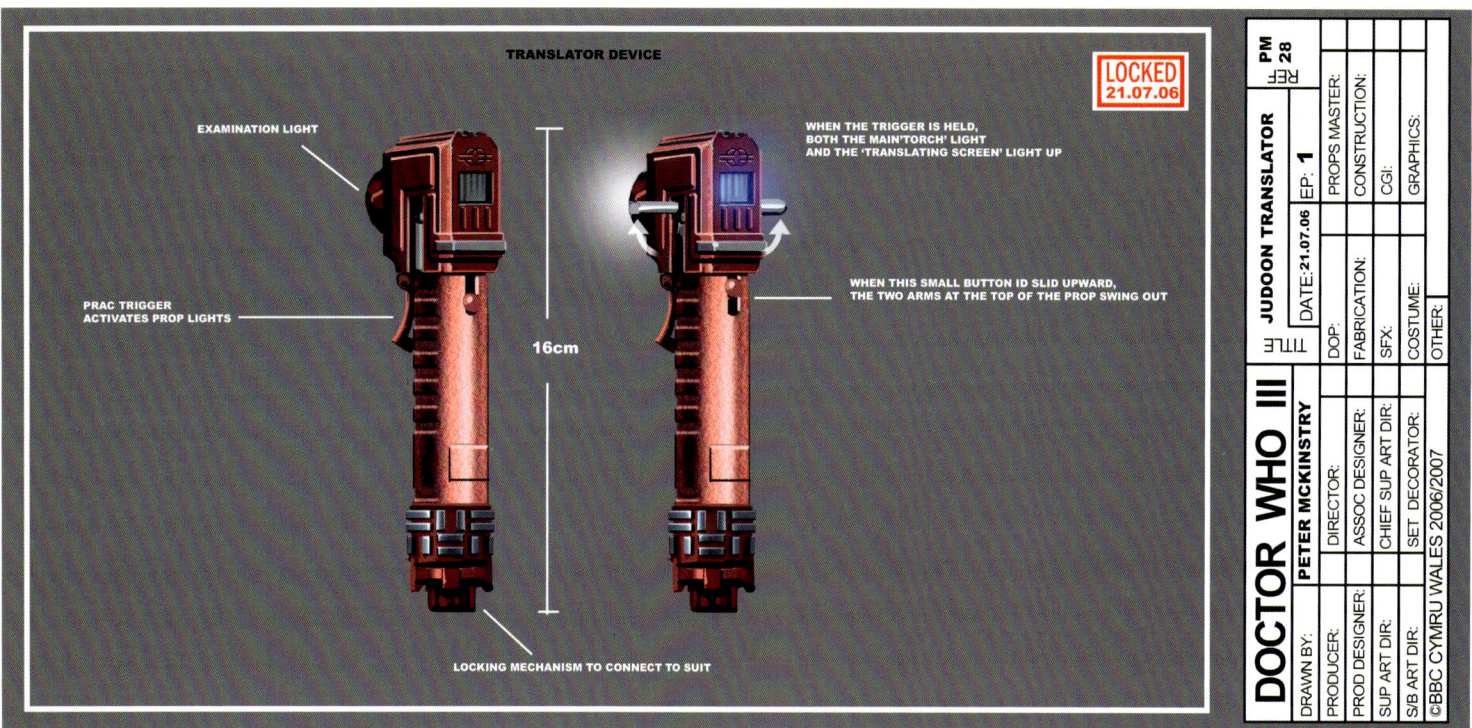

TRANSLATOR DEVICE

EXAMINATION LIGHT

WHEN THE TRIGGER IS HELD,
BOTH THE MAIN 'TORCH' LIGHT
AND THE 'TRANSLATING SCREEN' LIGHT UP

PRAC TRIGGER
ACTIVATES PROP LIGHTS

16cm

WHEN THIS SMALL BUTTON ID SLID UPWARD,
THE TWO ARMS AT THE TOP OF THE PROP SWING OUT

LOCKING MECHANISM TO CONNECT TO SUIT

LOCKED
21.07.06

DOCTOR WHO III	TITLE	JUDOON TRANSLATOR		REF	PM 28
		DATE: 21.07.06	EP: 1		
DRAWN BY: PETER MCKINSTRY					
PRODUCER:	DIRECTOR:	DOP:	PROPS MASTER:		
PROD DESIGNER:	ASSOC DESIGNER:	FABRICATION:	CONSTRUCTION:		
SUP ART DIR:	CHIEF SUP ART DIR:	SFX:	CGI:		
S/B ART DIR:	SET DECORATOR:	COSTUME:	GRAPHICS:		
©BBC CYMRU WALES 2006/2007		OTHER:			

JUDOON PROPS

The Judoon also needed their own props, specifically a translator device and a 'species identifier'. The translator, in fact, was a repurposed prop from Series 2 – Jake's scanner. That prop had been used on-screen but not in close-up, so it was possible to give it a second life here. It was a well-realised piece, with moving parts and functional lights, so rather than start from scratch, I created a new concept based on that prop. I showed how we could add a new covering for the grip and head area to match the Judoon's aesthetic, bringing it in line with their distinct look while saving time and resources.

The species identifier and communicator props were designed to tie in with the overall aesthetic of the Judoon spaceship. The goal was to imply that all Judoon equipment, from their tools to their vessels, followed the same brutal, utilitarian design philosophy, reinforcing their identity as a unified and efficient force.

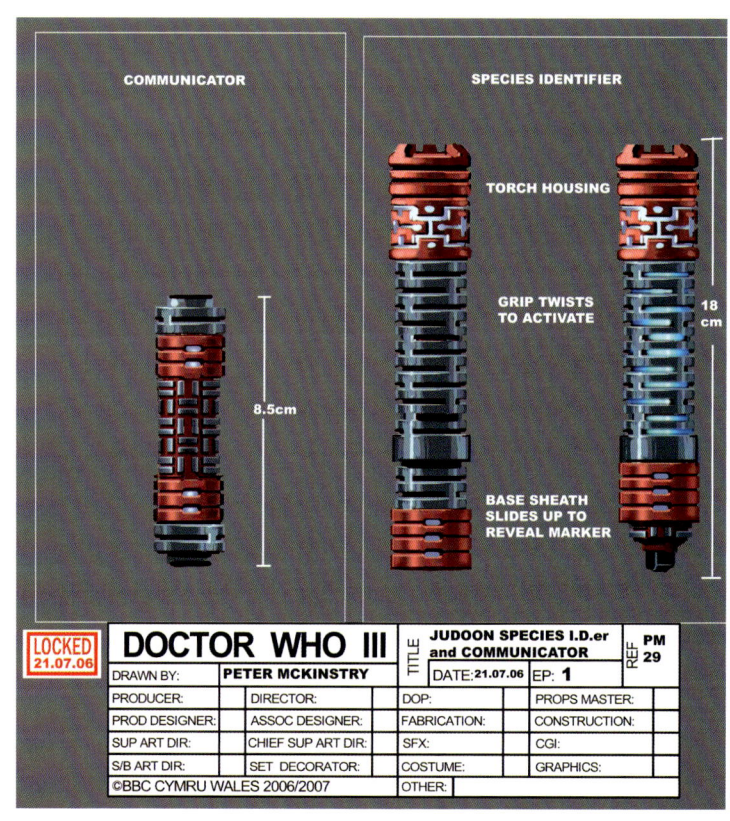

COMMUNICATOR

SPECIES IDENTIFIER

TORCH HOUSING

GRIP TWISTS
TO ACTIVATE

8.5cm

18 cm

BASE SHEATH
SLIDES UP TO
REVEAL MARKER

LOCKED
21.07.06

DOCTOR WHO III	TITLE	JUDOON SPECIES I.D.er and COMMUNICATOR		REF	PM 29
DRAWN BY: PETER MCKINSTRY		DATE: 21.07.06	EP: 1		
PRODUCER:	DIRECTOR:	DOP:	PROPS MASTER:		
PROD DESIGNER:	ASSOC DESIGNER:	FABRICATION:	CONSTRUCTION:		
SUP ART DIR:	CHIEF SUP ART DIR:	SFX:	CGI:		
S/B ART DIR:	SET DECORATOR:	COSTUME:	GRAPHICS:		
©BBC CYMRU WALES 2006/2007		OTHER:			

JUDOON TRANSLATOR – CUTAWAY

As shown here, it was almost as much fun to come up with the names for the various components as it was to produce the image. The purple wave pattern was a modified piece of the sixties *Doctor Who* title sequence. Originally created for GE Fabbri's *Doctor Who: The DVD Files* magazine.

THE SHAKESPEARE CODE

WITCH SWORD

I hadn't tackled a sword design before! My aim was to make sure the weapon felt connected to the character – and since the witch (or Carrionite) in the story had a habit of crafting disturbing little dolls, it seemed only fitting that her weapon would carry some similarly dark, personal touches.

I incorporated a trio of shrunken heads on the hilt for a sinister layer of detail. Past victims, perhaps, or ex-partners! I also wrapped the hilt in plaited hair which then fanned out, giving the sword an almost broomstick-like silhouette.

BODKIN AND STRAW DOLL

This wasn't the only time I had to create a rustic-looking doll. Years later, I was asked to do something similar for *Game of Thrones*. There's something so eerie about these kinds of handmade, crude figures. Despite their simplicity, they can carry a lot of emotional or narrative weight, adding an unsettling, folk-horror element to the story.

Russell felt the same: 'The doll is wonderful, really creepy. What is it about dolls?!'

CARRIONITE

I loved working on the Carrionite design. After reading the script, I began gathering reference images to find a direction and was particularly drawn to bird skulls and photos of freshly hatched birds. I started sketching, combining the two concepts, using the bird skull as a kind of exoskeleton that shields the fleshy parts beneath. The aim was to blend bird-like eeriness with classic witch features, such as the hook nose and elongated chin. I was thrilled when the design made it to the screen almost unchanged. (Though I wasn't a fan of the wobble they added to the chin – it was meant to be bone!)

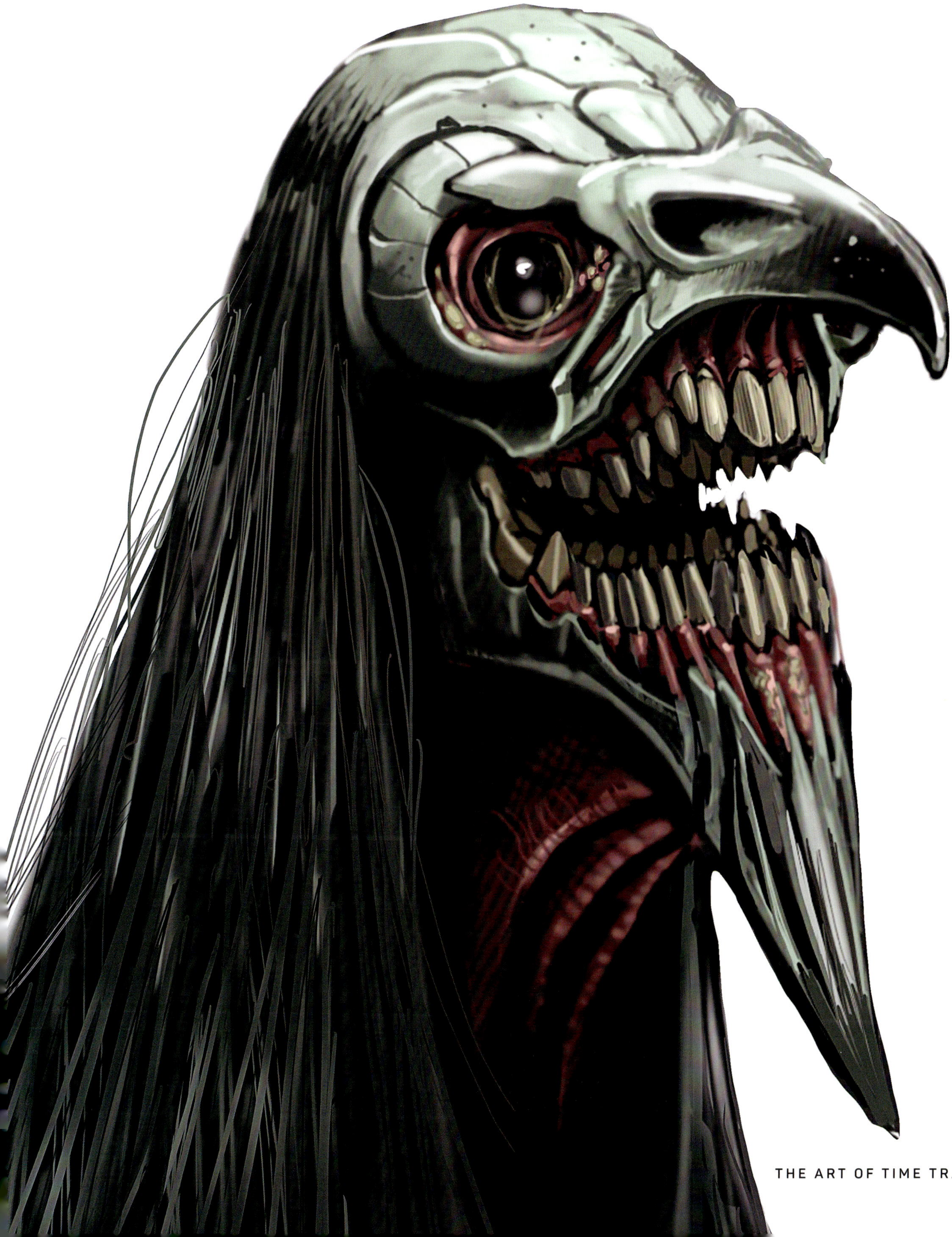

CARRIONITE CAULDRON

The design of the cauldron went through a few variations; if I remember correctly, the director, Charlie Palmer, requested the addition of an eye design. By the time we'd settled on their distinctive aesthetic, the cauldron had already been made, so I didn't get the chance to go back and apply that look to it, which was a bit of a shame.

LOCKED
16.08.06

CARRIONITE CRYSTAL BALL

My initial versions of these alien witches' scrying glasses were fairly traditional crystal balls cradled in iron stands. It worked, but it wasn't particularly interesting. Once the Carrionite design was approved, I revisited the crystal ball concept and infused it with the same eerie, witchy aesthetic. I warped the bone-like structure around the ball, making it feel more like an extension of their power, as though their dark magic was physically binding and shaping it. This approach gave the crystal ball a much more dynamic and fittingly sinister look, and it also offered a way to hide the wiring for the internal lights.

BECOMING BILL

'Has anyone here ever used a quill?' Steffan called out as he burst into the art department. 'We need to get a close-up of Shakespeare's hand.' He scanned the room, clearly on the hunt for a volunteer. 'We need someone who can actually write with it. Like, now!'

I had been happy to step in at zero notice as a Cyberman. But, writing with a quill?

Supervising Art Director Arwel Jones turned to me. 'Peter, you can do that sort of thing, right?' He ignored me shaking my head. 'I'm sure you'll manage.' On the way to set, we passed Dean outside the Blue Box Café. 'He's going to be your hand, Dean,' Arwel informed him. Dean glanced at his stand-in – or hand-in – gave a noncommittal nod, and went back to his script.

One minute, I'd been designing props; the next, I was in a ruffled shirt, sitting at a wooden desk, trying to look like I knew my iambic pentameter. The ink was temperamental, the quill scratchy and frankly useless, and I kept blotting the parchment in ways that looked more like ancient Gallifreyan than Elizabethan.

The director was hoping for the delicate hand of a literary genius. What they got was a man wrestling with a feather.

Somehow, a few takes later, I managed to make it look half-decent. Watching the scene back later, I had to laugh. I was supposed to be bringing authenticity to the shot. But let's be honest – I was basically just another prop.

GRIDLOCK

MOOD ALLEY

This was a location photo paint-over. Early in pre-production, the locations department scouted various potential sites for different scenes. In this instance, I received the location photographs and was tasked with creating a visual overlay to illustrate how the scene would look on-site, helping to convey the intended atmosphere and design elements.

LOCKED
30.08.06

LOCKED
28.08.06

MILO AND CHEEN'S GUNS

This gun concept was approved quickly and the prop was effective enough that it was later repurposed, receiving an updated paint job for use as one of River Song's weapons.

TELEPORT BANGLE

As shown in the concept, I approached the design of this bangle with its multi-functionality in mind. I envisioned it as a ring of connected modules, each with a distinct function that could be individually controlled.

Russell ultimately chose Version 1 because it struck the correct balance between futuristic tech and an accessory that someone might wear.

VERSION 1

FUNCTION KEYS MOUNTED
ON THE OUTER EDGES OF THE 'LINKS'

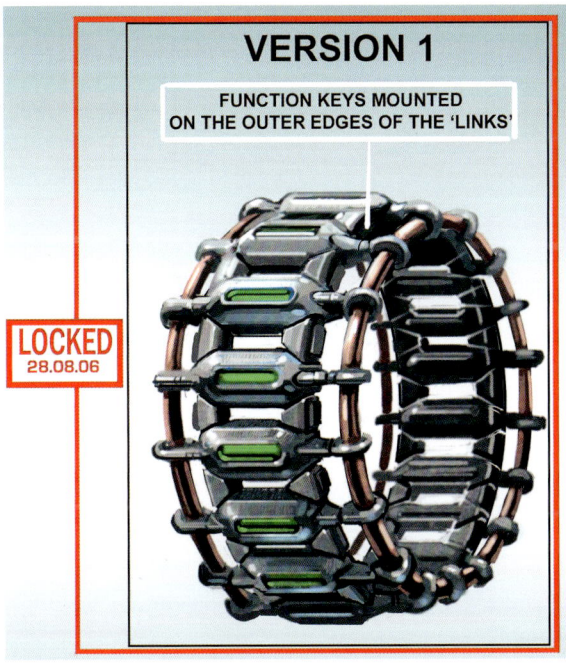

VERSION 2

FUNCTIONS KEYS FEATURED
MORE OBVIOUSLY

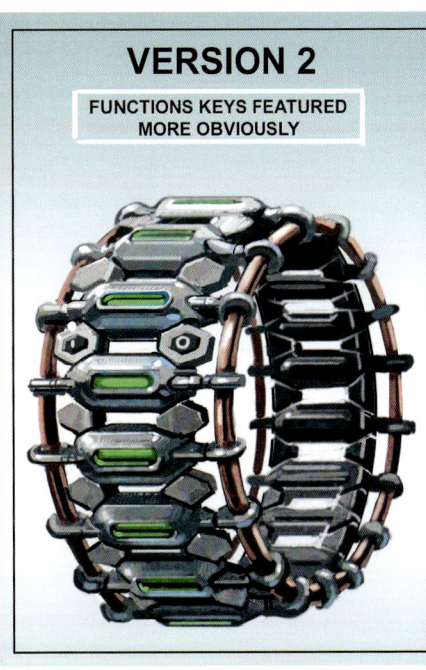

VERSION 3

BANGLE MADE UP OF DIFFERENT
FUNCTION NODES, INC TELEPORT,
REMOTE POWER CONTROL ETC

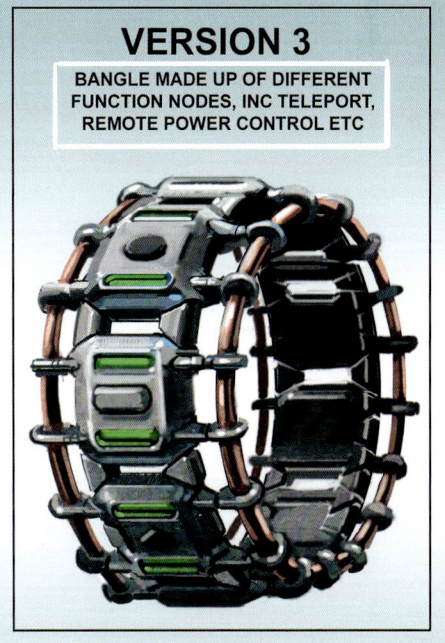

MOTORWAY TUNNEL

Series 3 concept designs had so far been quite prop-led, so I enjoyed this chance to visualise an actual environment.

Subject: Ep 3 Motorway Tunnel Interior
Sent: Monday, August 28, 2006 3.14 PM
To: Russell T Davies
From: Peter Mckinstry

Hello,

Attached is a version of the motorway interior. I've also attached a version with no traffic, to show the actual tunnel structure.

Thanks

Pete

Sent: Monday, August 28, 2006 3:40 PM
To: Peter Mckinstry
From: Russell T Davies

That looks amazing. Absolutely amazing. Brilliant.

A lot of the background is going to be obscured by the foreground cars, cos they need to be stacked choc-a-block in lines going horizontally and vertically, and not moving. But we must find some omniscient super-wide-shots (like the one at the end of the hymn) to really show the size and scale of that brilliant design.

Thank you, Peter!

R x

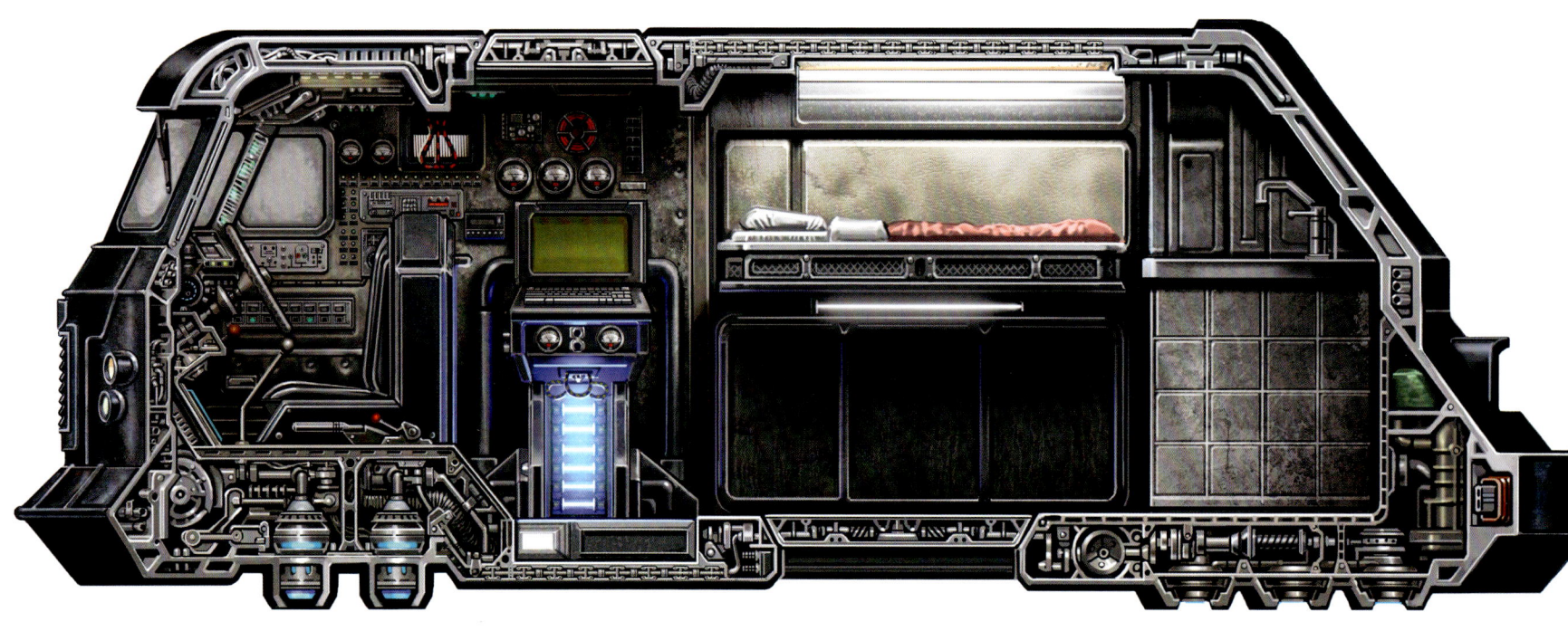

GRIDLOCK CAR – CUTAWAY

This illustration was done for GE Fabbri's *Doctor Who: The DVD Files* magazine and proved quite a challenge. The interior set, designed as a super compact travel home, left little room to depict the internal machinery typically found in a vehicle of this nature. As always with these cutaways I aimed to convey as much detail as possible, balancing the cramped living space with a set of imagined mechanical systems.

GRIDLOCK CAR CHAIR

A good sturdy driver's seat was essential for the never-ending traffic jams in *Gridlock*, but I made sure they were comfortable too!

THE FACE OF BOE

The Face of Boe, who in *Gridlock* has a warning for the Doctor, was first seen in the Series 1 episode *The End of the World*. I provided this illustration for the BBC Books title *A History of the Universe in 100 Objects* by James Goss and Steve Tribe.

DALEKS IN MANHATTAN / EVOLUTION OF THE DALEKS

DALEK IN EMPIRE STATE BUILDING OFFICE

This concept was designed to illustrate the contrast between the completed and unfinished sections of the office under construction. One side of the room features polished, high-finish marble, evoking the grandeur of the Empire State Building, while the other side remains unfinished, with exposed floorboards and girders.

NYC SEWER

This early concept was essential in conveying the overall tone, atmosphere, and structural layout of the sewer environment. I aimed to capture the gritty, claustrophobic feel of an underground labyrinth while ensuring the space could accommodate key scenes and action sequences – and, most importantly, a Dalek!

DALEK GRAPHICS AND SCREEN

This design for a Dalek screen was a bit of an experiment, but one that thankfully paid off. I had observed that when a flat screen display was placed under a Perspex hemisphere, its content would reflect onto the hemisphere's surface. I adopted the idea for the Daleks and was relieved to see that the final prop worked exactly as I had hoped, with the Dalek graphic shapes I'd supplied projecting seamlessly onto the plastic hemisphere. This effect was so successful that it was used in several other Dalek stories.

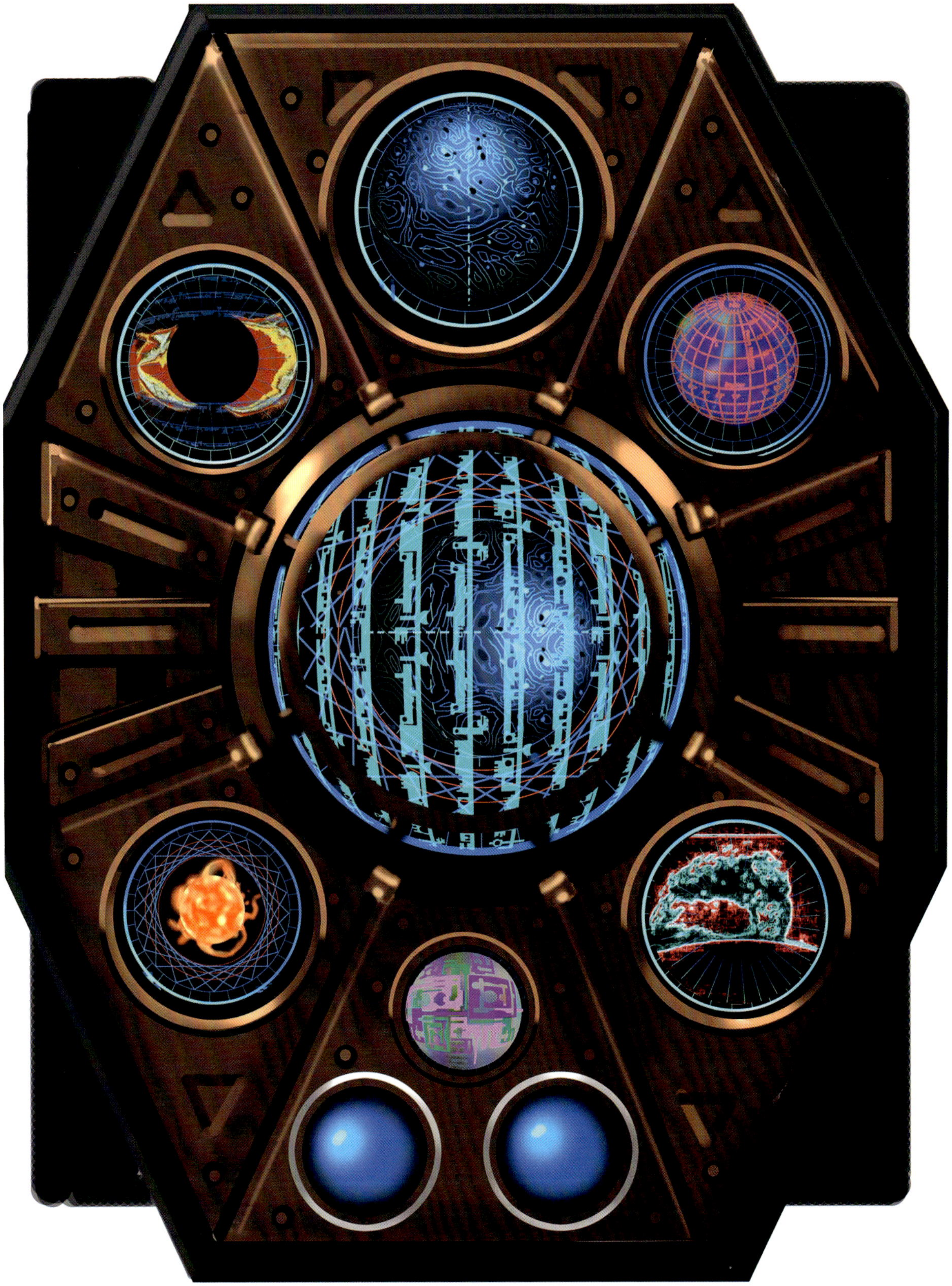

DALEK SYRINGE

What more could the discerning Dalek wish for to enhance its menacing appearance than a giant syringe arm attachment? My initial concept was to incorporate a visible winding mechanism, where you could see gears turning as the syringe's plunger was pulled back. However, for the approved version I took a different approach: I imagined the Dalek's iconic black plunger arm gripping a large syringe, moulding its sucker around it tightly to manipulate the plunger with precision. This gave it a more integrated look and kept the viewers' focus on the syringe needle itself.

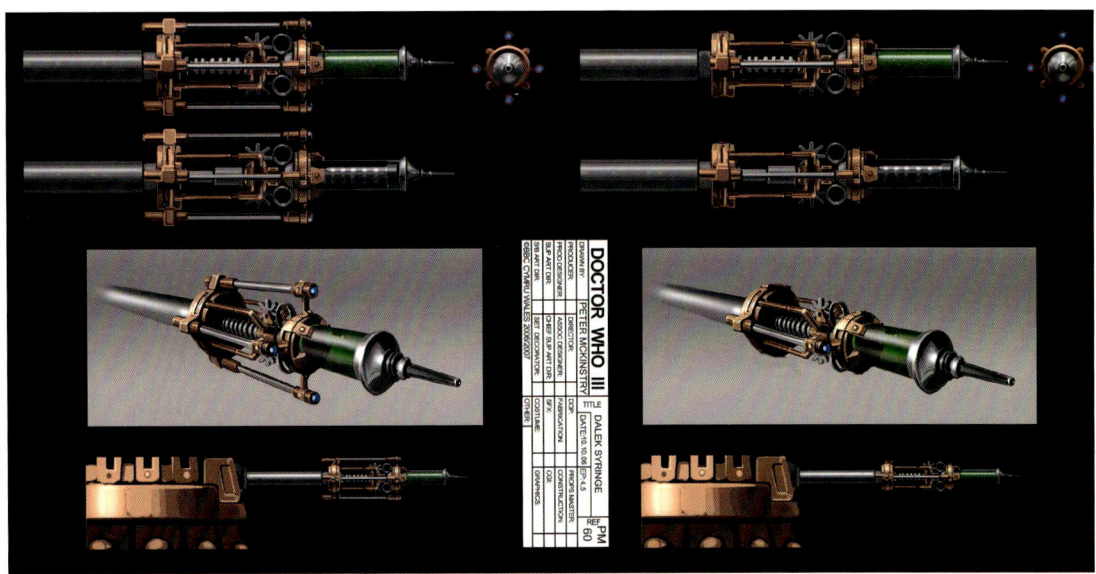

DALEK TOMMY GUN

I enjoyed creating a hybrid weapon that combined a Thompson machine gun – or Tommy gun – with Dalek technology. The concept was that the Daleks had upgraded the Tommy guns with their own tech, so I swapped out the original barrels for a Dalek gun and added covering elements in the bronze-like 'Dalekanium', to integrate the two designs. The result was a weapon that looked both familiar and otherworldly, fitting perfectly into the Whoniverse.

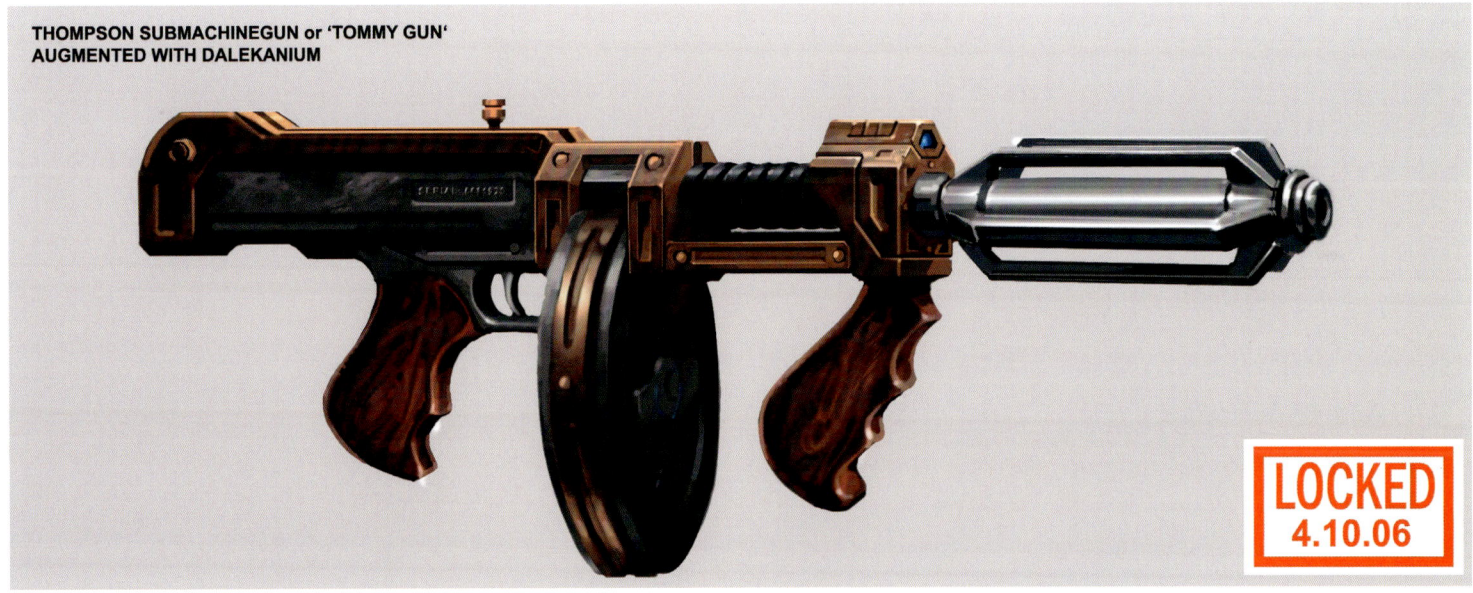

THOMPSON SUBMACHINEGUN or 'TOMMY GUN'
AUGMENTED WITH DALEKANIUM

LOCKED
4.10.06

THE LAZARUS EXPERIMENT

GENETIC MANIPULATION DEVICE

The design for Professor Lazarus's GMD went through several iterations before I found one that felt just right. Initially, I explored a very heavy industrial aesthetic, complete with flashing rotator beacons, but they looked more like Cyber-conversion units.

Russell suggested a more streamlined approach with sleek, modern technology infused with a touch of Apple's aesthetic. My first attempt in this direction veered too far into minimalism. So, I refined the concept further, incorporating clear glass tubes along the arms of the device to allow a glimpse of the technology housed within its shell. The final prop struck my hoped-for balance between futuristic elegance and functionality most successfully, and was very cool to see on-set!

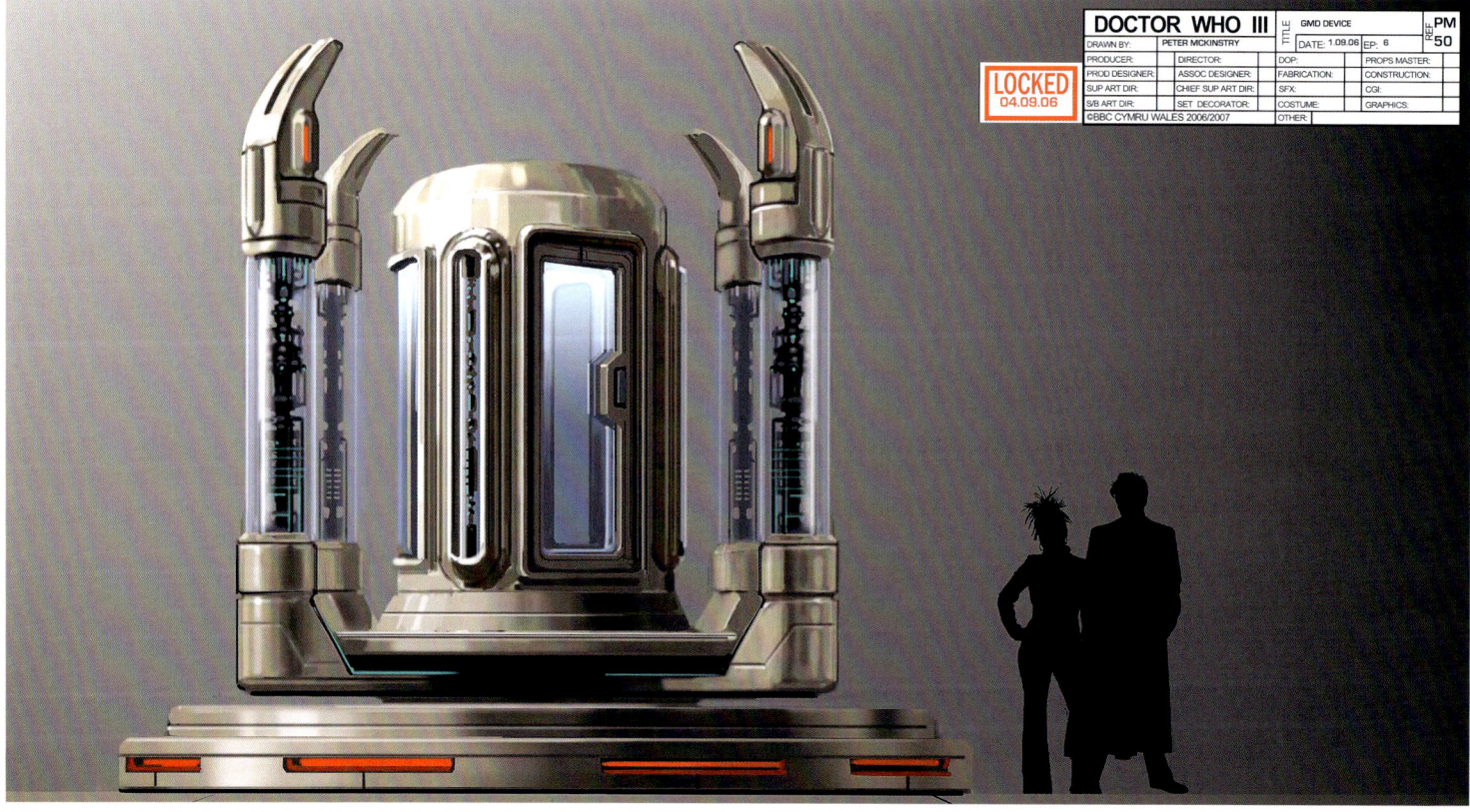

DOCTOR WHO III		GMD DEVICE		PM
DRAWN BY:	PETER MCKINSTRY	DATE: 1.09.06	EP: 6	50
PRODUCER:	DIRECTOR:	DOP:	PROPS MASTER:	
PROD DESIGNER:	ASSOC DESIGNER:	FABRICATION:	CONSTRUCTION:	
SUP ART DIR:	CHIEF SUP ART DIR:	SFX:	CGI:	
S/B ART DIR:	SET DECORATOR:	COSTUME:	GRAPHICS:	
©BBC CYMRU WALES 2006/2007		OTHER:		

LOCKED
04.09.06

PROFESSOR LAZARUS'S CANE

Here's a design that didn't make it off the digital drawing board...

Subject: Lazarus's Cane
Sent: Wednesday, September 13, 2006 12:56 PM
To: Russell T Davies
From: Peter Mckinstry

Hi Russell,

Attached is a visual of Lazarus's cane.

Essentially it's a glass rod with the DNA double helix running along the outside.

As shown, it originally had a ball top, a bit too disco pimp style, so I've altered it to a more traditional walking stick handle, which is a bit more in-keeping perhaps for a frail old man.

Let us know your thoughts,

Pete

Sent: Wednesday, September 13, 2006 2:08 PM
To: Peter Mckinstry
From: Russell T Davies

Now. Hmm. I'm not sure. That's brilliant work, as ever, Peter... but I worry that we'd never get a proper close up on the cane, and that from a distance, it's gonna look like an odd glass/silver sci-fi thingy. I can't help thinking that an old man should be using a nice, classy, proper wooden cane. Less is more!

Sorry, that's a great design. We'll publish it in a book one day!

R x

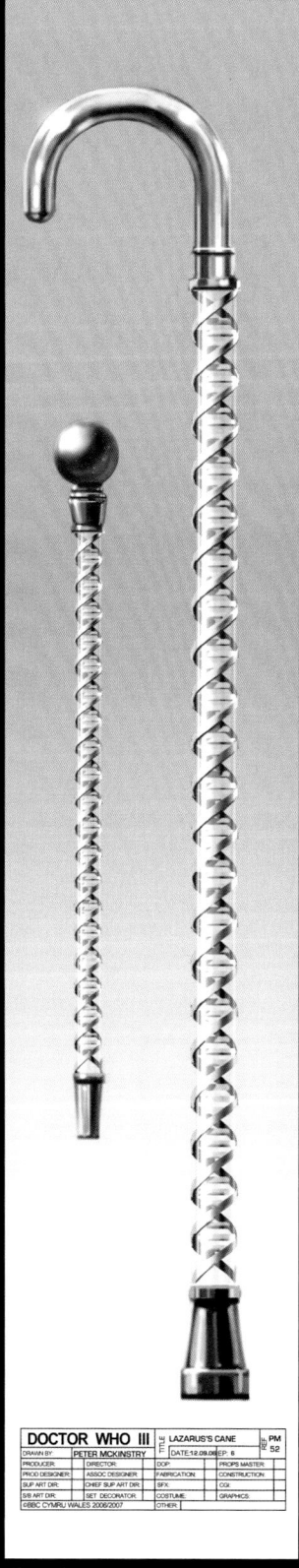

DOCTOR WHO III · LAZARUS'S CANE · PM 52

GMD – CUTAWAY

I had the opportunity to dive deeper into the GMD's design when I created this cutaway illustration for GE Fabbri's *Doctor Who: The DVD Files* magazine. This was a chance to really open up the device and show its inner workings. I was careful to ensure the illustration maintained continuity with the on-screen version. I even included the Laz Labs logo as a manufacturer's mark on the inner components.

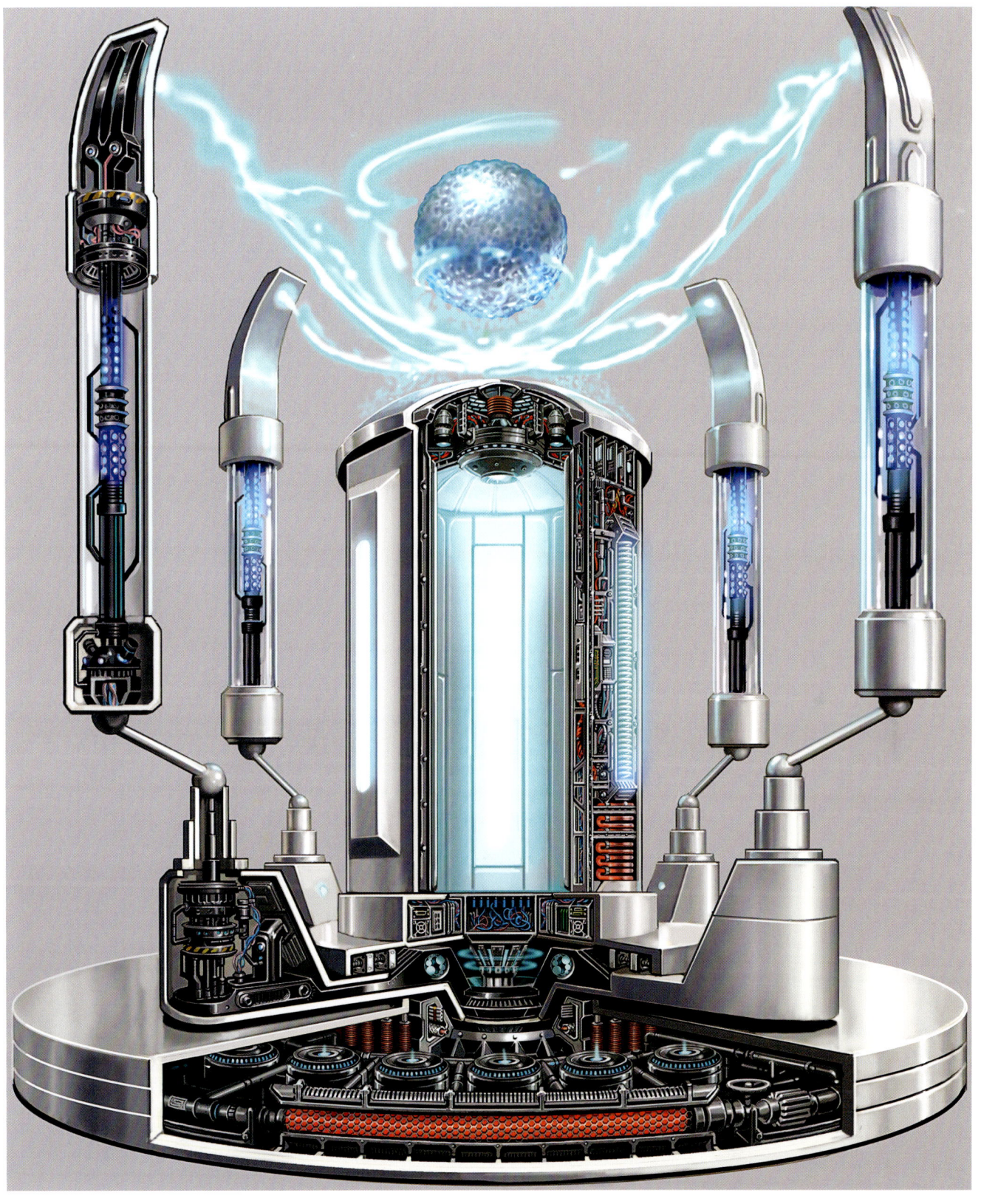

SS *PENTALLIAN* SPACESHIP

The story required a cargo ship with a long corridor section, linking the command centre at the front with the engine and fuel tanks at the rear. This structural requirement gave me a foundation from which I could experiment with form and function.

Initially, my designs leaned toward a more traditional, bulky spacecraft. But as the concept evolved, I explored the idea of a ship that looked rather fragile and worn, as if it had seen better days and was barely holding together.

This beat-up aesthetic added a layer of character to the ship, suggesting it had endured countless journeys and become something of a relic, and gave it a distinctive feel. I sent it off to Russell. He replied 'Ooh, yes, that's much more interesting. Feels new! Lovely!'

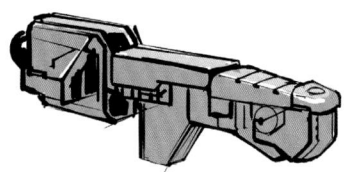
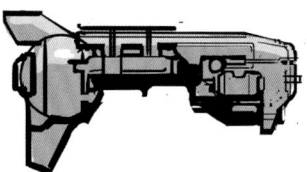
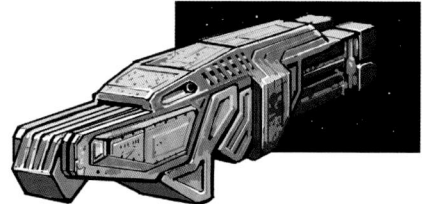

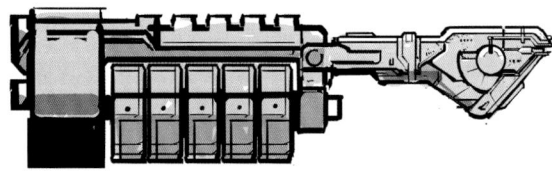

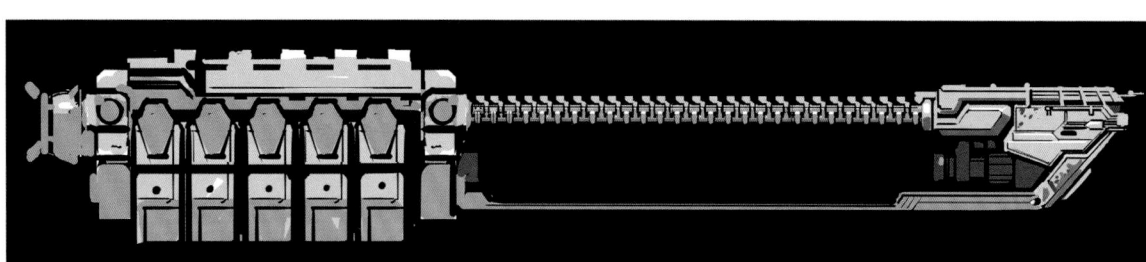

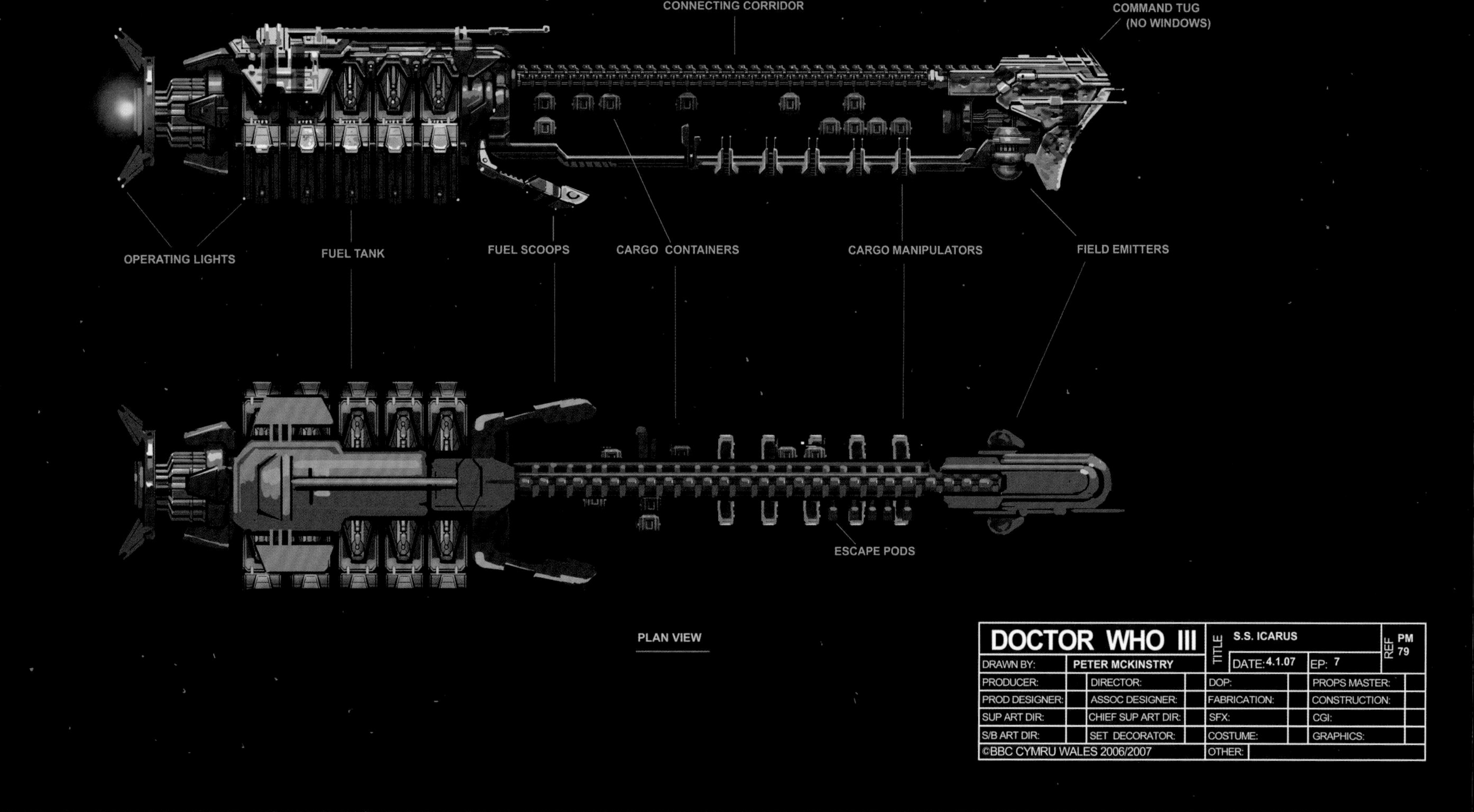

CONNECTING CORRIDOR

COMMAND TUG
(NO WINDOWS)

OPERATING LIGHTS FUEL TANK FUEL SCOOPS CARGO CONTAINERS CARGO MANIPULATORS FIELD EMITTERS

ESCAPE PODS

PLAN VIEW

DOCTOR WHO III			S.S. ICARUS		REF PM 79
DRAWN BY:	PETER MCKINSTRY	TITLE	DATE: 4.1.07	EP: 7	
PRODUCER:	DIRECTOR:	DOP:		PROPS MASTER:	
PROD DESIGNER:	ASSOC DESIGNER:	FABRICATION:		CONSTRUCTION:	
SUP ART DIR:	CHIEF SUP ART DIR:	SFX:		CGI:	
S/B ART DIR:	SET DECORATOR:	COSTUME:		GRAPHICS:	
©BBC CYMRU WALES 2006/2007		OTHER:			

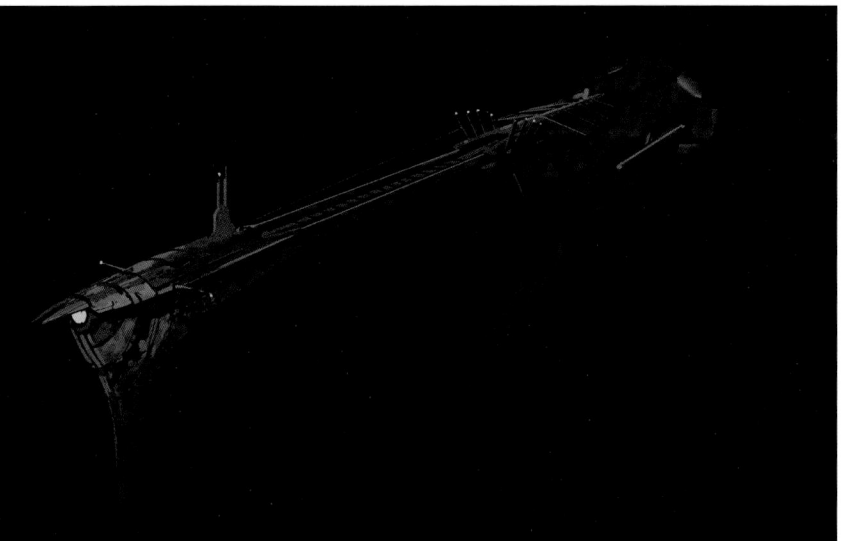

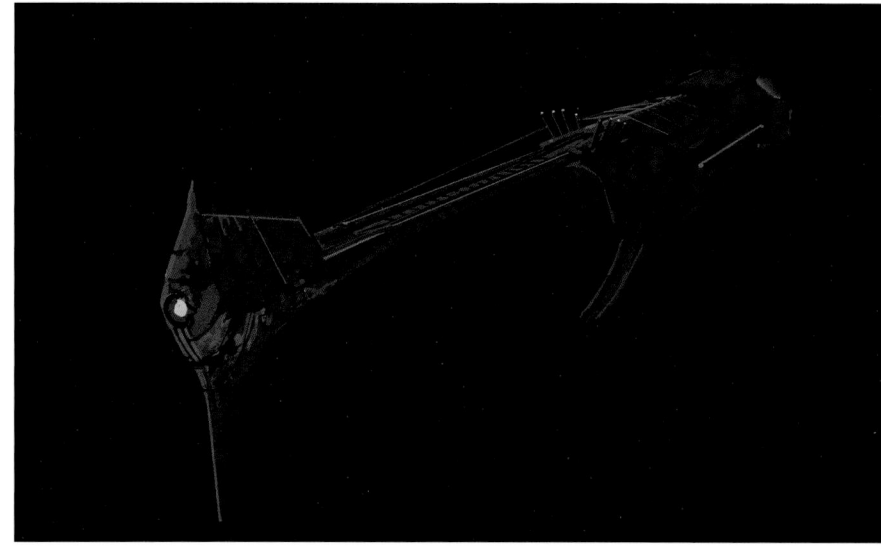

LOCKED
5.1.07

DOCTOR WHO III		TITLE	S.S. ICARUS version 2		REF	PM 80
DRAWN BY:	PETER MCKINSTRY		DATE: 5.1.07	EP: 7		
PRODUCER:	DIRECTOR:	DOP:		PROPS MASTER:		
PROD DESIGNER:	ASSOC DESIGNER:	FABRICATION:		CONSTRUCTION:		
SUP ART DIR:	CHIEF SUP ART DIR:	SFX:		CGI:		
S/B ART DIR:	SET DECORATOR:	COSTUME:		GRAPHICS:		
©BBC CYMRU WALES 2006/2007		OTHER:				

SS *PENTALLIAN* EXT DETAIL

The escape pods played a crucial role in the narrative. Their design and placement on the hull had to make sense within the context of the ship's architecture, adding to the realism of the world we were building while supporting the narrative tension of the escape sequence.

DOCTOR WHO III		ESCAPE POD		PM 84
DRAWN BY:	PETER MCKINSTRY	DATE: 11.1.07	EP: 7	
PRODUCER:	DIRECTOR:	DOP:	PROPS MASTER:	
PROD DESIGNER:	ASSOC DESIGNER:	FABRICATION:	CONSTRUCTION:	
SUP ART DIR:	CHIEF SUP ART DIR:	SFX:	CGI:	
S/B ART DIR:	SET DECORATOR:	COSTUME:	GRAPHICS:	
©BBC CYMRU WALES 2006/2007		OTHER:		

LOCKED
12/01/07

ESCAPE POD

While I focused on designing the exterior of the ship, Set Designer Al Roberts constructed a detailed card model for the interior of the escape pod. I photographed Al's model and then painted over the photograph in Photoshop.

By combining Al's practical model with my digital artwork, I was able to visualise how the escape pod would look from the outside, ensuring a harmonious fit with the ship's fragile and worn design.

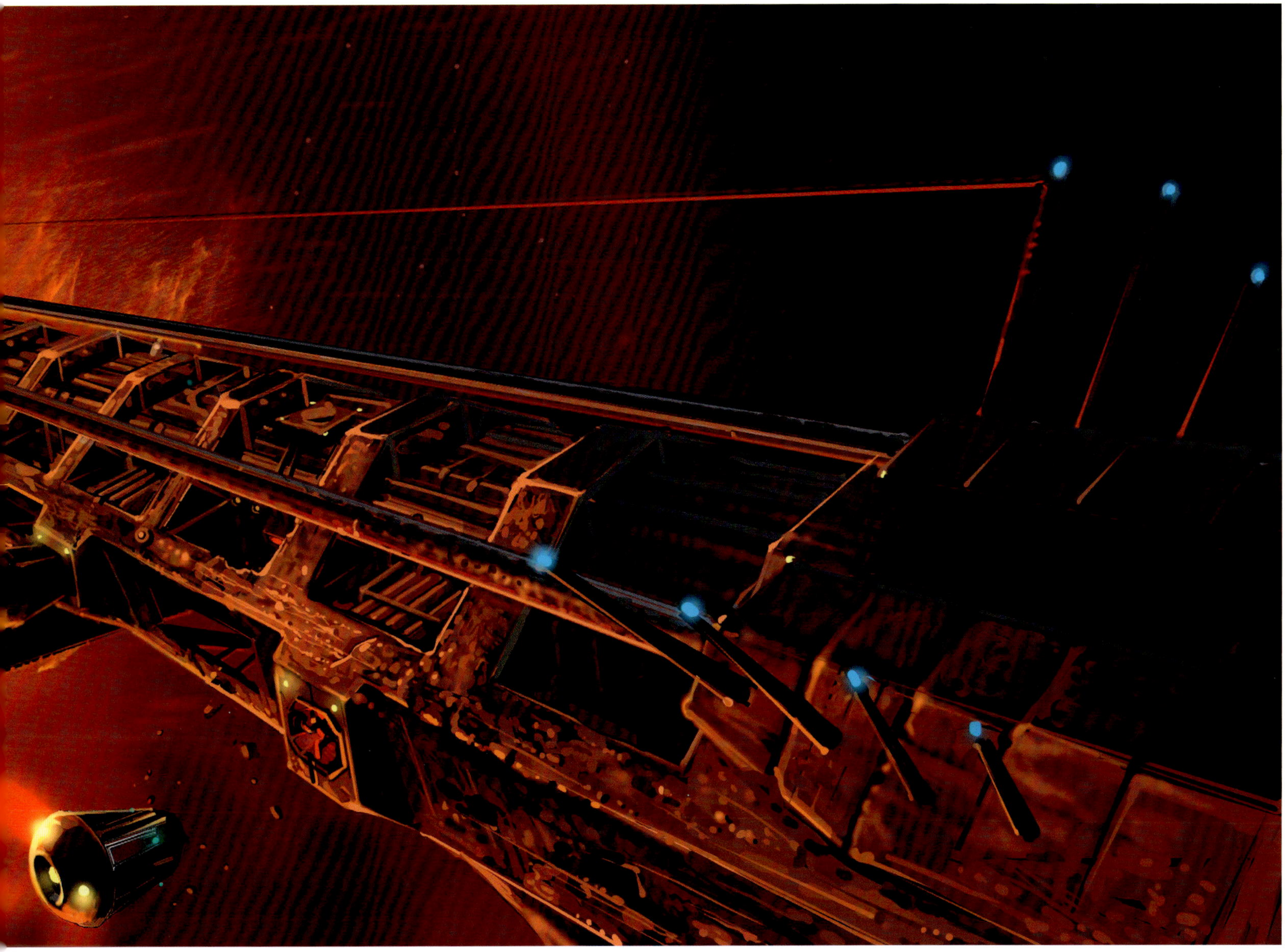

2

THE ART OF TIME TRAVEL   143

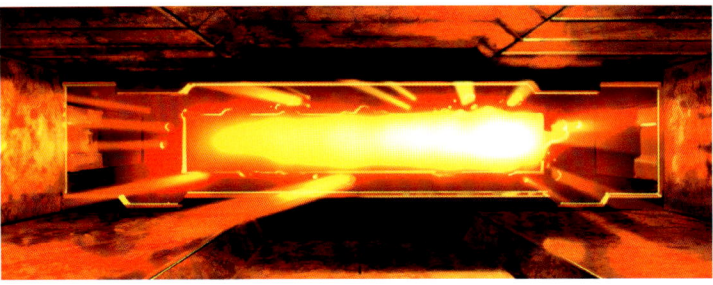

PORTHOLE VIEW

Subject: View from the Icarus
Sent: Friday, January 12, 2007 4:07 PM
To: Russell T Davies
From: Peter Mckinstry

Hello Russell,

Ed asked me to do a visual of what the view from the Icarus porthole might look like.

Given that the outer hull is pitted with holes, perhaps it would be nice to suggest the movement of the ship by showing beams of light passing through from one side to another.

Pete

Sent: Saturday, January 13, 2007 1:27 PM
To: Peter Mckinstry
From: Russell T Davies

Oh, that's gorgeous, that's got exactly the heat and intensity we want!

R x

SS *PENTALLIAN* – CUTAWAY

I created this cutaway illustration for GE Fabbri's *Doctor Who: The DVD Files* magazine. It was one of the more involved cutaway illustrations, providing a detailed look inside the ship and showcasing the layout of various sets featured in the episode. I wanted to show how the different areas connected with one another.

HUMAN NATURE / FAMILY OF BLOOD

FOB WATCH

The fob watch design went round the houses a little. The first design with the circular apertures is a subtle nod to the TARDIS roundels, suggested by Ed. But while Russell liked it, he felt 'It's got to be watch first, sci-fi second. It should still look old and traditional.' He also wanted it to be silver: 'silver watches are classy, while gold ones are a bit bling.'

I worried that the silver design with the filigree cover might be a bit too much; ditto with the three discs on the watch face inside denoting hours, minutes, and seconds. Russell felt that it was too thought-out and reiterated that he wanted 'a nice, plain, old-fashioned watch'. He had the idea of taking the back of the watch – silver, closed off and with the Gallifreyan pattern which wouldn't attract attention in 1913. Much more subtle and appropriate.

fob chain plugs into TARDIS console

filigree cover over glass

charging point/connecting port to the TARDIS console

front (closed)

front (open)

FRONT (CLOSED)

OPEN

BACK

8CM

ALIEN GUN

With this gun, used by the cruel hunters known as the Family of Blood, I wanted to go beyond the simple mechanical blaster.

Subject: Alien Guns

Sent: Monday, November 6, 2006 10:45 AM

To: Russell T Davies

From: Peter Mckinstry

Hello

Here's where we are at with the alien guns for 8 and 9. Part metallic, part organic, the idea is that this is actually a creature who is cruelly trapped inside the thing, when the trigger is pulled it pricks a blister on the handle, which prompts it to emit its death ray/venom... let us know what you think.

Pete

LOCKED
6.11.06

DOCTOR WHO III		TITLE	ALIEN GUN		REF	PM 68
DRAWN BY:	PETER MCKINSTRY		DATE: 6.11.06	EP: 8/9		
PRODUCER:	DIRECTOR:		DOP:		PROPS MASTER:	
PROD DESIGNER:	ASSOC DESIGNER:		FABRICATION:		CONSTRUCTION:	
SUP ART DIR:	CHIEF SUP ART DIR:		SFX:		CGI:	
S/B ART DIR:	SET DECORATOR:		COSTUME:		GRAPHICS:	
©BBC CYMRU WALES 2006/2007			OTHER:			

Sent: Monday, November 6, 2006 11:38 AM

To: Peter Mckinstry

From: Russell T Davies

Ha ha, that's brilliant! They're using outer-space sea-horses as a power supply!

Love 'em. Like the middle one best, I think.

R x

CHAMELEON ARCH

The Chameleon Arch allows its wearer to hide in plain sight by changing their biology and personality. The wearer's real personality is stored within the fob watch, which is equipped with a perception filter in case it is discovered.

When designing a prop that an actor has to wear on their head, the golden rule is that it mustn't look silly. That's why there were a few designs of this bit of tech before we landed on the right one.

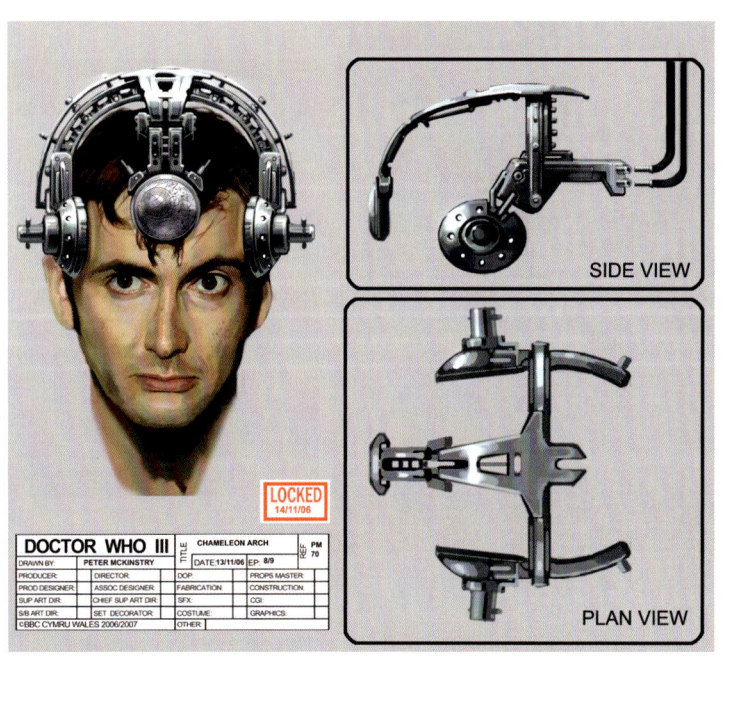

SIDE VIEW

PLAN VIEW

LOCKED
14/11/06

DOCTOR WHO III		CHAMELEON ARCH		PM 70
DRAWN BY: PETER MCKINSTRY		DATE:13/11/06 EP: 8/9		
PRODUCER:	DIRECTOR:	DOP:	PROPS MASTER:	
PROD DESIGNER:	ASSOC DESIGNER:	FABRICATION:	CONSTRUCTION:	
SUP ART DIR:	CHIEF SUP ART DIR:	SFX:	CGI:	
S/B ART DIR:	SET DECORATOR:	COSTUME:	GRAPHICS:	
©BBC CYMRU WALES 2006/2007		OTHER:		

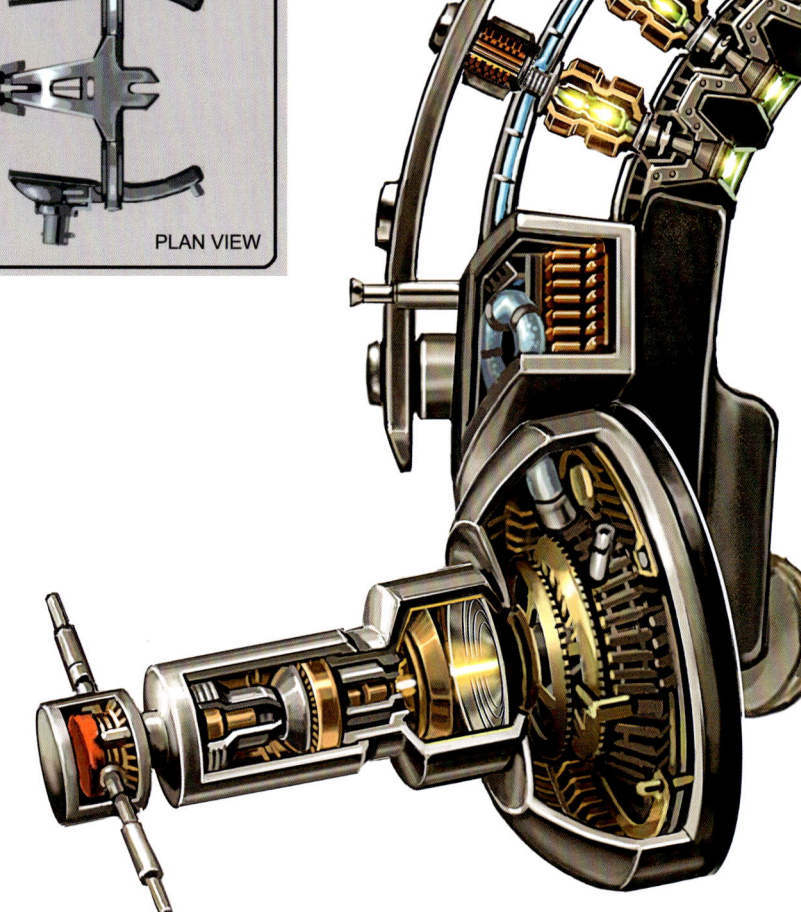

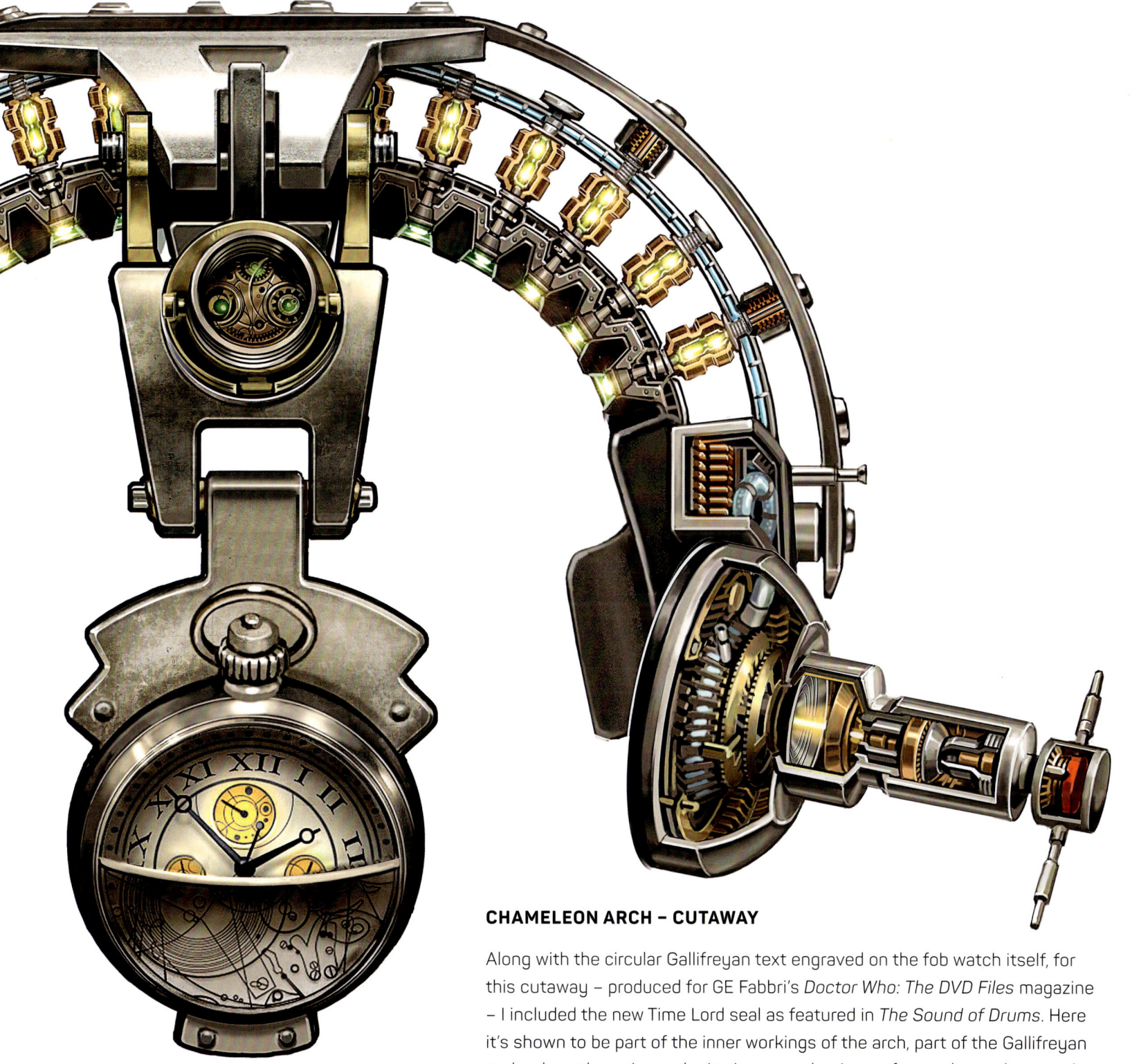

CHAMELEON ARCH – CUTAWAY

Along with the circular Gallifreyan text engraved on the fob watch itself, for this cutaway – produced for GE Fabbri's *Doctor Who: The DVD Files* magazine – I included the new Time Lord seal as featured in *The Sound of Drums*. Here it's shown to be part of the inner workings of the arch, part of the Gallifreyan technology that mirrors the intricate mechanisms of a regular pocket watch.

UTOPIA

CHANTHO'S GUN

I based the first version of Chantho's pistol to tie in with the character's appearance. However, a second design was required...

Subject: Chantho's Pistol
Sent: Monday, January 22, 2007 6:14 PM
To: Russell T Davies
From: Peter Mckinstry

Please find attached a visual for Chantho's pistol. I've based the shape on a mini Dillinger type purse gun. I've also been looking at the prosthetic for the character's head and tried to tie it slightly with that.

Do you think it's too biological looking, especially so soon after the Family of Blood gun?

Thanks,

Pete

Sent: Monday, January 22, 2007 10:15 PM
To: Peter Mckinstry
From: Russell T Davies

Oh, it's lovely but you've second-guessed me – it's not that it's too biological, it's just too BEAUTIFUL for ep.11, where everything is downgraded and useless and the cities have collapsed and even the computers don't work. A nice, basic stubby blaster would be better. Sorry, I feel like I'm stamping down on lovely work! But it just doesn't feel... 11ish.

R x

'Not a problem,' I replied. 'We'll save it for the Sea Devils!'

CORAL CITY

The remnants of the coral city of Malcassairo to be realised with CGI. Although the design was approved, the city didn't make it to the screen in this form. This happens from time to time; sometimes the CGI companies have their own idea of how they want to realise a setting, and sometimes changes are requested in post-production.

YANA CONSOLE

Given that Yana is a renegade Time Lord who has forgotten his own identity and yet is haunted by vague recollections of his past, I thought it would be fun to give his control consoles a vague visual resemblance to a worn-down version of a TARDIS console; as if Yana has subconsciously arranged the elements in such a way that, from a certain angle, they evoke the silhouette of the iconic console.

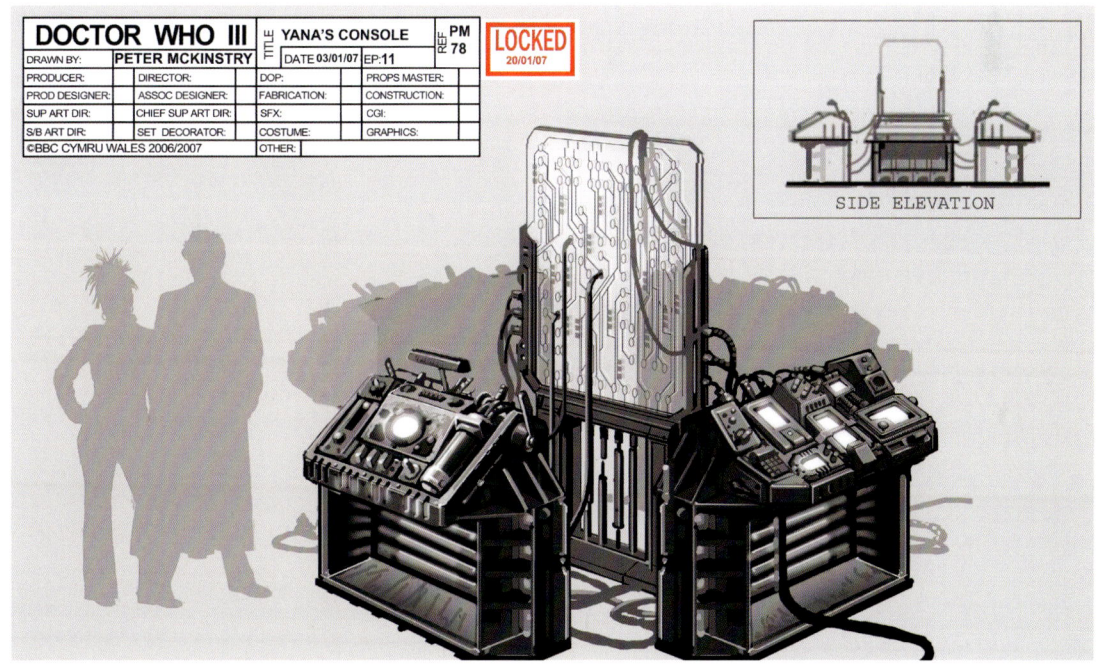

FUTUREKIND

Designing the Futurekind offered an exciting opportunity to explore a devolved tribal culture emerging from the remnants of an advanced civilisation – our own future.

I began with a full-body concept illustration (which I painted over a photo of Props Buyer Ben Morris) that depicted the Futurekind's aesthetic: a mishmash of leather and chains that reflected their rugged existence. Initially, based on early script drafts I incorporated motorcycles into their cultural identity, which led to the decision to integrate various headlamps into their costumes – practical tools that also served as symbols of their resourcefulness.

I got in some dental design too, creating three different options for the appearance of the Futurekind's teeth, which would further define their tribal look. Additionally, I explored the idea of facial tattoos, presenting a selection to Russell that captured the raw essence of their character. The standout choice was inspired directly by the motorcycle theme, blending the futuristic with the tribal.

As I explained to Russell:

The thought process behind the visual is that this feral tribe have their own rites of passage, one of which is a ceremony where the young brave is made to lie on the ground and have a bike ridden over him, marking him forever!

And he replied:

You sick bastard. That is brilliant!

Love it. R x

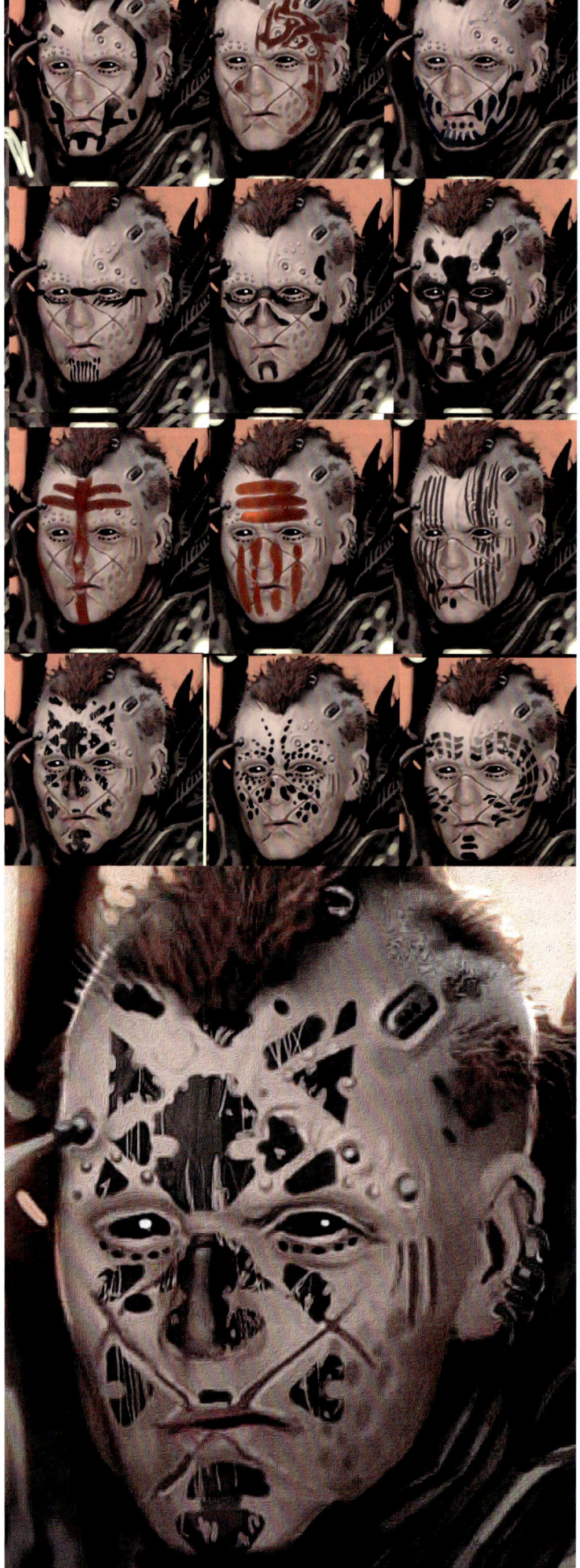

MUDGUARDS AS SHOULDER PIECES
PADDED UNDERNEATH

LOCKED
08/12/06

DOCTOR WHO III		TITLE	FUTUREKIND SHOULDERS		REF	PM 78
DRAWN BY:	PETER MCKINSTRY		DATE 8/12/06 EP:11			
PROD DESIGNER:	ASSOC DESIGNER:		FABRICATION:	PROPS MASTER:		
SUP ART DIR:	CHIEF SUP ART DIR:		SFX:	CONSTRUCTION:		
S/B ART DIR:	SET DECORATOR:		COSTUME:	CGI:		
©BBC CYMRU WALES 2006/2007			OTHER:	GRAPHICS:		

LOCKED
08/12/06

DOCTOR WHO III		TITLE	FUTUREKIND		REF	PM 72
DRAWN BY:	PETER MCKINSTRY		DATE 6/12/06 EP:11			
PRODUCER:	DIRECTOR:		DOP:	PROPS MASTER:		
PROD DESIGNER:	ASSOC DESIGNER:		FABRICATION:	CONSTRUCTION:		
SUP ART DIR:	CHIEF SUP ART DIR:		SFX:	CGI:		
S/B ART DIR:	SET DECORATOR:		COSTUME:	GRAPHICS:		
©BBC CYMRU WALES 2006/2007			OTHER:			

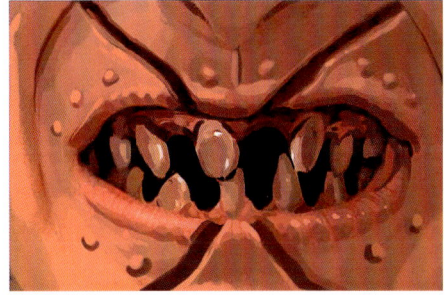

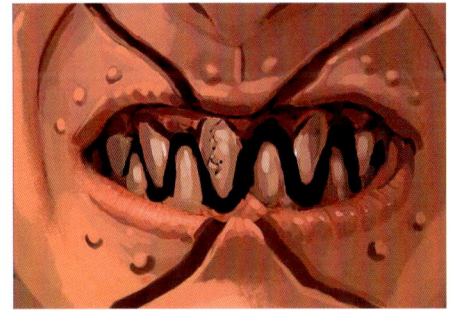

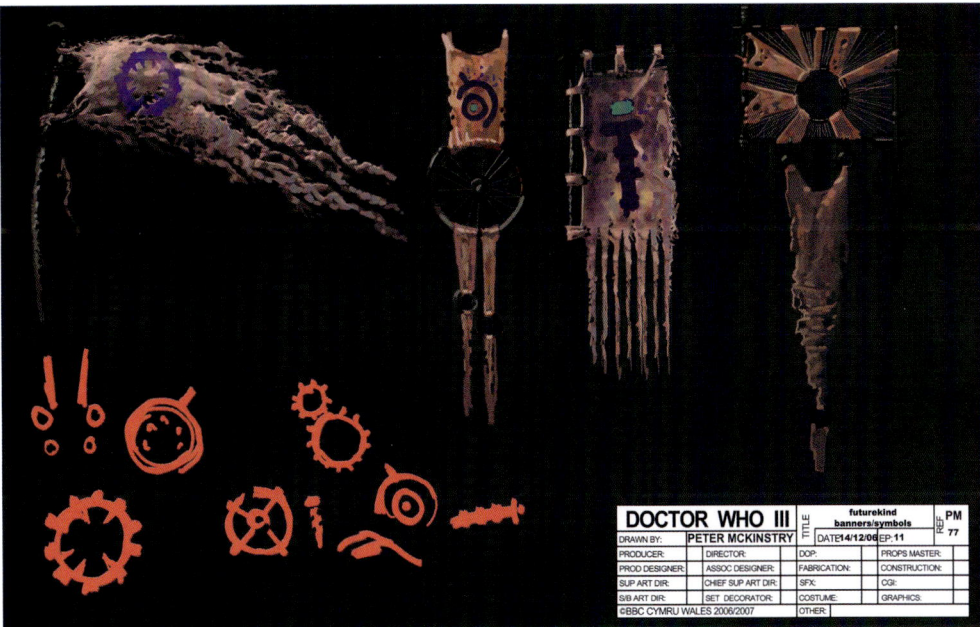

DOCTOR WHO III		TITLE	futurekind banners/symbols		REF	PM 77
DRAWN BY:	PETER MCKINSTRY		DATE 14/12/06 EP:11			
PRODUCER:	DIRECTOR:		DOP:	PROPS MASTER:		
PROD DESIGNER:	ASSOC DESIGNER:		FABRICATION:	CONSTRUCTION:		
SUP ART DIR:	CHIEF SUP ART DIR:		SFX:	CGI:		
S/B ART DIR:	SET DECORATOR:		COSTUME:	GRAPHICS:		
©BBC CYMRU WALES 2006/2007			OTHER:			

DOCTOR WHO III		TITLE	FUTUREKIND TEETH		REF	PM 73
DRAWN BY:	PETER MCKINSTRY		DATE 7/12/06 EP:11			
PRODUCER:	DIRECTOR:		DOP:	PROPS MASTER:		
PROD DESIGNER:	ASSOC DESIGNER:		FABRICATION:	CONSTRUCTION:		
SUP ART DIR:	CHIEF SUP ART DIR:		SFX:	CGI:		
S/B ART DIR:	SET DECORATOR:		COSTUME:	GRAPHICS:		
©BBC CYMRU WALES 2006/2007			OTHER:			

THE SOUND OF DRUMS / LAST OF THE TIME LORDS

TOCLOFANE

The Toclafane design was one I initially thought would be a bit of a challenge. Not only would these props require electronics to run the lights and an opening mechanism, but there were also the bladed elements to consider.

However, when I showed the concept to Barry Jones – *Doctor Who*'s senior prop maker from *The Runaway Bride* right through to Series 5's *The Big Bang* – he assured me that my design could be executed practically. Even the 'chocolate orange' opening style would work so long as we kept the segments down to four. Barry's ability to translate complex designs into tangible props was always impressive (and a huge relief!).

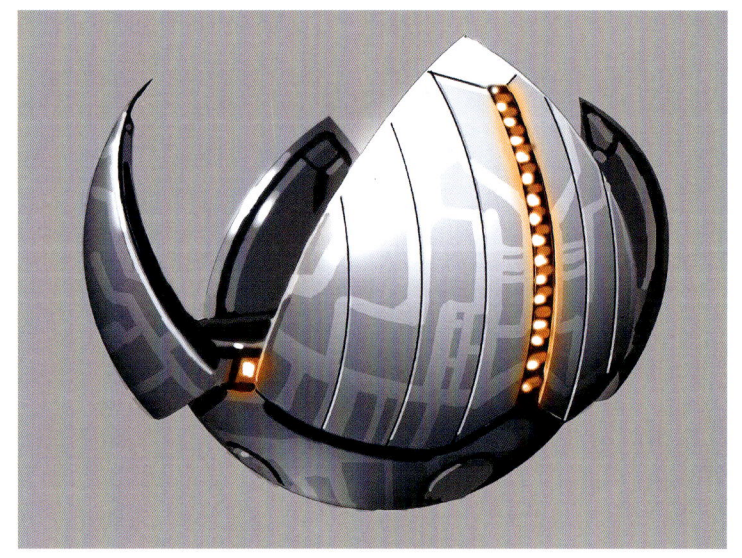

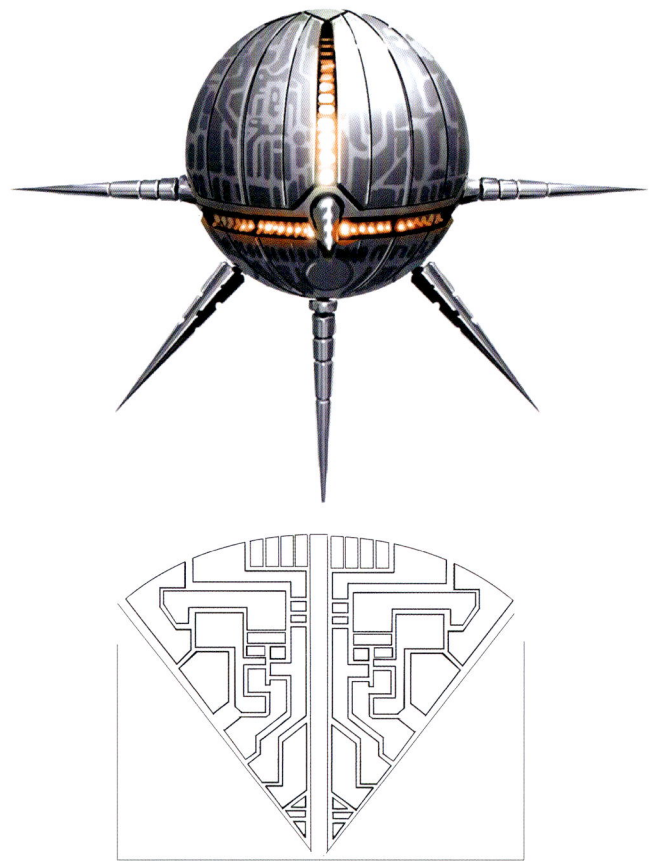

ANCIENT DOCTOR

As a purely CGI creation, the final appearance of the ancient Doctor was always going to be the responsibility of The Mill. However, I had a strong vision for how he might look, so I got involved. I gathered images of the oldest living people and noticed that very often they have areas where the skin sags heavily. I applied this to the Doctor's face, particularly under the eyes. My experience with portrait work and drawing from life models helped in capturing these subtleties.

The key was to maintain David Tennant's recognisable facial proportions, ensuring that even in this aged state, you could still see him beneath the transformation.

APPROACHING THE *VALIANT*

I later had the opportunity to revisit the HMS *Valiant* when I was commissioned to create an illustration for BBC Books' *Doctor Who: Starships and Space Stations* by Justin Richards. For this piece, I included a private jet in the foreground, ready to land on board the *Valiant*, which added a dynamic sense of scale and movement. The composition was influenced, in part, by the work of Syd Mead, whose futuristic designs often blend sleek modern technology with vast, imposing structures.

SAXON'S RING

I was looking at Saxon's ring and wondering what to use for the seal, the part where a coat of arms might usually go. I remembered in the episode *The Lazarus Experiment* we had introduced the Laz Labs logo, a circular pattern of spiralling rings designed by Sarah Payne, who had joined us for Series 3. At the time, this reminded me a little of our Gallifreyan text. Now, seeing as Saxon had funded Lazarus, this was a perfect opportunity to tie the two together. I added some Gallifreyan symbols into the Laz Labs logo design and Russell approved the finished result enthusiastically.

VALIANT INSIGNIA

The HMS *Valiant*, a base of operations in the clouds, was designed and built by the Master during his time posing as British Prime Minister Harold Saxon, capitalising on a perceived need to strengthen homeland security. Given its military nature, the *Valiant* and its staff needed their own insignia.

I had the Union Jack flag open on my screen, and by cropping the flag strategically, I found that the intersection of the red, white, and blue elements formed a stylised 'V' shape. It was perfect for the *Valiant*'s 'V' insignia, linking the ship to its British origins while giving it a distinct and bold identity.

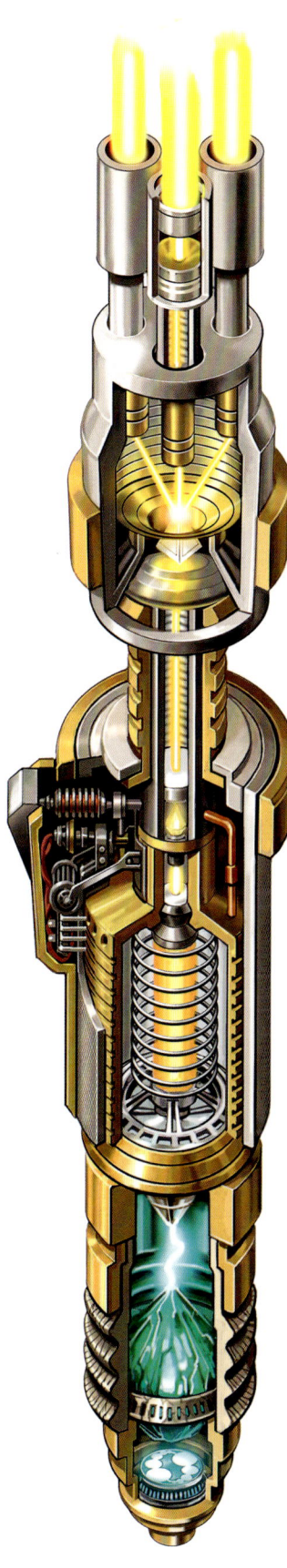

LASER SCREWDRIVER

My thinking with this design was that the Master built his laser screwdriver not with Gallifreyan tech, but with components and materials available to him on Earth. I wanted to contrast it with the Doctor's quite elegant-looking sonic screwdriver, so I made this a more tactile, chunky piece; something of a blunt instrument, reflecting its creator's viciousness. The inner workings are visible in an open section on the shaft, and there are three laser barrels at the tip which extend and rotate.

The prop was built by the amazing Nick Robatto and completed just in time for its first scene. As Russell headed to set, he spotted me and suggested I personally present the laser screwdriver to John Simm, who was playing the Master. John was in position on the *Valiant* set, getting some last-minute makeup applied, when Russell introduced me. 'John, we have something special for you!' he announced.

With a playful, ceremonious flair, I presented the prop. John took it and narrowed his eyes as if slipping into character. He slowly turned it over in his hands, weighing it carefully, then let out a quiet, sinister 'Heh, heh, heh,' under his breath, followed by a nod of approval. Russell laughed and nudged me: 'I think he likes it!'

LASER SCREWDRIVER – CUTAWAY

This design was done for *Doctor Who: The DVD Files* magazine by GE Fabbri.

PARADOX MACHINE

This device – in story-terms created by the Master and built around the TARDIS console – had to look like brutal, invasive technology, distorting the TARDIS into something dark and dangerous. Before a simpler budget-friendly option was chosen, I produced several designs and think version three would have worked brilliantly. I wanted the Paradox Machine to feel chaotic, as though it was barely holding its immense power together, which would have helped sell the intensity of the story's climactic moment.

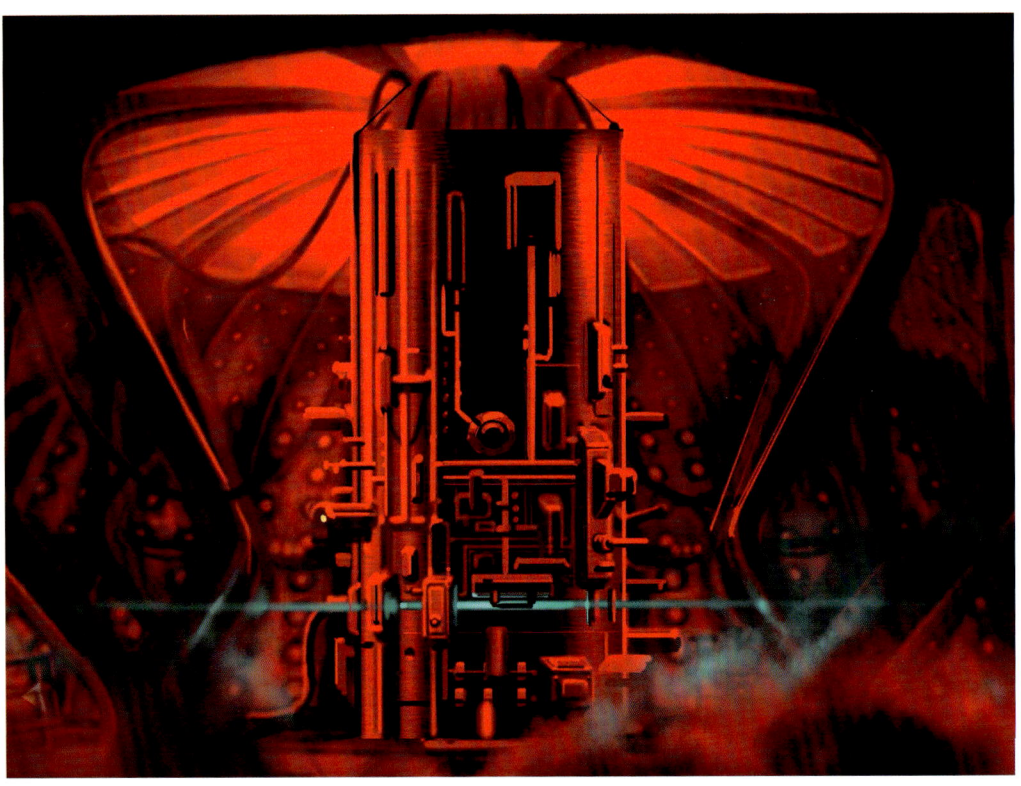

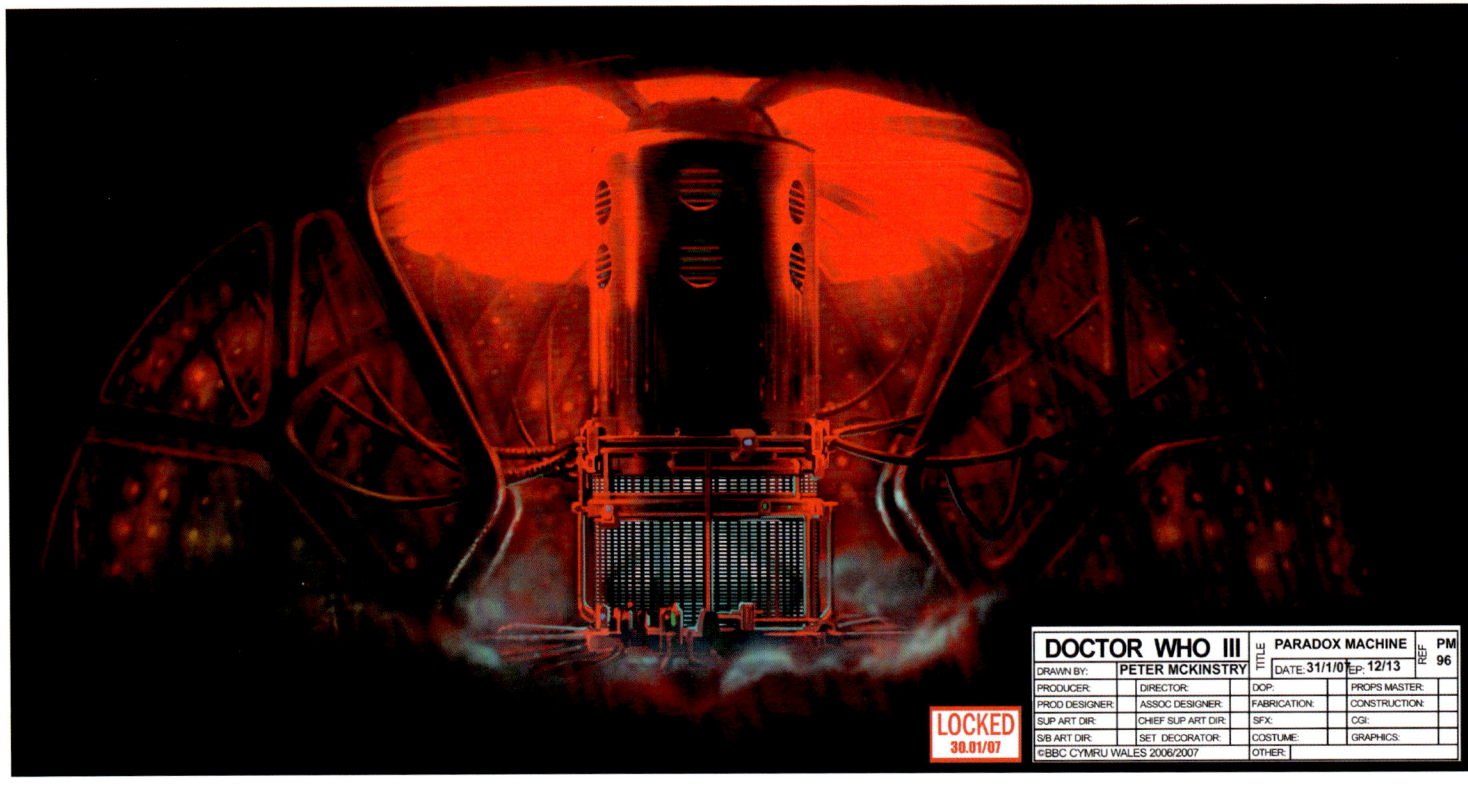

DOCTOR WHO III		TITLE	PARADOX MACHINE	REF.	PM 96
DRAWN BY: PETER MCKINSTRY		DATE: 31/1/07	EP: 12/13		
PRODUCER:	DIRECTOR:	DOP:	PROPS MASTER:		
PROD DESIGNER:	ASSOC DESIGNER:	FABRICATION:	CONSTRUCTION:		
SUP ART DIR:	CHIEF SUP ART DIR:	SFX:	CGI:		
S/B ART DIR:	SET DECORATOR:	COSTUME:	GRAPHICS:		
©BBC CYMRU WALES 2006/2007		OTHER:			

LOCKED 30.01/07

GALLIFREY CITADEL

Gallifrey, the homeworld of the Time Lords, is an important part of *Doctor Who* lore. While the planet was first seen in *The War Games* (1969) it was not named until *The Time Warrior* (1973–4). And while the Time Lords' Citadel was first mentioned in the 1978 story *The Invasion of Time*, it had never been seen from the outside – until now!

My first design was a domed city as mentioned in the script. But I felt it wasn't distinctive enough. I tried again, extended the scripted dome into a sphere, to emphasise the isolated nature of the Time Lords: a remote, self-contained mountaintop city.

For its internal structure I borrowed the shapes of the TARDIS struts, to make a subtle visual link between the two. The ring-halo effect around the suns was a nod to the graphic design of the Gallifreyan language, a series of complex circles and intersecting curves, which had been devised by graphic designer Jenny Bowers for Series 1.

I mentioned to Russell how exciting it was to work on the look of the Gallifrey citadel. 'Imagine how I felt typing it!' he replied. 'Gallifrey looks AMAZING. Thank you, what brilliant, brilliant work.'

With Russell's approval on the concepts, Gallifrey and its Citadel made the first of many appearances in the programme.

TIME LORD SEAL

Ed wasn't a fan of the classic *Doctor Who* Time Lord seal, the Seal of Rassilon, feeling it looked too Celtic. I disagreed and reasoned that its appearance in the show would be a callback to the original that would be appreciated by the fans. The decision had been made, however, and I was happy to be put to work on a new design. This fresh take would be applied to the Time Lord collar for the Gallifrey Citadel flashback. Shortly after the episode aired, I was surprised to receive a message on social media from someone who had got the new design tattooed on his chest! It was a great reminder of how deeply these visual elements can resonate with fans.

NEW BEGINNINGS

Work on Series 3 flew by in a flash, but it's a time I look back on with incredible fondness. As I settled into the rhythm of life in Cardiff, I was deeply engaged not only in my work but in building a life outside of it.

I had been living in a lively shared house in Canton, around the corner from the Chapter Arts Centre. The housemate interview, with a trio of them assessing my suitability, felt like a scene straight out of a TV show. As it turned out, living there wasn't far off from a soap opera, with each of us cohabiting while on our own career paths.

Weekends in Cardiff were something special. The city's nightlife and social scene were lively and welcoming, filled with laughter, music, and long, late nights. It was at one particular party that I met Chris, the person who would later become my civil partner. He knew Cardiff like no one else – and it seemed as though everyone in Cardiff was his friend. He lit up the room wherever he went, leaving an impression as striking as the city itself.

So, this period really was a crossroads for me on a personal level. The path I took with Chris, and the life we've built together, is one I wouldn't trade for anything.

Presenting some of the fascinating inventions that have helped – or hindered – the Doctor on his travels.

K-9 – CUTAWAY

Like many kids back in the day, I built my own version of K-9 using cardboard boxes and felt-tip markers, after the robot dog's debut in *The Invisible Enemy* (1977). Naturally, I was delighted to see the character return during my own days on the series (in *School Reunion* (2006)).

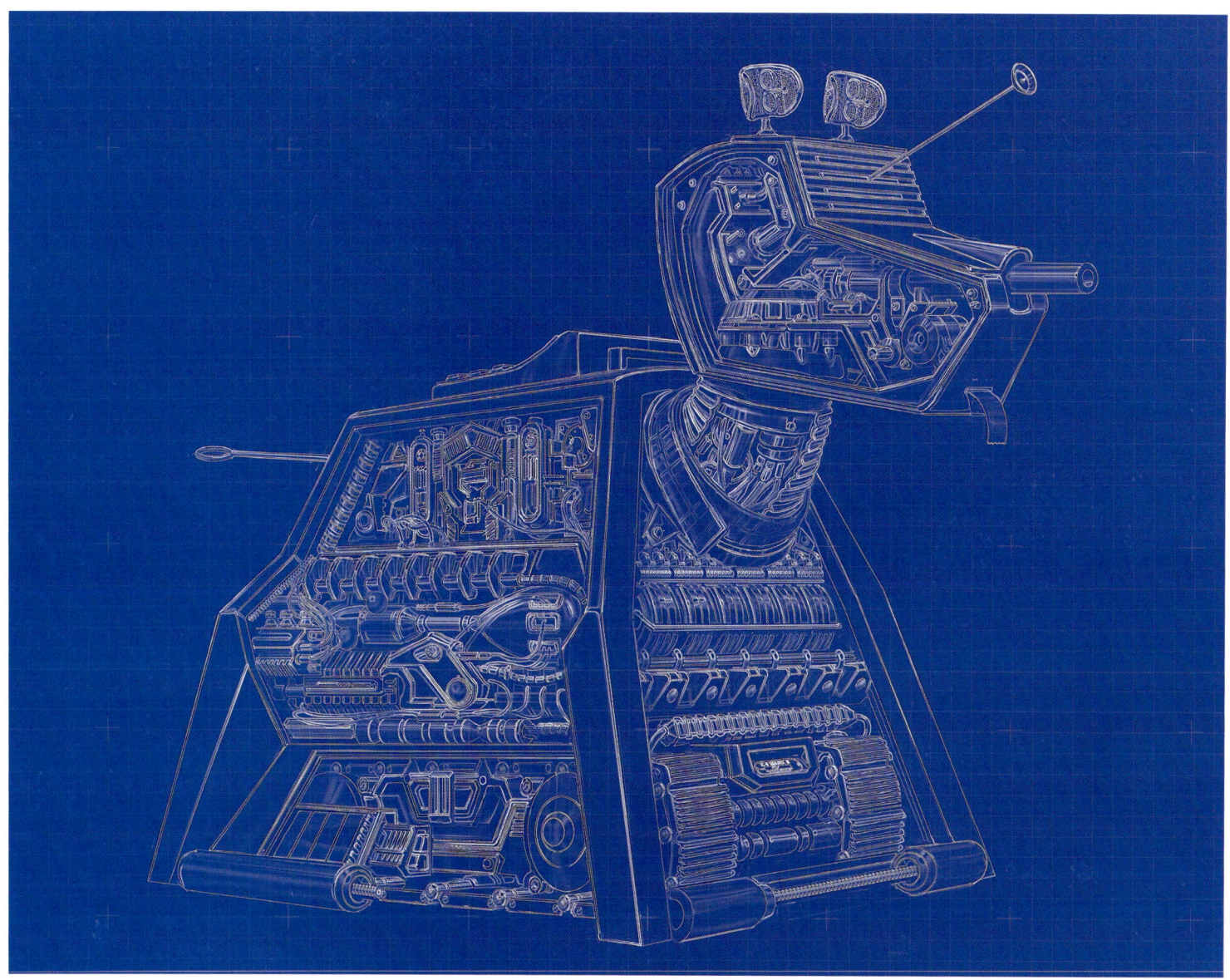

While developing this illustration of K-9 I was working on a film at Pinewood Studios. As I worked on the illustration during lunchbreaks, the film's production buyer glanced at my screen and exclaimed, 'That's my husband you're drawing!' To my surprise, her husband was none other than John Leeson, the talented voice actor behind K-9. This unlikely coincidence resulted in a large print of my K-9 illustration being auctioned for charity, kindly signed by John himself.

(Source: *Doctor Who: The DVD Files* magazine, GE Fabbri)

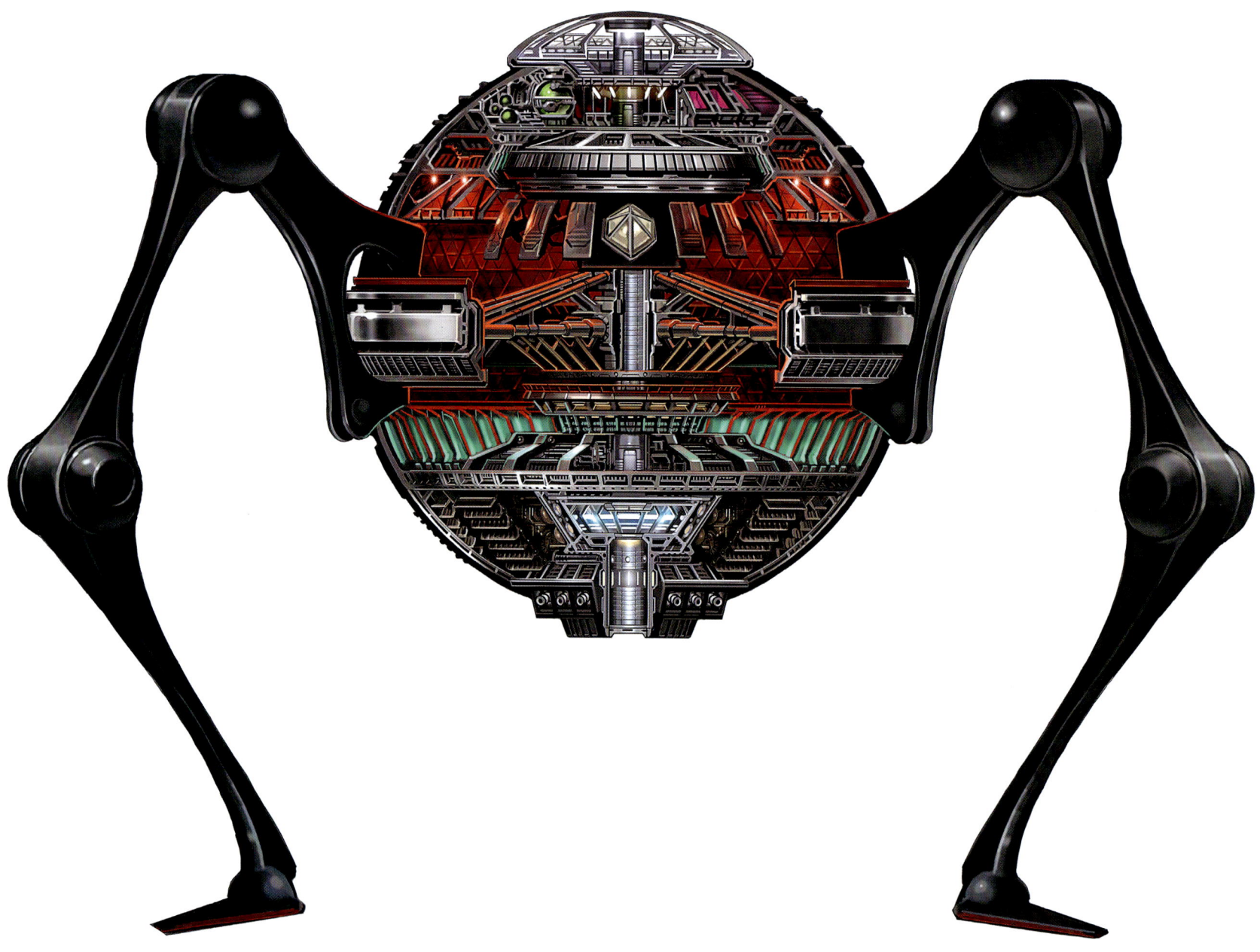

JAGAROTH SPACESHIP – CUTAWAY

This spherical, three-legged vessel from *City of Death* (1979) has long been a fan favourite. In the episode's opening scene, we catch a glimpse inside the ship's cockpit, with the villain Scaroth at the controls, so I used those details as a starting point to create a more complete, detailed vision of the rest of the ship's interior.

(Source: *Doctor Who: The DVD Files* magazine, GE Fabbri)

TISSUE COMPRESSION ELIMINATOR – CUTAWAY

A signature weapon of the Master, the TCE shrunk his victims to a fraction of their original size.

(Source: *Doctor Who: The DVD Files* magazine, GE Fabbri)

THE TIME LORD SPACE STATION

The spectacular opening shot of *The Trial of a Time Lord* (1986), showing the TARDIS being drawn into this space station, remains one of the most impressive effects sequences in all *Doctor Who*.

(Source: *A History of the Universe in 100 Objects* by James Goss and Steve Tribe, BBC Books)

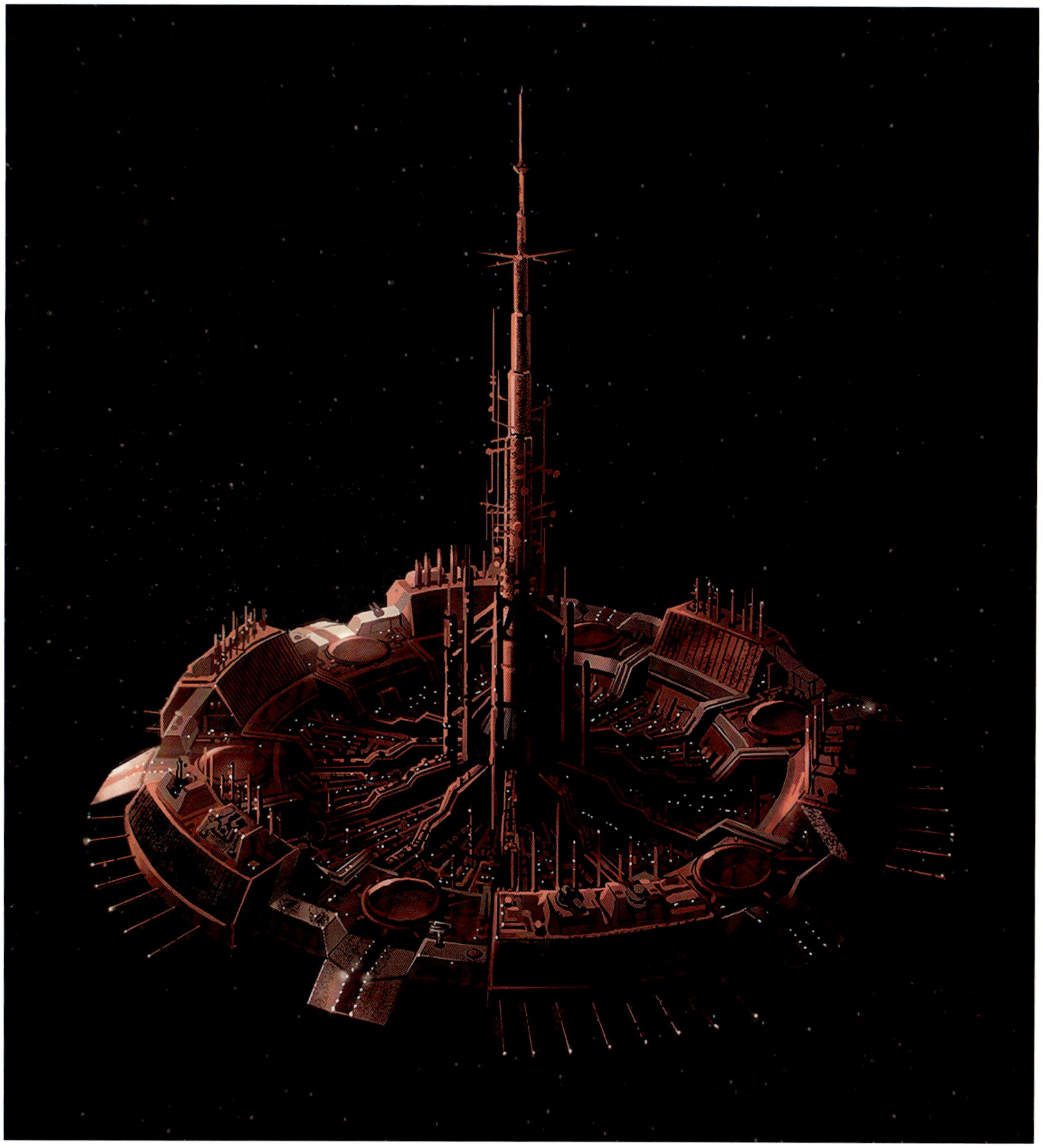

THE WHOMOBILE – CUTAWAY

The Third Doctor's incredible flying car! Combining futuristic technology with a distinctive hovercraft design, this one-of-a-kind vehicle was a symbol of the Doctor's style and ingenuity.

(Source: *Doctor Who: The DVD Files* magazine, GE Fabbri)

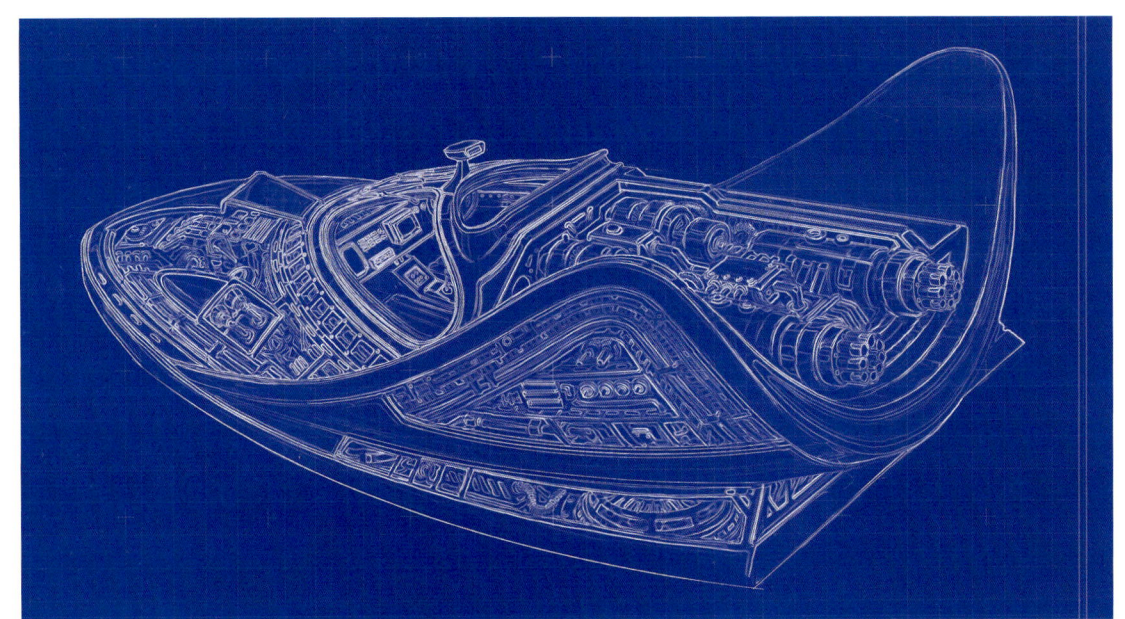

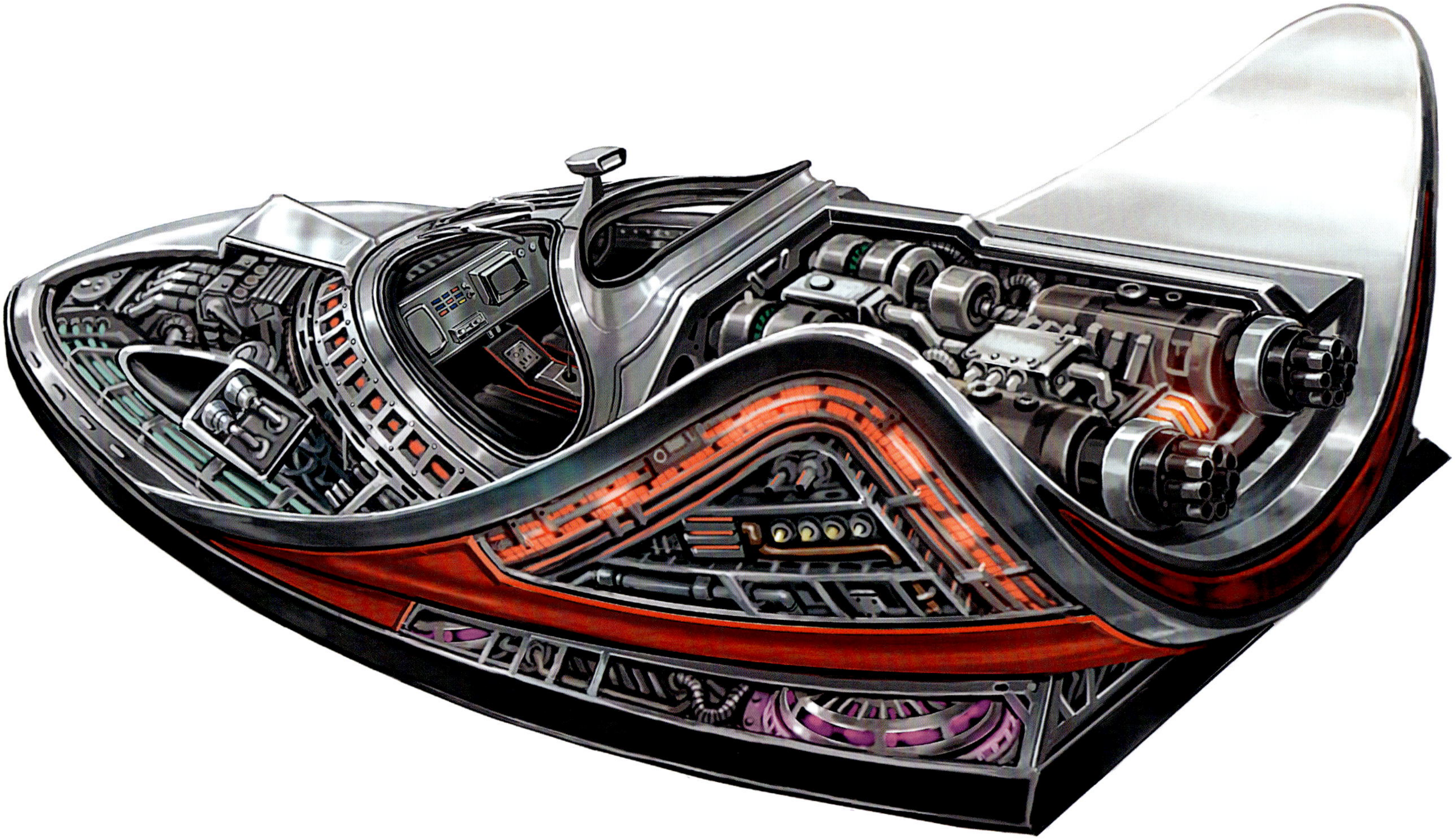

BESSIE – CUTAWAY

First appearing in *Doctor Who and the Silurians* (1970), Bessie was the Doctor's beloved Edwardian roadster, equipped with advanced and quirky technology that made her more than just a vehicle. She was a character in her own right, a reflection of the Doctor's eccentric personality and his connection to both the past and future.

(Source: *Doctor Who: The DVD Files* magazine, GE Fabbri)

SONIC SCREWDRIVER (1975–82) – CUTAWAY

The sonic screwdriver is an emblem of the Doctor's resourcefulness and ingenuity: a versatile tool that helps him and his companions escape endless tricky situations. For this version, used by the Fourth and Fifth Doctors, I included the 'function drums' from my previous cutaways – a carousel of small discs, each programmed with various capabilities.

(Source: *Doctor Who: The DVD Files* magazine, GE Fabbri)

THE GALVANIC BEAM – CUTAWAY

This UNIT weapon plays a pivotal role in *The Giggle* (2023), triggering the Doctor's bi-generation. All I had for reference when recreating it in 3D were screengrabs from varying angles and a schematic of the weapon, momentarily visible on-screen. For the inner workings, I researched modern military tech for the appropriate laser componentry – fascinating stuff!

(Source: *Doctor Who: The Gold Archive* by Mike Tucker and Steve Cole, BBC Books)

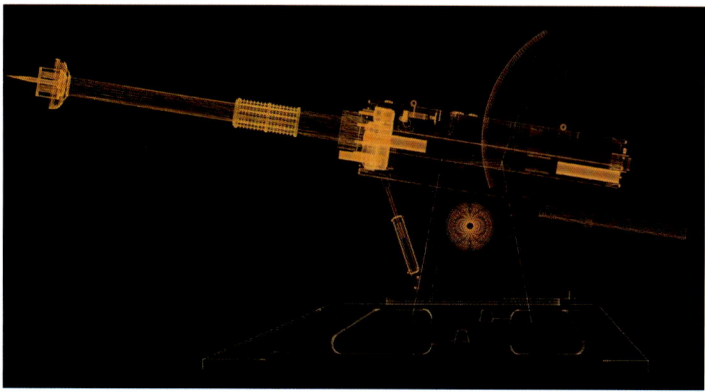

MEANWHILE, BACK AT THE HUB...

A selection of concept art and designs for Series 2
of *Torchwood* (2008).

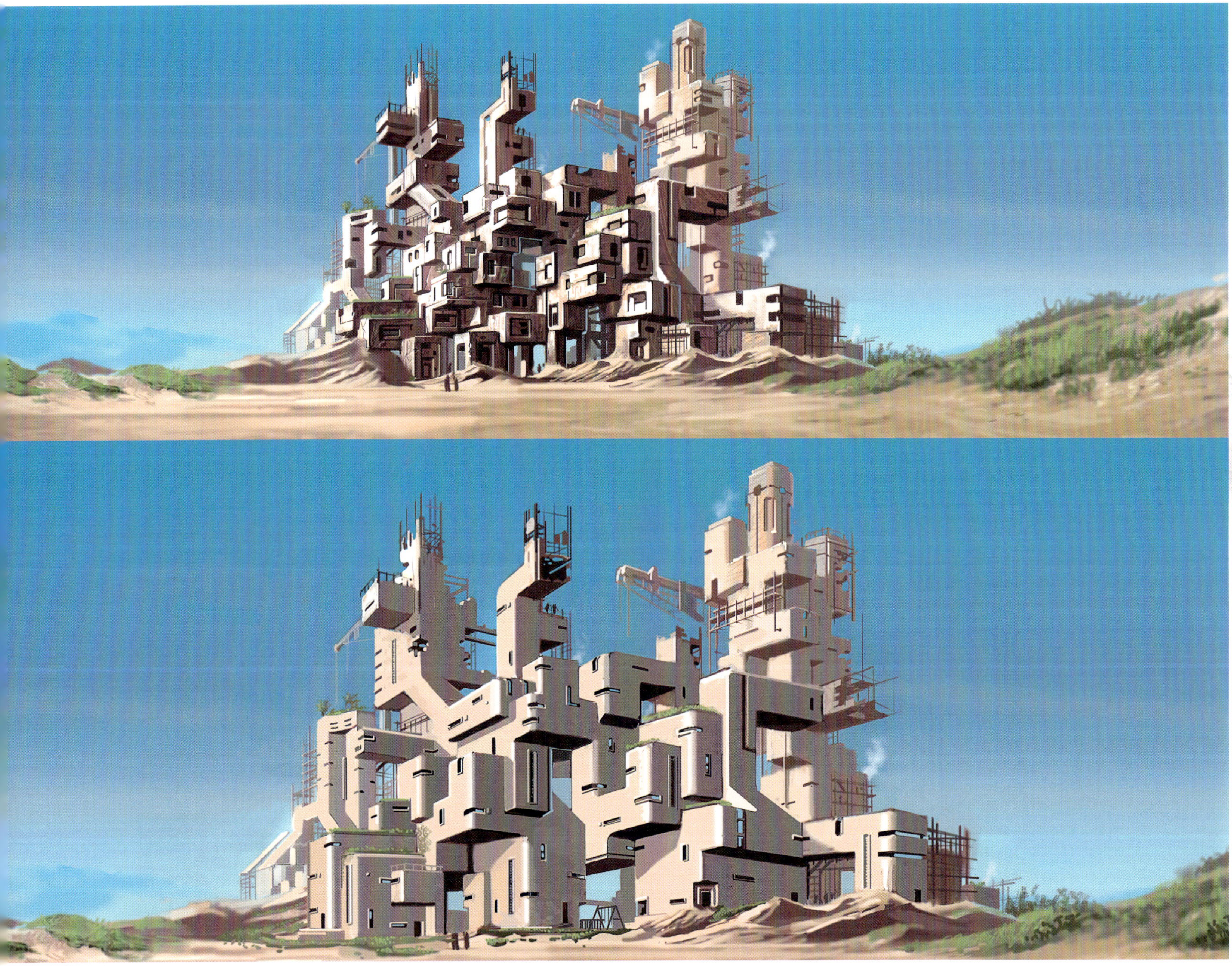

THE BOESHANE COLONY DESIGN DEVELOPMENT (*ADAM*).

TOSHIKO'S POLICE PORTRAIT AND THE RIFT MANIPULATOR PROP DESIGN (*TO THE LAST MAN*).

TIME GAUGE FINAL DESIGN (*MEAT*).

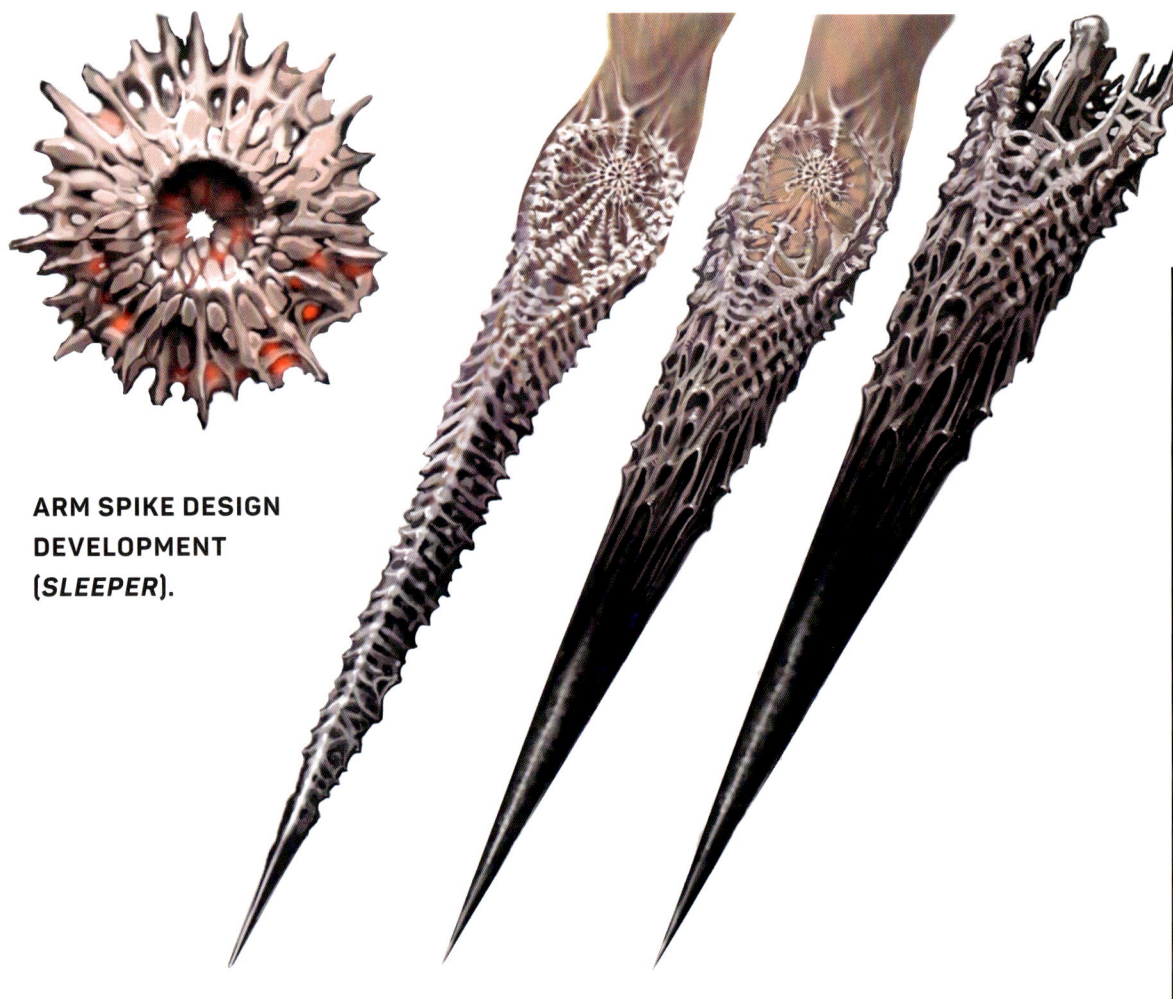

ARM SPIKE DESIGN DEVELOPMENT (*SLEEPER*).

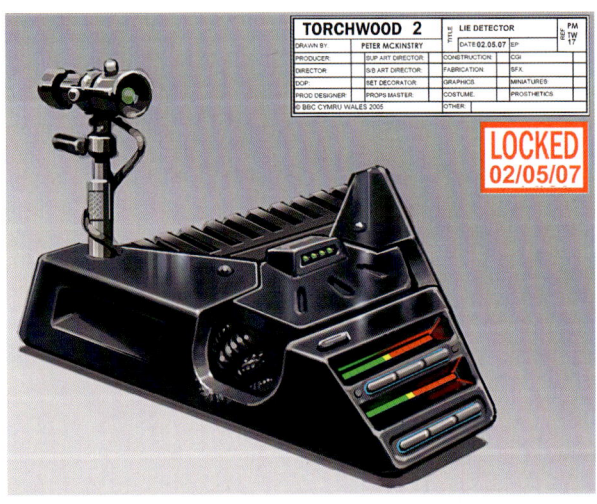

LIE DETECTOR PROP (*ADAM*).

RIFT DISC PROP FINAL DESIGN.

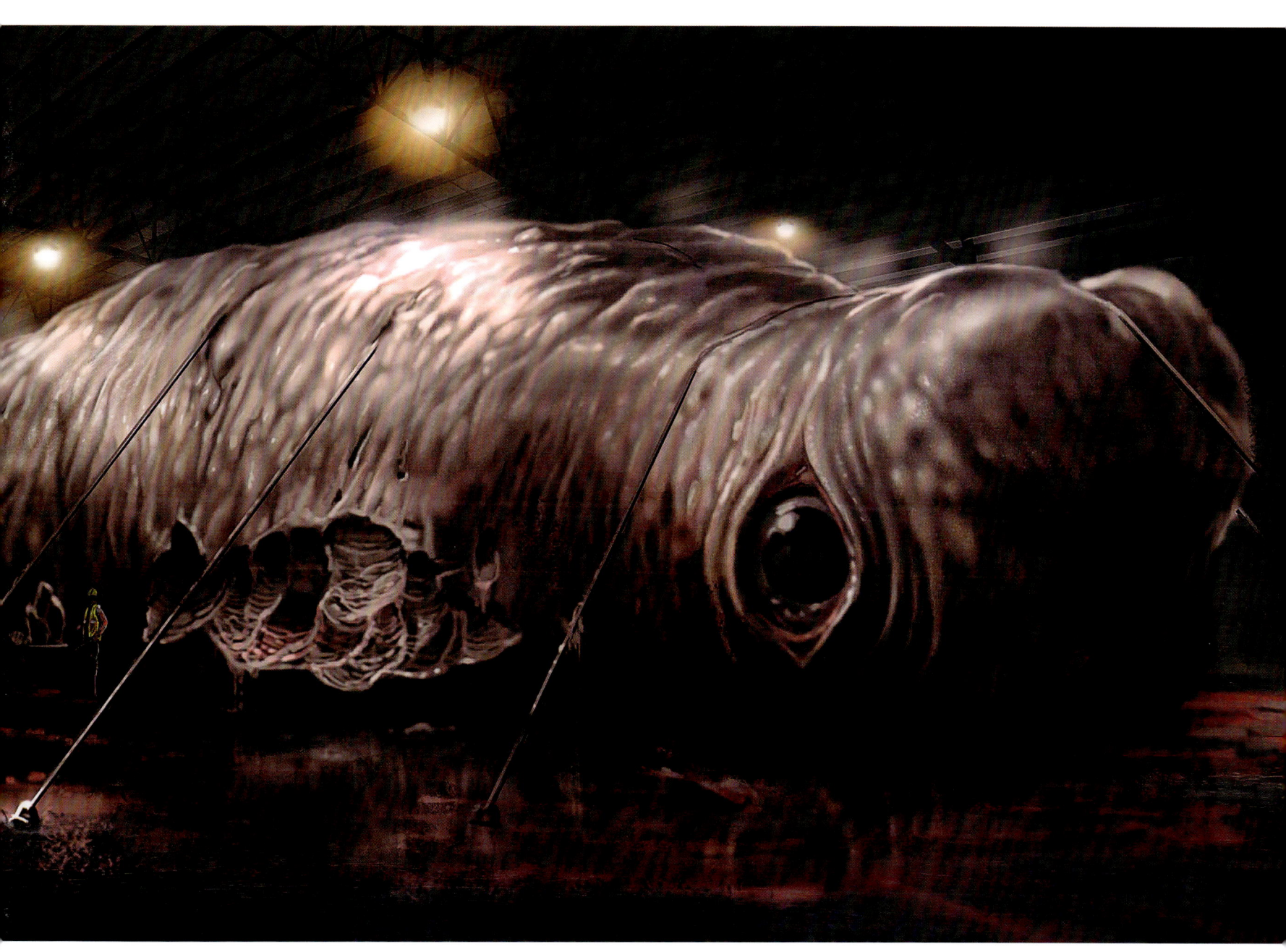

THE LEVIATHAN, FINAL APPROVED DESIGN (*MEAT*).

As a young viewer it was the trans-dimensional magic of the TARDIS that really caught my imagination. So much more than just a ship, this unassuming vessel is the Doctor's greatest ally, and a gateway to all of time and space…

THE ORIGINAL CONTROL ROOM

Otherworldly and expansive, Peter Brachacki's iconic design for the TARDIS control room, as seen in the very first episode, *An Unearthly Child* (1963), conveys technological sophistication beyond human understanding. Its clean, minimalist design was a huge contrast from the cluttered junkyard outside the TARDIS doors and remains a landmark in television and science fiction. Although I grew up with the Fourth Doctor's TARDIS on TV, I was always intrigued to see the grainy black-and-white photos of that original console and its environs in the pages of *Doctor Who Weekly*. It's the template for every control room that has followed it and remains a personal favourite.

(Source: *A History of the Universe in 100 Objects* by James Goss and Steve Tribe, BBC Books)

TARDIS ON THE MOON
(PREVIOUS PAGE)

While the Doctor has visited the Moon many times, on TV the TARDIS was seen to land on the lunar surface only once, in *The Moonbase* (1967).

(Source: *A History of the Universe in 100 Objects* by James Goss and Steve Tribe, BBC Books)

'ENGINE DECK' TARDIS CONTROL ROOM

I created this purely for my own amusement while I was teaching myself to use a new 3D modelling software program. I like the dark feel of it, with steps leading down to a swelteringly hot, 'below decks' engine room.

PART 3 | SERIES 4

THE MEASURE OF TIME

As the production gears kept turning and work began on Series 4, I found myself wondering how long the good times could last.

By now, I'd designed all manner of things for *Doctor Who*, but I'd also learned that in the freelance world, nothing lasts forever. Teams shift, faces change. Some people in the art department had already moved on, replaced by new colleagues. At the same time, we were edging ever closer to the end of the Tenth Doctor's tenure. What I didn't know was that even bigger changes were on the horizon – not only a new Doctor, but also a new showrunner.

Still, there was no time to think of farewells just yet. While Series 3 had felt like a new chapter, Series 4 was business as usual. Long days and short deadlines were what we were used to, and *Torchwood* Series 2 had kept us all in work, so we were still happily barrelling along. By the time we received the first scripts for the new run of *Doctor Who*, it felt like we'd never stopped.

Series 4 was full of special moments both on-screen and behind the scenes. One standout memory was when members of my own family were able to visit Upper Boat Studios, including my mum and Heather and Owen, my young niece and nephew. While I was deep in the work – obsessing over teleport bracelets or the precise shade of Supreme Dalek red – watching their reactions was like seeing the show through fresh eyes.

Another special day was when Raymond Cusick, the original designer of the Daleks, visited the studio. Ed and I showed him round the art department. He had designed so many stories in the show's early days and here we were, still building on that foundation decades later. It was an inspiring reminder that great design transcends time.

One of the most exciting challenges for me this year was the chance to design a brand new Dalek Supreme; a great example of the delicate balance between innovation and tradition that defined my work on *Doctor Who*.

Series 4 builds to a brilliant finale with all the Doctor's friends teaming up to save the day – and even piloting the TARDIS together. Watching it now, it still tugs at my heart. Not just because of how well it works on-screen, but because behind the scenes, it wasn't so different. In the art department, we had our challenges, our moments of frustration. But that was all part of the process. We were a team, all working hard to make something we loved the best it could be.

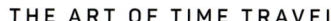

VOYAGE OF THE DAMNED

TITANIC SPACESHIP

For the Christmas special *Voyage of the Damned* (2007), my first task was designing a spaceship version of the *Titanic*. This was needed for the closing moments of *Last of the Time Lords*, which had ended Series 3, and my initial design was for a luxury star-cruiser on a vast scale, with long elegant lines.

Russell quickly set me right. 'It should be REALLY Titanicky (what a good word.)… Your casual viewer should go, oh look, the *Titanic*, and then, stares closer… oh, it's got spaceship engines too. But with prow and four funnels and deck and everything… I love this ship though, save it for something else!'

So, I started over, using the original *Titanic* as my anchor.

Once the overall design was approved, I needed to create an additional image: a ship's painting to hang in the *Titanic*'s main hall. So, I digitally repainted the concept image so it appeared to have been done in oils. I had done plenty of real oil paintings at art school – a fairly messy and time-consuming way of working – and when the image was printed onto canvas, framed, and placed on set, it looked surprisingly effective. I sometimes wonder what happened to that canvas!

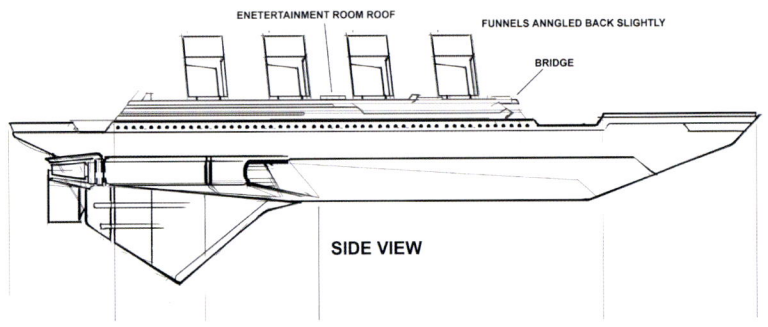

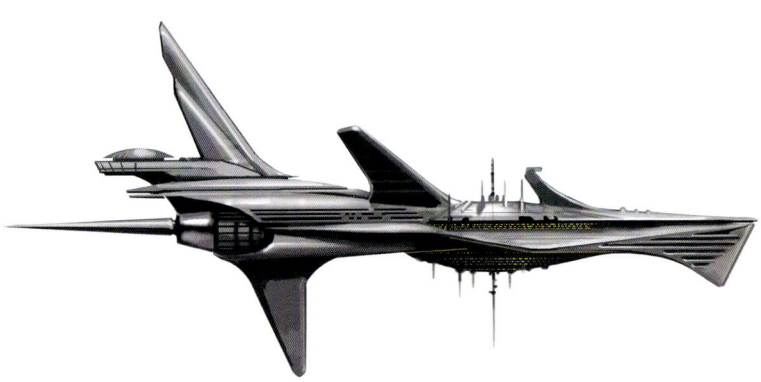

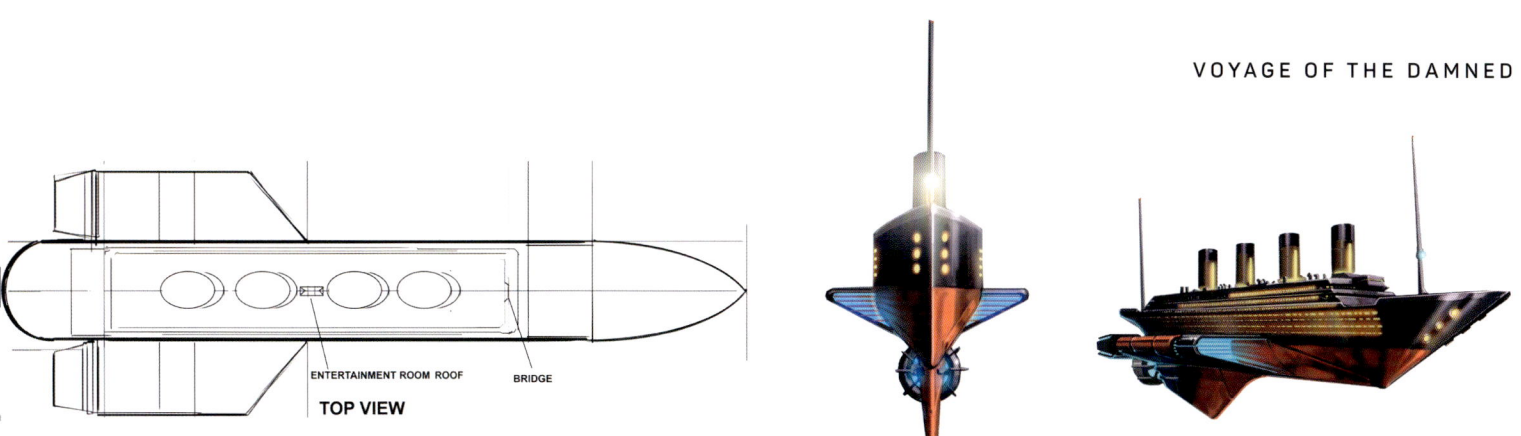

ENTERTAINMENT ROOM ROOF   BRIDGE

TOP VIEW

BATON BASE
NAVEL ON BANNAKAFFALATTA'S TORSO?

FUNCTION KEYS

THIS END PLUGS IN TO CHARGE BATON

FULLY EXTENDED TO EMIT EMP PULSE

CHARGE POINT

EMP PULSE EMITTERS

MANUAL ON/OFF

ON ACTIVATION,
BATON EXTENDS
FOR MANUAL USE

SLIGHTLY RECESSED
CONTROL PANEL

CHARGE LIGHT

LOCKED
27/06/07

BANNAKAFFALATTA'S EMP BATON

There's something really fun in designing small hand props, especially when you know they'll feature in a dramatic close-up shot. On 26 June 2007 I sent off my design for Bannakaffalatta's Electromagnetic Pulse generator, which is used to defeat the deadly angelic Host. Producer Phil Collinson responded first, saying that although he liked it, he felt it too close in appearance to a sonic screwdriver. Russell agreed, so I designed a new version in black. When the prop arrived it had a metallic finish, which ironically made it look more like a sonic than the original design!

MAX CAPRICORN PORTRAIT

The canvas print of the *Titanic* painting had worked so well that I was asked to do a portrait of the villain, Max Capricorn, which would also be framed and hung on set. The portrait of Max was based on a photo of actor George Costigan in costume and designed to resemble the self-assured style of portraits typically done for company CEOs. I tried to capture his calculating, confident expression, with a subtle hint of arrogance – all capped off by Max's glinting gold tooth!

THE MAX BOX

Max needed a means of transport – one that would conceal the fact that the actor wasn't *really* a disembodied head kept alive by a mobile life-support unit. This first 'industrial' version was just a starting point, my attempt to create something that suggested a contrast between his harsh, reclusive existence and the grandeur of the *Titanic*.

The next version, which ended up being the final design, was driven by the need to stay within budget. This more compact version kept the industrial feel but allowed the actor to kneel in position, with his head placed in the Perspex 'incubator chamber'.

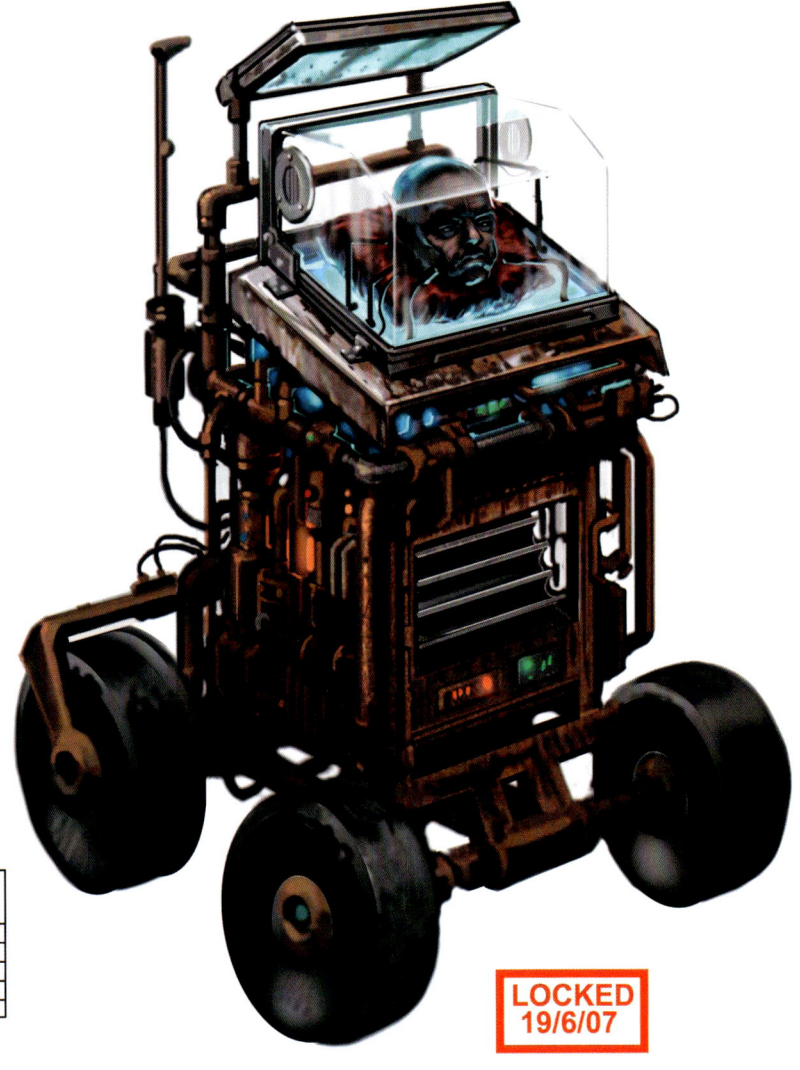

DOCTOR WHO IV	TITLE	MAXBOX	v.2		REF	PM 03
DRAWN BY:	PETER MCKINSTRY		DATE 19/6/07	EP: X		
PRODUCER:	DIRECTOR:	DOP:		PROPS MASTER:		
PROD DESIGNER:	ASSOC DESIGNER:	FABRICATION:		CONSTRUCTION:		
SUP ART DIR:	CHIEF SUP ART DIR:	SFX:		CGI:		
S/B ART DIR:	SET DECORATOR:	COSTUME:		GRAPHICS:		
©BBC CYMRU WALES 2006/2007		OTHER:				

LOCKED
19/6/07

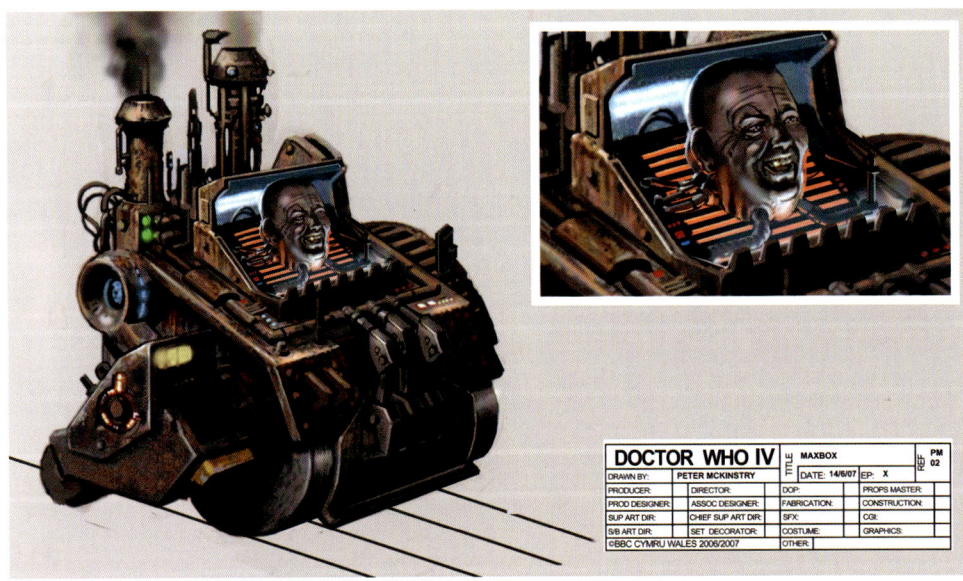

DOCTOR WHO IV	TITLE	MAXBOX		REF	PM 02
DRAWN BY:	PETER MCKINSTRY		DATE: 14/6/07	EP: X	
PRODUCER:	DIRECTOR:	DOP:		PROPS MASTER:	
PROD DESIGNER:	ASSOC DESIGNER:	FABRICATION:		CONSTRUCTION:	
SUP ART DIR:	CHIEF SUP ART DIR:	SFX:		CGI:	
S/B ART DIR:	SET DECORATOR:	COSTUME:		GRAPHICS:	
©BBC CYMRU WALES 2006/2007		OTHER:			

COMMS UNIT AND DOOR CONTROL

These comms units gave us another chance to tell the story through design. Below decks, everything had a more industrial, sci-fi steampunk feel, while the front-of-house comms units and controls featured a more brassy, ornate design to complement the opulent decor.

ASTRID'S FORKLIFT

In the episode's conclusion, Astrid Peth (played by Kylie Minogue) carries Max's box over the edge of a deadly precipice in a forklift, perishing along with him. We had a forklift in the studio, but it really needed dressing up in order to be fit for the screen. This concept shows the exact forklift with added panels and other details to transform it and make it fit into our *Doctor Who* world. Poor Max, he really did get carried away!

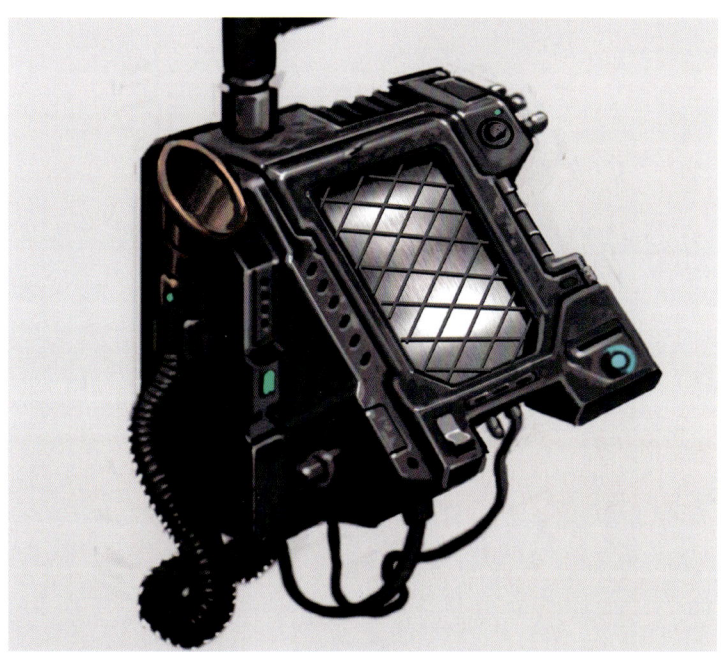

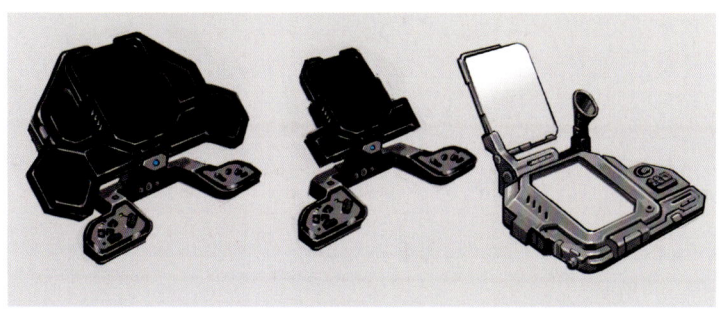

TELEPORT BRACELET AND PLINTH

The first version of the teleport bracelet came from an idea Ed had – that it should resemble Novice Hame's device from Series 3's *Gridlock*. It would also save the production the cost of making a brand new prop! However, Russell reminded us that Novice Hame existed in the year Five Billion, far beyond this time, and told us to try something new.

My revised design was a chunkier bracelet, partly inspired by the teleport devices in *Blake's 7*, which I'd loved as a child. Indeed, I still remember following *Blue Peter*'s instructions as a kid to make my own, using just a pair of scissors and an empty plastic squash bottle. (That's likely where I got the bright idea to cut open my talking Dalek!)

Ed suggested the bracelets be carried on a tray like a cinema usherette's ice creams. However, Russell pointed out that this wouldn't be secure: 'bracelets on a tray would be thrown everywhere.' A structure was needed to hold them in place, so I proposed a raised plinth where the bracelets could be securely stored. This concept was then refined into a simpler lectern, which served the same function while better complementing the *Titanic*'s wood and brass interior.

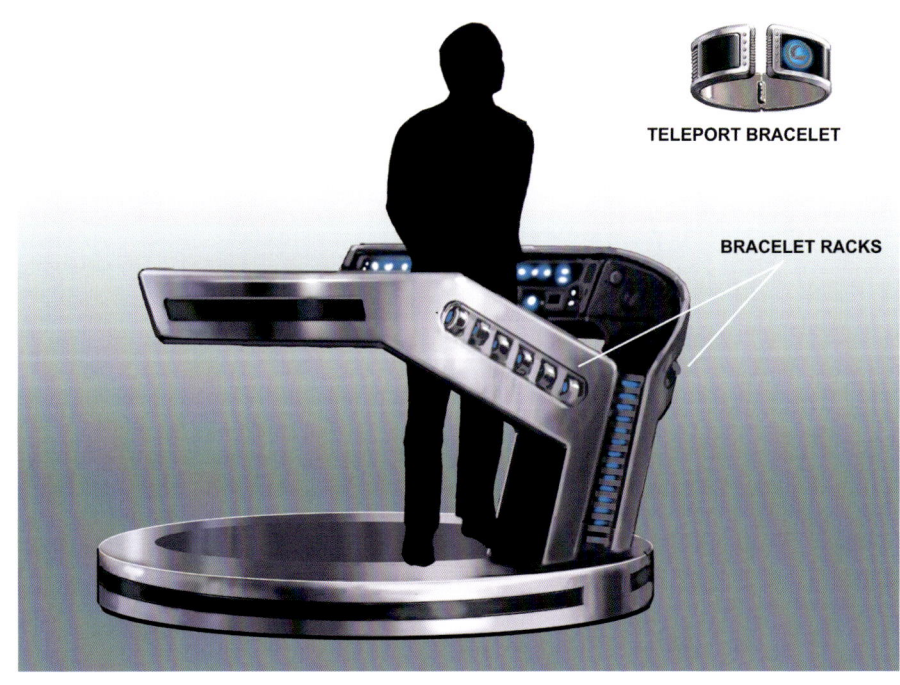

TELEPORT BRACELET

BRACELET RACKS

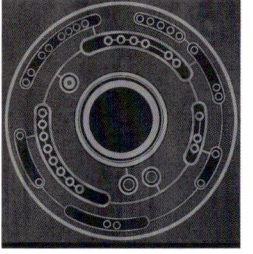

KEYPAD

BRACELET RACK

FUNCTION KEYS

LOCKED
4/7/07

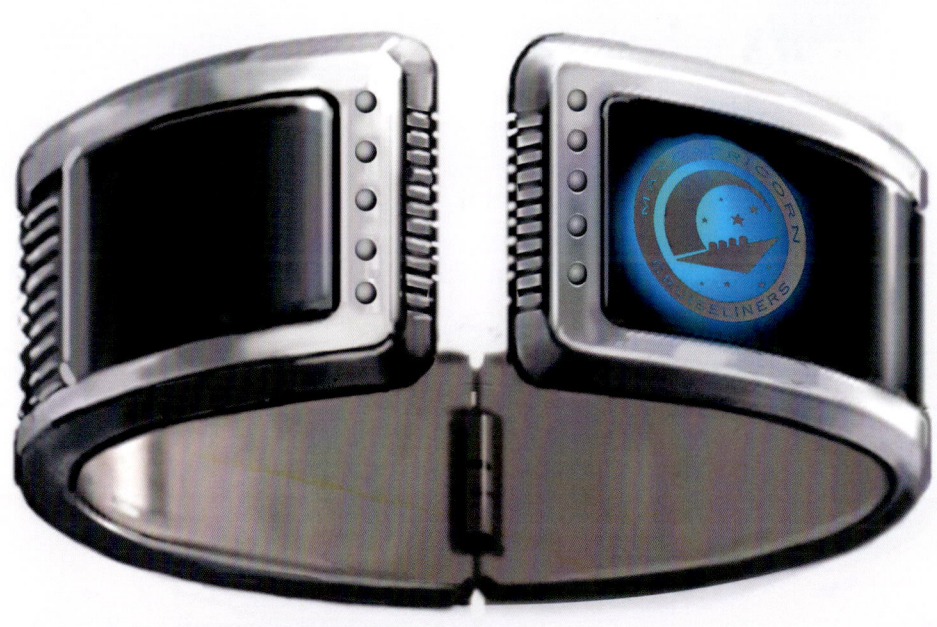

BRIDGE OF DOOM

We called this image the Bridge of Doom. It's a scene very much in the vein of the classic disaster movies like *The Poseidon Adventure* and *The Towering Inferno*, showing the survivors making a perilous crossing inside one of the *Titanic*'s funnels. It's another example of providing a visual touchstone for a moment that would be largely CGI, but incorporating practical elements, like the actual set of the bridge itself, filmed against green screen. Once an image like this received Russell's approval, it was shared with both the VFX team and set builders to guide discussions on how the final shot would be achieved and how it might look on screen.

Subject: Bridge of Doom
Sent: Friday, June 29, 2007 5:43 PM
To: Russell T Davies
From: Peter Mckinstry

Hello,

Completed version of this visual, the precarious crossing from above. So much fun to paint it should be illegal. Let us know if this works for you all!

I was thinking the other day how it'd be great to visit myself as a kid, and whisper in my 8-year-old ear, 'You're learning to draw by drawing pictures of the Doctor and the TARDIS, one day, it'll be your job.' Now, I'm thinking, no need to take me back that far. If I could go back 2 years, to when i started on *Who*, and convey the massive amount of joy it would bring me, GOOD GOD! I'm so grateful to be part of it.

Ahem, anyway, yeah, not bad! Carry on :)

Pete

Sent: Sunday, July 1, 2007 10:17 AM
To: Peter Mckinstry
From: Russell T Davies

You're right, imagine knowing we'd do this, as a kid. We'd never have been able to comprehend it. Our little heads would have exploded!!

R x

PARTNERS IN CRIME

ADIPOSE LOGO

The starting point for the Adipose logo was the pill-shaped outline surrounding the text, symbolising the weight-loss pills sold by Adipose Industries. The next step was designing the typography to fit within the pill shape, creating a graphic style reminiscent of contemporary corporate logos.

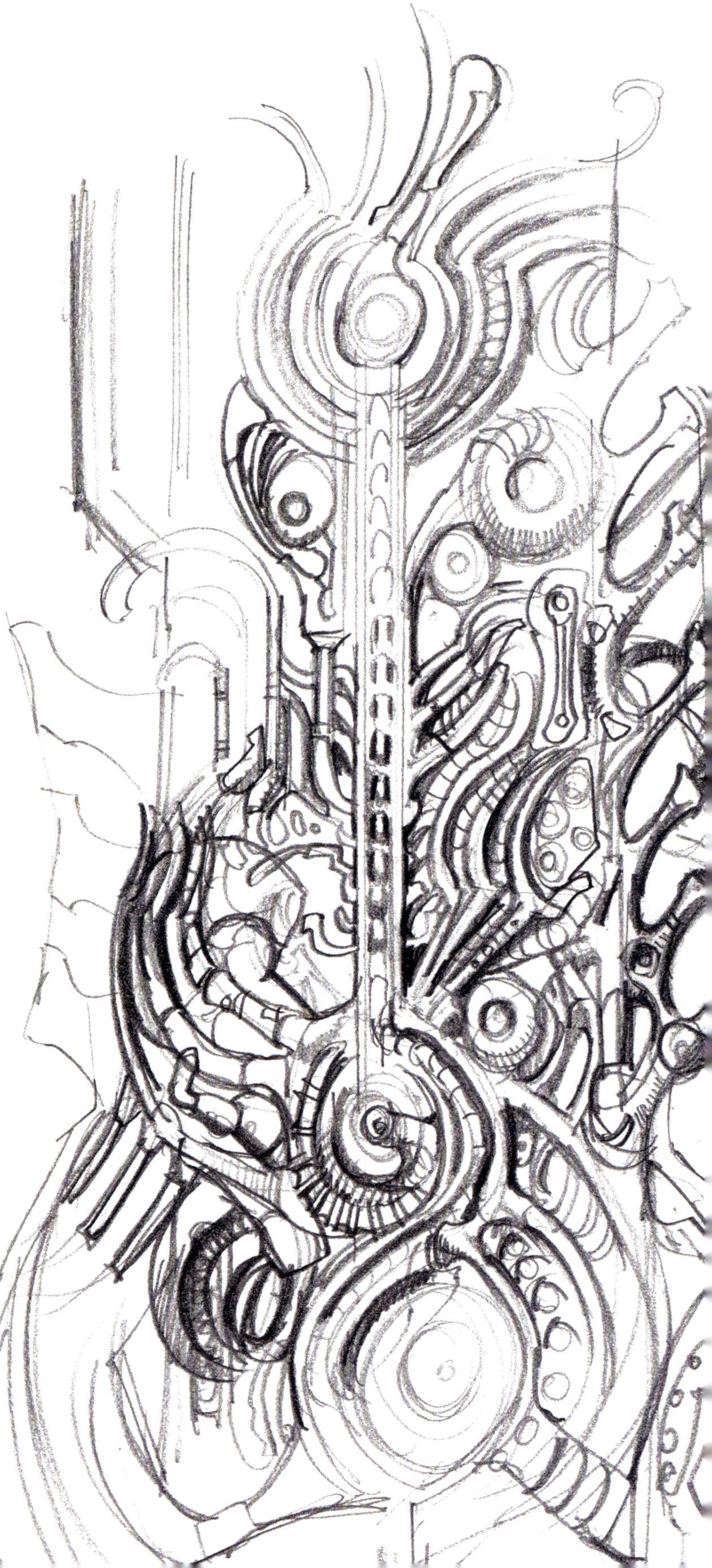

COMPUTER WALL

I enjoyed ensuring that every new alien species the Doctor encounters has its own unique technology, culture, and design language. The final design for the Adipose computer wall evolved through several iterations – starting with a more organic look before shifting to a structure resembling a spinal column. This repeating vertebrae-like form helped to suggest that the computer extended throughout the entire building.

To ensure the Doctor could interact with it, I introduced a column of rotating levers positioned horizontally. It's fun to find interesting new ways to reinvent levers and buttons for the Doctor to use!

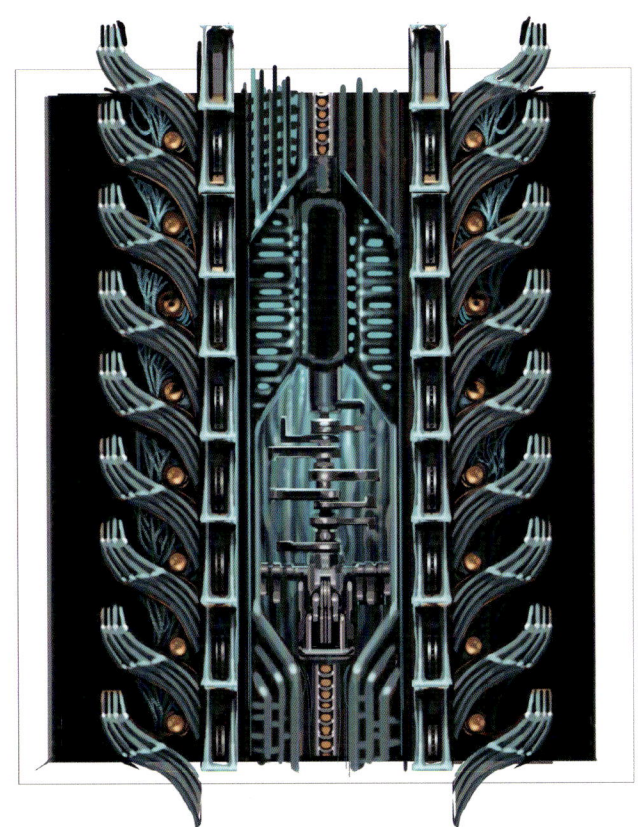

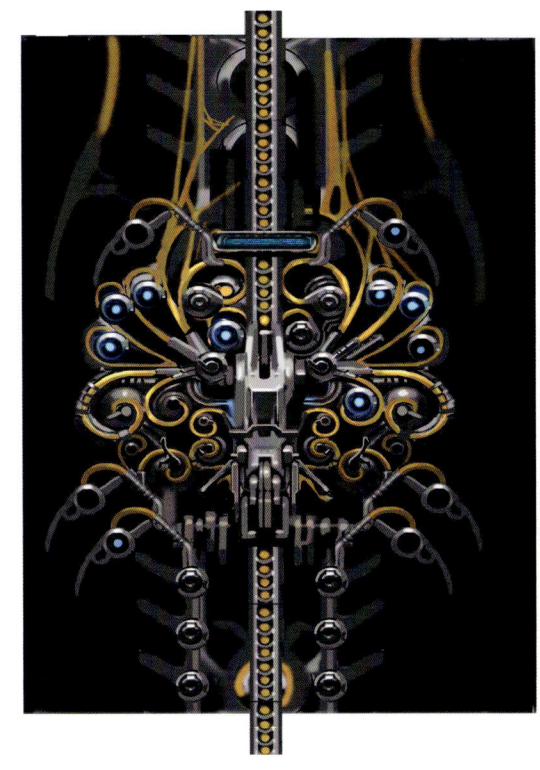

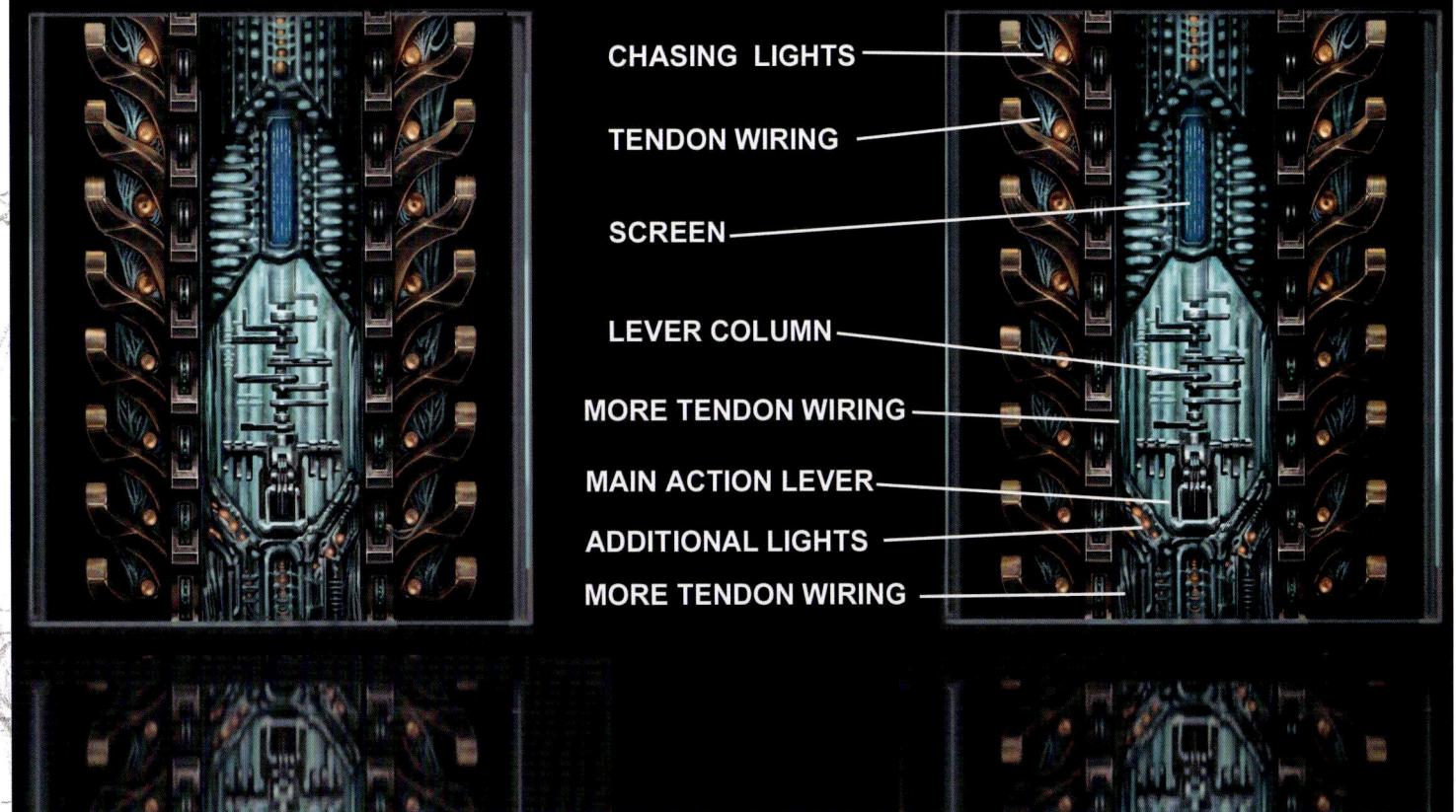

CHASING LIGHTS

TENDON WIRING

SCREEN

LEVER COLUMN

MORE TENDON WIRING

MAIN ACTION LEVER

ADDITIONAL LIGHTS

MORE TENDON WIRING

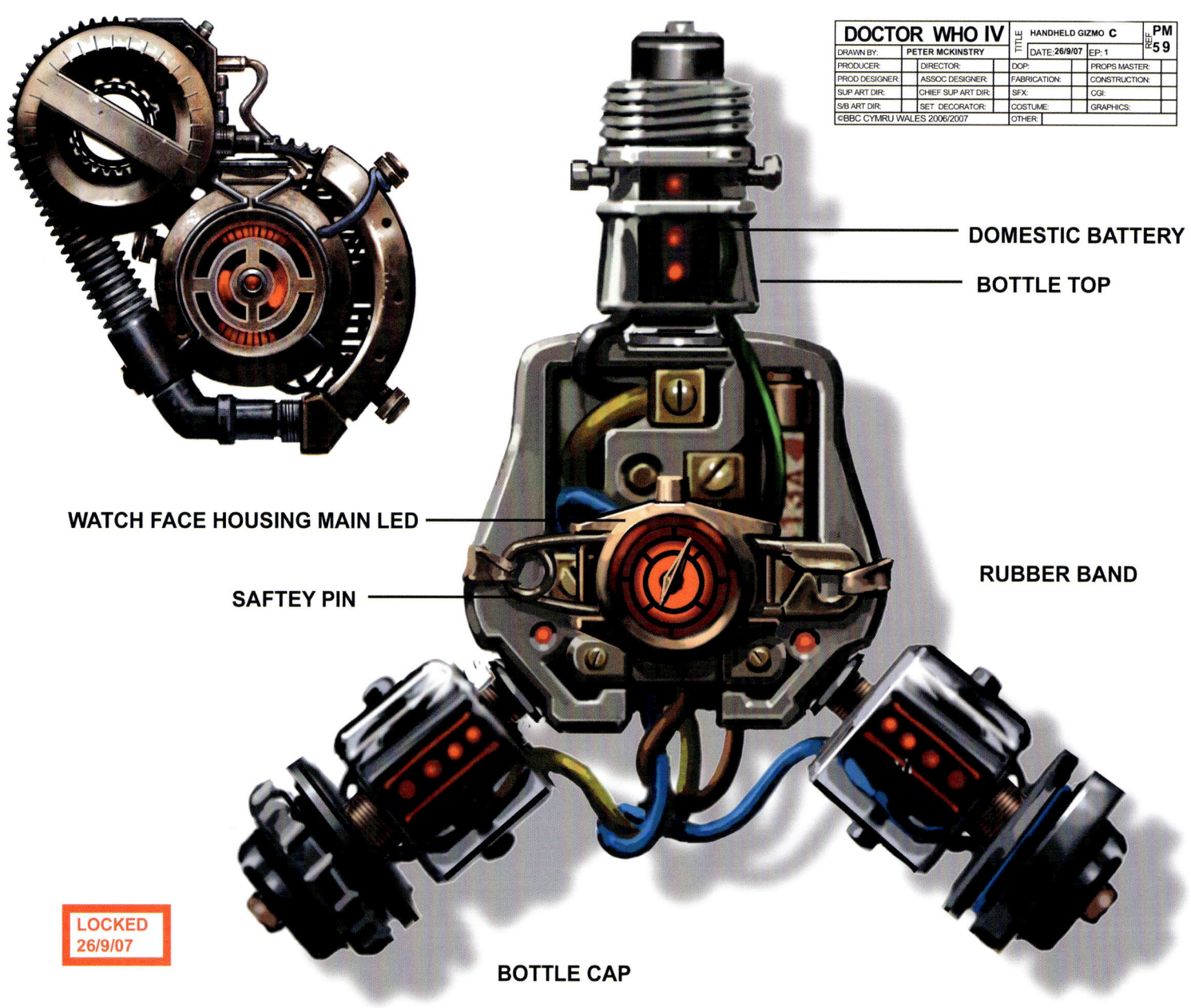

DOMESTIC BATTERY

BOTTLE TOP

WATCH FACE HOUSING MAIN LED

SAFTEY PIN

RUBBER BAND

LOCKED
26/9/07

BOTTLE CAP

HANDHELD TRACKING DEVICE

Russell felt my first design for this handheld prop looked too similar to the circular rift manipulator from *Torchwood*, which prompted a rethink. I moved toward an object that would fit in the palm, pieced together from different bits of tech.

Russell encouraged me to push it further and make it look even more thrown together. The key was to find a central piece, something simple that the Doctor might pick up and start tinkering with. I took inspiration from an electrical three-pin plug in the prop store; the three additional pieces, which point outwards from the centre, suggested a sense of triangulation – perfect for a signal-tracking device.

SONIC PEN – CUTAWAY

This cutaway of Miss Foster's sonic pen was created for GE Fabbri's *Doctor Who: The DVD Files* magazine. I included design elements from the Adipose computer wall, along with some nods to the sonic screwdriver, while ensuring the internal workings were distinct. The blue from the Adipose logo – later used in the design of the Adipose ship – was also included to tie everything together visually.

And, of course, it still had to function as an actual pen! Turning the barrel one way extends the nib, while twisting it the other way activates the sonic function. A simple but stylish instrument with a hidden side – very Miss Foster!

ADIPOSE WALL ART

Miss Foster's Adipose office spaces needed some wall art. Instead of traditional corporate artwork, we took imagery of fat cells as a starting point, using their shapes and textures to create organic biological-looking designs. The result, painted from these images by Scenic Artist John Pinkerton, was something that subtly reflected the nature of the Adipose without being too on-the-nose.

THE FIRES OF POMPEII

MARBLE SQUARES

The story is set in Ancient Pompeii, so large slabs of marble circuitry were an intriguing story element. I started my design by collecting images of printed circuit boards. I mixed and matched their intricate patterns and lines, adding a maze-like quality that felt a little off-beat and otherworldly.

Subject: Who Ep3 Marble Cubes
Sent: Tuesday, August 28, 2007 2:48 PM
To: Russell T Davies
From: Peter Mckinstry

Another ep3 image for your feedback please. This shows all six cubes together as in sc 17.

Thanks

Peter

Sent: Tuesday, August 28, 2007 3:48 PM
To: Peter Mckinstry
From: Russell T Davies

Excellent, that's brilliant. They're squares, not cubes, but I think that's what you meant.

Russell T Pedant

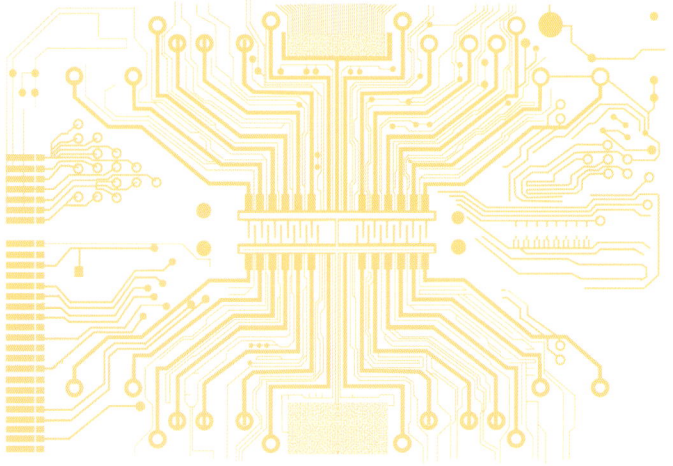

SIBYLLINE SISTERS' FACE MARKINGS

As with the Beast's markings in *The Satan Pit*, I knew my design for the soothsayer sisterhood's facial makeup had to balance striking visual impact with practicality, since multiple actors – three principal members, a soothsayer, and six additional sisters – would require full makeup.

While I enjoyed leaning into the mystical, ominous nature of the sisterhood, Director Colin Teague highlighted the need to maintain consistency across so many characters. So, I created a simpler set of options, with the top-right design emerging as a strong contender – bold yet simple enough to work efficiently in makeup.

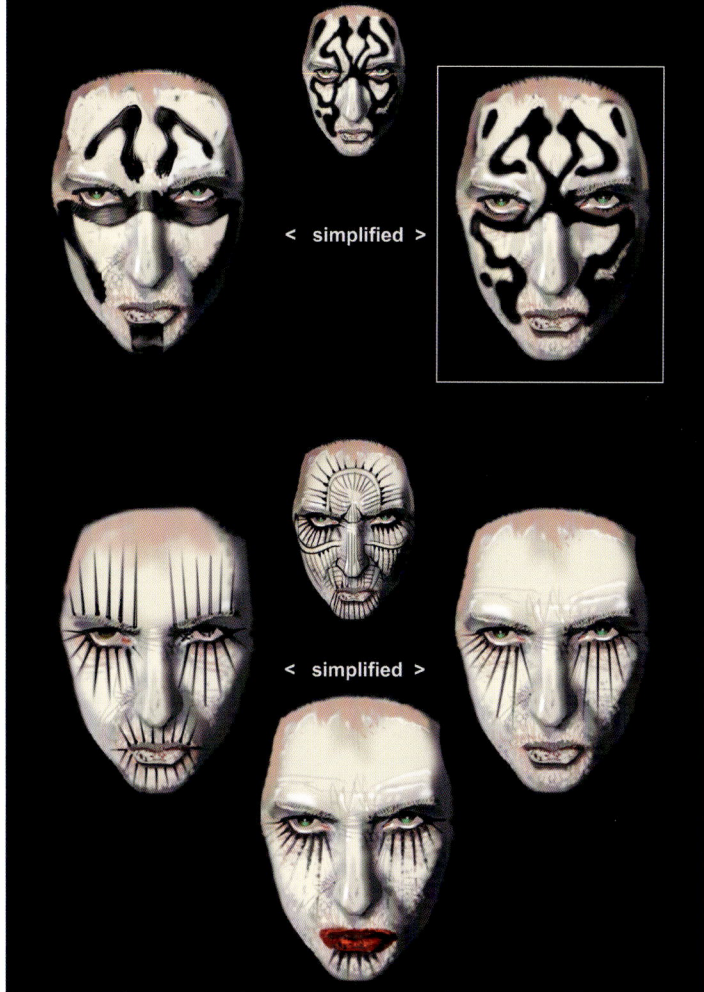

PYROVILE POD

My early designs reflected the Pyroviles' rock-based technology. I intended the angular elements of the circuit to be continued in the overall design language of the Pyrovile Pod, drawing inspiration from naturally formed geometric rock structures, such as the basalt columns of the Giant's Causeway.

However, for filming reasons, the final design eventually took the form of a sphere – something I'd tried to avoid so as not to clash with the spherical Sontaran spacecraft (first seen in 1973-4's *The Time Warrior*) which would be seen later in the season.

The interior did include the basalt formations. Built upon these formations were 'rock buttons' and spaces for the marble circuit boards.

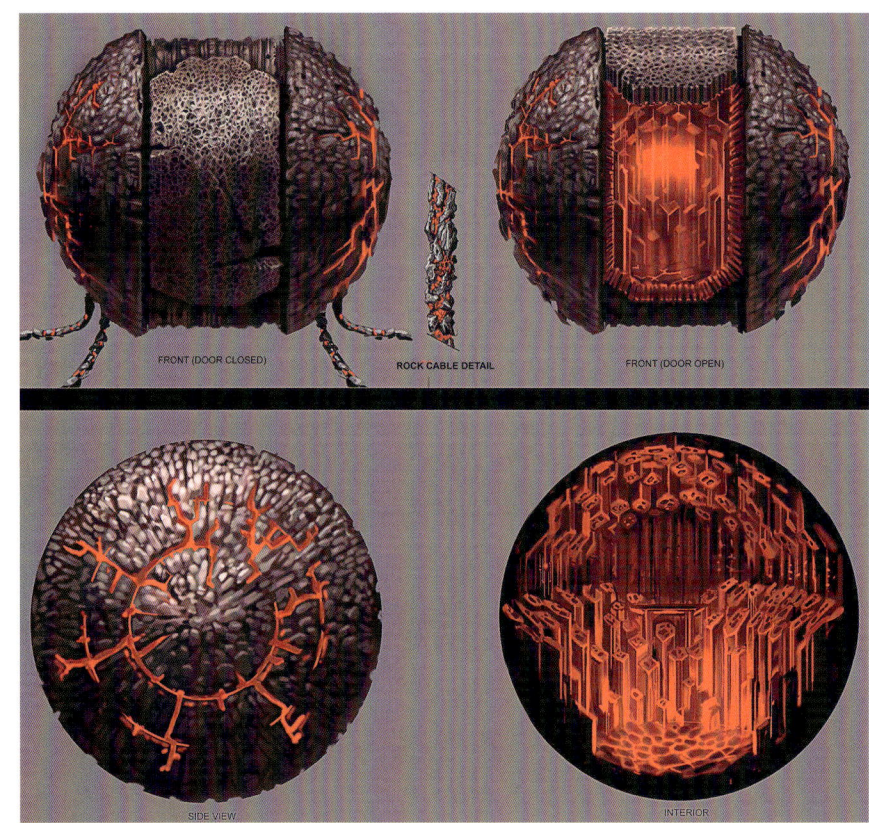

FRONT (DOOR CLOSED)   ROCK CABLE DETAIL   FRONT (DOOR OPEN)

SIDE VIEW   INTERIOR

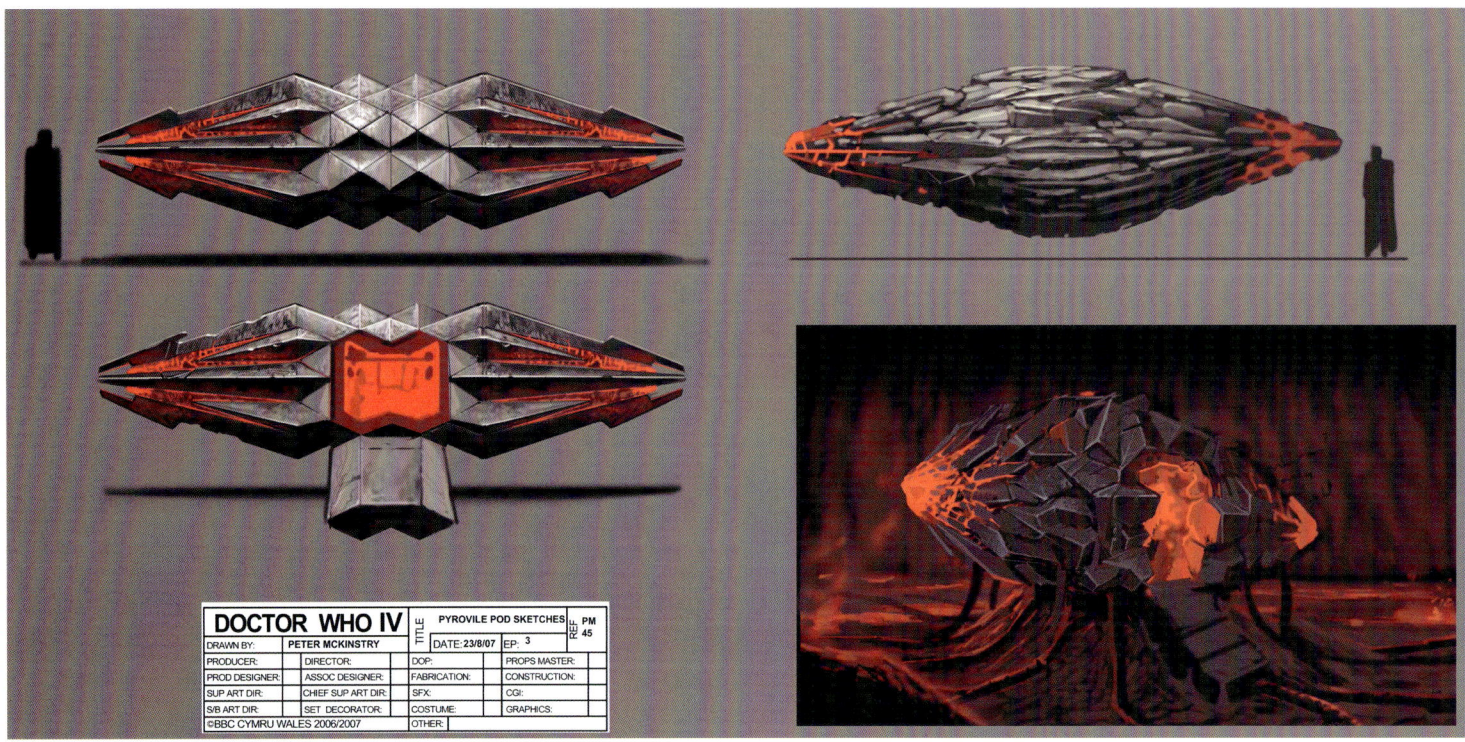

DOCTOR WHO IV		TITLE	PYROVILE POD SKETCHES	REF.	PM 45
DRAWN BY:	PETER MCKINSTRY		DATE: 23/8/07	EP: 3	
PRODUCER:	DIRECTOR:	DOP:	PROPS MASTER:		
PROD DESIGNER:	ASSOC DESIGNER:	FABRICATION:	CONSTRUCTION:		
SUP ART DIR:	CHIEF SUP ART DIR:	SFX:	CGI:		
S/B ART DIR:	SET DECORATOR:	COSTUME:	GRAPHICS:		
©BBC CYMRU WALES 2006/2007		OTHER:			

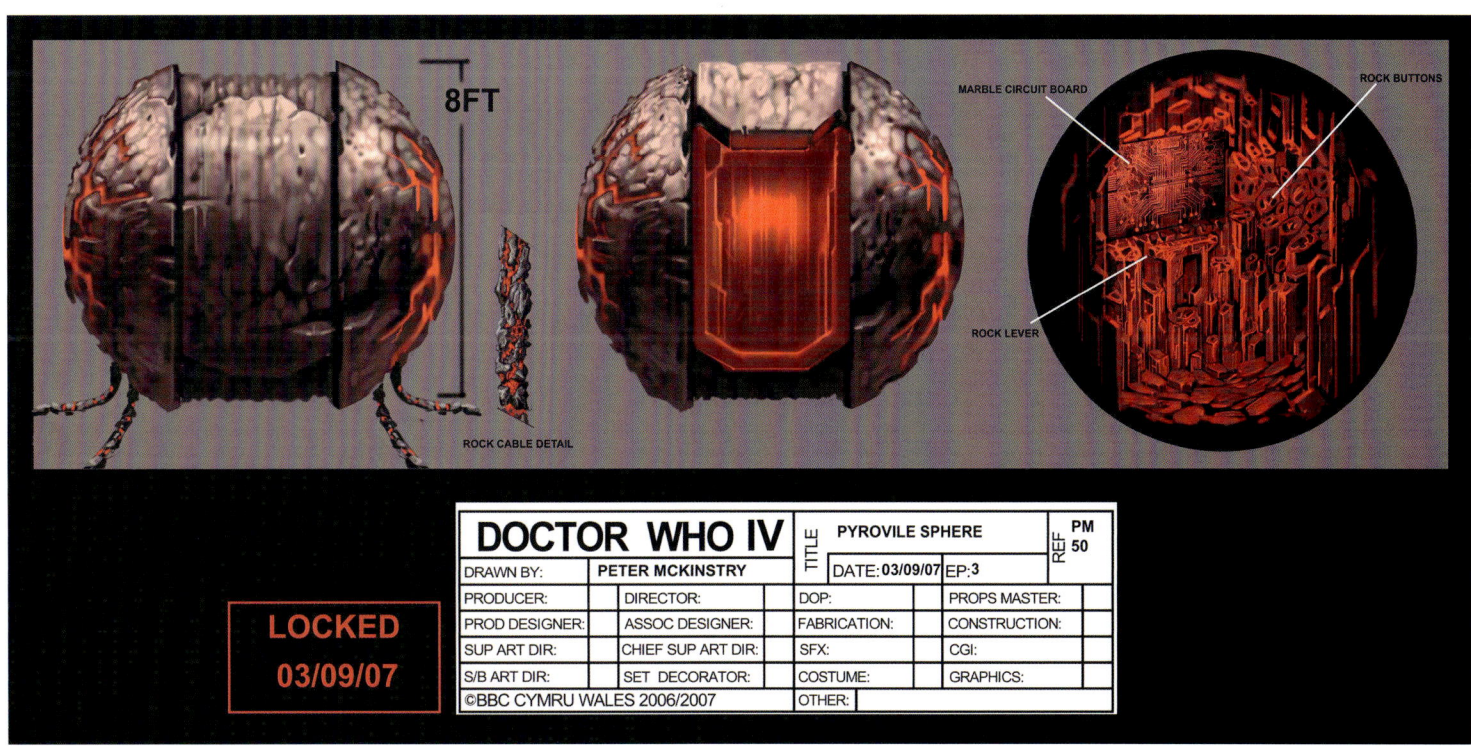

8FT

ROCK CABLE DETAIL

MARBLE CIRCUIT BOARD

ROCK BUTTONS

ROCK LEVER

DOCTOR WHO IV	TITLE	PYROVILE SPHERE		REF	PM 50
DRAWN BY:	PETER MCKINSTRY		DATE: 03/09/07 EP: 3		
PRODUCER:		DIRECTOR:	DOP:	PROPS MASTER:	
PROD DESIGNER:		ASSOC DESIGNER:	FABRICATION:	CONSTRUCTION:	
SUP ART DIR:		CHIEF SUP ART DIR:	SFX:	CGI:	
S/B ART DIR:		SET DECORATOR:	COSTUME:	GRAPHICS:	
©BBC CYMRU WALES 2006/2007			OTHER:		

LOCKED
03/09/07

POMPEII STREET IMAGES

These visuals were created at top speed to demonstrate how we could adapt and utilise the pre-existing standing sets from the TV show *Rome*. In addition to showing where our CGI volcano should go in relation to the main street where filming would take place, it was also important to capture the overall look and atmosphere of the episode before production began, not least to highlight how our interpretation of the period would differ visually.

THE SONTARAN STRATAGEM / THE POISON SKY

SONTARAN

Having brought back the Daleks for Series 1, the Cybermen for Series 2 and the Master for Series 3, Series 4's returning foes were the Sontarans. Since ultimately the Sontaran prosthetic design would be handled by Millennium FX, this design was presented at the Tone Meeting to spark initial discussions. I kept it faithful to the Sontaran Linx in *The Time Warrior* – my instinct was to update it only in a subtle way, enhancing the details of the originals.

SONTARAN CONTROL STATION

For the overall look of Sontaran technology, we began by creating a series of moodboards. We drew references from Brutalist architecture and Eastern European Constructivism, both of which are known for their bold, sculptural forms. Working on the control station, I used shapes from the moodboards that caught my eye: broken circles and curves, contrasting with large, imposing blocks. This approach felt right for the Sontarans, who in all their appearances are stark, militaristic, and formidable. These shapes created a distinct look for the Sontarans across the entire series.

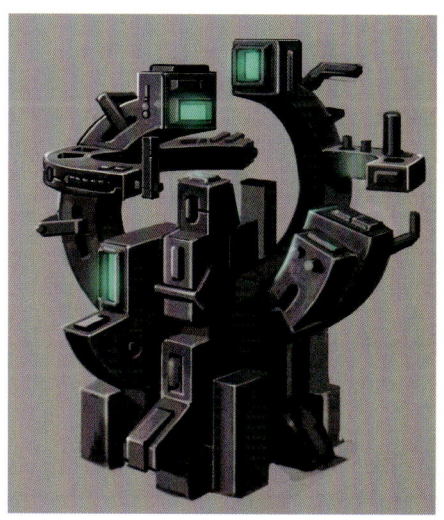

CLONING TANK

I intended the cloning tank to resemble a huge sarcophagus, giving the viewer a hint of its function before the reveal of its opening. Its design ties in with the Sontarans' cold, militaristic society, where every aspect of their existence is stripped of individuality and treated like a machine-driven ritual.

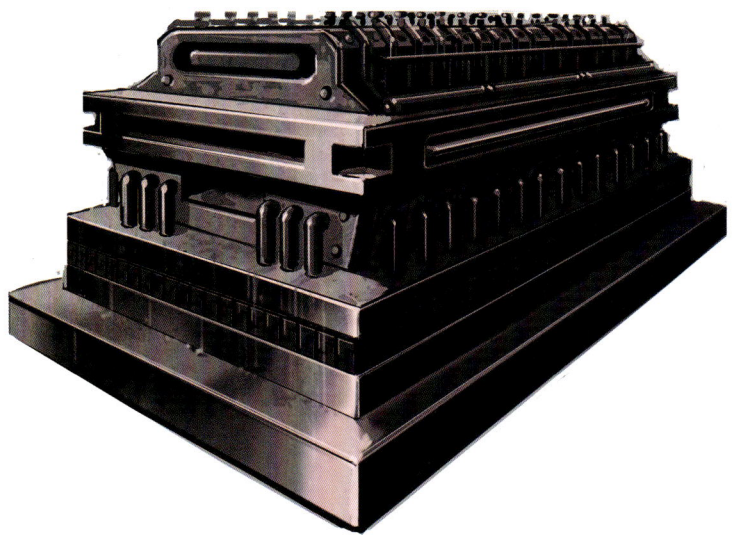

GAS ANALYSER AND TELEPORT HEMISPHERES

I was quietly pleased with the gas analyser; the goal was to create a 'modern' piece of technology that did its job on screen and looked convincing in its setting. The Teleport hemispheres were a fun callback to the Sontaran ships featured in the classic series.

ATMOSPHERIC CONVERTER

The entire climax of the Sontaran story revolved around the atmospheric converter. It needed to be sturdy enough to be dropped onto grass without wobbling! To ensure this, one version of the design even incorporated the base of a swingball set!

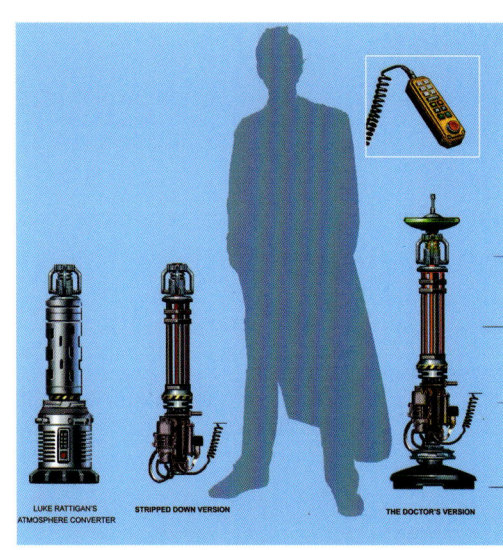

LUKE RATTIGAN'S ATMOSPHERE CONVERTER   STRIPPED DOWN VERSION   THE DOCTOR'S VERSION

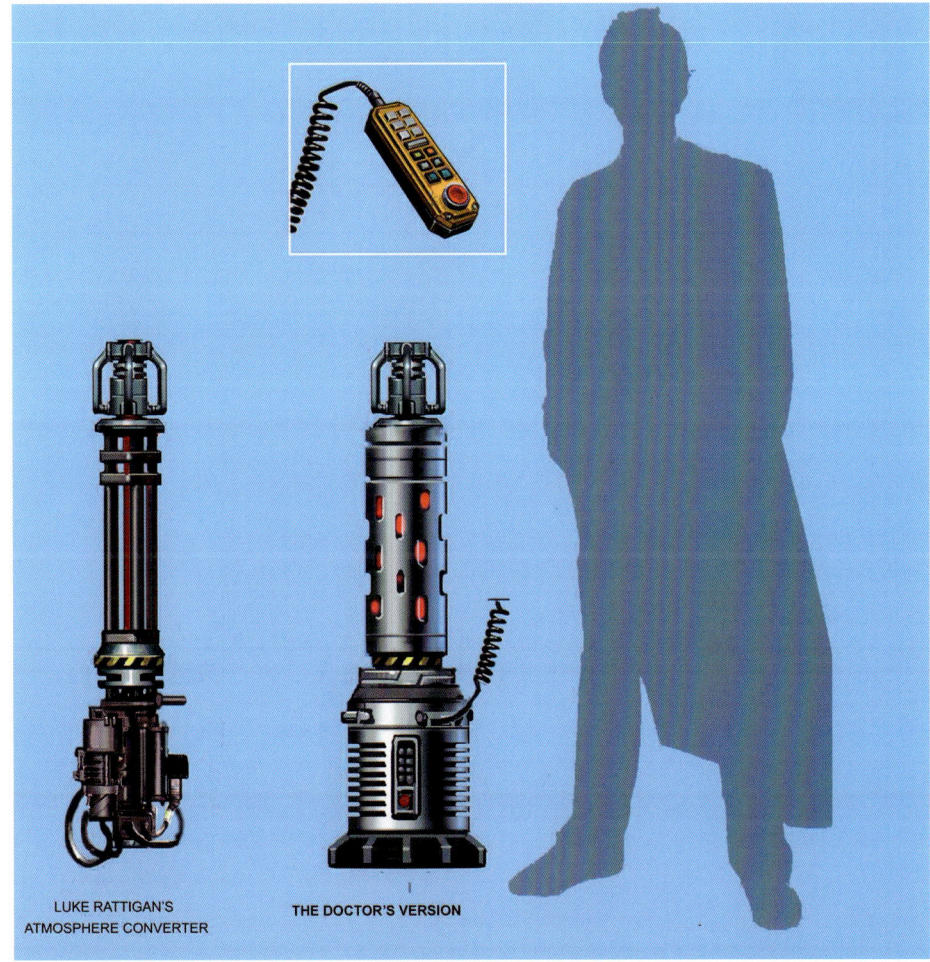

LUKE RATTIGAN'S ATMOSPHERE CONVERTER   THE DOCTOR'S VERSION

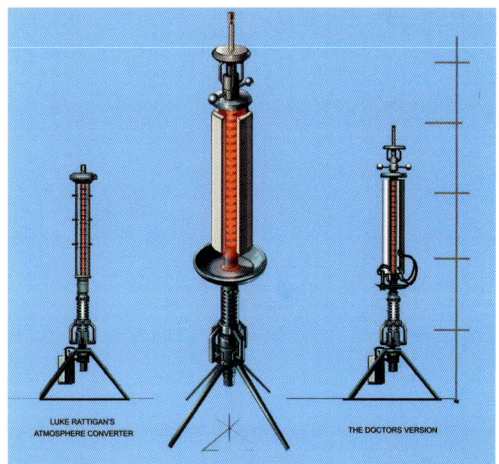

LUKE RATTIGAN'S ATMOSPHERE CONVERTER   THE DOCTORS VERSION

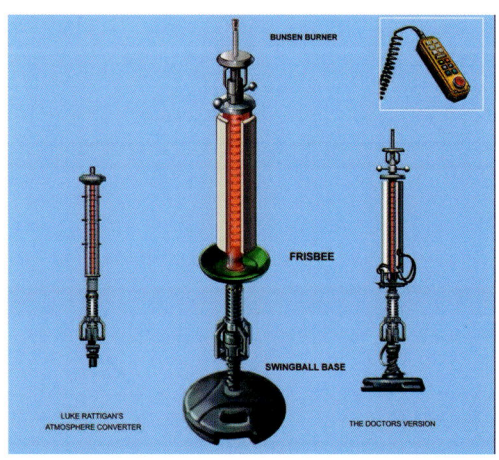

BUNSEN BURNER

FRISBEE

SWINGBALL BASE

LUKE RATTIGAN'S ATMOSPHERE CONVERTER   THE DOCTORS VERSION

JUNCTION FEED

In the story, Donna has to locate a piece of Sontaran technology from a description given by the Doctor. Originally, a 'C' with a line through it was suggested – but my first design wasn't clear enough for Donna to spot. Of course, a 'C' with a line through it risked looking like the Cybus Industries logo… and a suggestion to flip the 'C' horizontally would make it resemble the Preachers' logo! The answer was to switch to another letter – 'O'!

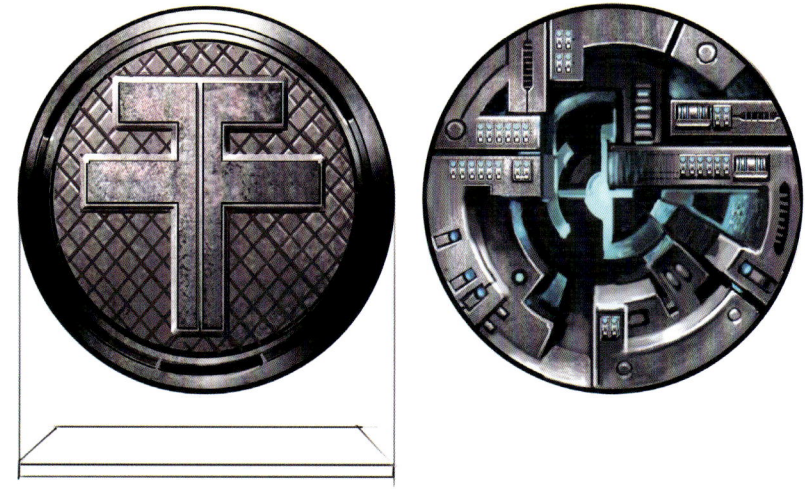

SONTARAN HANDPRINT READER

For the Sontaran handprint reader, I saw an opportunity to subtly nod to the classic series. The old Sontaran sphere ships were always a favourite of mine, and when I discovered we weren't bringing them back, I wanted to weave in a small design element that acknowledged their iconic look.

SONTARAN DEVICE

I designed the device to feel like an extension of the Sontaran control station, making it instantly recognisable as part of the Sontaran arsenal.

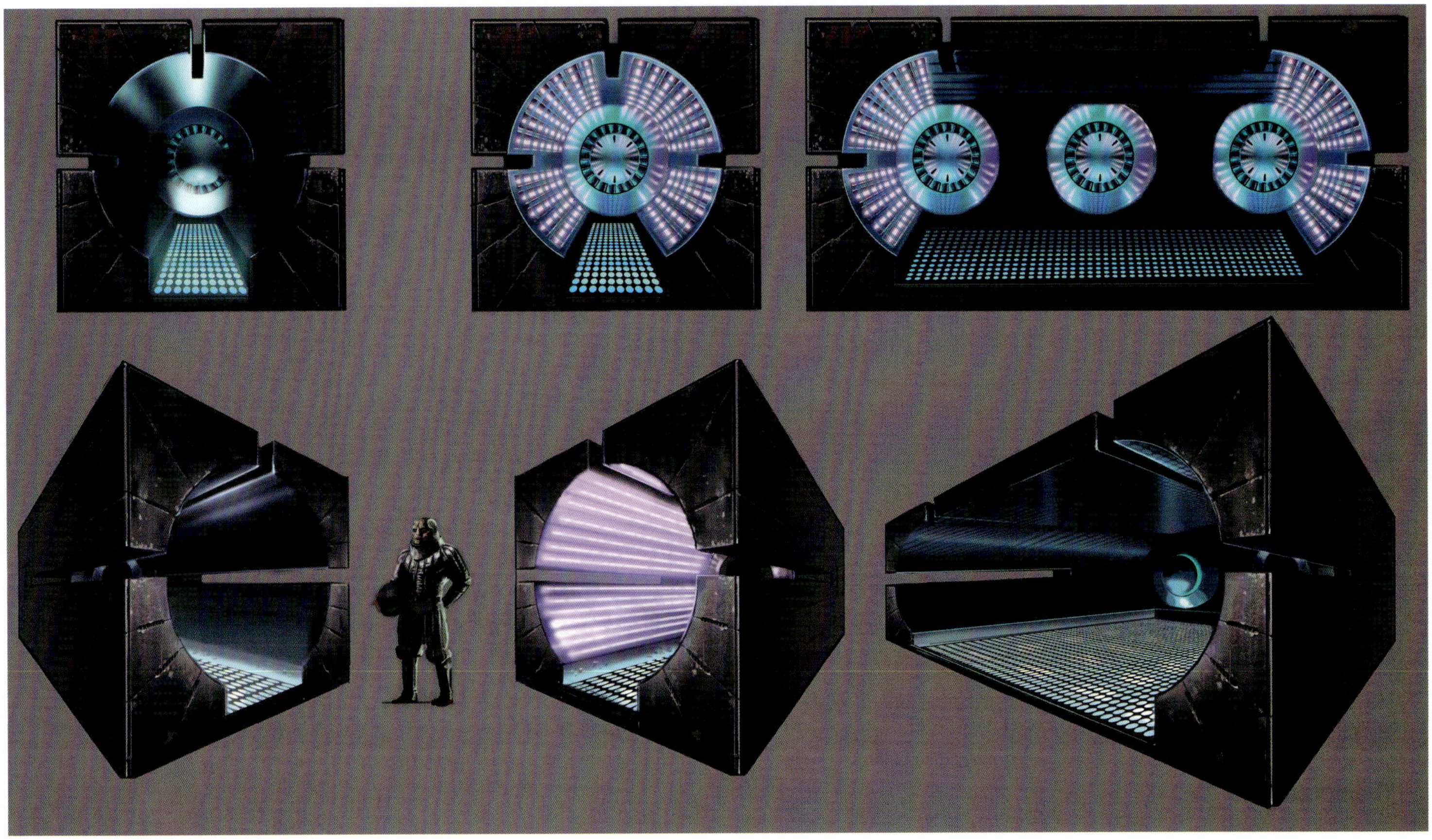

TELEPORT ARCH

The Sontaran teleport arch
was originally a simple
standalone piece similar
to the control station.
Ed suggested I make it
an integrated part of the
whole set. It became wide
enough to accommodate
entire squads teleporting
in unison, shoulder to
shoulder, ready to battle.

SONTARAN RANK PIPS

This subtle but important design detail
helped reinforce a sense of hierarchy
within the Sontaran army. For the
Lieutenant, the pip was a single squat
diamond. The Commander had the same
pip flanked by two larger diamonds,
giving a sense of higher status. The
General's rank was signified by the
addition of two smaller diamonds placed
either side of the larger ones. This
tiered structure created a clear, visual
hierarchy displayed on the collar of the
Sontaran helmets – noticeable without
overshadowing the rest of the costume.

LEUITENANT

COMMANDER

GENERAL

SONTARAN RIFLE

The earliest designs show how closely related it was to the Control Station, which I was working on simultaneously. I wanted these to reflect the brute-force efficiency of the Sontaran war fleet – heavy-duty, solid, functional and deadly. Give any concept artist a brief to design alien weaponry, and they'll be happy sketching away indefinitely—until they're told to stop!

Subject: Sontaran Rifle
Sent: Tuesday, October 16, 2007 3:10 PM
To: Russell T Davies
From: Peter Mckinstry

Hi,

Here's our Sontaran assault rifle design, shall we super-size them? Turn them into bazookas?

Thanks as ever

Peter

Sent: Tuesday, October 16, 2007 4:25 PM
To: Peter Mckinstry
From: Russell T Davies

Great guns! Don't make 'em bigger – they're only little, our Sontarans!

R x

DOCTOR WHO IV		TITLE	SONTARAN RIFLE		REF	PM 71
DRAWN BY:	PETER MCKINSTRY		DATE:16/10/07	EP: 4/5		
PRODUCER:		DIRECTOR:		DOP:	PROPS MASTER:	
PROD DESIGNER:		ASSOC DESIGNER:		FABRICATION:	CONSTRUCTION:	
SUP ART DIR:		CHIEF SUP ART DIR:		SFX:	CGI:	
S/B ART DIR:		SET DECORATOR:		COSTUME:	GRAPHICS:	
©BBC CYMRU WALES 2006/2007				OTHER:		

UNIT TACTICAL TRUCK INTERIOR

For this early cutaway illustration of the UNIT truck interior, the goal was to create a practical yet tactical space; something that felt functional but also visually engaging on screen. Every element had to be placed to maximise efficiency, making it clear that this was a fully operational command centre.

SONTARAN WARSHIP – CUTAWAY

By peeling back the exterior of the warship, we could showcase its inner workings – reinforcing the idea that every inch of the ship was built for efficient warfare. Created for GE Fabbri's *Doctor Who: The DVD Files* magazine.

SONTARAN POD – CUTAWAY

For this cutaway illustration of the Sontaran scout ship, featured in GE Fabbri's *Doctor Who: The DVD Files* magazine, I gathered as many screengrabs as possible from *The Time Warrior* and its follow-up, *The Sontaran Experiment* (1975), so I could include the key design elements. At the same time, I incorporated aspects of the updated Sontaran technology from the new episodes, culminating in a design that connected both the classic series and the modern show.

PLANET OF THE OOD

OOD OPERATIONS FACTORY EXTERIOR

This is one of a pair of early production illustrations depicting the exterior of the Ood Operations facility. My brief was to show a sleek skyscraper frontage within the very industrial real-world location used for filming; this particular rear view emphasises the contrast between the front-of-house office area and the more industrial factory section at the back.

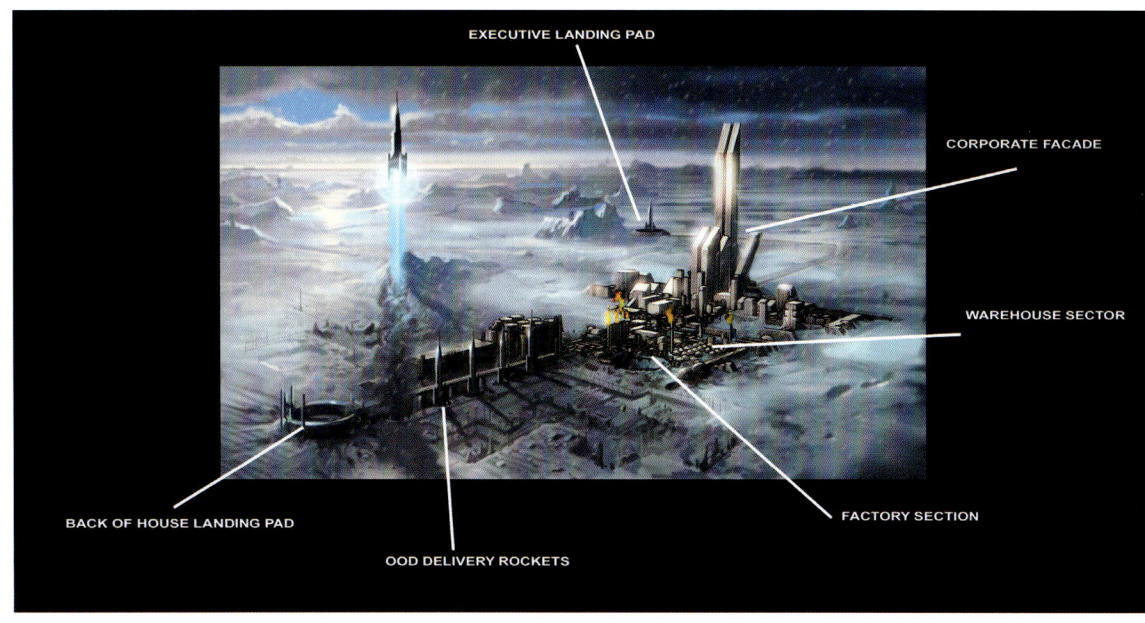

EXECUTIVE LANDING PAD

CORPORATE FACADE

WAREHOUSE SECTOR

FACTORY SECTION

BACK OF HOUSE LANDING PAD

OOD DELIVERY ROCKETS

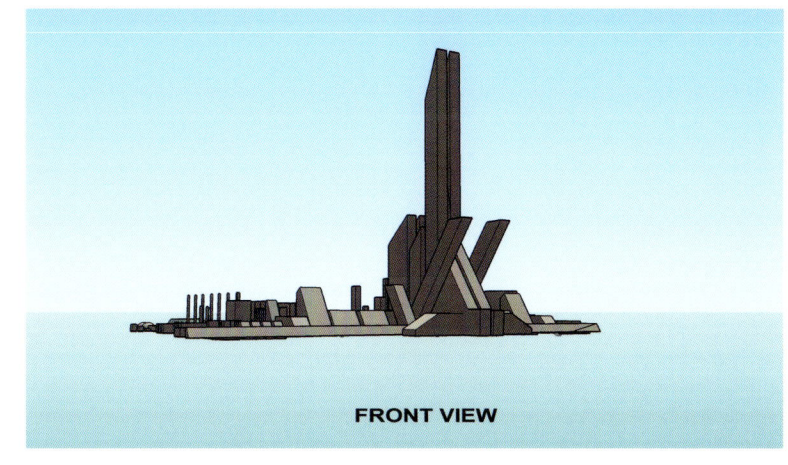

FRONT VIEW

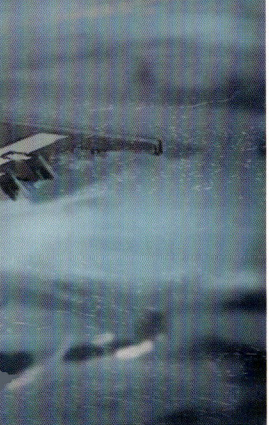

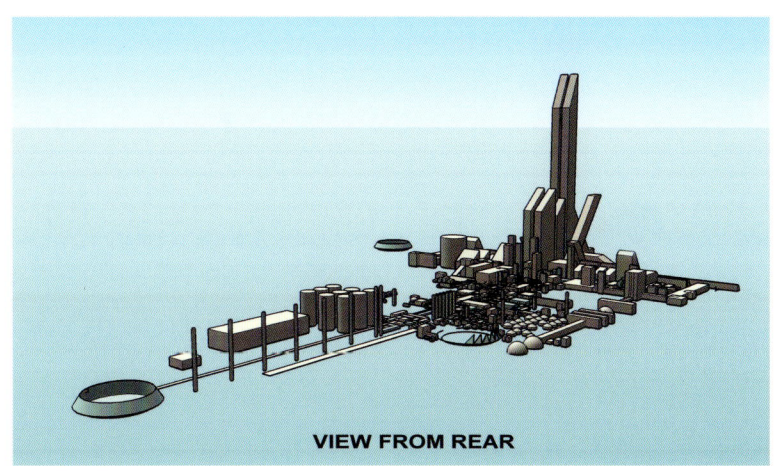

VIEW FROM REAR

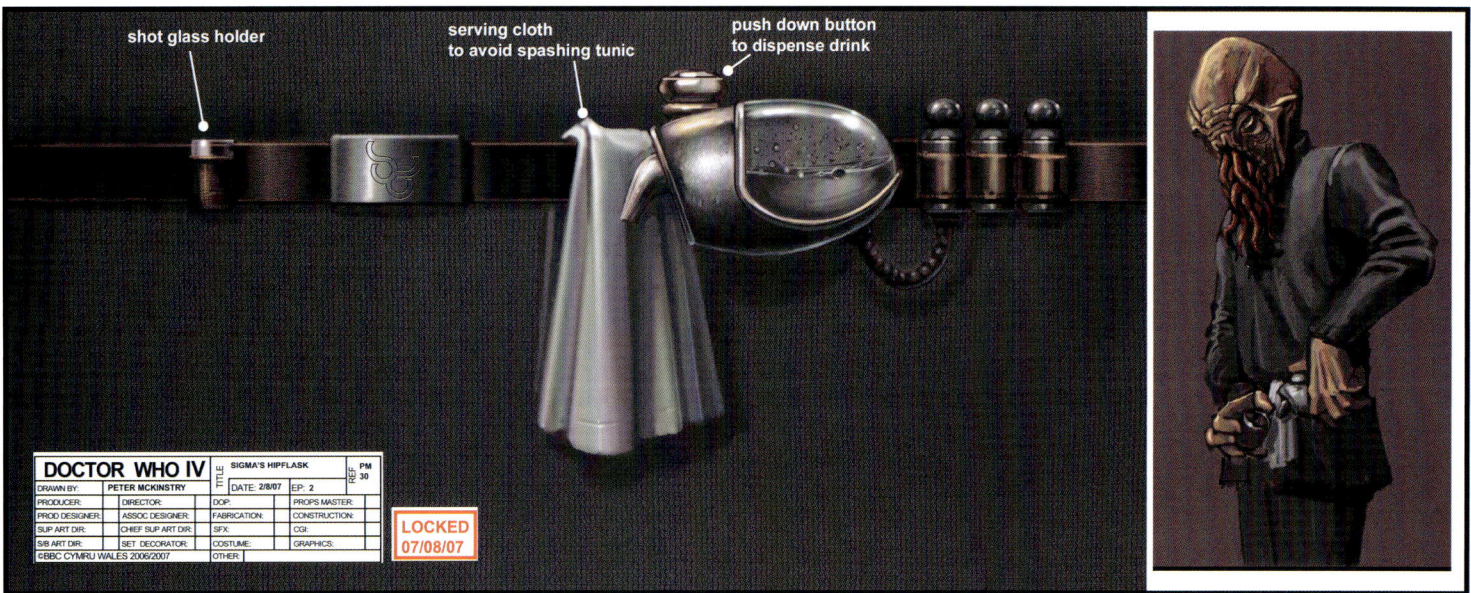

shot glass holder

serving cloth to avoid spashing tunic

push down button to dispense drink

DOCTOR WHO IV		SIGMA'S HIPFLASK		REF PM 30
DRAWN BY: PETER MCKINSTRY		DATE: 2/8/07	EP: 2	
PRODUCER:	DIRECTOR:	DOP:	PROPS MASTER:	
PROD DESIGNER:	ASSOC DESIGNER:	FABRICATION:	CONSTRUCTION:	LOCKED 07/08/07
SUP ART DIR:	CHIEF SUP ART DIR:	SFX:	CGI:	
S/B ART DIR:	SET DECORATOR:	COSTUME:	GRAPHICS:	
©BBC CYMRU WALES 2006/2007		OTHER:		

OOD SIGMA'S FLASK

Ood Sigma's belt flask was a small prop with a pivotal role in the episode. The 'hair tonic' in the flask proved to be a liquid compound that was slowly transforming Klineman Halpen, Chief Executive of Ood Operations, into an Ood himself!

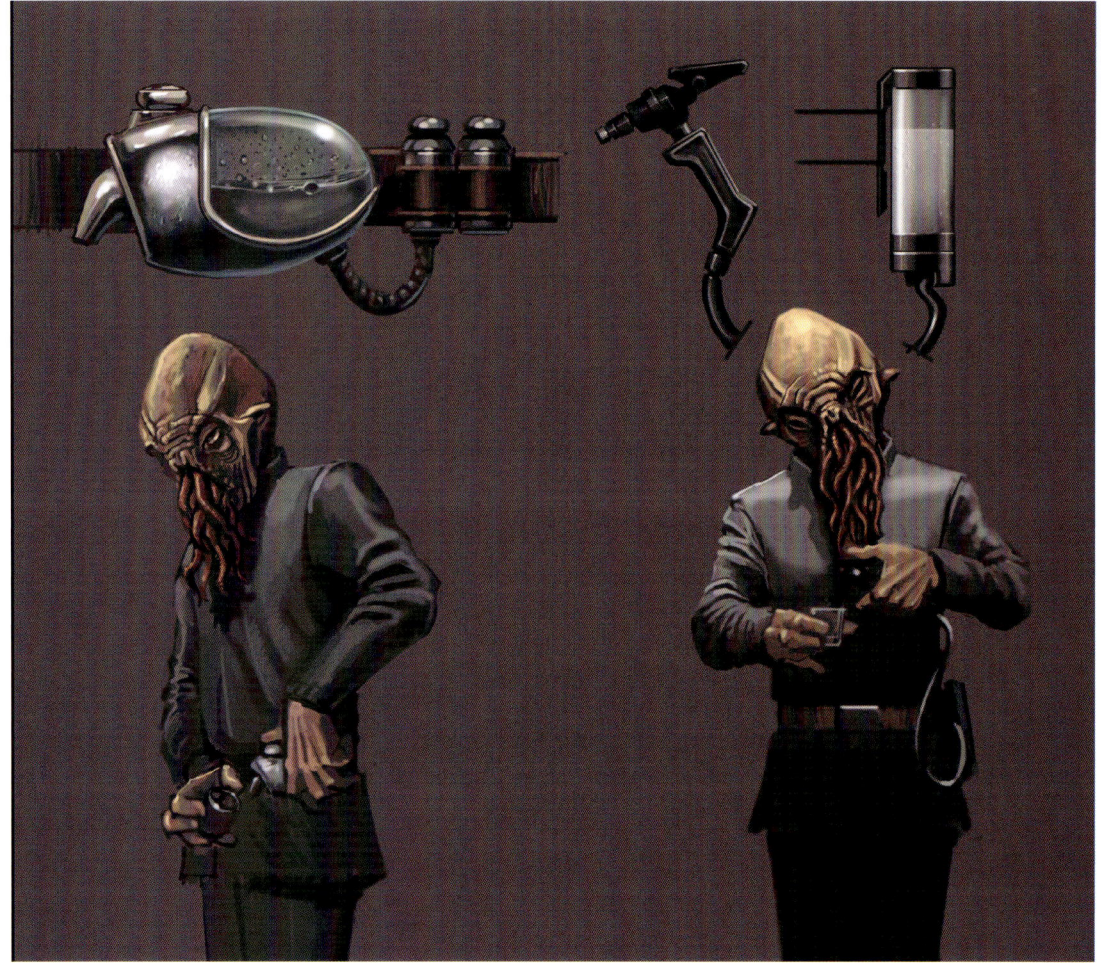

OOD ART

For this project, I had limited time and a lot of wall space to cover. I suggested something like Warhol's Marilyn Monroe screen prints or Richard Avedon's psychedelic portraits of The Beatles. Ed liked this idea but suggested a cooler colour palette to match the chilly atmosphere of Ood Operations.

OOD MANACLES

The manacles were used to restrain the Ood during their wild 'red-eyed' phase. These are meant to feel oppressive and uncomfortable to highlight the cruelty the Ood were expected to endure.

OOD BRAIN

The giant Ood Brain in Warehouse 15 needed to feel both scientific and macabre; something that could plausibly exist within the dystopian factory feel of Ood Operations. In these versions of the Ood Brain, I worked in the shapes of Ood facial features within the folds and wrinkles of the brain, in an attempt to make it look more sympathetic, and so we could perhaps show through its expression how much it was suffering.

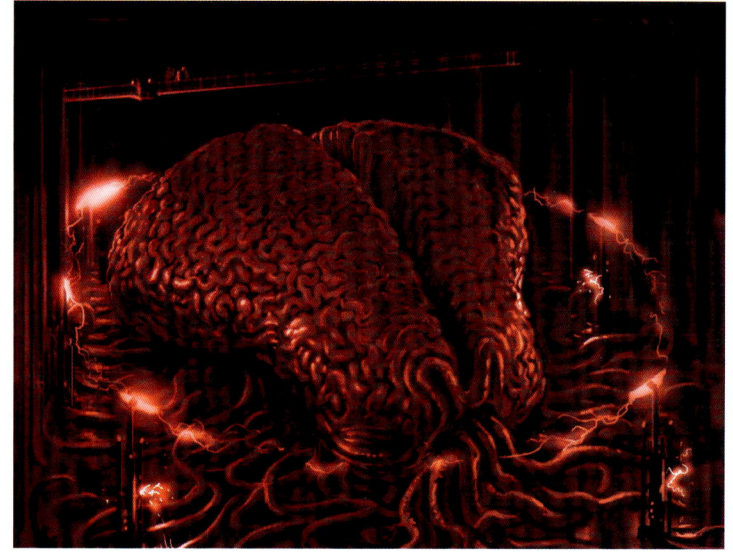

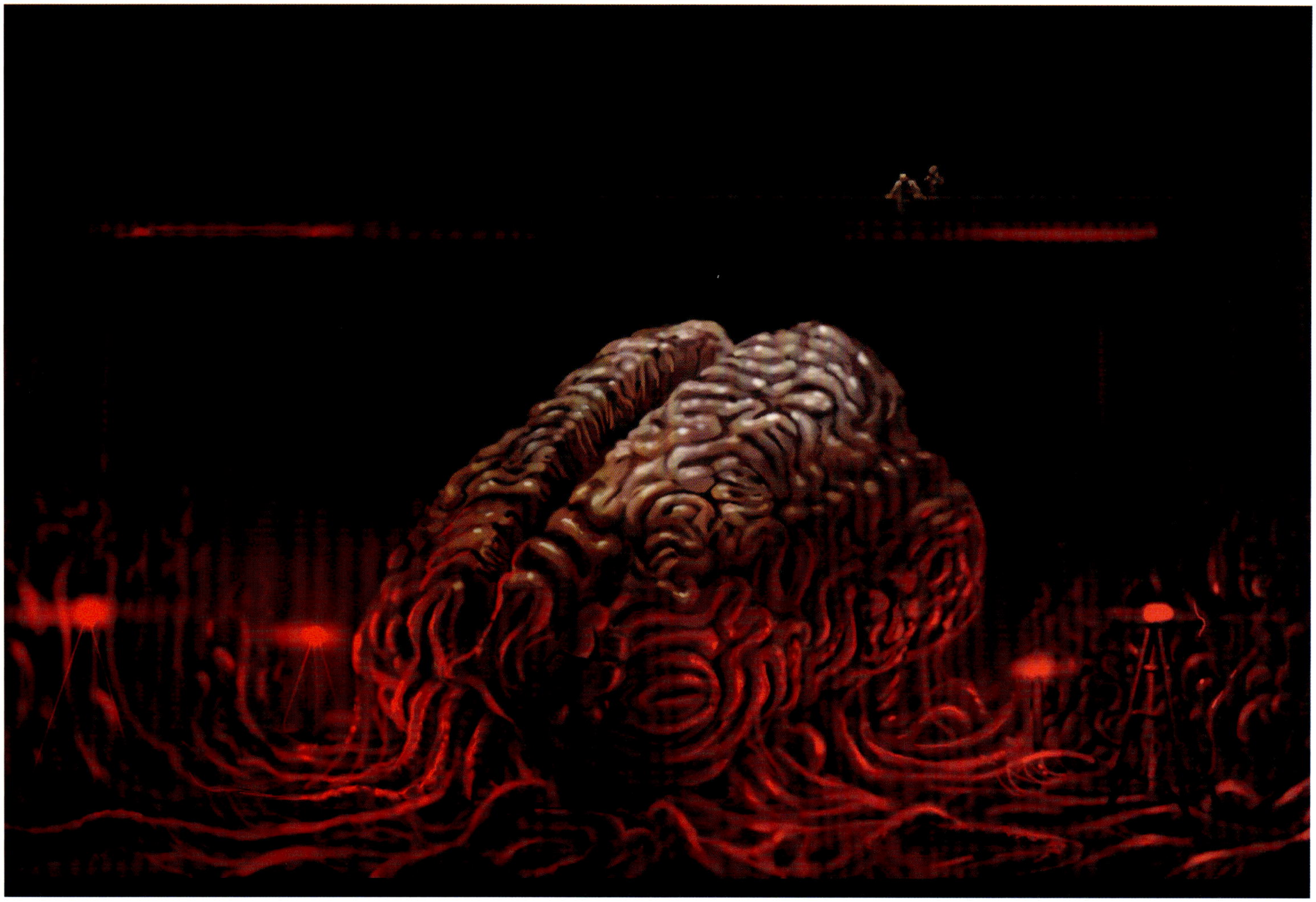

OOD OPERATIONS LOGO

The Ood Operations logo evolved from experimenting with the various graphic elements, moving the shapes around on different layers in Photoshop and seeing what emerged. The 'Double O' naturally stood out as a chance to reference the Ood translator devices with their connecting wires. They also resemble the Ood's hind-brains, which serve a key story point in the episode.

DISC BOMB

These disc bombs, or 'detonation packs' as Halpen calls them, are another example of taking inspiration from real life – in this case, various landmine designs – and developing them into something fitting for our *Doctor Who* world.

THE DOCTOR'S DAUGHTER

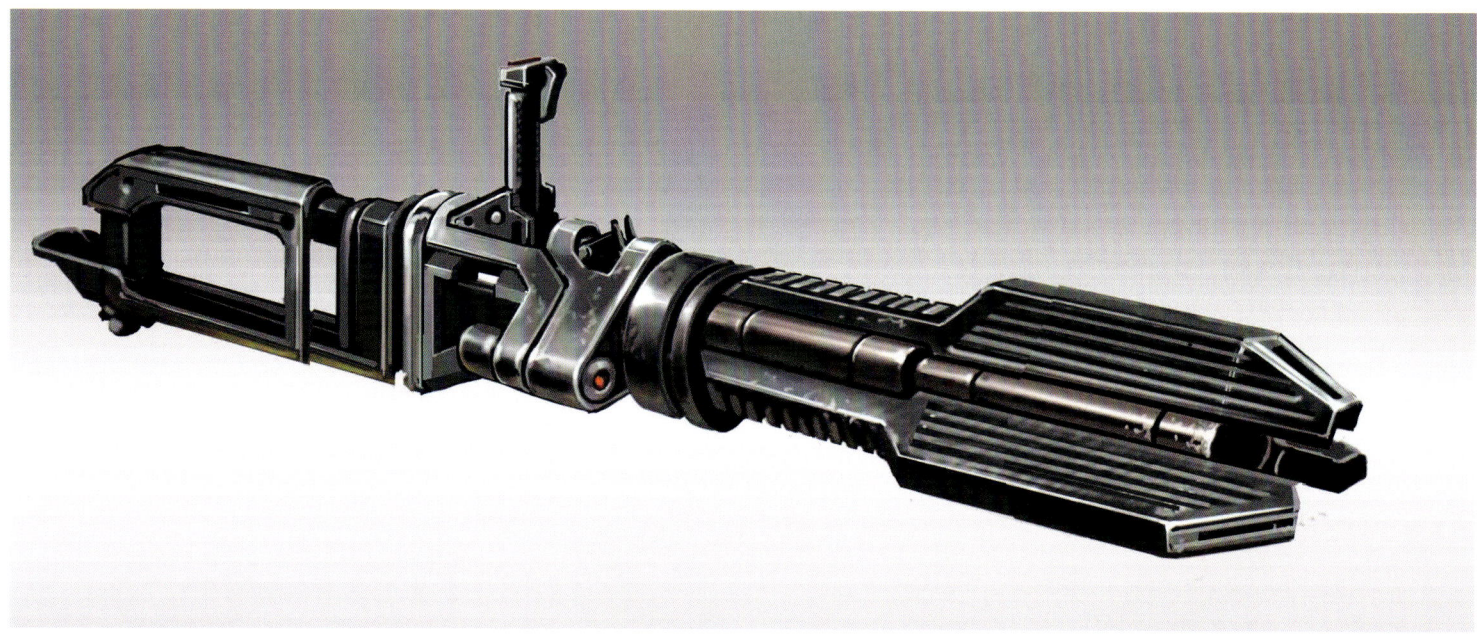

JENNY'S GUN

The first thing I tackled for this episode was the gun to be wielded by Jenny, the titular character. I had in mind a hefty sci-fi assault weapon that wouldn't have looked out of place in the hands of the *Alien* franchise's Ellen Ripley. My initial design took a bold approach: a sci-fi take on a Gatling gun, complete with muzzle flare and a rotating barrel, purely because they always look incredible on screen, and partly to leave the Doctor horrified that his 'daughter' was wielding something so vicious for that 'Hello, Dad!' moment.

Russell requested the weapon be made chunkier, and the revised design was quickly approved. Unfortunately, it never made it to screen: cut before it even had a chance to be fired. The first casualty in war is not always innocence – sometimes it's the massive gun!

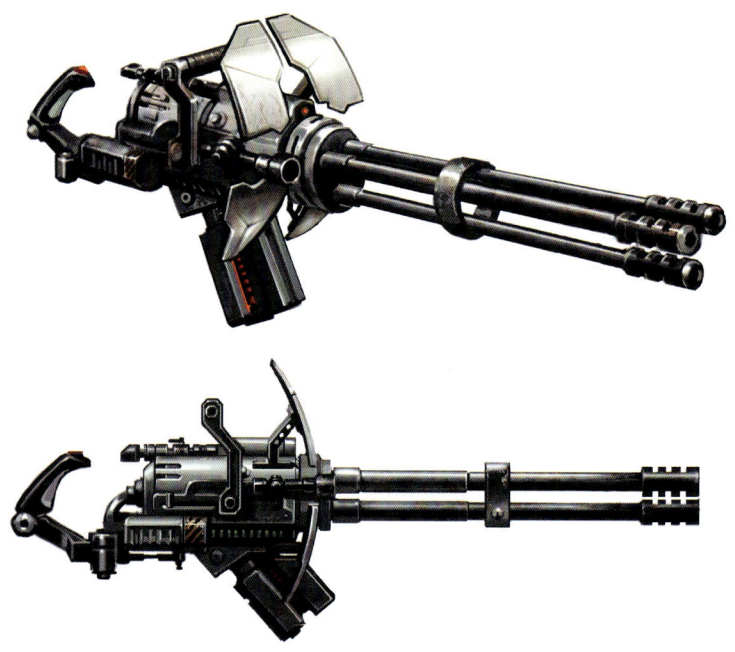

DOCTOR WHO IV	TITLE	JENNY'S HUGE GUN		REF	PM 78
		DATE: 1/11/07	EP: 6		
DRAWN BY: PETER MCKINSTRY					
PRODUCER:	DIRECTOR:	DOP:		PROPS MASTER:	
PROD DESIGNER:	ASSOC DESIGNER:	FABRICATION:		CONSTRUCTION:	
SUP ART DIR:	CHIEF SUP ART DIR:	SFX:		CGI:	
S/B ART DIR:	SET DECORATOR:	COSTUME:		GRAPHICS:	
©BBC CYMRU WALES 2006/2007		OTHER:			

PROGENITOR

The Progenitor booth – a transparent cubicle large enough to house a person – proved to be one of the more complicated builds of the entire series. The door mechanism had to function smoothly on cue, while the prop had to be robust enough to be transported between various shooting locations, including disused railway tunnels and an abandoned theatre.

The booth's glass windows were meant to be transparent, with the interior filling with smoke so the viewer could see the silhouette of the person set to emerge. Unfortunately, the construction team forgot to remove the blue film from the glass on set, leaving everything inside obscured.

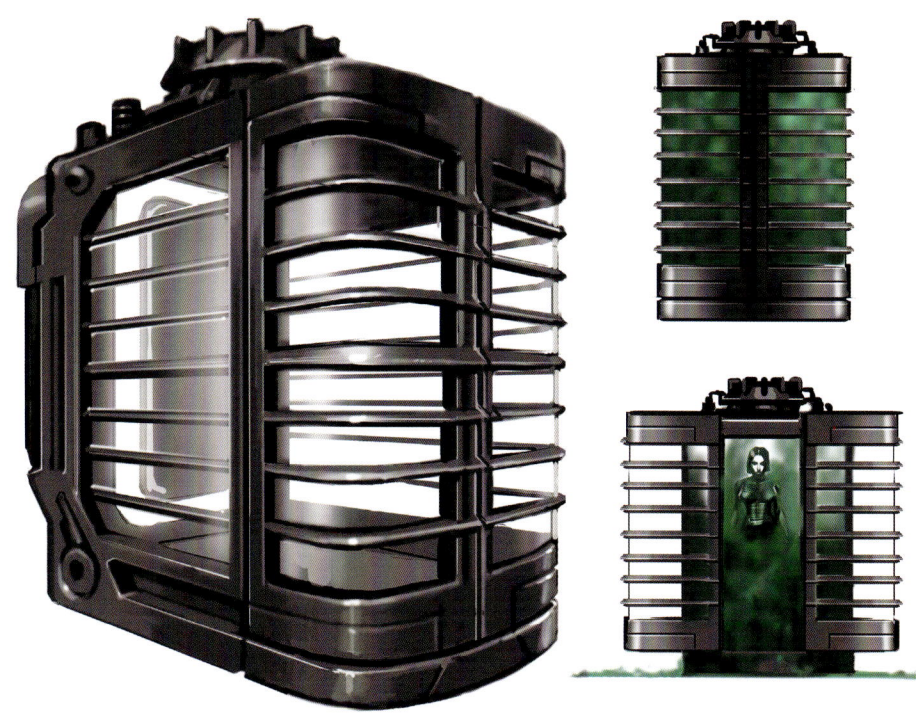

PROGENITOR TISSUE SAMPLER

The Tissue Sampler was designed to be a large, intimidating, very *user-unfriendly* apparatus. The Doctor's arm would be placed inside it, and to address the obvious question of why he couldn't just pull it out, I added 'grippers' that tightened around the arm. Within the logic of the story, this would be required for taking a clean sample, but it also served the plot by trapping the Doctor's arm against his will, ramping up the drama.

HATH BULB

The bulb itself was a warm, glowing device, giving off heat and light to keep the Hath comfortable in the colder, deeper parts of their world. It was one of those props that, despite its simplicity, helped add an extra layer of realism to the episode's sparse environment.

HOLO-PROJECTOR

This small holographic projector became a nice little dynamic prop. I discussed its design with Senior Prop Maker Barry Jones, securing a little moment of visual interest when the Doctor sonics it to display hidden layers of data – the top section rotates and rises up slightly.

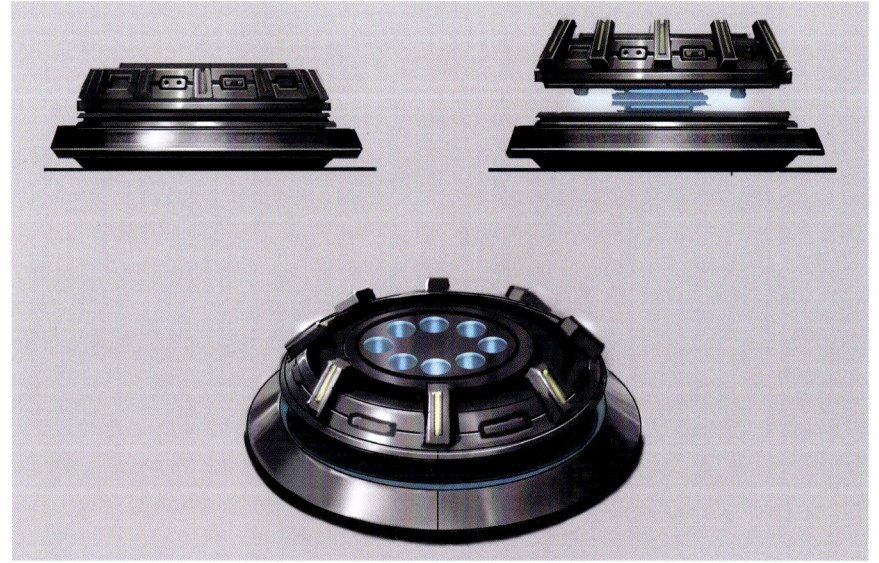

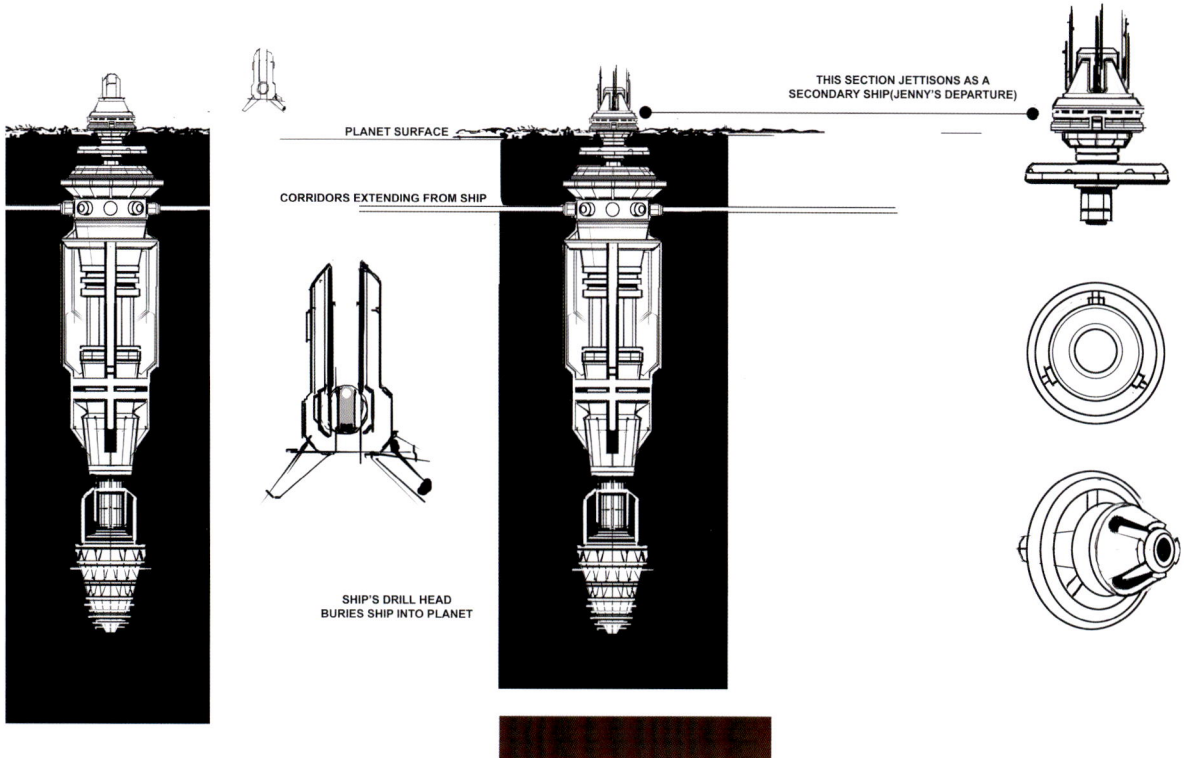

PLANET SURFACE

CORRIDORS EXTENDING FROM SHIP

THIS SECTION JETTISONS AS A
SECONDARY SHIP (JENNY'S DEPARTURE)

SHIP'S DRILL HEAD
BURIES SHIP INTO PLANET

TERRAFORMING SHIP AND SHUTTLE

This design shows the terraforming ship that had drilled down into the planet. From here the drone-built structures would have radiated out from the ship into the planet's crust. The shuttle which Jenny makes her exit in is docked at the top of the structure, like a rocket ready to blast off – only half-hidden so it looks like part of the larger ship. The idea was that the crew would initiate the terraforming process and then depart via the shuttle, which from ground level would look to be a towering structure. This setup would have given us a striking visual moment for Jenny's exit, but the budget would not allow for it.

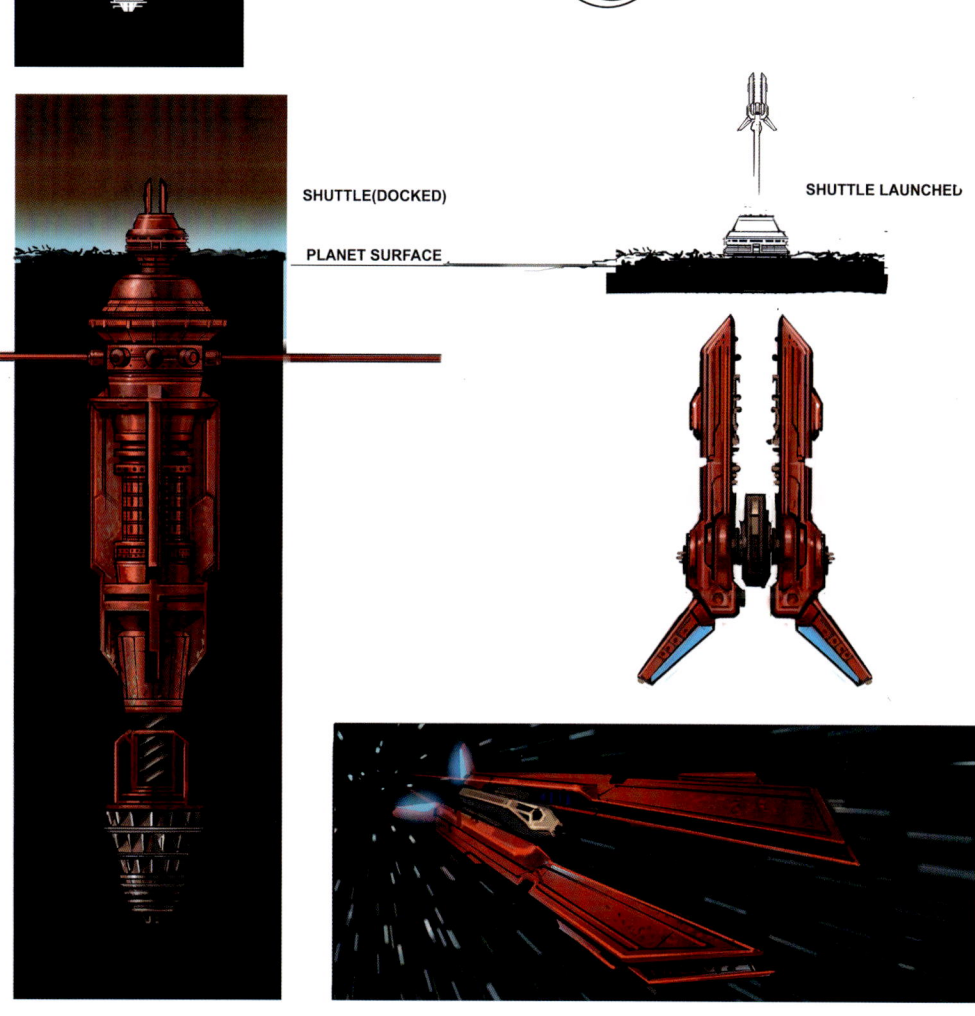

SHUTTLE (DOCKED)

SHUTTLE LAUNCHED

PLANET SURFACE

HEAT LANCE

This was a prop required for an earlier draft of the script.

THE SOURCE

The Source was the terraforming MacGuffin at the heart of the story. The metallic bracing on the orb served to hide the seams in the actual sphere prop while suggesting some function of the orb itself. It also left space for The Mill to add a clear, radiating glow from within.

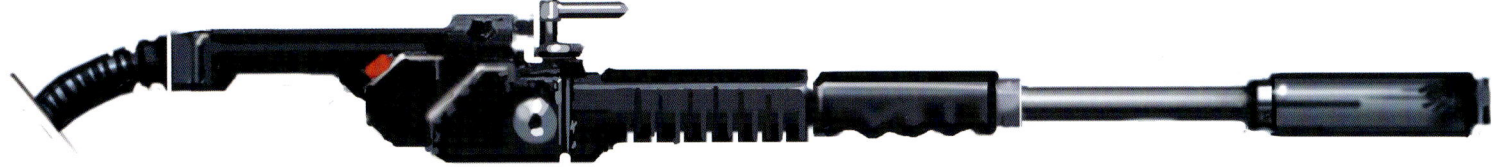

THEATRE INTERIOR / MILITARY BASE

This is another quick paint-over of a location photograph, used to illustrate how the space could be transformed into the main area for colonist Cobb's fighting force. The goal was to give the area a gritty, utilitarian feel that matched the rough, military nature of the characters.

PLANET SURFACE

This was a bird's-eye view of the planet Messaline's surface, also known as Margam Opencast Mine in Bridgend. It made for quite an unpleasant walk for Martha and her new Hath friend!

THE UNICORN AND THE WASP

VESPIFORM AND STINGER

The titular wasp – in fact the alien Vespiform – required a practical stinger for use on-set that had to blend seamlessly with the CGI-rendered body. To achieve this, I took inspiration from real-world wasp species, studying their exoskeleton structures, colour patterns, and the mechanics of their stingers.

The trick was finding the right balance between entomological accuracy and the heightened drama of the show. The stinger had to feel anatomically plausible but also menacing and convey a sense of acute threat, adding to the creature's intimidating presence on screen.

DOCTOR WHO IV	TITLE	VESPIFORM & STINGER	REF	PM 23
DRAWN BY:	PETER MCKINSTRY		DATE 20/7/07 EP: 7	
PRODUCER:		DIRECTOR:	DOP:	PROPS MASTER:
PROD DESIGNER:		ASSOC DESIGNER:	FABRICATION:	CONSTRUCTION:
SUP ART DIR:		CHIEF SUP ART DIR:	SFX:	CGI:
S/B ART DIR:		SET DECORATOR:	COSTUME:	GRAPHICS:
©BBC CYMRU WALES 2006/2007			OTHER:	

SILENCE IN THE LIBRARY / FOREST OF THE DEAD

RIVER SONG'S SONIC

The arrival of River Song, played so wonderfully by Alex Kingston, felt like a significant event in the overall arc of the new series, even more so when I read the script and found she owned a future version of this Doctor's sonic screwdriver.

The goal of this design was to adapt and age the Ninth and Tenth Doctors' sonic screwdriver while still preserving its recognisable shape. The updated design features an oxidised copper colour and texture, hinting at a long history of other adventures — which remained a mystery right through till the era of the Twelfth Doctor, as played by Peter Capaldi.

LIBRARY RECEPTION

A production illustration showing what we could achieve at the chosen location, which was Brangwyn Hall in Swansea. The hall provided a large, open space that helped convey the epic scale of the library planet's reception.

The desk itself was a custom build and Set Dresser Dave Morrison provided the centrepiece – a huge brass armillary – that added to the grandeur of the setting.

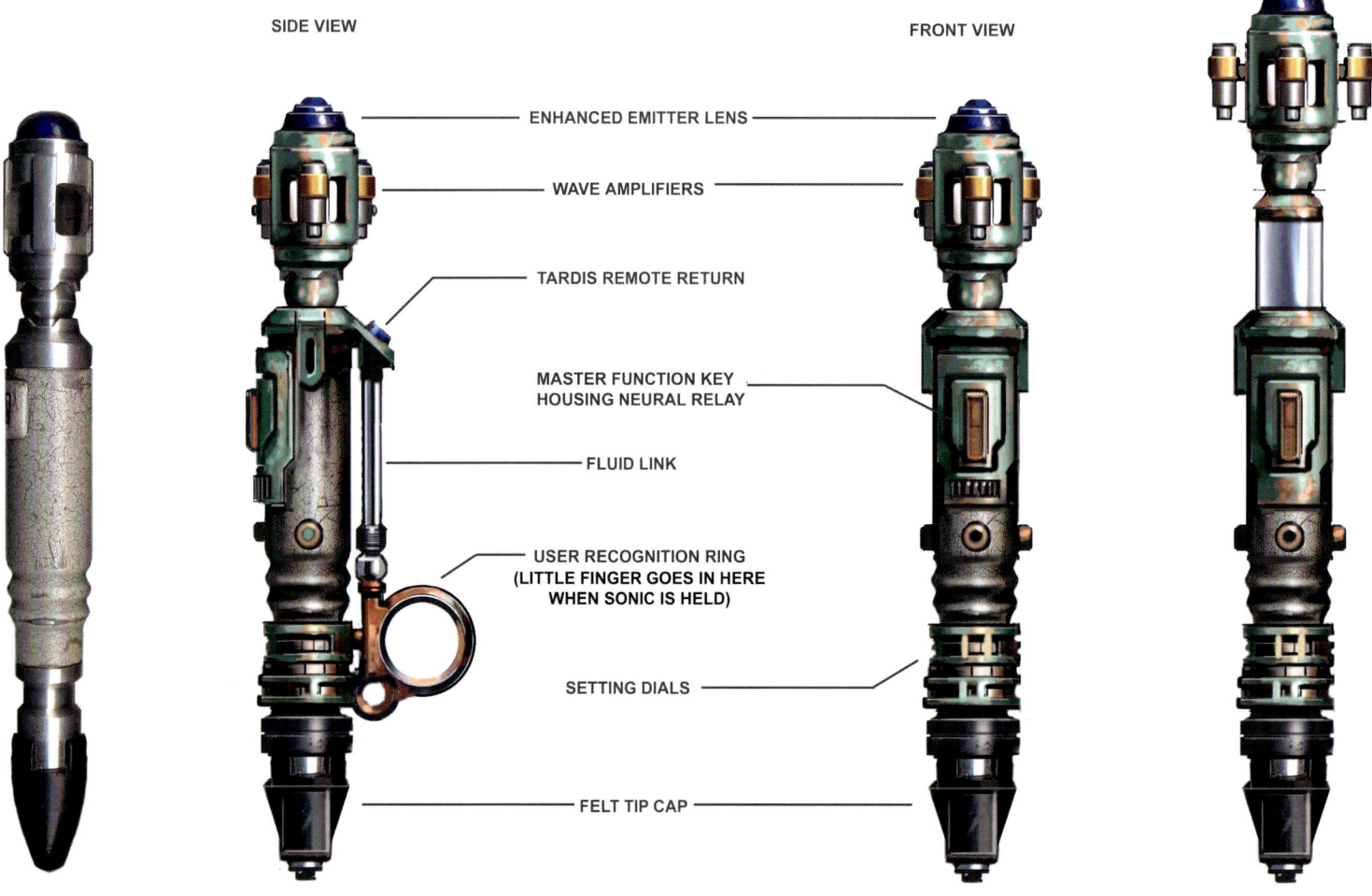

SIDE VIEW

FRONT VIEW

ENHANCED EMITTER LENS

WAVE AMPLIFIERS

TARDIS REMOTE RETURN

MASTER FUNCTION KEY
HOUSING NEURAL RELAY

FLUID LINK

USER RECOGNITION RING
(LITTLE FINGER GOES IN HERE
WHEN SONIC IS HELD)

SETTING DIALS

FELT TIP CAP

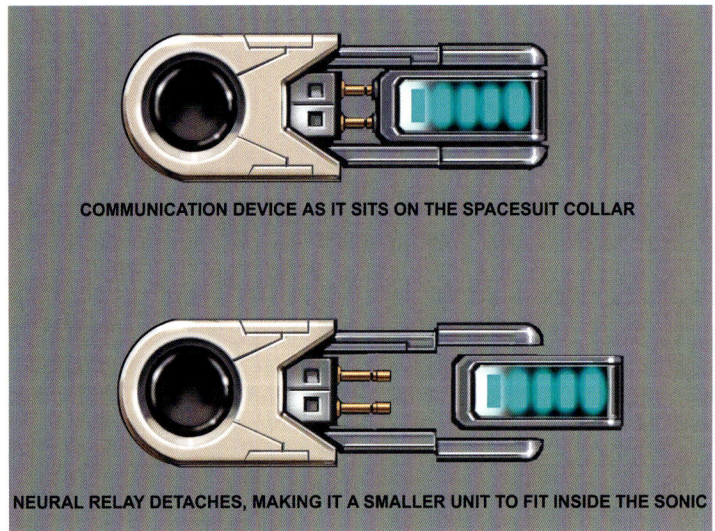

COMMUNICATION DEVICE AS IT SITS ON THE SPACESUIT COLLAR

NEURAL RELAY DETACHES, MAKING IT A SMALLER UNIT TO FIT INSIDE THE SONIC

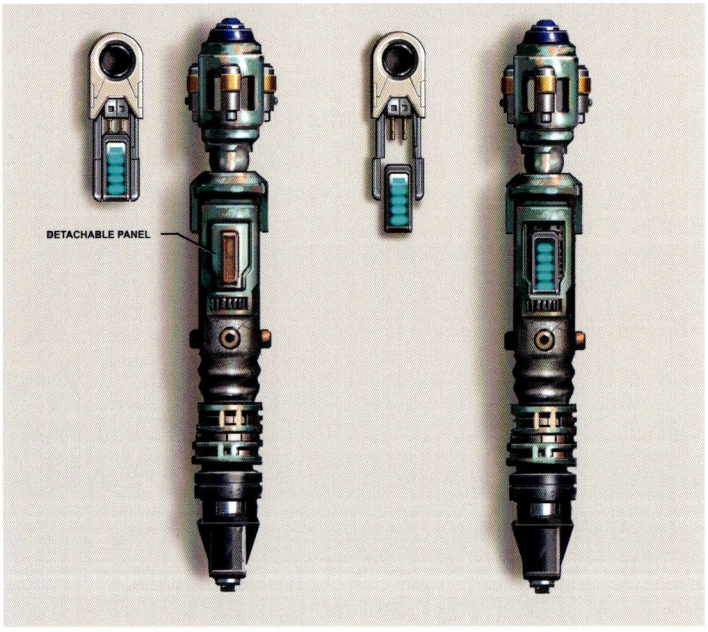

DETACHABLE PANEL

CAMERA WALL MOUNT

The Library contains large spherical camera devices as if carved from wood – so I designed a suitably ornate wall mount for each to sit on.

COMMUNICATOR / NEURAL RELAY

To keep this multi-function prop visually cohesive, I tied it into the design language of the story's space suits, carrying over the same colour scheme and materials. As shown in the concept, the neural relay was designed as a detachable component – allowing it to be fitted inside River's sonic.

LOCKED
10/1/087

DOCTOR WHO IV		TITLE	CAMERA ARM		REF	PM 109
DRAWN BY:	PETER MCKINSTRY		DATE: 10/1/08	EP: 9/10		
PRODUCER:	DIRECTOR:		DOP:		PROPS MASTER:	
PROD DESIGNER:	ASSOC DESIGNER:		FABRICATION:		CONSTRUCTION:	
SUP ART DIR:	CHIEF SUP ART DIR:		SFX:		CGI:	
S/B ART DIR:	SET DECORATOR:		COSTUME:		GRAPHICS:	
©BBC CYMRU WALES 2006/2007			OTHER:			

RIVER'S JOURNAL

River's journal of her many adventures with the Doctor was described in the script only as 'a big, ancient, leather-bound book... bound in police box blue'. I understood the subtle but meaningful connection to the TARDIS, hinting at adventures we were yet to see, but as I sketched, I started thinking about how I could enhance the links a little more. That's when the panelling of the TARDIS Police Box came to mind; it felt like a perfect fit for the cover, hinting at the book's mysterious origins.

COMPUTER WALL COVER

This design incorporates a big boxy structure on location as a foundation for revealing the Library's computer.

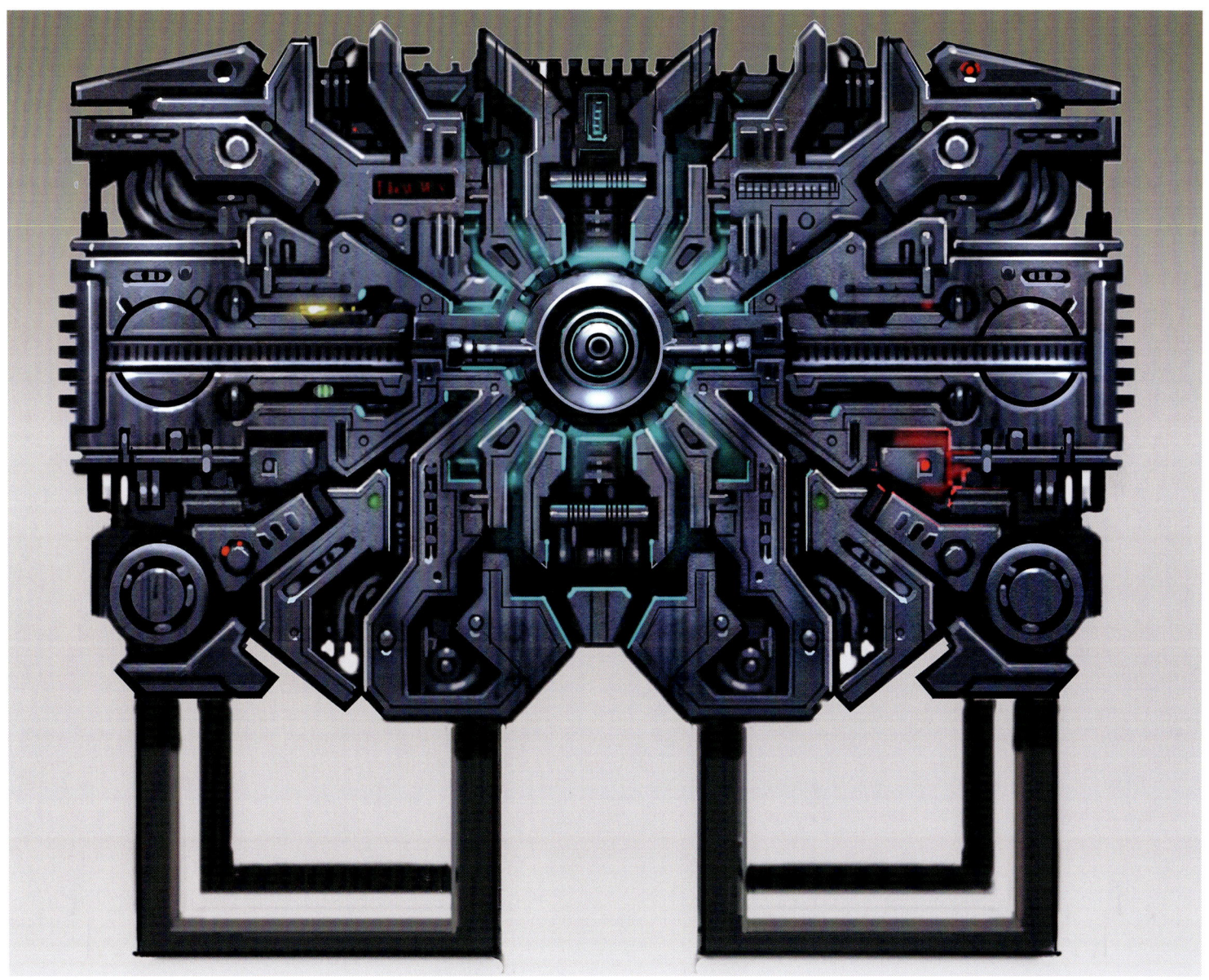

RIVER'S CHAIR

This is the throne upon which River Song makes her ultimate sacrifice. The first version was an attempt to build onto an interesting old dentist's chair we had, but Russell pointed out that it just wasn't grand enough. My revised design connected visually with the computer wall behind it, and my intention when creating this symmetrical pattern radiating from the centre was to get a dramatic, striking shot that enhances the moment's emotional impact.

DOCTOR WHO IV	TITLE	THRONE FOR SONG	REF	PM 114
DRAWN BY:	PETER MCKINSTRY	DATE: 17/1/08	EP: 10	
PRODUCER:	DIRECTOR:	DOP:	PROPS MASTER:	
PROD DESIGNER:	ASSOC DESIGNER:	FABRICATION:	CONSTRUCTION:	
SUP ART DIR:	CHIEF SUP ART DIR:	SFX:	CGI:	
S/B ART DIR:	SET DECORATOR:	COSTUME:	GRAPHICS:	
©BBC CYMRU WALES 2006/2007		OTHER:		

LOCKED
17/01/08

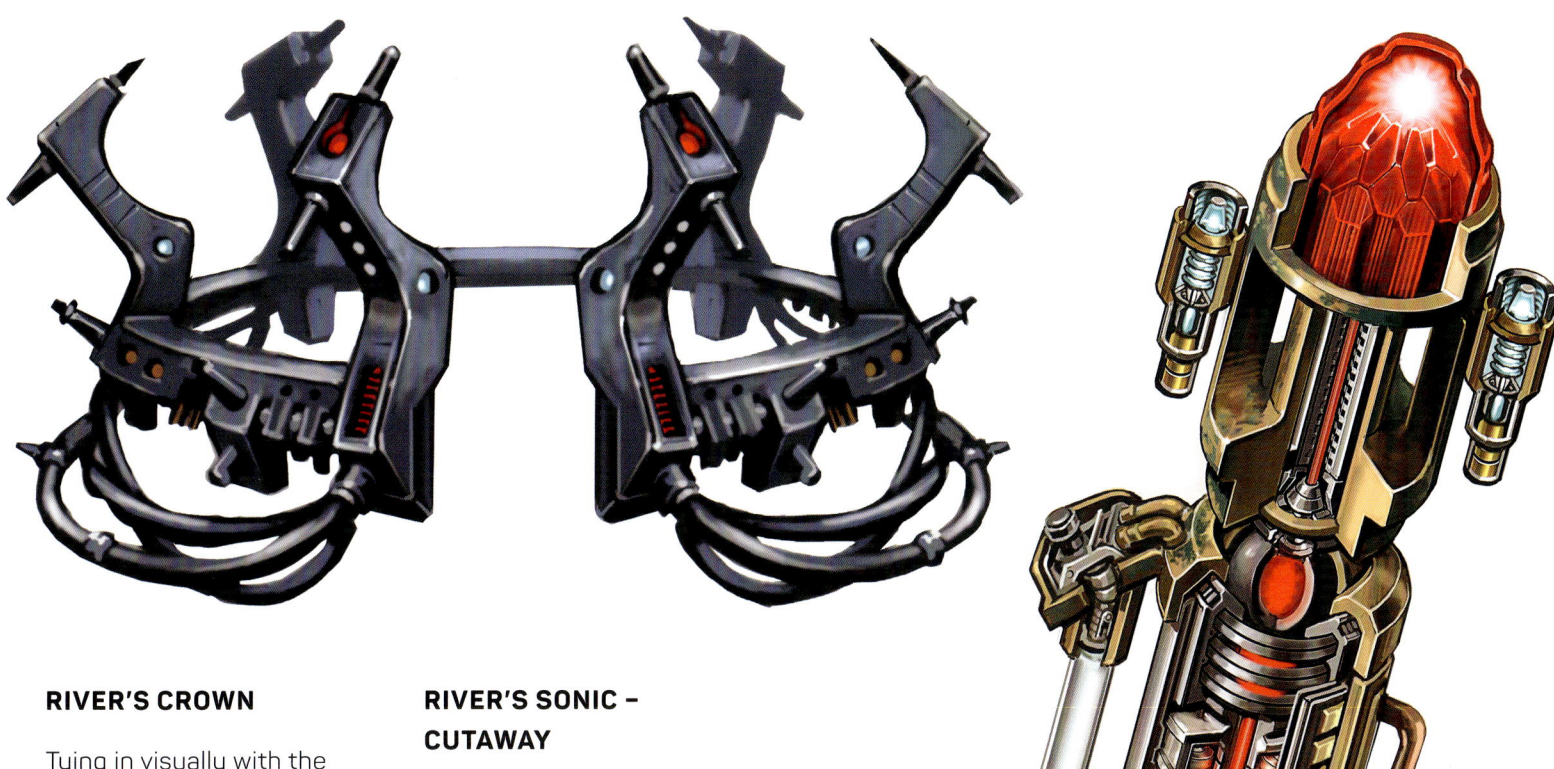

RIVER'S CROWN

Tying in visually with the throne and the computer wall, the design for this coronet of wires was intended to evoke a sense of unease. I focused on making it look uncomfortable, with sharp, thin metallic points that resemble a crown of thorns; just enough to suggest the potential for pain, but with a nod to the nobility of River's sacrifice.

RIVER'S SONIC – CUTAWAY

This cross-section cutaway reveals the inner workings of River Song's iconic sonic screwdriver. The internal components show a layered construction, while the exposed elements suggest modifications made over time, reinforcing the idea that this sonic has a history of its own, shaped by River's adventures. The piece's personality is unmistakably River Song's – sophisticated and enigmatic. Created for GE Fabbri's *Doctor Who: The DVD Files* magazine.

TURN LEFT

TARDIS ECG

These devices attached to the TARDIS exterior, assessing its functional health, were designed to evoke the feeling of a stethoscope – nothing too threatening or overtly alien, more like advanced secret military tech. We spent time discussing their origin, debating whether they might be reverse-engineered alien tech or perhaps direct from the UNIT labs (or even from Torchwood!).

TARDIS CIRCLE OF MIRRORS

The purpose of this illustration was to establish how the set would come to life, offering a visual blueprint for its layout, lighting, and overall composition. The intention was for the set to feel as if it had history, as though it had been used and worn over time. Paying attention to the small details – such as the distance between mirrors, the angle of the lights, the texture of the surfaces – helps the image feel grounded, real, and dramatic.

LOCKED
3/12/07

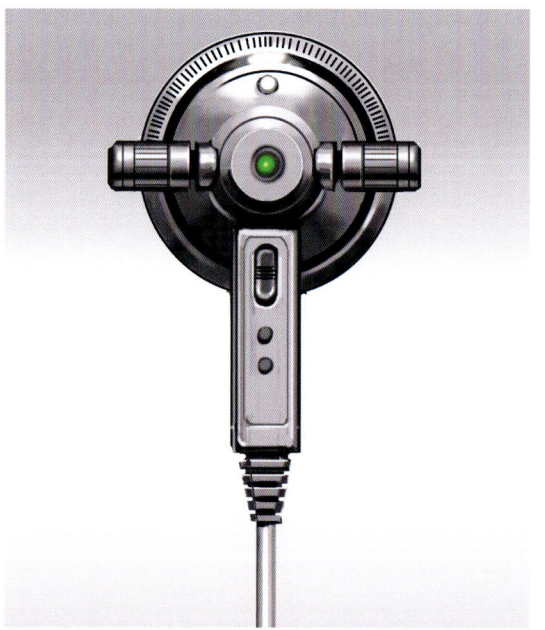

SHAN SHEN ALLEY

Another fast turnaround was required here. I was sent a photo of a potential filming location for Shan Shen Alley, and had to quickly paint in some loose set dressing details to help visualise the space, ensuring the setting captured the right tone and energy for the scene. Hot from the printer it went straight into the Tone Meeting – where those swift adjustments helped the team refine the visual direction of the scenes to be set on this colourful alien street.

THE STOLEN EARTH / JOURNEY'S END

THE DALEK SUPREME

At first, the Supreme was to be plugged into his own throne-like structure, giving him a much more imposing presence on set – a bit like the towering Dalek Emperor in *Evil of the Daleks* (1967). That idea was abandoned as it could prove restrictive during shooting. It was soon decided that for budgetary reasons, the Supreme should be created by building *onto* one of the pre-existing Daleks, rather than creating something from scratch.

'New Daleks. Is there anything more exciting?' was Russell's reply to my first batch of concept sketches. Ed had suggested that I look at designs from the era of the original Daleks, so that I might be influenced by the same things that Raymond Cusick would have been aware of when devising the classic Daleks in 1963. This led me to the Sputnik 1, the first artificial Earth satellite. I took the spherical body of Sputnik and tried something similar as the Dalek head, applying the satellite's distinctive angled antennae so that they connected the head to the body. I included this design as option 5 within this first round of concepts. Russell responded to it immediately. 'I like... those metal bars going all the way down to the waist. "Waist"! Daleks have waists. But if option 1 could have those waist-extensions incorporated somehow, that'd be good.'

This led to a more refined design, favoured now by both Russell and Producer Phil Collinson.

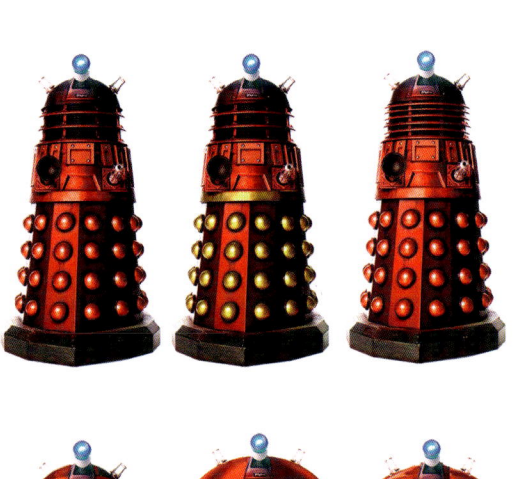

DOCTOR WHO IV	TITLE	SUPREME DALEK X		REF	PM 126
		DATE: 29/1/08	EP: 12/13		
DRAWN BY:	PETER MCKINSTRY				
PRODUCER:	DIRECTOR:	DOP:	PROPS MASTER:		
PROD DESIGNER:	ASSOC DESIGNER:	FABRICATION:	CONSTRUCTION:		
SUP ART DIR:	CHIEF SUP ART DIR:	SFX:	CGI:		
S/B ART DIR:	SET DECORATOR:	COSTUME:	GRAPHICS:		
©BBC CYMRU WALES 2006/2007		OTHER:			

A wild card option was presented, inspired by the Special Weapons Dalek from *Remembrance of the Daleks* (1988). 'I think the Supreme is clever and cunning,' Russell pointed out. 'This looks like a big, thumping war machine.'

I felt that the 'Sputnik' arms looked a little weak and spindly, so I created a new version with the same feature but thicker and more integrated with the overall Dalek design. They suggested a function and hierarchy without being explicit or obvious about it; and they were almost crown like, befitting a Supreme Dalek. I added a third light to the back of the Dalek head to add more emphasis to the crown idea.

Finally, the exact shade of red was discussed. 'I really think we need a radical, strong red,' said Russell. 'Not primary! But deep and sexy and strong.' I suggested a 'Morse red' (referring to Inspector Morse's Jaguar Mark II) and the design was eventually finalised.

'BEAUTIFUL' came Russell's response on 30 January 2008. 'Peter, that's magnificent. That Dalek is... supreme!'

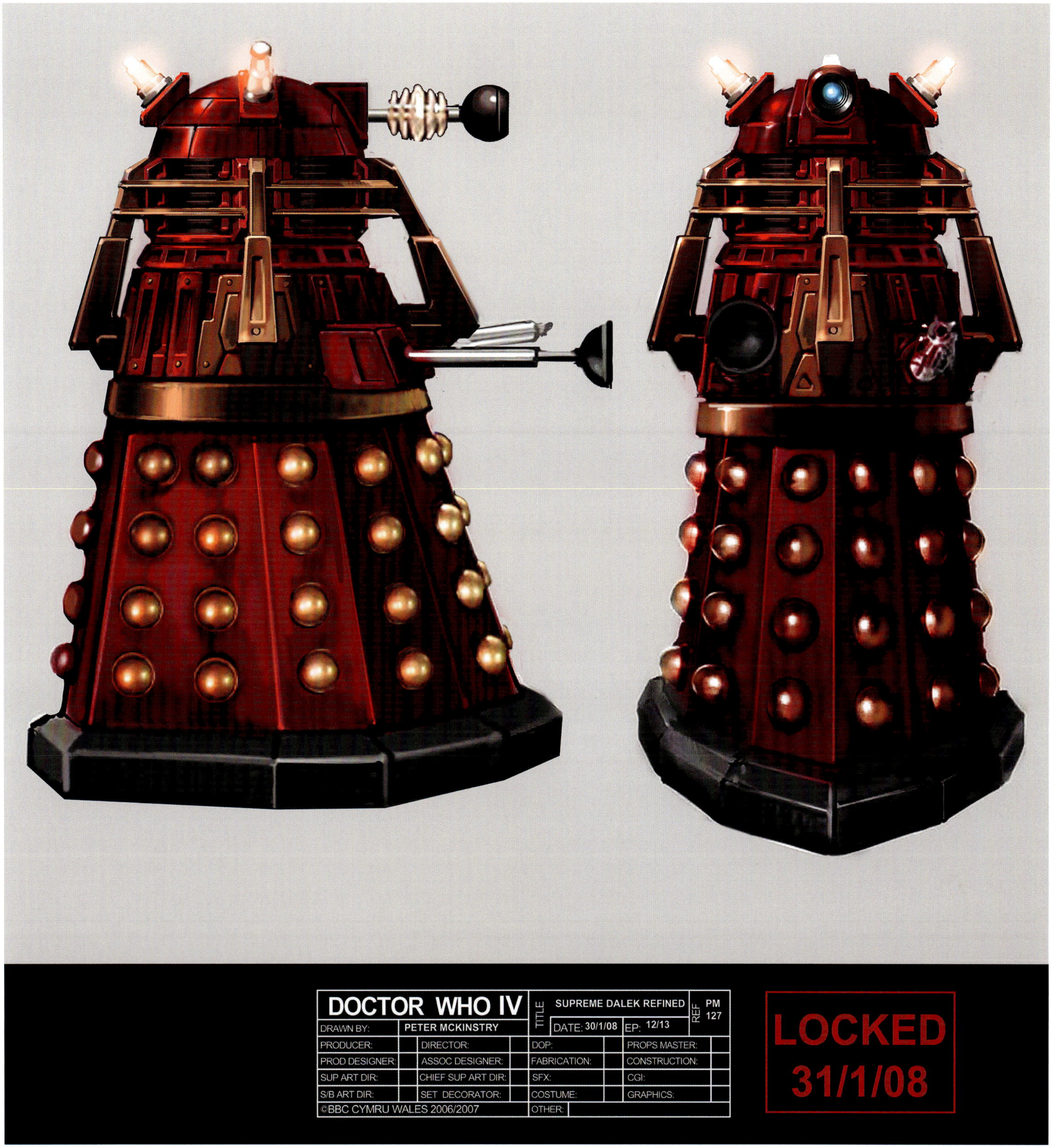

DOCTOR WHO IV		TITLE	SUPREME DALEK REFINED	REF	PM 127
DRAWN BY:	PETER MCKINSTRY		DATE: 30/1/08	EP: 12/13	
PRODUCER:	DIRECTOR:	DOP:		PROPS MASTER:	
PROD DESIGNER:	ASSOC DESIGNER:	FABRICATION:		CONSTRUCTION:	
SUP ART DIR:	CHIEF SUP ART DIR:	SFX:		CGI:	
S/B ART DIR:	SET DECORATOR:	COSTUME:		GRAPHICS:	
©BBC CYMRU WALES 2006/2007		OTHER:			

LOCKED
31/1/08

DAVROS

Davros's last appearance in a new *Doctor Who* story had been fleetingly in the final episode of *Remembrance of the Daleks*, where he'd been in disguise. Now he was to come back in an updated version of his original form.

His prosthetic mask and hand would be provided by Millennium FX and his tunic would come from Costume Designer Louise Page. *My* role in the megalomaniac's return focused on designing his Dalek chair, aligning it with the aesthetic that Ed and Matt had introduced to the Daleks in 2005. Even with these established elements in place, there was still plenty for me to sink my teeth into. Just the opportunity to draw Davros at all was a thrill.

The section behind his head was a deliberate addition to ensure that, even in close-up shots, there would be a recognisable Dalek element present. I also included the new back piece – a rib-like structure that gave the impression of Davros almost being held prisoner within his own chair.

Unlike the Supreme Dalek, which went through multiple iterations, this design emerged fully formed and was approved immediately. Russell remarked, 'Half the problem with the old Davros was that he often looked so flimsy. And this is gonna make him look really strong and enthroned. Especially when Julian [Bleach, who has played the character multiple times since 2008] has such a massive physical presence.'

PREACHER GUN MARK 2 AKA THE ROSE GUN

My intention for Rose's big gun was to give her something easy to carry while still allowing her to hold a cool, heroic stance. Since we had previously used heavy assault rifles, which suggest brute-force firepower, I opted for a sleeker, more refined design. The cone-shaped emitter reinforced the idea of a high-powered, precise weapon. I envisioned it as a laser harpoon gun, capable of firing energy bolts strong enough to rip through Dalekanium.

However, Director Graeme Harper and Russell were keen on the heavy assault weapon look, so I happily adapted the Preacher gun design, adding more detail and features to enhance its presence. Even so, I carried over the cone-shaped emitter from my original version, ensuring that the idea of it being modified for greater power and precision remained a part of the final design.

DALEK WALLCAM

This is a callback to the design of the Dalek scanner-lenses seen way back in 1963 during their first story.

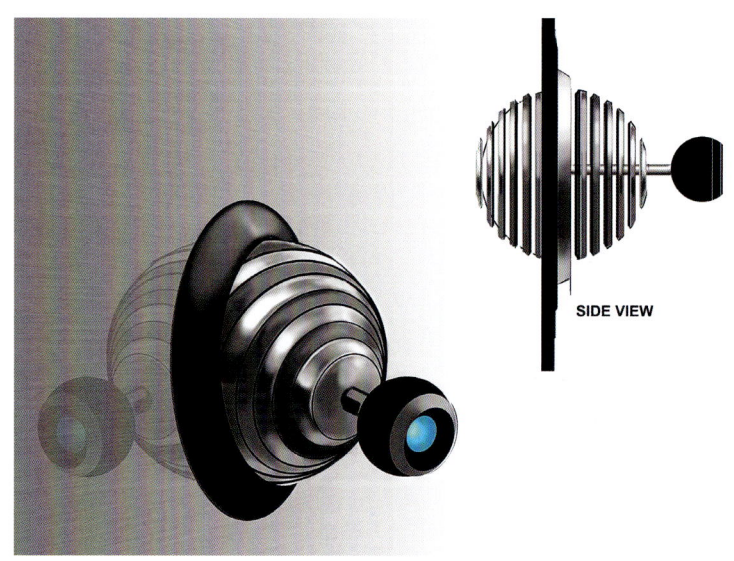

SIDE VIEW

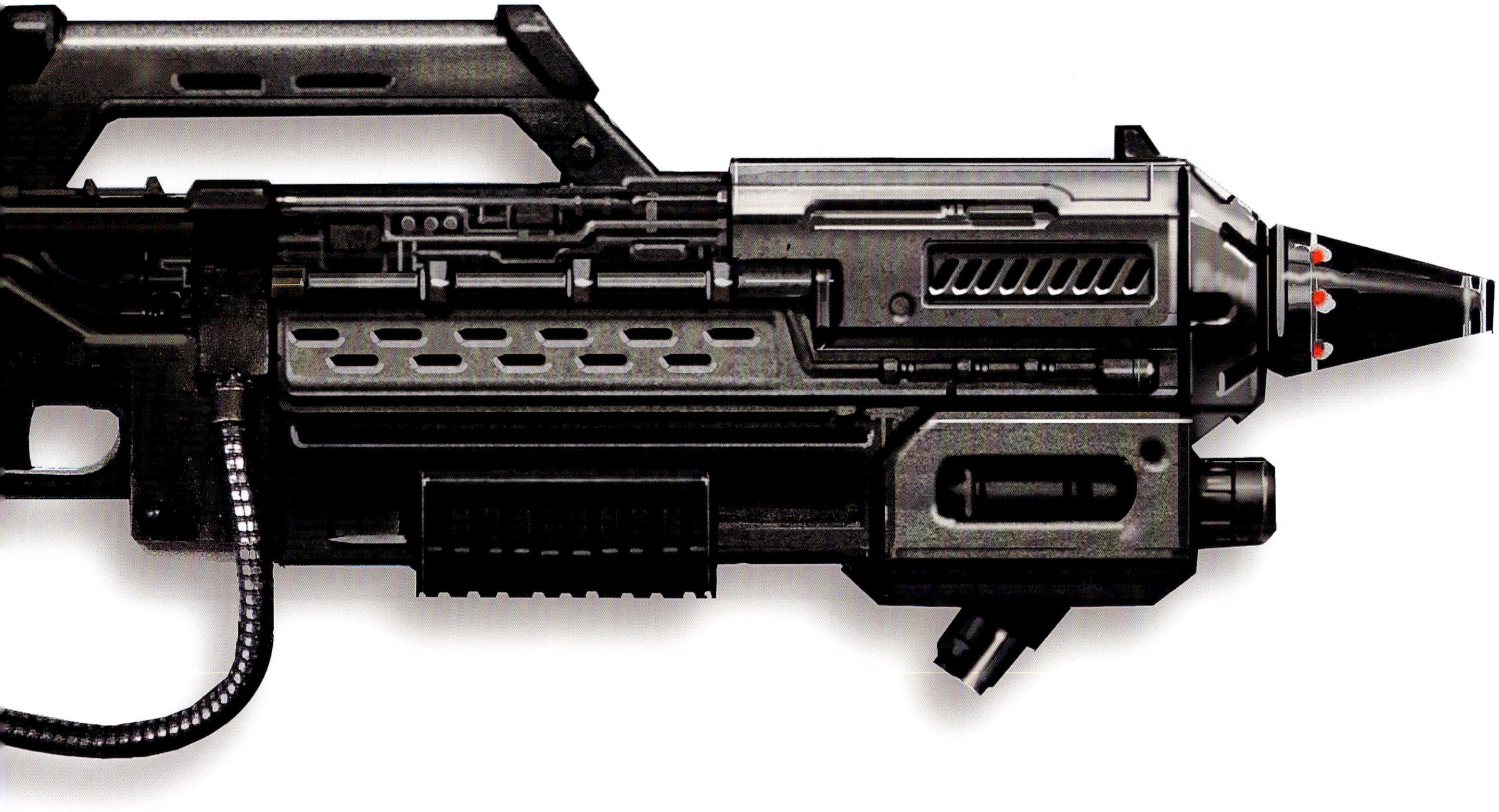

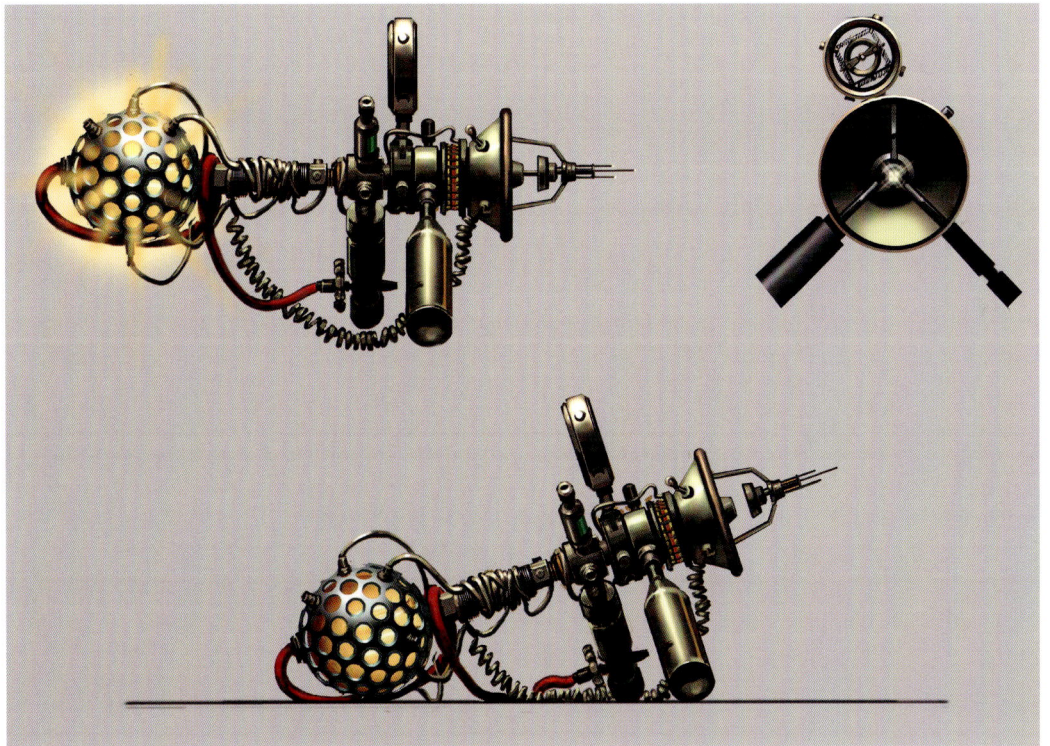

DOCTOR'S DEVICE

This prop, above all else, had to be 'actor proof' as it was going to get thrown around on set a lot. We see it being built by the Doctor, carried by Donna and then dropped onto the floor before being blown to bits.

To emphasise the idea of it being lashed together from different parts, I wanted this prop to be asymmetrical. The angled cylinders that jut out from the centre made the prop easy to hold, and also meant it could sit on the floor pointing up, thus looking more interesting when not in use.

WARPSTAR

For the Warpstar, five different designs were initially presented. My aim was to create something that felt like a piece of technology – perhaps a component of a warp core – that just happened to resemble a piece of jewellery. On closer inspection, the metallic elements weren't intended to be decorative; instead, they were a part of its functional design.

However, Russell was clear that the final prop should reflect Sarah Jane's character. Instead of industrial steel, he insisted it be gold; less of a futuristic gadget and more of a magical charm.

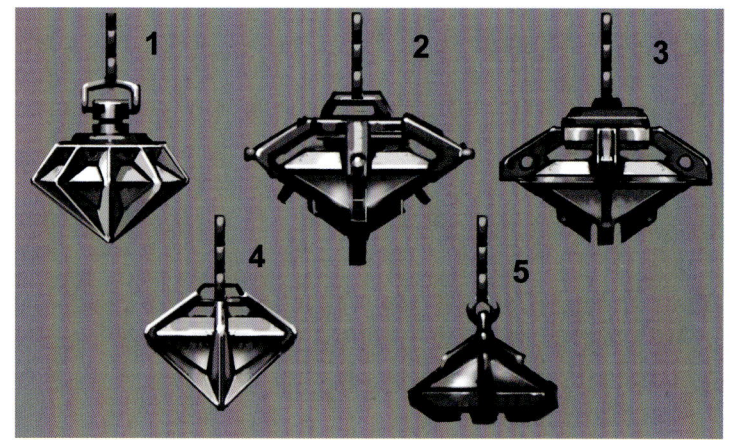

SHADOW PROCLAMATION HANGAR

This was a location photograph which I painted over to create a digital set extension so the interior matched the grand scale of the exterior.

THE DOCTOR'S HAND

The Doctor's hand in a jar, created for *A History of the Universe in 100 Objects* by James Goss and Steve Tribe, for BBC Books.

SHADOW PROCLAMATION (OVERLEAF)

The Shadow Proclamation was a chance to create a grand, spectacular setting that I hoped would become iconic within the Whoniverse, suspecting it was a place the show would return to time and time again.

DALEK ARM

The script called for a new Dalek arm design – a multi-digit, grasping appendage to be worked by the Dalek operators that could plug directly into various sockets fitted on the Dalek control panels. These sockets were sized so that a human could also fit their fingers inside and twist them.

SHADOW PROCLAMATION COMPUTER

The only specially created prop for the Shadow Proclamation interior, this computer terminal allows the Shadow Architect to show the Doctor and Donna all the planets that had been stolen from the universe.

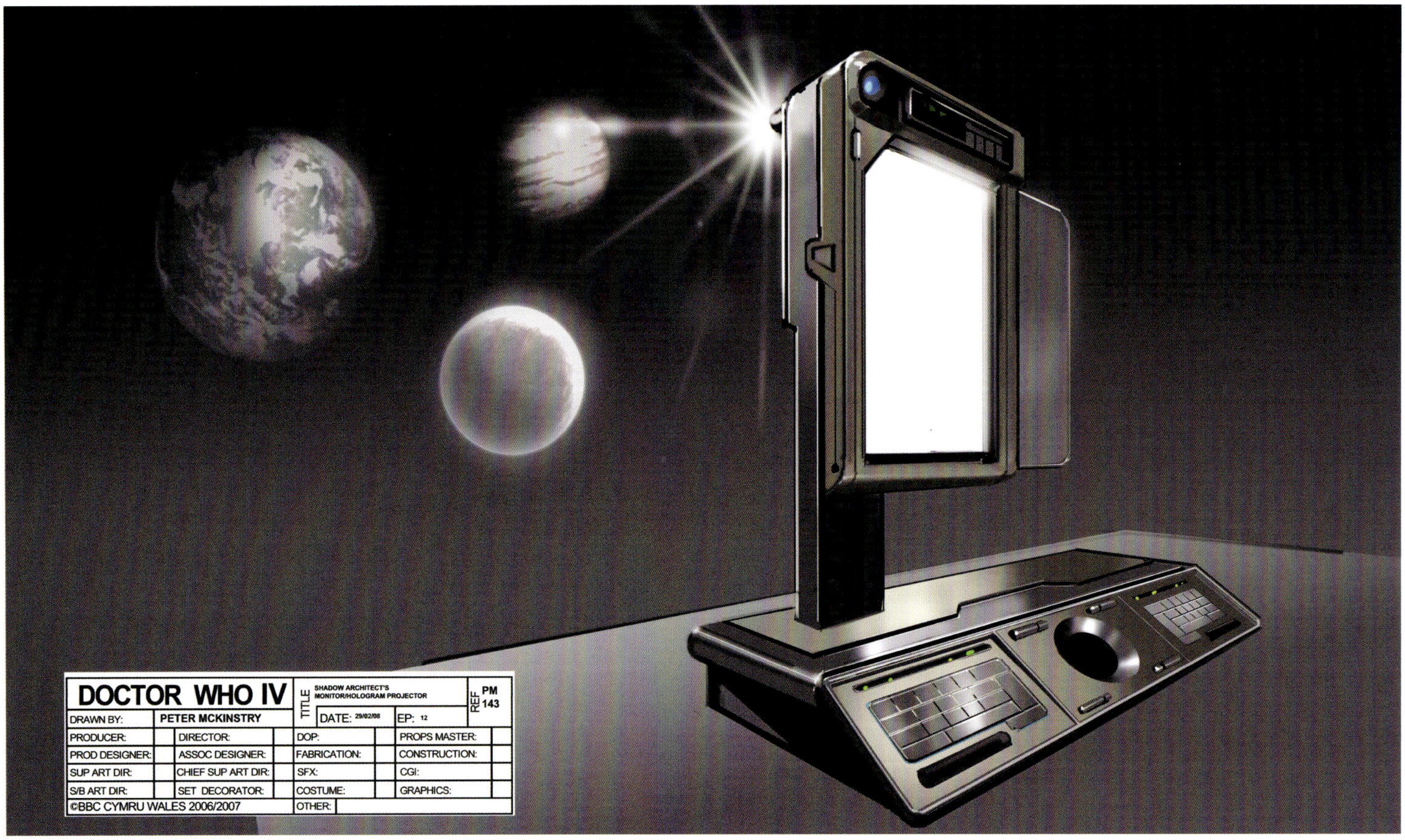

DOCTOR WHO IV		SHADOW ARCHITECT'S MONITOR/HOLOGRAM PROJECTOR		REF PM 143
DRAWN BY:	PETER MCKINSTRY	DATE: 29/02/08	EP: 12	
PRODUCER:	DIRECTOR:	DOP:	PROPS MASTER:	
PROD DESIGNER:	ASSOC DESIGNER:	FABRICATION:	CONSTRUCTION:	
SUP ART DIR:	CHIEF SUP ART DIR:	SFX:	CGI:	
S/B ART DIR:	SET DECORATOR:	COSTUME:	GRAPHICS:	
©BBC CYMRU WALES 2006/2007		OTHER:		

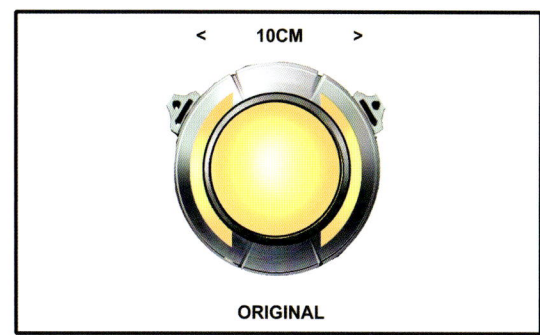

< 10CM >

ORIGINAL

TELEPORT DISC MARK 2

This was a welcome chance to improve the teleport discs designed for Series 2. I wanted to make them chunkier and give them some extra weight. It was a case of taking the original props, dirtying them down and incorporating this new element – like a heavy protective brace.

UNIT SCANNER

This was a sleek yet functional piece of advanced military technology, ensuring only authorised personnel (or the right actors!) gained access to whatever it guarded.

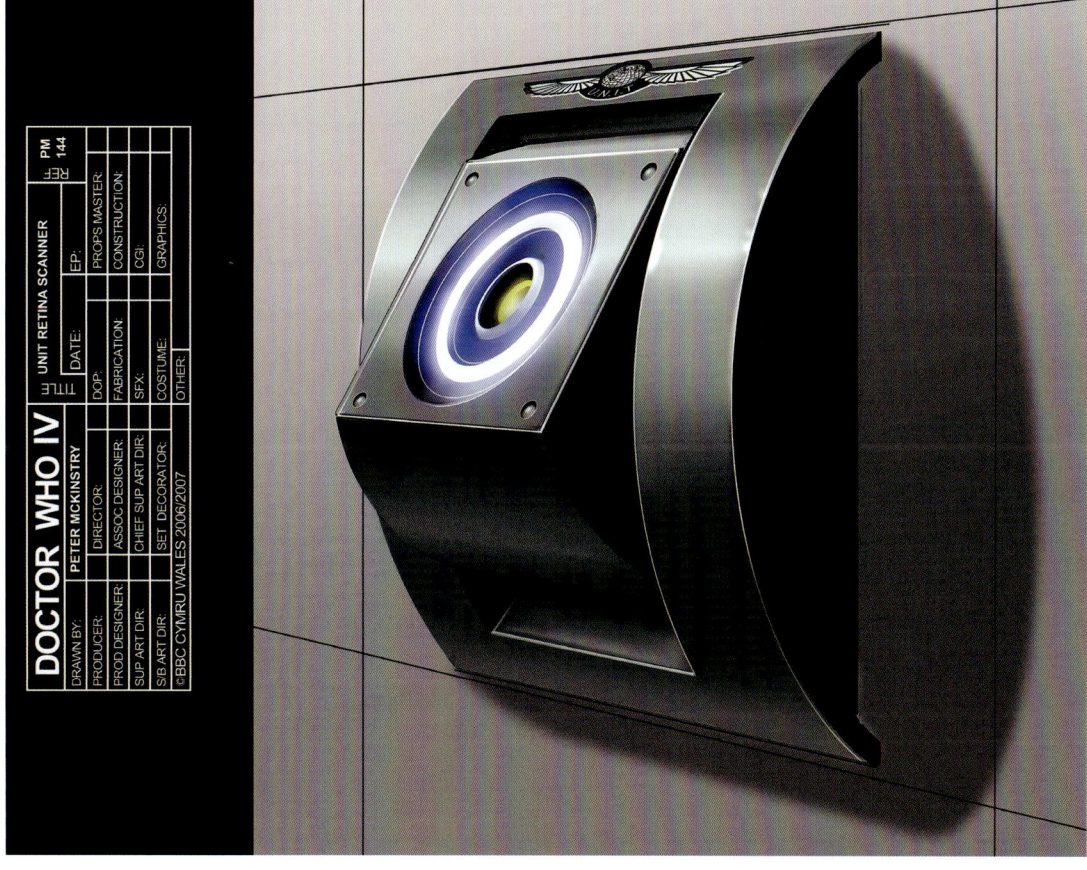

THE NEXT DOCTOR

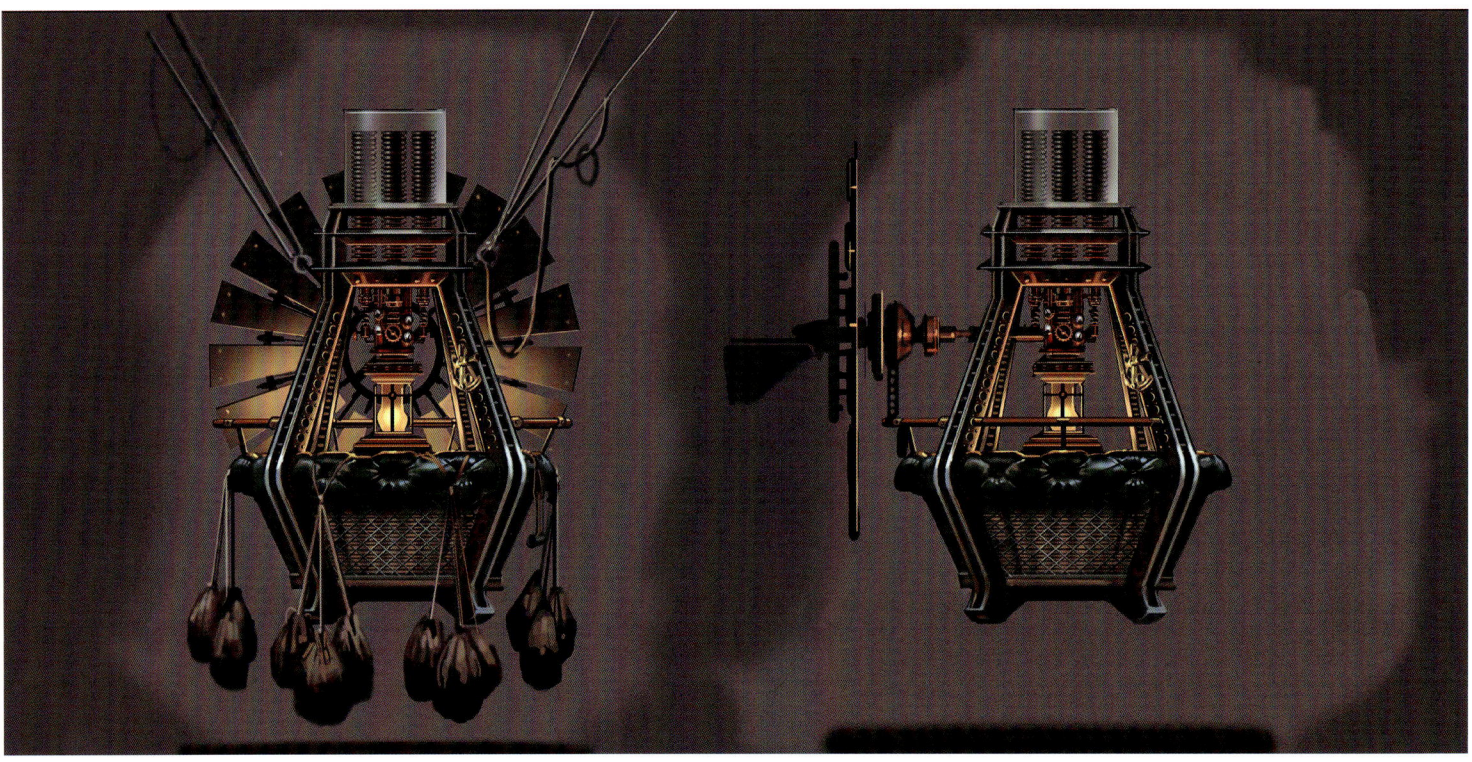

BALLOON BASKET

One of the many things I loved about working on the show was the sheer variety of stories told; after the epic space opera of the Dalek two-parter, 2008's Christmas special, *The Next Doctor*, took us to Victorian London. Here, an ordinary human, Jackson Lake, has a run-in with Cybermen and comes to believe that he is the Doctor.

Jackson's version of the TARDIS is in fact a hot air balloon – 'Tethered Aerial Release Developed in Style'. This design was an exploration into how we might subtly echo some real TARDIS design elements into the balloon's basket.

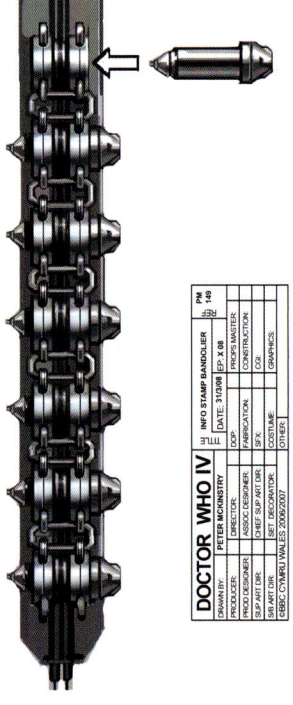

INFO STAMP AND BANDOLIER

The info stamps are examples of Cyber-technology, so they needed to be steel, sleek and simple. The Info Stamp prop follows a 'less is more' design philosophy – its clean, metallic look feels strikingly foreign in the period setting.

HUGE MACHINE

I really loved working on these designs for the 'huge machine'. It was so engrossing, painting all the cannibalised systems of cogs and gears and boilers and turbines – elements working together bring the awe-inspiring Cyber King to being!

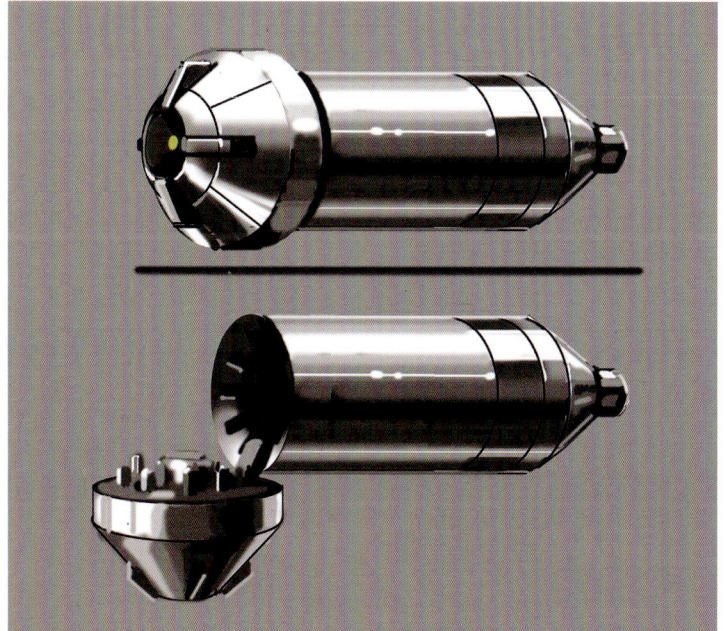

DIMENSION VAULT AND ROD

The Doctor instantly recognises the Dimension Vault as Dalek technology, giving me a strong starting point for the design. I revisited my early concepts for the Dalek Supreme's throne, adapting key elements and miniaturising it to create this new piece of Dalek technology.

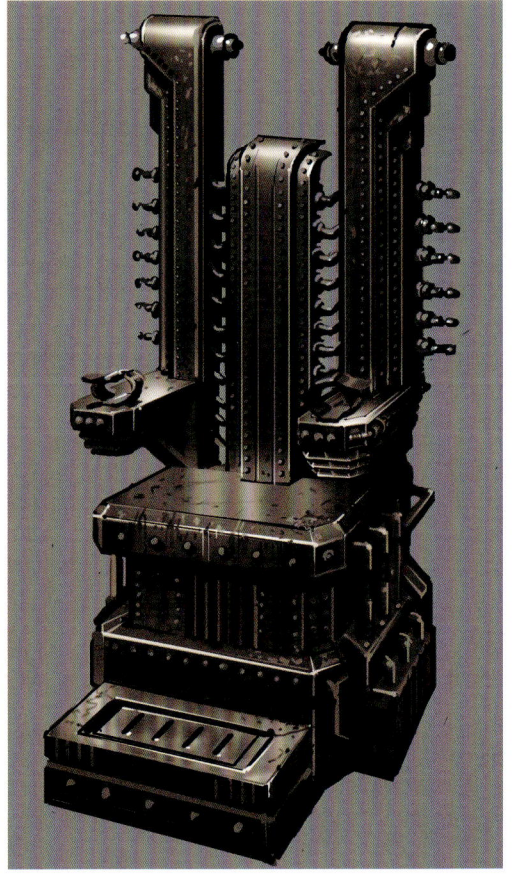

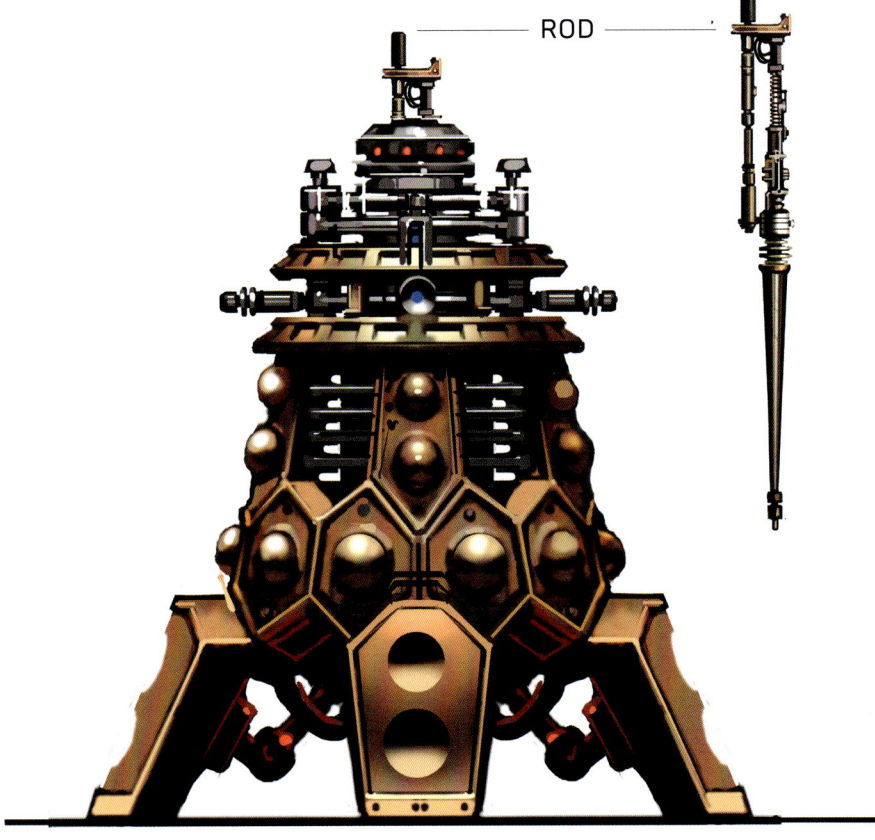

ROD

THRONE

The first design for the Cyber-throne was the one which was finally approved. But I also offered an alternative version. However, Producer Susie Liggat felt it looked a little too much like an electric chair. Director Andy Goddard agreed, suggesting that 'it look a bit more imperious and regal. I think if it looks too much like an electric chair the audience are going to be a step ahead in pre-empting Miss H being dragged to it…'

CYBER KING

The Cyber King was to be a fully CGI creation, but this early concept drawing was developed for the episode's Tone Meeting, well before any specifics were finalised. It was later passed to The Mill as a starting point from which the final version was developed.

CYBER HQ PERISCOPE

Since the Cybermen were hiding under the Thames, Ed suggested we base their scanner on a periscope shape, with the screens being head height to a Cyberman. Andy Goddard described it as 'a steampunk dream', with Russell adding, 'If Andy's happy, I'm happy. Wonderful work!'

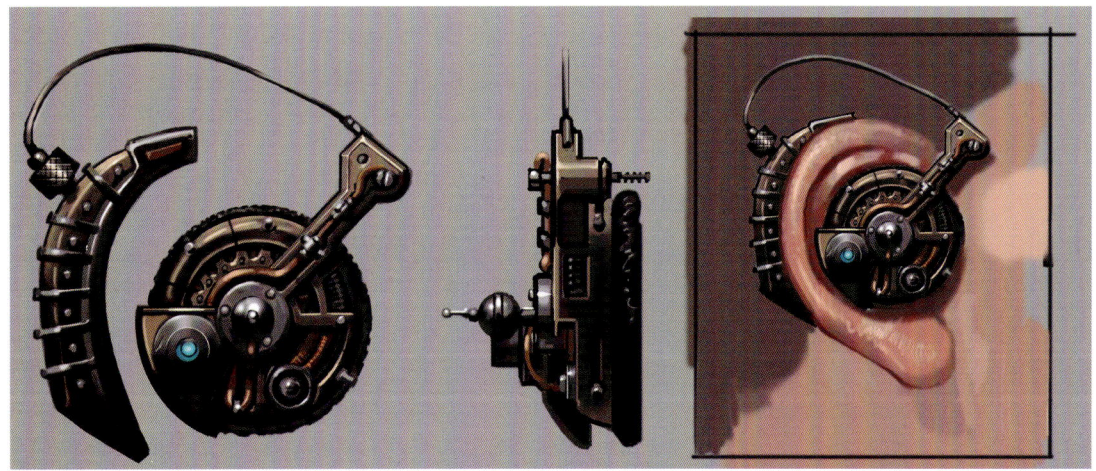

EARPIECE

This was a chance to revisit the Cyber-earpods from Series 2. Here they're less sleek, more in keeping with the industrial tech look of the huge machine and the Cyber King.

VANISHING POINT

The end of Series 4 had a real end-of-school feeling. There was to be a break in production for a while, then work on a succession of further specials would commence. But all that was in the future. For many of us, it was time to find new challenges – myself included.

Another opportunity had come along that I simply couldn't let slip by. I'd been invited to join the concept design team in the *Harry Potter* art department, and went on to work for *The Half-Blood Prince* and both *Deathly Hallows* films.

On my last day at Upper Boat, I was presented with a print of the fob watch I'd designed during Series 3, personally signed by David Tennant. It was an unexpected but deeply appreciated parting gift, and of course, it still hangs on my wall to this day.

Receiving such a perfect gift really felt like the end of my *Doctor Who* experience. I'd had an amazing time, loved the work, and had always felt honoured to be part of something so special. I don't remember feeling sad that day, simply grateful. Happy that it had happened at all, rather than sad that it was over. Wait. Did I say over...?

Subject: Cheerio then!
Sent: Monday, 28 April, 2008 1:46 PM
To: Russell T Davies
From: Peter Mckinstry

Hi Russell,

I've just finished my *Doctor Who* contract, and just wanted to say thanks. It's been fantastic. It's been a genuinely magical experience. No matter what I do in the future, I'll always be proud to say I was a part of it.

So, thank you!! and I hope we work together again!

All the best

Peter

Sent: Monday, 28 April, 2008 2:35 PM
To: Peter Mckinstry
From: Russell T Davies

Oh, lovely Peter!

THANK YOU FOR EVERYTHING. A million times over. I hope we work together again, I'm sure we will. And if ever I can help – references or anything – then just give's a call.

You have been BRILLIANT.

R x

A gallery of some of the most memorable foes the Doctor has faced throughout his adventures – some personal favourites among them!

THE NUCLEUS OF THE SWARM

This intelligent virus-creature from *The Invisible Enemy* (1977) was originally realised as a practical prop, prawn-like in appearance with long metallic whiskers. My brief was to redesign the alien as if it were a creation for the new series. I kept some of the crustacean feel of the original while making it appear more sinister and sentient.

(Source: *Doctor Who Magazine*, Issue 510)

THE K-1 ROBOT – CUTAWAY

For me, the K-1's design is one of those classic elements of *Doctor Who* that perfectly captures the charm of the era. I was only one year old when *Robot* (1974–5) was transmitted, so perhaps my nostalgia for the character comes from seeing it on the box of my Denys Fisher TARDIS toy or pictures in *Doctor Who Weekly* as I grew up. Rewatching *Robot* before starting work on this cutaway, I realised how helpful the dialogue was, containing as it does references to parts of the K-1's design – the inhibitor, living metal, neural relays, etc. This was an unusual leg-up in terms of what to include in my illustration.

(Source: *Doctor Who: The Gold Archive* by Mike Tucker and Steve Cole, BBC Books)

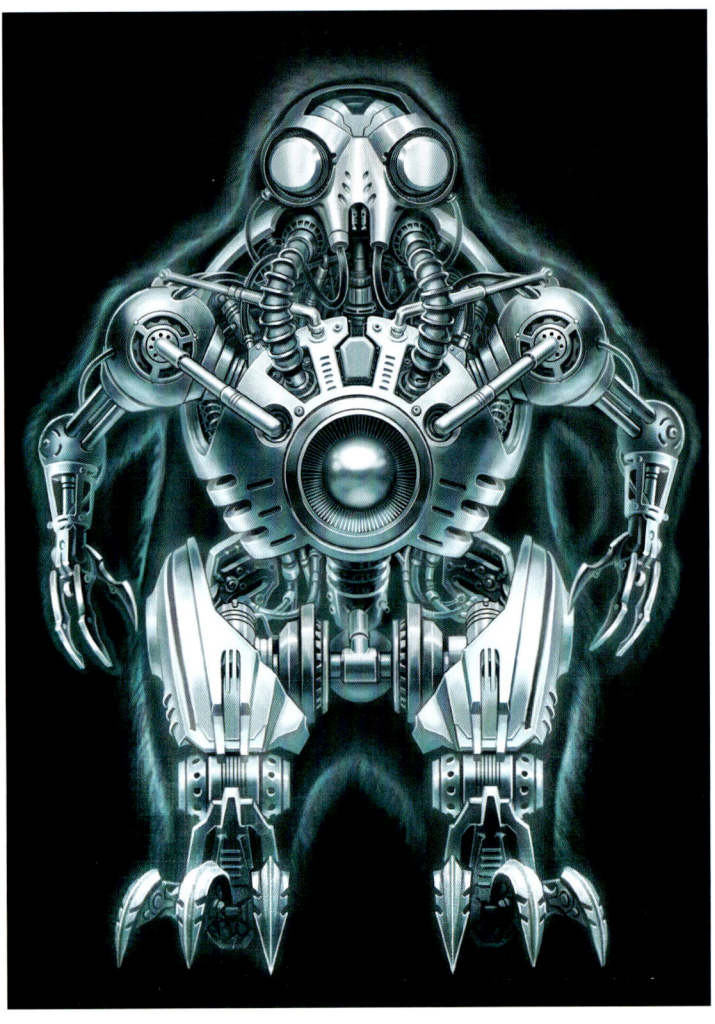

VOC ROBOT – CUTAWAY

The Voc Robots, with their elegant yet eerie aesthetic, are another iconic *Doctor Who* design. In *The Robots of Death* (1977) we are shown only fleeting glimpses of their inner workings; I was keen to capture as much detail as possible for this cutaway.

(Source: *Doctor Who: The DVD Files* magazine, GE Fabbri)

THE YETI

The Yeti present as fearsome, furry beasts but in fact they are robots in disguise, tools of the disembodied Great Intelligence. First appearing in Tibet in *The Abominable Snowmen* (1967), they are redeployed to modern England to menace the London Underground in *The Web of Fear* (1968).

(Sources: *Doctor Who: The DVD Files* magazine, GE Fabbri (cutaway) and *Doctor Who: The Secret Lives of Monsters* by Justin Richards, BBC Books)

RASTON WARRIOR ROBOT – CUTAWAY

This 'perfect killing machine' from *The Five Doctors* (1983) could move at incredible speed and launch built-in spears from its hands with deadly precision. For this illustration, I stripped away its outer skin to show how this might work. I imagined a system in which cartridges are created and stored within a compartment in the robot's upper arm. When the robot prepares to fire, these cartridges are propelled through a superheated filament at the elbow joint. This filament not only ignites the cartridge but also reshapes it into a sleek spear form as it exits the arm through the wrist. Simple really!

(Source: *Doctor Who: The DVD Files* magazine, GE Fabbri)

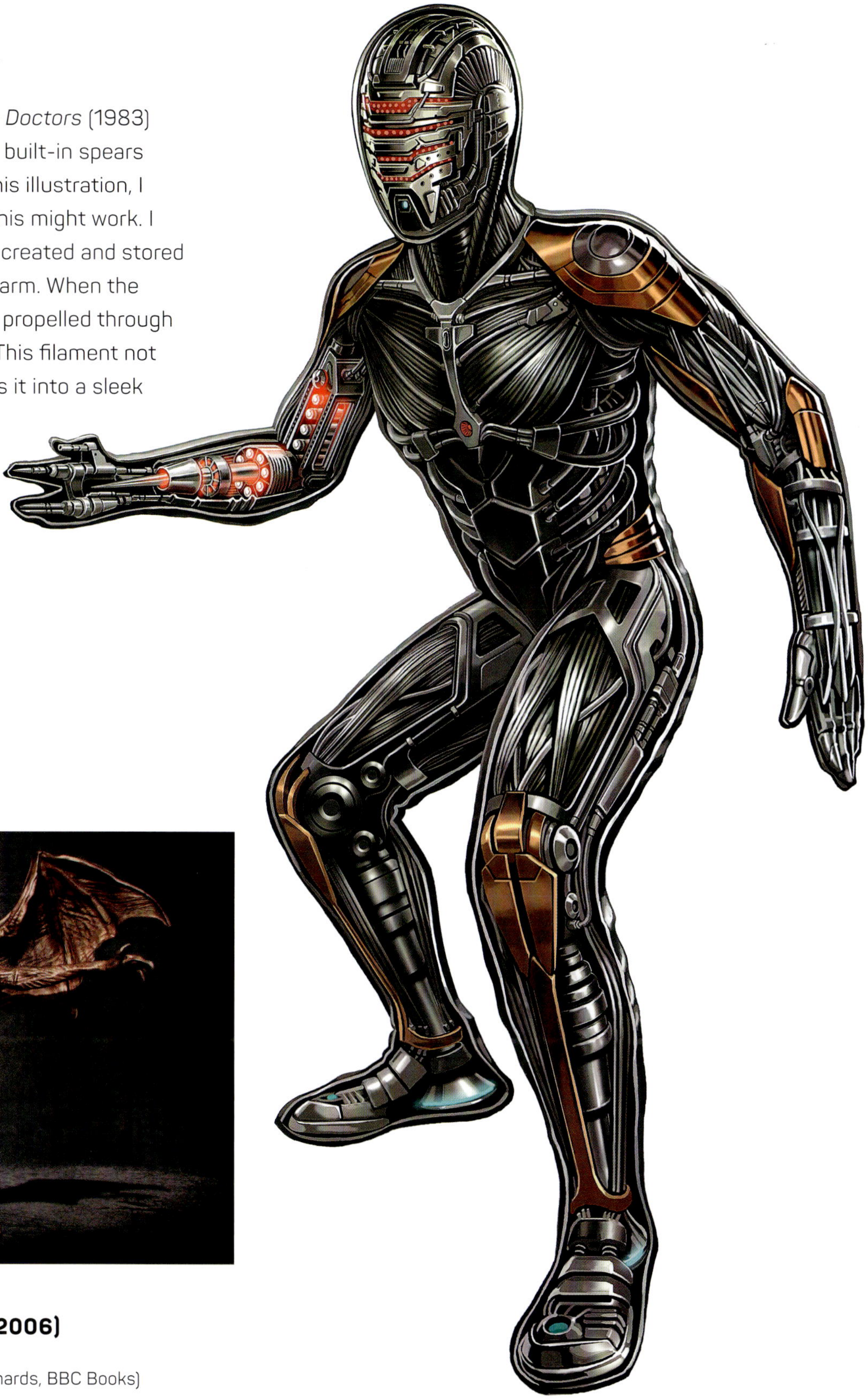

KRILLITANE FROM *SCHOOL REUNION* (2006)

(Source: *The Secret Lives of Monsters* by Justin Richards, BBC Books)

THE DARKSMITH LEGACY

For this assignment I had to design and illustrate brand-new monsters dreamed up by the writers of this ten-book adventure: Justin Richards, Colin Brake, Richard Dungworth, Steve Cole, Trevor Baxendale, Jacqueline Rayner and Mike Tucker.

(Source: *Doctor Who: The Darksmith Legacy*, various titles, BBC Children's Books)

KRAAL ANDROID – CUTAWAY

While there are some clear shots of these androids' hidden faces in *The Android Invasion* (1975), catching details of their other workings is like trying to watch a Weeping Angel move – blink and you miss it! I pieced together screengrabs and used them as reference while building my 3D model, but getting the uniform right took even longer. A military friend suggested it was a made-up outfit thrown together by the costume department, but after further research, I discovered that the correct term for this uniform style is 'barrack dress'.

(Source: *Doctor Who: The Gold Archive* by Mike Tucker and Steve Cole, BBC Books)

SIL

This cruel and manipulative individual, first seen in *Vengeance on Varos* (1985), relished the suffering of others. A corporate capitalist obsessed with profit margins, his eccentric voice translator added a layer of dark comedy to his tirades. His favourite food was marsh minnows – as revolting as his outlook on life!

(Source: *A History of the Universe in 100 Objects* by James Goss and Steve Tribe, BBC Books)

PART 4 | SERIES 5

A NEW PARADIGM

Having been kept busy at Hogwarts for a while, I discovered there was an upside to not working on *Doctor Who* – I was able to enjoy *Planet of the Dead*, *The Waters of Mars* and *The End of Time* without spoilers, which was a real treat.

By now, Chris and I were living in a flat in Cardiff Bay, which often felt like living inside an episode of *Doctor Who* or *Torchwood*. Owen Harper's flat was next door, and Mount Stuart Square – where I'd once played a Cyberman – was just around the corner. The Torchwood Hub tower stood gleaming outside the Millennium Centre and nearby was Ianto Jones' shrine in Mermaid Quay.

Then, as my time on Harry Potter was winding down, the phone rang. It was the *Doctor Who* production office. Was I available to jump back on board for another adventure?

How could I resist!

The first thing I saw when I returned to Upperboat was Ed's

new multi-level TARDIS control room set. It was a bold departure from the Eccleston/Tennant version, and filled a whole studio stage. And of course, that wasn't the only thing that had changed. Russell T Davies was no longer at the helm; Steven Moffatt had arrived as showrunner, and the show was entering a new phase.

Adapting to any change, including leadership, is part and parcel of freelance work. Every showrunner has their own approach, and it's up to the team to bring that vision to life. Change, after all, is in the DNA of the Whoniverse.

An early highlight of production commencing was the afternoon when Matt Smith and Karen Gillan popped into the art department. They were going around the whole studio, saying hello to each and every person they met before filming started – a lovely, unexpected gesture. It gave us all a real buzz. A new era was about to begin, and I couldn't wait to get stuck in!

THE ELEVENTH HOUR

PRISONER ZERO TENDRIL

The 'tendril' – part of Prisoner Zero's true form – was described in the script as 'a translucent tendril with a bunched, little face, the whole thing transparent'. This led me to think of deep-sea creatures with their internal organs visible through their skin. A bioluminescent creature had not previously been seen in *Doctor Who*, so the novelty also appealed to me.

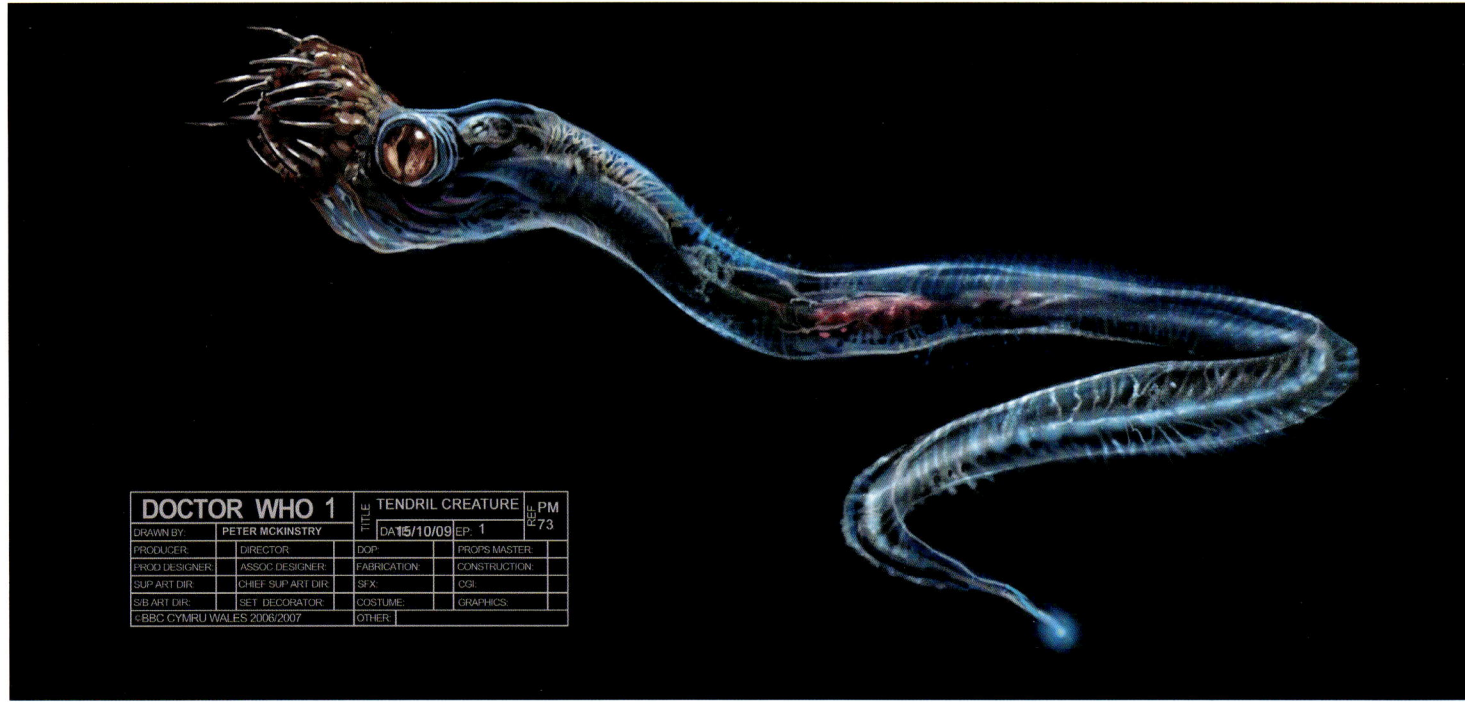

DOCTOR WHO 1		TITLE	TENDRIL CREATURE	REF	PM 73
DRAWN BY:	PETER MCKINSTRY		DATE 15/10/09	EP: 1	
PRODUCER:	DIRECTOR:	DOP:		PROPS MASTER:	
PROD DESIGNER:	ASSOC DESIGNER:	FABRICATION:		CONSTRUCTION:	
SUP ART DIR:	CHIEF SUP ART DIR:	SFX:		CGI:	
S/B ART DIR:	SET DECORATOR:	COSTUME:		GRAPHICS:	
©BBC CYMRU WALES 2006/2007		OTHER:			

STARFISH SHIP

Prisoner Zero's jailers were the Atraxi, and the script described their ship as having a starfish shape with a huge eye at its centre. I explored the concept with a fluid, organic design to see if it could work. After all, a strange alien spaceship shouldn't have to conform to human ideas of form or function. I also created a more structured design that kept the central eye framed within a more solid spacecraft silhouette. Little did I know, Steven simply wanted a floating eyeball!

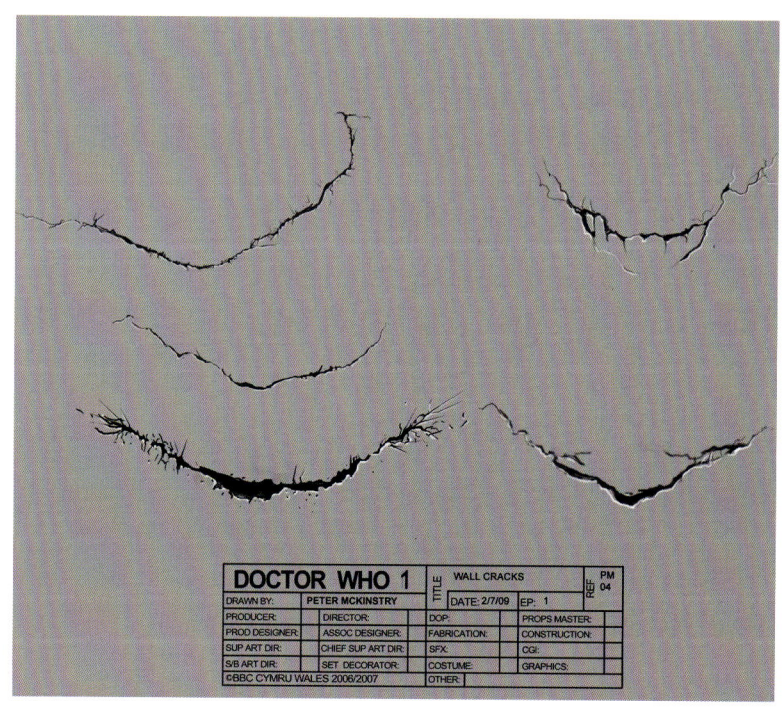

TARDIS MONITOR GRAPHICS

These updated Gallifreyan characters were required for display on the console's monitor screen. The new graphic elements resemble ghostly bokeh artifacts, yet their arrangement on the screen suggests they are conveying the complex information necessary to navigate the time vortex.

WALL CRACKS

The crack on Amy's wall was both an eerie anomaly and an ominous portent of impending disaster. As such, its shape needed to be instantly recognisable since it was to reappear in multiple episodes as Series 5 progressed.

DOCTOR WHO 1		TITLE	WALL CRACKS		PM 04
DRAWN BY:	PETER MCKINSTRY		DATE: 2/7/09	EP: 1	REF
PRODUCER:	DIRECTOR:		DOP:	PROPS MASTER:	
PROD DESIGNER:	ASSOC DESIGNER:		FABRICATION:	CONSTRUCTION:	
SUP ART DIR:	CHIEF SUP ART DIR:		SFX:	CGI:	
S/B ART DIR:	SET DECORATOR:		COSTUME:	GRAPHICS:	
©BBC CYMRU WALES 2006/2007			OTHER:		

DESTROYED SONIC

The Ninth and Tenth
Doctors' sonic screwdriver
had survived a few
near misses since its
introduction, but this time,
it really was the end of
the road. The brief for this
concept was to depict
the sonic as having well
and truly shuffled off
its electromagnetic coil.
In an effort to maintain
consistency with the
cross-section illustrations
I had done for *The Visual
Dictionary* and *The
DVD Files* magazine, I
incorporated elements
from those images into this
design.

THE ELEVENTH
DOCTOR'S SONIC –
CUTAWAY

For this cutaway of the new
sonic screwdriver, I again
aimed to maintain continuity
with the inner workings
of my previous sonic
illustrations while further
evolving the design. From
previous versions, I included
the 'function drums': a
carousel of multiple tiny
discs which are programmed
with the sonic's various
astounding capabilities.
The organic shapes I've
introduced within the rest of
this sonic mirror the blown
glass shapes seen in the
central rotor column of the
Eleventh Doctor's TARDIS
console, tying the two
designs together.

Please note: 'It doesn't
do wood!'

THE BEAST BELOW

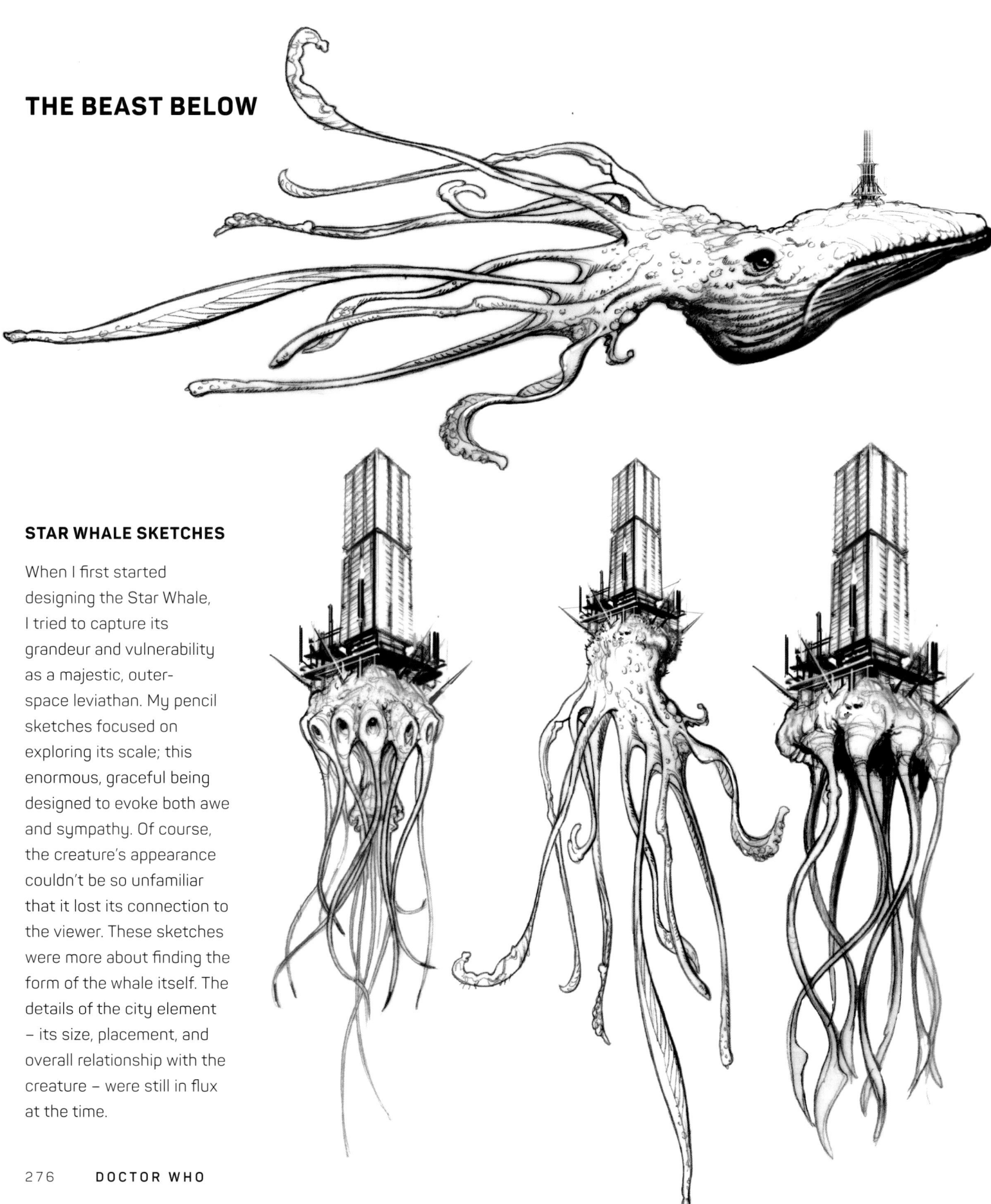

STAR WHALE SKETCHES

When I first started designing the Star Whale, I tried to capture its grandeur and vulnerability as a majestic, outer-space leviathan. My pencil sketches focused on exploring its scale; this enormous, graceful being designed to evoke both awe and sympathy. Of course, the creature's appearance couldn't be so unfamiliar that it lost its connection to the viewer. These sketches were more about finding the form of the whale itself. The details of the city element – its size, placement, and overall relationship with the creature – were still in flux at the time.

DOCTOR WHO 1			LIZ 10's PISTOLS		REF	PM	LOCKED
		TITLE	DATE: 10/8/09	EP: 2		32	12/8/09
DRAWN BY:	PETER McKINSTRY						
PRODUCER:		DIRECTOR:		DOP:		PROPS MASTER:	
PROD DESIGNER:		ASSOC DESIGNER:		FABRICATION:		CONSTRUCTION:	
SUP ART DIR:		CHIEF SUP ART DIR:		SFX:		CGI:	
S/B ART DIR:		SET DECORATOR:		COSTUME:		GRAPHICS:	
©BBC CYMRU WALES 2006/2007				OTHER:			

LIZ 10'S PISTOLS

It was refreshing to approach a sci-fi weapon from a slightly new angle. The ornate design was perfect for her regal character, while the overall retro-futuristic silhouette paid homage to classic sci-fi serials like *Buck Rogers*. I especially enjoyed adding the teardrop pearl to the hilt – a subtle finishing touch that added elegance and sophistication.

WINDER KEY

Everything on Starship UK was intended to hark back to a kind of nostalgic and whimsical idea of Great Britain. For the Winder Key, the prop's silhouette had to convey its function, so I made it reminiscent of a key for an old grandfather clock or wind-up toy. Then, in the style of the details and the material finish, I was able to place it visually in the context of the episode.

8cm

MONITOR CABINET AND MONITOR BANK

Another design in the vein of nostalgic Britain began with a riff on old-fashioned TV corner cabinets, once again using something from the prop store. However, this design felt a bit too retro, so for the next iteration I tried a more stylised approach. This version was well-received, but I later revised it to bring back that nostalgic feel. I reshaped the various monitors so that they formed the shapes of the Union flag. It's pure whimsy but, sometimes, that's exactly what's required.

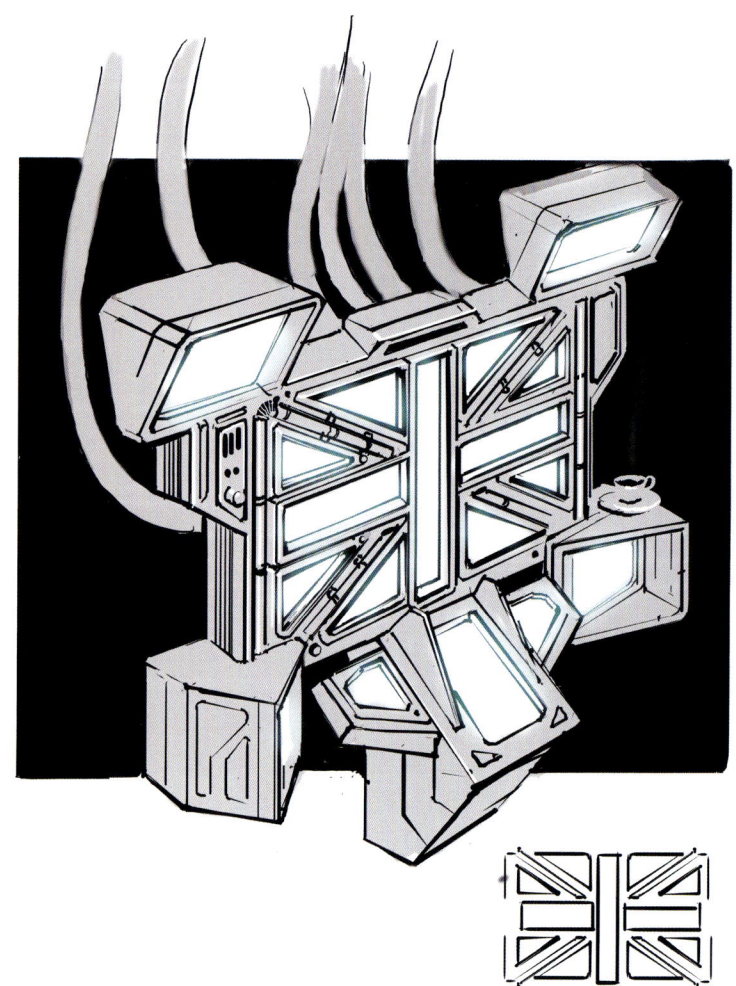

'OCCUPIED' SIGN

Not every design is exciting, but each one is necessary to build the world, piece by piece!

REPLICATOR

This design started with a large cylindrical set of drawers from the prop store and evolved into a kind of meeting spot or multi-directional signpost. I figured that if all that's left of your country is a spaceship, you might want to surround yourself with paraphernalia that reminds you of where you came from. I took inspiration from the black and white stripes of UK zebra crossings, and had far too much fun filling out the signs!

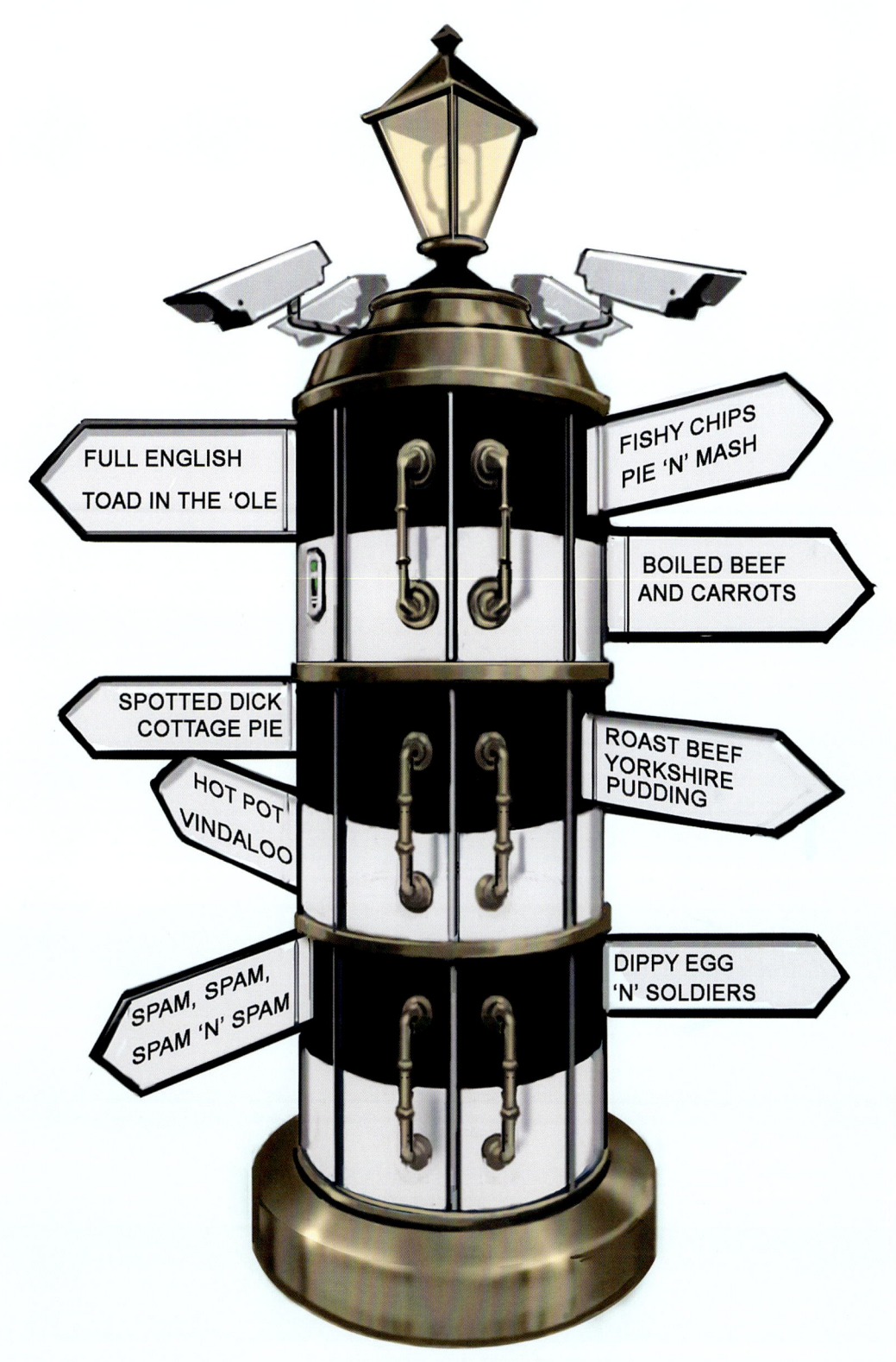

WINDOW VIEW

I enjoyed this chance to illustrate a story moment: the Doctor and Amy looking out over the expanse of Starship UK. I was given a low-resolution, off-screen photo taken during filming, and used it to create the view outside the window.

WORK TENT (INTERIOR)

I produced this image to convey the interior layout of the work tent in which Amy finds herself.

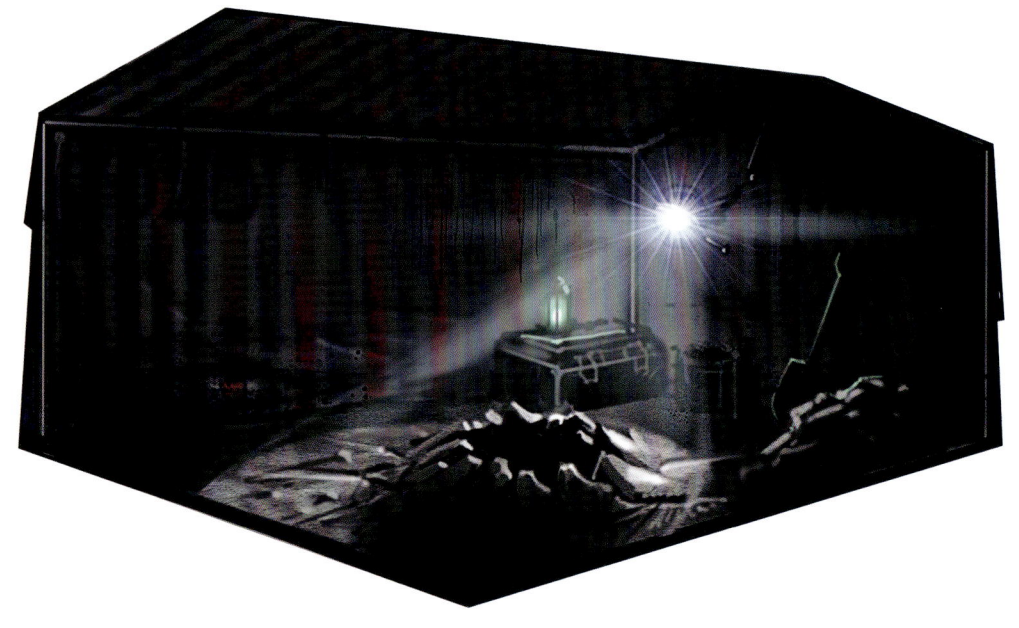

SMILER – CUTAWAY

This cutaway illustration shows the inside of one of the grotesque Smilers, the menacing automatons that sat in carnival-style booths. I produced it for GE Fabbri's *Doctor Who: The DVD Files* magazine.

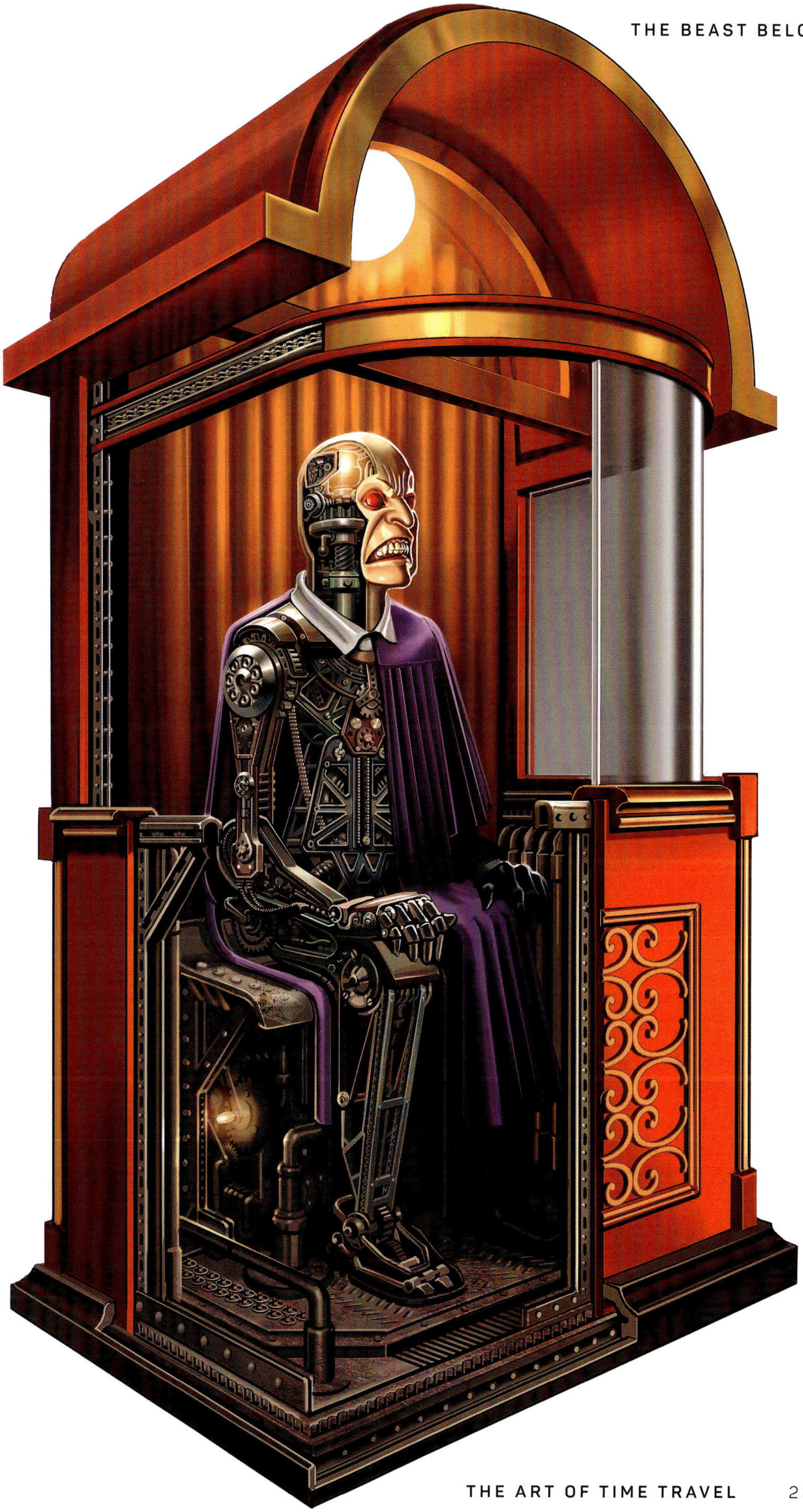

STARSHIP UK (OVERLEAF)

While the original sketches laid the foundation for the design of the Star Whale, this illustration, done for BBC Books' *A History of the Universe in 100 Objects* by James Goss and Steve Tribe, shows the final design in all its strange glory.

VICTORY OF THE DALEKS

NEW DALEK PARADIGM

The concept design process for the Daleks' new paradigm was an exciting opportunity to push the boundaries of these foes' iconic look. The team wanted to create a more imposing silhouette, making them tank-like yet devoid of studs and rivets to suggest a more advanced level of Dalek technology. With sharp edges and cold, smooth surfaces, even the fins on the eyestalk were designed to make them less grabbable. Steven also wanted a new organic feel to the eye, giving it a distinct, more alien look and hinting at the organism sealed inside.

The height of the bronze Daleks had been based on Billie Piper's eye level, so for this redesign, we used Matt Smith's eye level as a guide, allowing him to go toe-to-toe with them. I broadened the shoulder section so that with their increased height, they would tower over the bronze Daleks, giving them a more muscular, intimidating presence. This was inspired by the original brief from Steven and the episode's writer, Mark Gatiss, who pointed out how well the scaled-up Daleks from the 1960s movies worked on screen.

Steven suggested the new Daleks might have a special, unexpected feature – something that could allow for a dramatic reveal or surprise twist. Loving the idea, I suggested adding a spinal section to the back of the design, from which a new appendage could emerge at a future point. This was inspired by an idea I'd had when entering a competition to redesign the Daleks for *SFX* magazine, a couple of years before I'd joined the show; my entry featured various mutant appendages to supplement the usual plunger and gun arm.

The overall aim of the redesign was for the Daleks to maintain their fearsome presence while introducing a bold, bombastic aesthetic. Steven requested a range of bright colours to denote hierarchy and roles. Red became Drone; blue, Strategist; orange, Scientist; yellow, Eternal and white, Supreme. All these Daleks were initially intended to have a

metallic finish to add a layer of build realism, but the idea was lost due to budget constraints. Thankfully, the metallic look was reinstated in later episodes, to the props' benefit. Initially, the fan reaction was mixed. The 'shock of the new' played its part but, over time and with alterations to their colouring and surface finishes in later appearances, they've grown more popular. And I'm happy to say they had one very important fan from the start...

Subject: Victory!
Sent: Saturday, April 17, 2010 6:51 PM
To: Peter Mckinstry
From: Russell T Davies

Hello there, Peter,

I hope this is still your email address!

A little bird tells me that those new Daleks tonight were yours. I thought they were GLORIOUS! I fully expected to hate them – I'm an old Dalek purist (which is a very Dalek thing to be) but they looked stunning. The yellow one was my favourite! So big and bold and movie-like.
Oh, just gorgeous!

R x

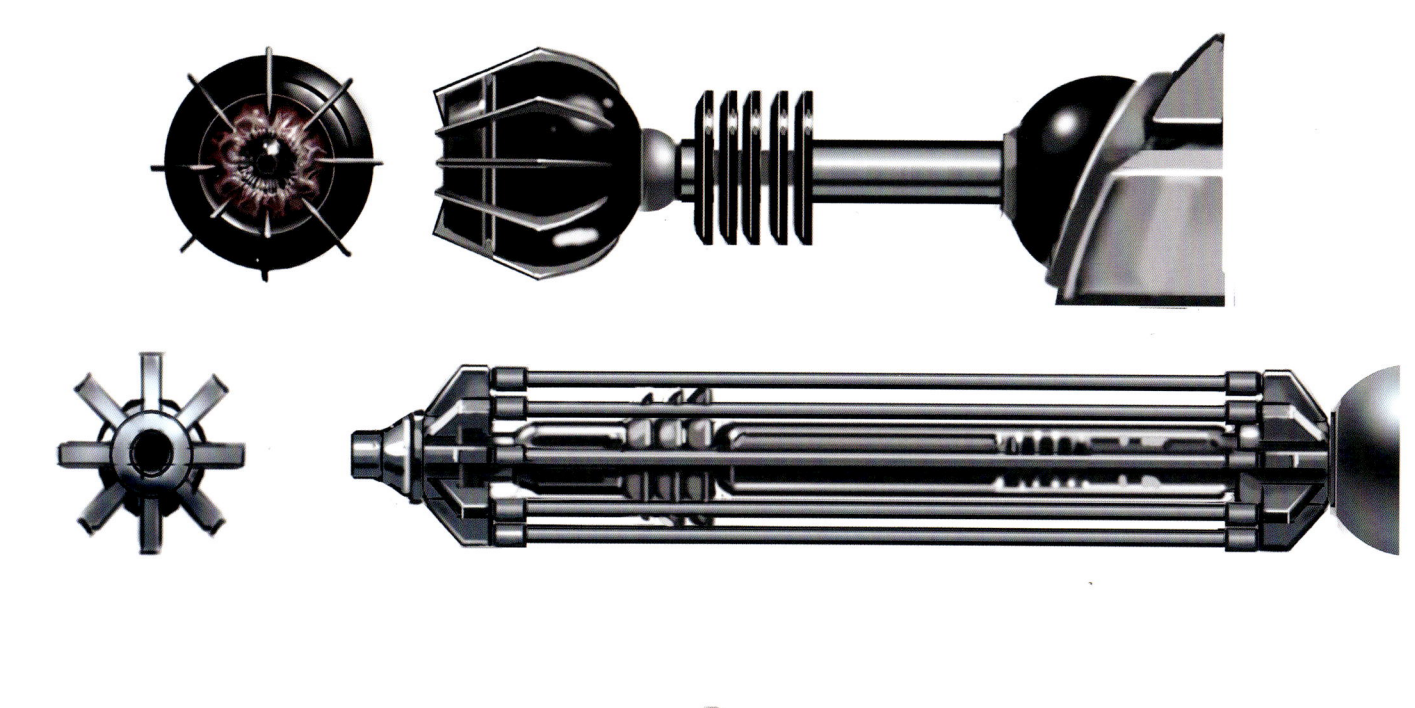

DOCTOR WHO 1		TITLE	DALEK		REF	PM 22	LOCKED
DRAWN BY:	PETER MCKINSTRY		DATE: 28/7/09	EP:			29/7/09
PRODUCER:	DIRECTOR:		DOP:		PROPS MASTER:		
PROD DESIGNER:	ASSOC DESIGNER:		FABRICATION:		CONSTRUCTION:		
SUP ART DIR:	CHIEF SUP ART DIR:		SFX:		CGI:		
S/B ART DIR:	SET DECORATOR:		COSTUME:		GRAPHICS:		
©BBC CYMRU WALES 2006/2007			OTHER:				

IRONSIDE

Designing the 'Ironside' Dalek was an exercise in 'less is more'. The Dalek itself is as much a design icon of Britain as red telephone boxes and black taxi cabs, making it a natural fit for this wartime variation. The drab olive paint and canvas utility pouches hinted at a practical, multi-purpose role, and helped the Ironsides integrate into Churchill's war room.

DALEK PROGENITOR

This piece of Dalek technology stores pure Dalek DNA and can reproduce fully grown Daleks. Since it symbolised the rebirth of the Daleks in their purest form, I shaped it somewhere between a Dalek and an egg, representing the promise of a new beginning.

DOCTOR WHO 1		TITLE	'IRONSIDE' DALEK	REF	PM 25
DRAWN BY:	PETER MCKINSTRY		DATE: 30/7/09	EP: 3	
PRODUCER:	DIRECTOR:		DOP:	PROPS MASTER:	
PROD DESIGNER:	ASSOC DESIGNER:		FABRICATION:	CONSTRUCTION:	
SUP ART DIR:	CHIEF SUP ART DIR:		SFX:	CGI:	
S/B ART DIR:	SET DECORATOR:		COSTUME:	GRAPHICS:	
©BBC CYMRU WALES 2006/2007			OTHER:		

LOCKED 12/8/09

DALEK SHIP INTERIOR STRUCTURE

This image was intended to give the viewer an understanding of the central control room's position within the overall structure of the Dalek spaceship.

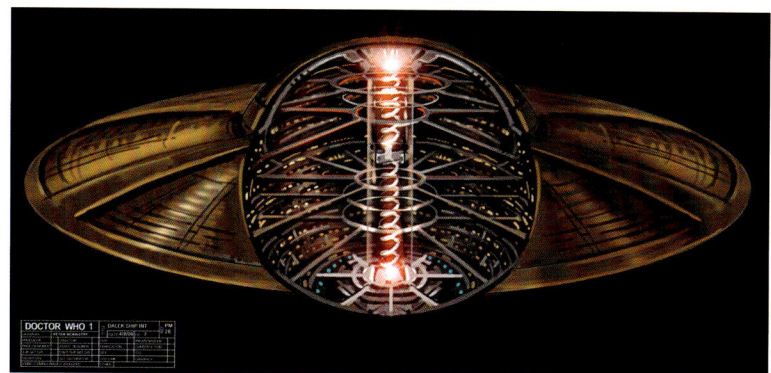

DALEK CORE AND CONTROL UNIT

The Dalek scenes were filmed inside an old cigar humidor chamber – a big metal box, essentially – so we needed to design standalone pieces of Dalek hardware that would fit within that context. Size – and a believable level of Dalek complexity – were key.

TO VICTORY!
POSTER AND DALEK BLUEPRINTS

I designed the Dalek blueprints and the *To Victory!* poster as paper props, to be used as set dressing for shooting, but happily they took on a life of their own beyond the episode. Both the poster and blueprints were used on T-shirts, mugs, prints, and posters. (I'm still patiently waiting for the royalties!) In the small print at the bottom of the Victory poster, I included a few personal Easter eggs, like the name of the small village I grew up in. I like to think that some of the people who bought the poster noticed and wondered, 'What or where on Earth is... *Fillongley*?'

Printed by the MOD Ministry of Defense Room 73,Public Relations Office, Fillongley Warks .Test Print awaiting approval,Not for public display until further notice.
Ref: 20773/04021985

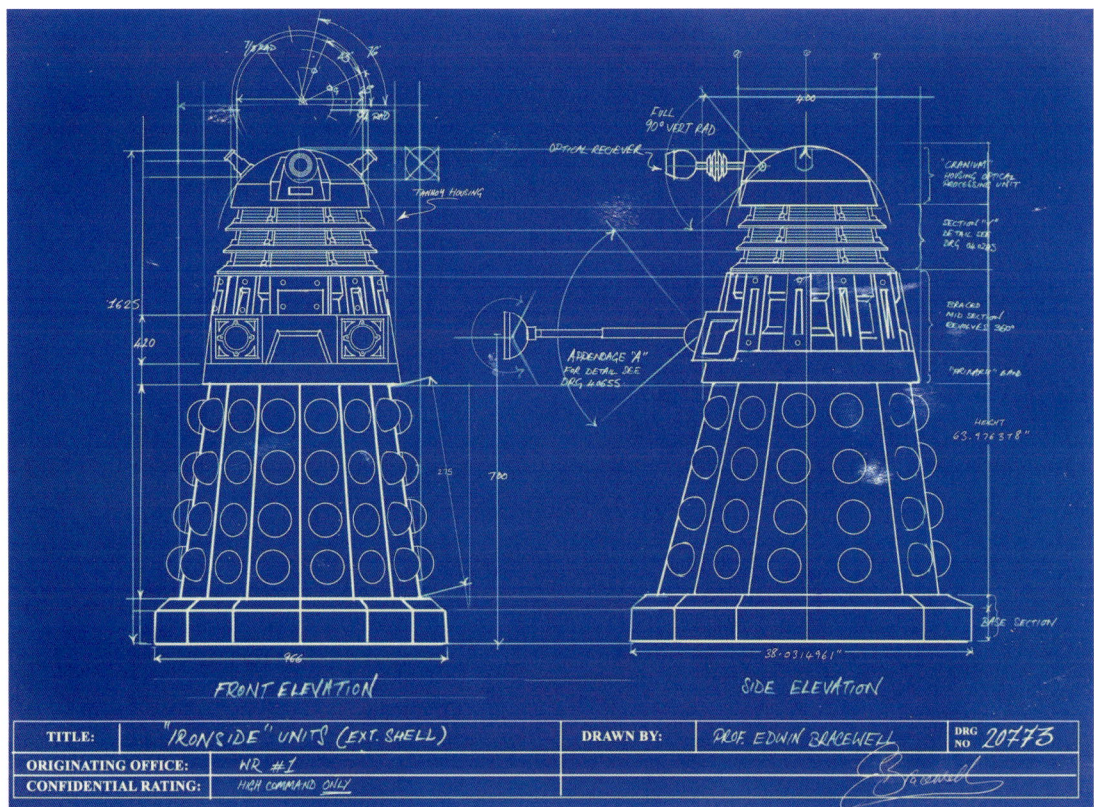

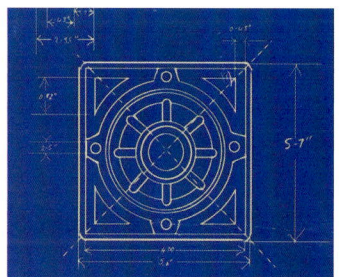

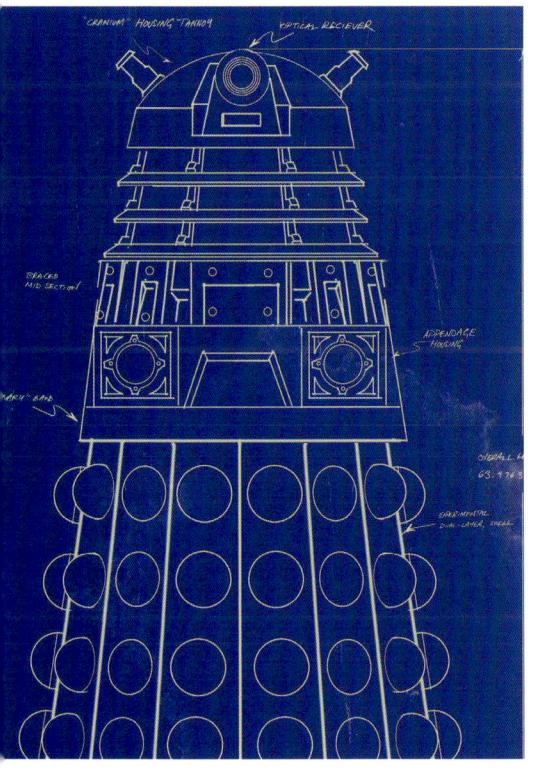

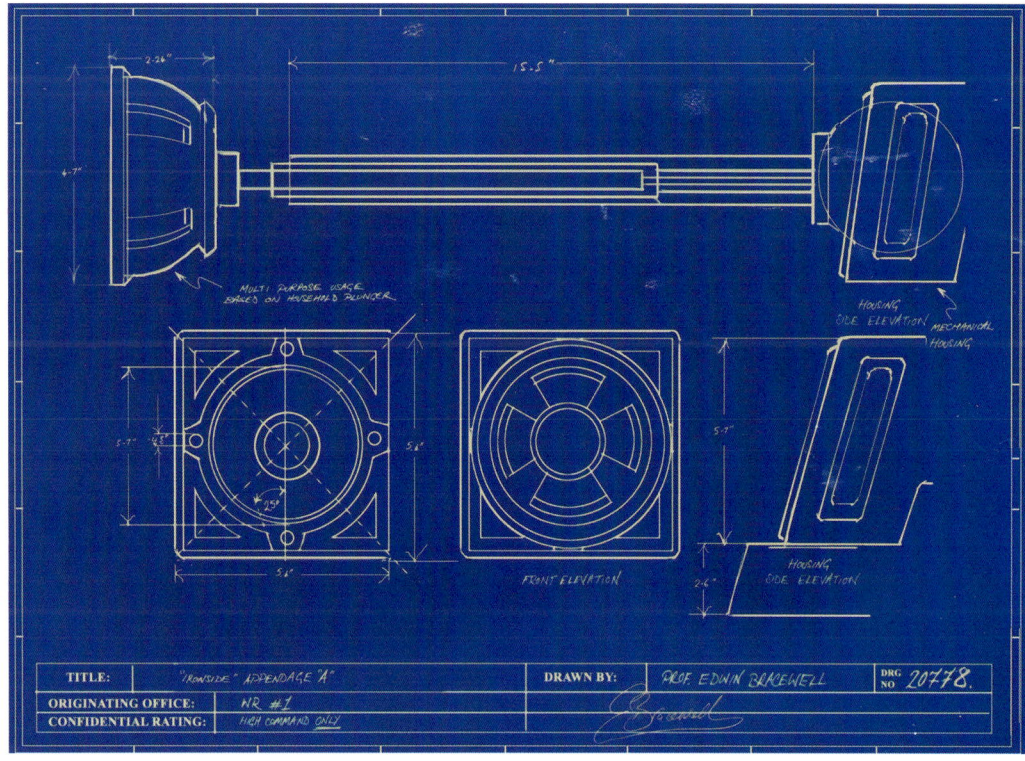

THE TIME OF ANGELS / FLESH AND STONE

BYZANTIUM STARLINER

The *Byzantium* was a sleek, futuristic starliner. 'The director, Adam Smith, knows exactly what he wants,' I was told after the Tone Meeting. *Oh good*, I thought. *Clarity is always helpful*. So, Adam came to see me. 'You know what'd look good?' he said. 'My orange juicer...'

Now, inspiration can come from anywhere: nature, architecture and, yes, even household objects. But this was a particularly distinctive juicer, and my concern was that the ship would inevitably resemble, well... a juicer. I suggested we explore some alternative designs that captured the essence of the juicer's shape while still feeling like a starship. But the director's vision was clear; this specific juicer was the way forward. Sometimes, you just have to smile, nod, and say, 'Here's your interstellar juicer.'

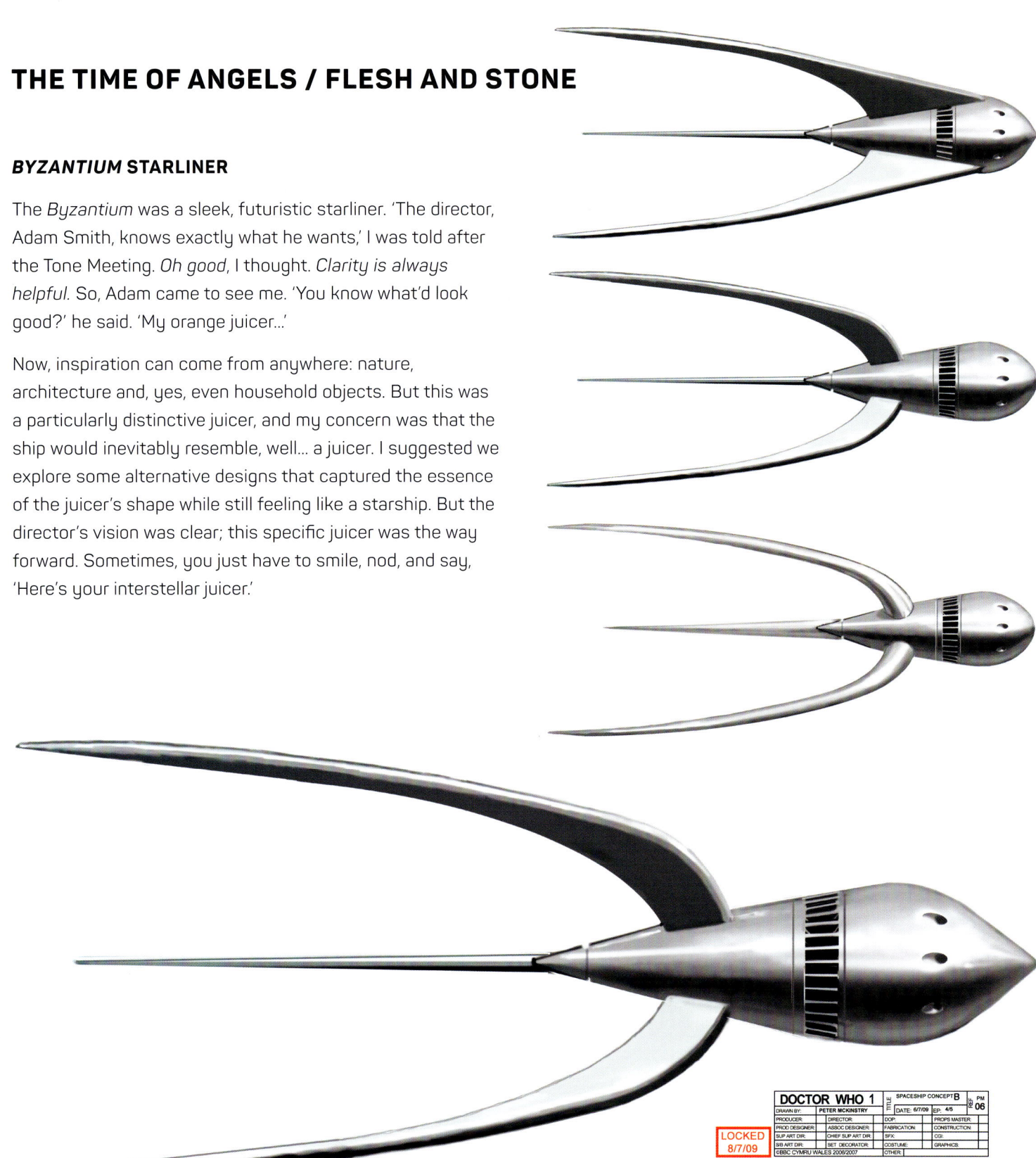

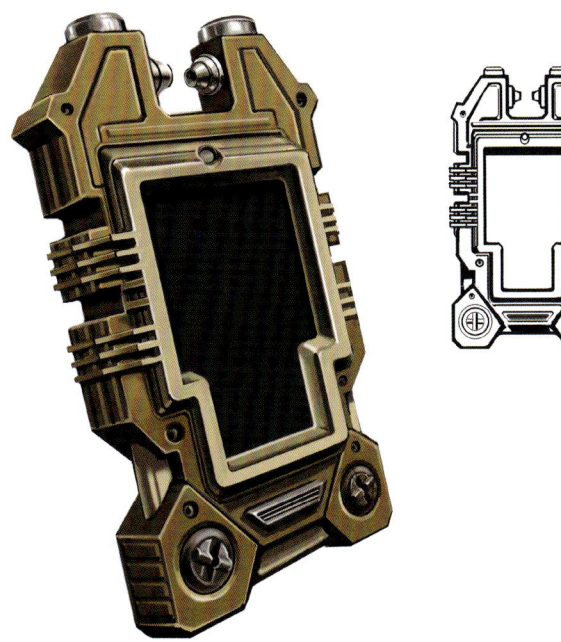

CLERIC CLAMP

Since this anti-gravity technology functions similarly to the magnaclamps used in Series 2's *Army of Ghosts / Doomsday*, I suggested that the Cleric clamp could be a more advanced, powerful yet compact military version of the same equipment.

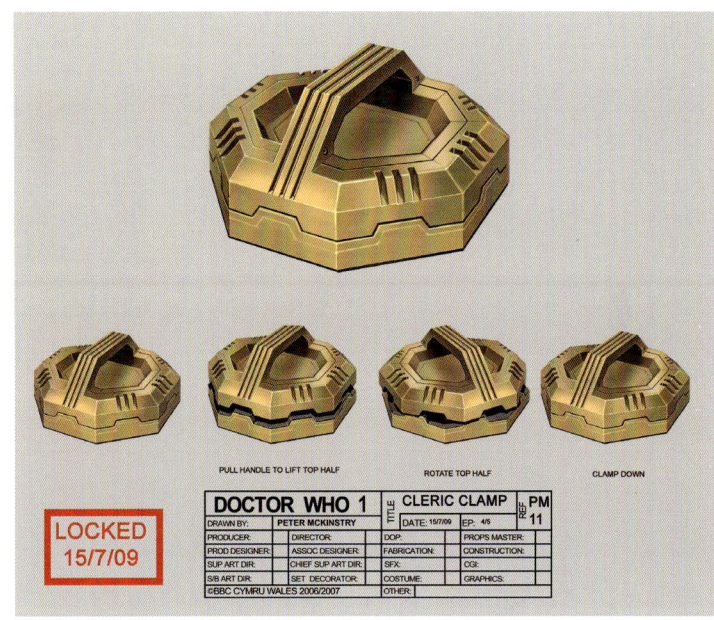

PULL HANDLE TO LIFT TOP HALF   ROTATE TOP HALF   CLAMP DOWN

LOCKED 15/7/09

DOCTOR WHO 1		TITLE	CLERIC CLAMP		REF	PM 11
DRAWN BY:	PETER MCKINSTRY		DATE: 15/7/09	EP: 4/5		
PRODUCER:	DIRECTOR:		DOP:		PROPS MASTER:	
PROD DESIGNER:	ASSOC DESIGNER:		FABRICATION:		CONSTRUCTION:	
SUP ART DIR:	CHIEF SUP ART DIR:		SFX:		CGI:	
S/B ART DIR:	SET DECORATOR:		COSTUME:		GRAPHICS:	
©BBC CYMRU WALES 2006/2007			OTHER:			

CLERIC PDA

The Personal Digital Assistant used by the military Clerics was designed around a pre-existing miniature screen, allowing it to display various graphics and enhance the illusion of functionality. The rugged, hard-wearing design suggests the durability needed for field use while the choice of colour complemented the Clerics' beige camouflage-style costume.

CLERIC HANDCUFFS

The handcuffs continue the chunky, heavy-duty Cleric military aesthetic.

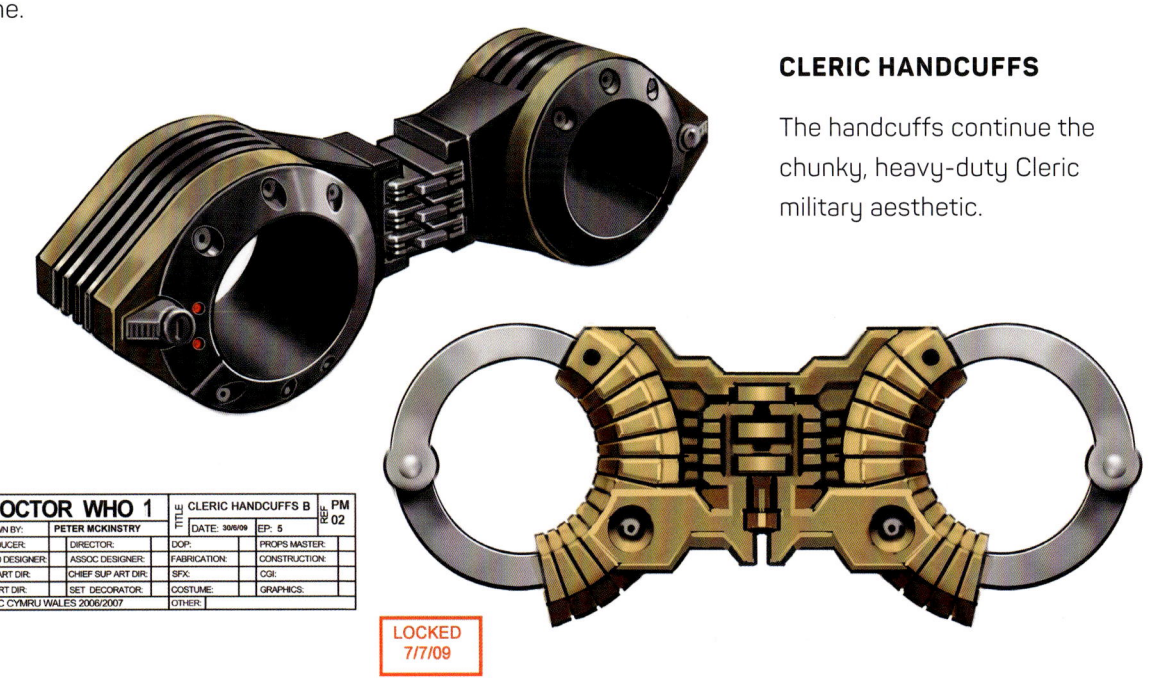

DOCTOR WHO 1		TITLE	CLERIC HANDCUFFS B		REF	PM 02
DRAWN BY:	PETER MCKINSTRY		DATE: 30/6/09	EP: 5		
PRODUCER:	DIRECTOR:		DOP:		PROPS MASTER:	
PROD DESIGNER:	ASSOC DESIGNER:		FABRICATION:		CONSTRUCTION:	
SUP ART DIR:	CHIEF SUP ART DIR:		SFX:		CGI:	
S/B ART DIR:	SET DECORATOR:		COSTUME:		GRAPHICS:	
©BBC CYMRU WALES 2006/2007			OTHER:			

LOCKED 7/7/09

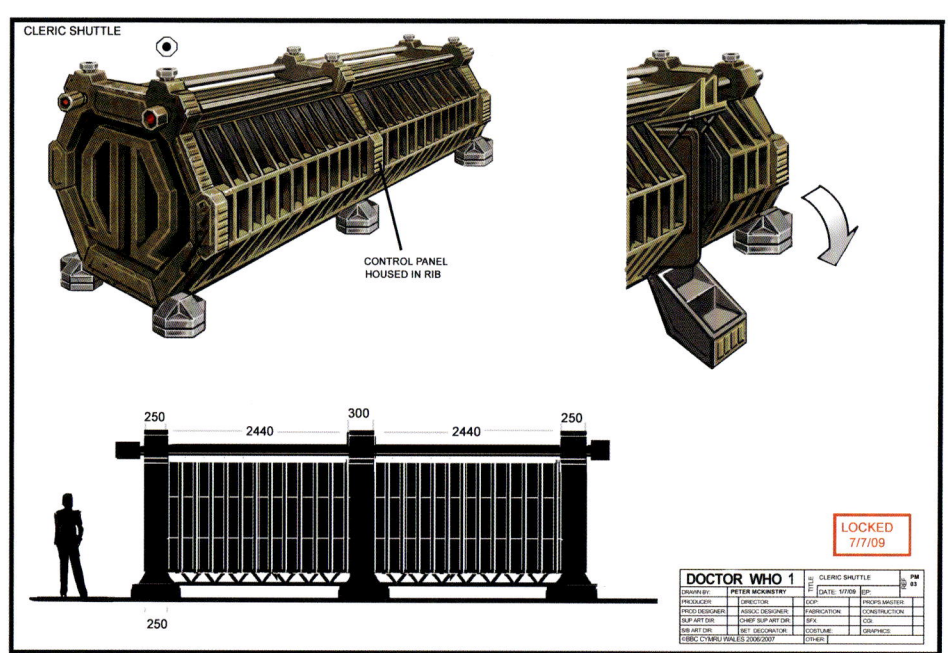

CLERIC SHUTTLE AND CONTROL PANEL

The Clerics' shuttle design was an example of function over form. I envisaged it as a mass-produced reinforced troop carrier/dropship: pure (and budget friendly!) utilitarian design.

RIVER'S GUN

River's gun was inspired by the compact pistols often associated with femme fatales of *film noir* (a genre which suited the character), the type they'd discreetly tuck away in their handbags, ready for a dramatic reveal.

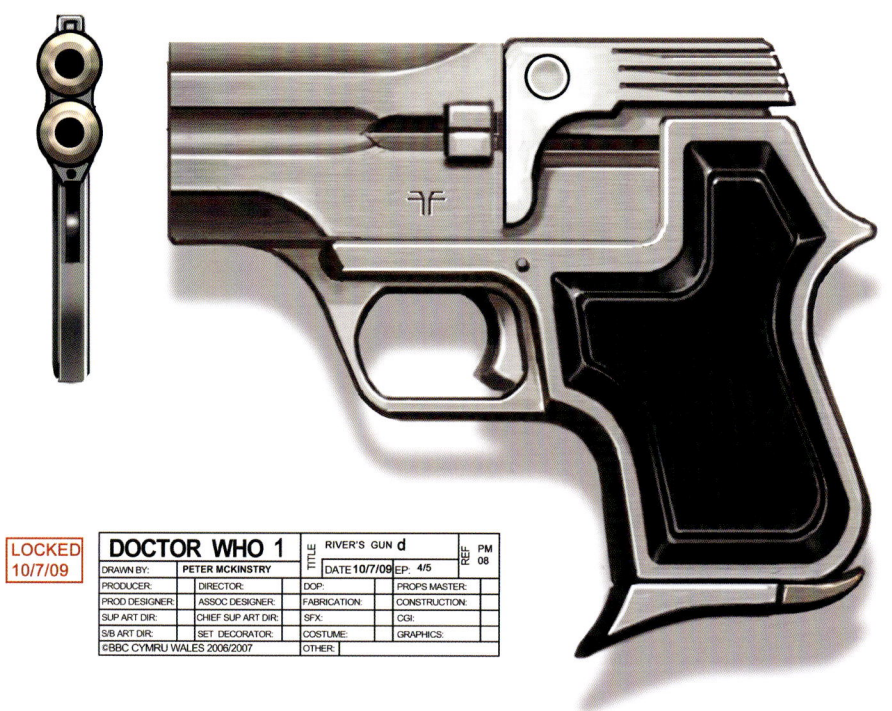

RIVER'S BOMB

Bond-style gadgets like this are fun to design, and I'm always happy to put on my Q hat and produce variations. After all, any unused designs can be squirrelled away for the next time you need to produce something at short notice!

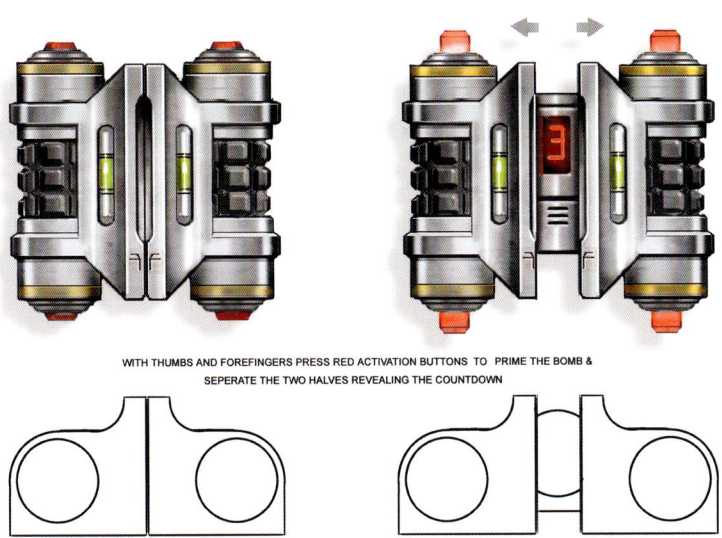

WITH THUMBS AND FOREFINGERS PRESS RED ACTIVATION BUTTONS TO PRIME THE BOMB &
SEPERATE THE TWO HALVES REVEALING THE COUNTDOWN

PLAN VIEW

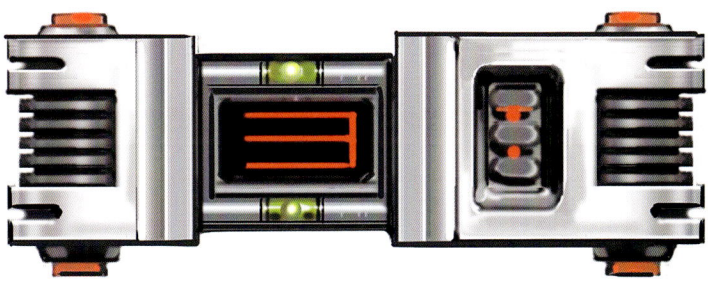

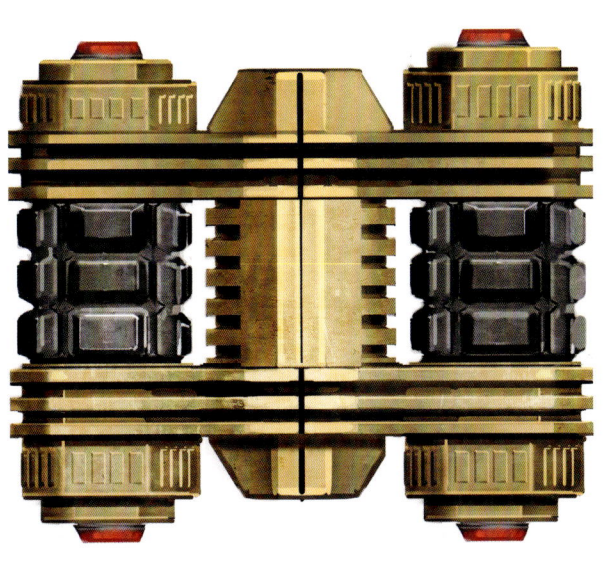

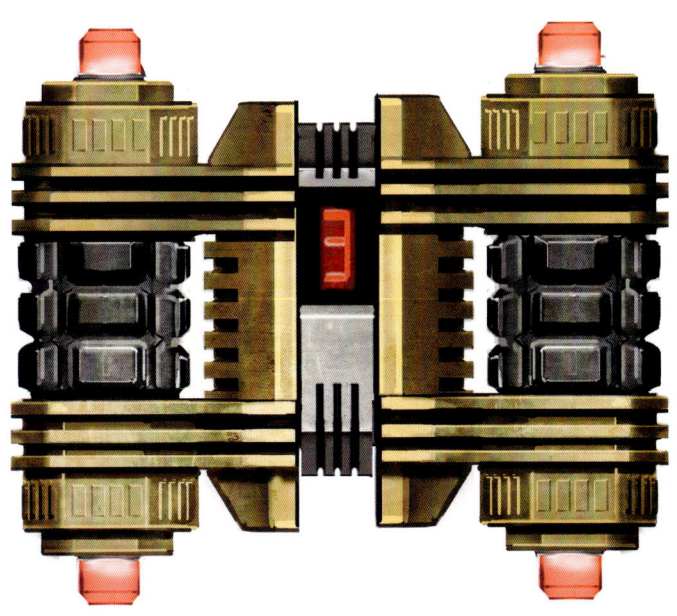

ON-BOARD FOREST AND ACCESS PANEL

This concept for the on-board forest housed within the vast *Byzantium* spacecraft was a welcome opportunity to design something completely different, blending nature with technology in a way that I hadn't explored before.

BYZANTIUM NOSE

The position of the *Byzantium* – specifically this section of the exterior on which the Doctor and friends are standing upside down at the start of the second episode – meant it was important to define exactly how the ship's nose should be oriented in relation to the surrounding environment.

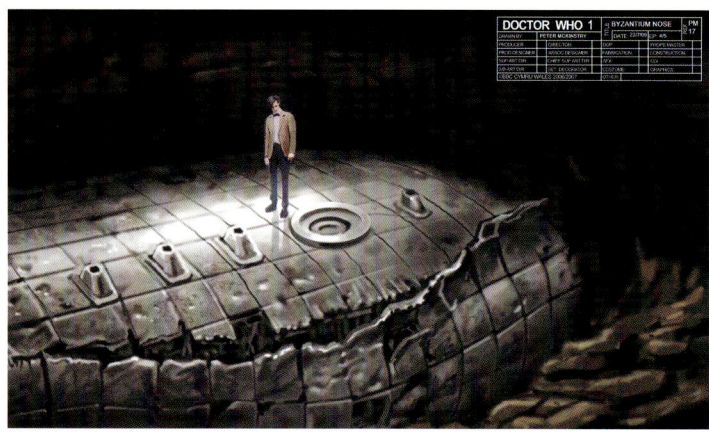

TEMPLE RUINS

I produced this image
simply by painting over a
location photograph.

BYZANTIUM – CUTAWAY

Despite my reservations on the exterior design of the *Byzantium*, creating the cutaway for GE Fabbri's *Doctor Who: The DVD Files* magazine was a fun challenge. I wanted to make sure it included all the key areas seen on-screen while also making the ship's layout feel logical. The vast artificial forest, housed in the main body of the ship, was a major focal point, alongside the more industrial sections like the bridge, walkways, stairwell, and airlock. The trick was placing everything in a way that made sense when referring back to the episode – no easy task, but a rewarding one!

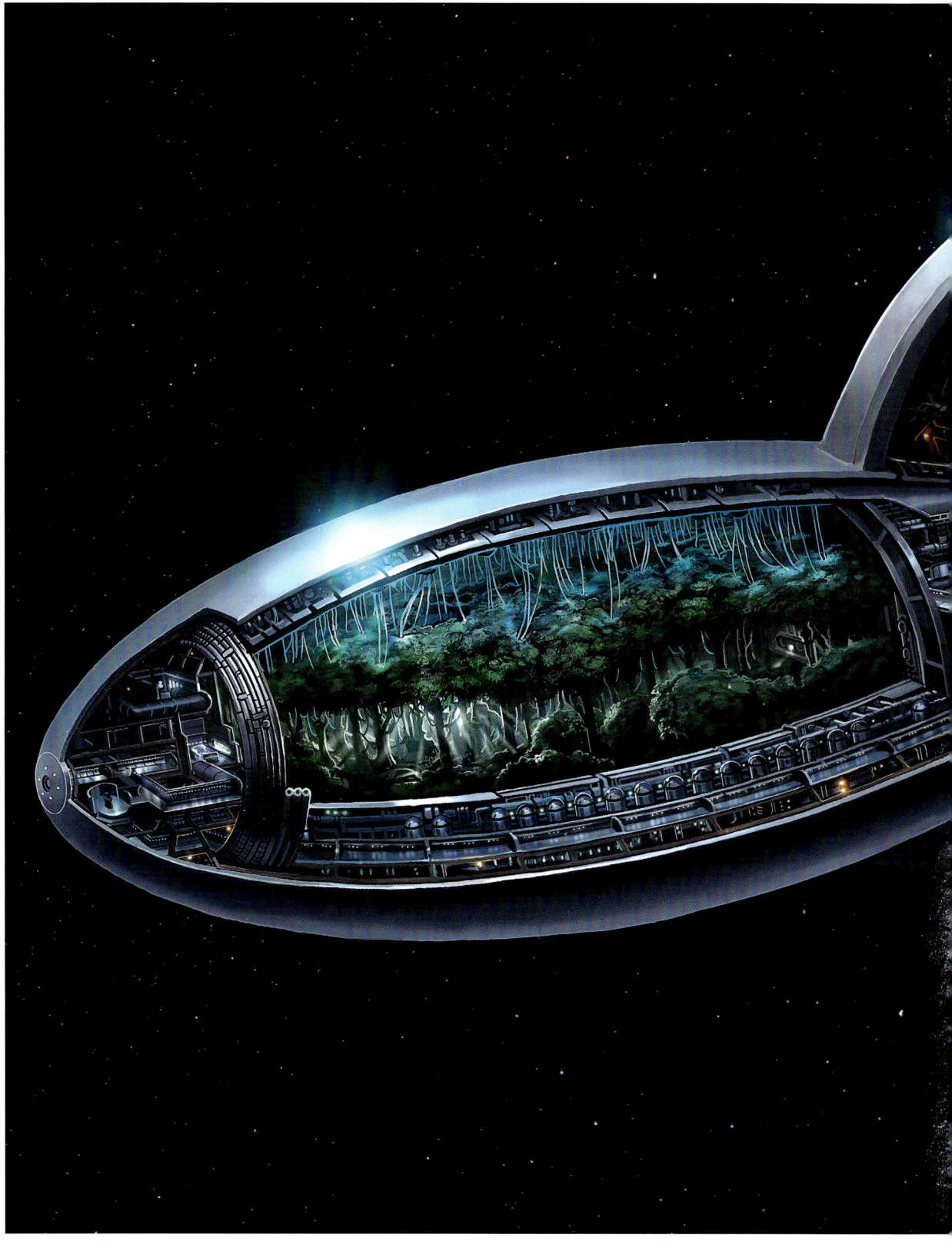

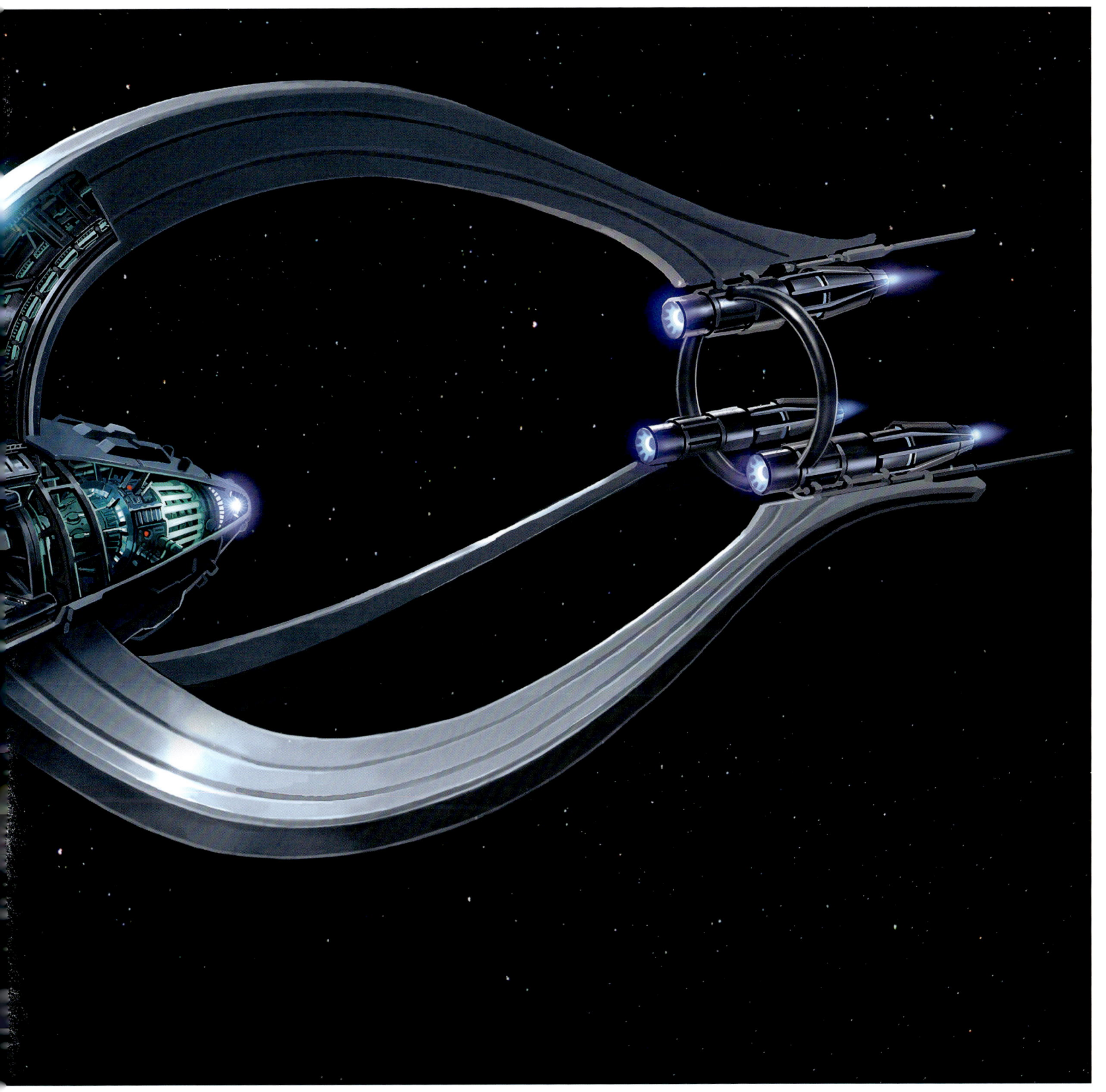

VAMPIRES OF VENICE

COAT OF ARMS

The Calvierri coat of arms, or crest, was included as background set dressing on location to reflect the family's standing and anchor them in the history of Venice within the story. Of course, it also hints at the characters' true nature.

DOCTOR WHO 1			COAT OF ARMS		REF 87	PM
DRAWN BY:	PETER MCKINSTRY		DATE: 4/11/09	EP: 6		
PRODUCER:		DIRECTOR:		DOP:		PROPS MASTER:
PROD DESIGNER:		ASSOC DESIGNER:		FABRICATION:		CONSTRUCTION:
SUP ART DIR:		CHIEF SUP ART DIR:		SFX:		CGI:
S/B ART DIR:		SET DECORATOR:		COSTUME:		GRAPHICS:
©BBC CYMRU WALES 2006/2007			OTHER:			

LOCKED 4/11/09

WELL

The well itself was a real feature on location, so my task was to create a design for its surroundings, including a metal archway that would blend in seamlessly. At the same time, I incorporated elements of our Saturnyan design language, as seen in the family crest.

GARGOYLES

The design for the stone gargoyles shows the true form of the Saturnyns; their secret on display, hiding in plain sight.

ORB

The orb forms a pivotal part of the story's climax, when it's revealed that the Saturnyns will use it to flood Venice. For this design, I envisioned that when its outer shell was uncovered, the orb would be full of movement – its internal components revolving and spinning – helping to amplify the chaotic tension of the moment.

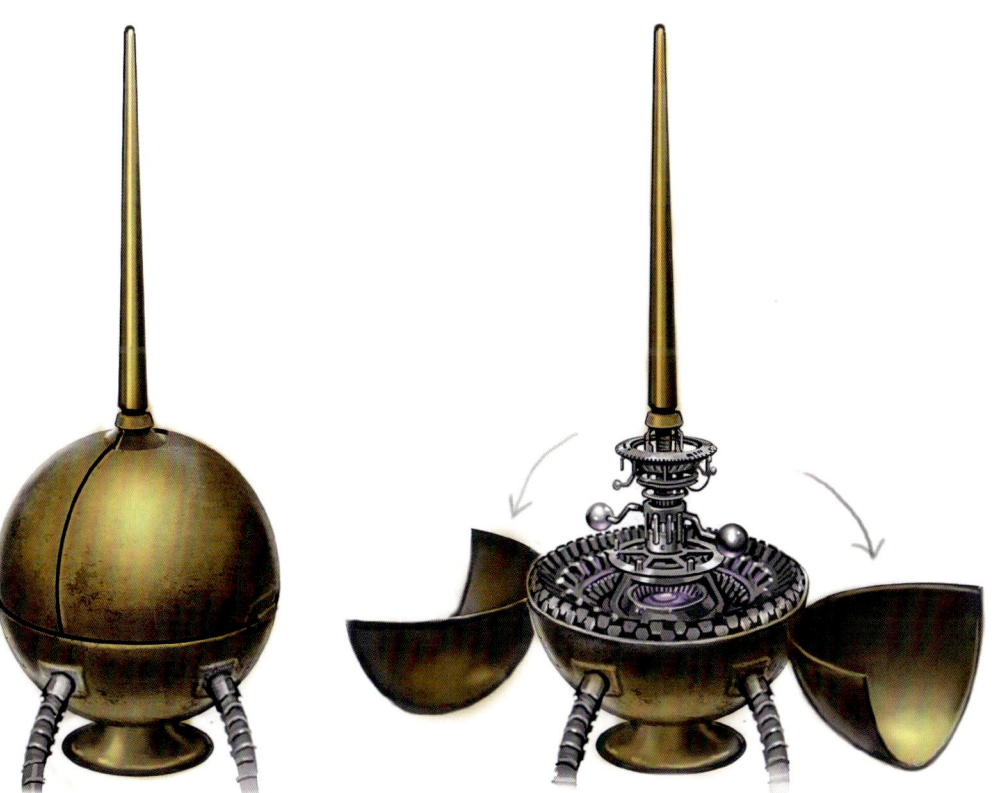

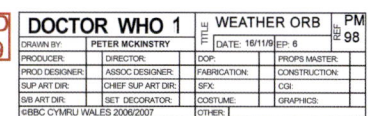

AMY'S CHOICE

EKNODINE MOUTH-EYEBALL CREATURES

Production Buyer Ben Morris was always game for a laugh and willing to be photographed to help create a concept. It was Ben who had posed as a model for me to start the design for the Futurekind in Series 3. I used a photographic basis for these images as I knew Steven and co. would want to see the idea presented as realistically as possible.

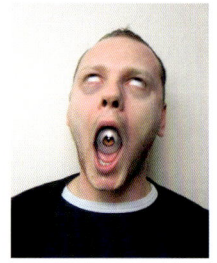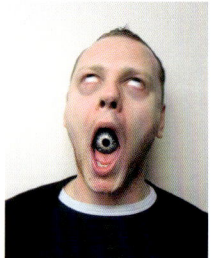
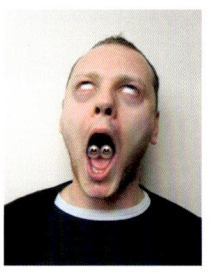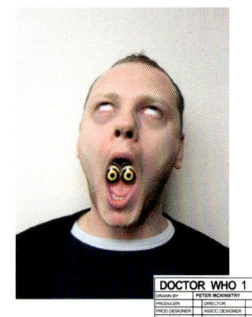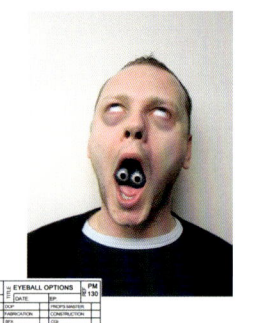

KETTLE

This 'bells and whistles' kettle is a fun design that, due to budget constraints, didn't make it to the screen. I've included it here as an example of creative exploration, a playful take on functionality and design with character.

TARDIS SHIPBUILDERS' PLAQUE

I was asked to produce a simple metal plaque as a bit of extra set detail, seen for a moment when the Doctor is underneath the main console area. Typically, such plaques record details such as the shipyard where the vessel was constructed, the year of completion, and a name or identification number, so there was scope to include some references to established lore. I suggested it should be written in Gallifreyan, but English was chosen – perhaps the TARDIS was translating!

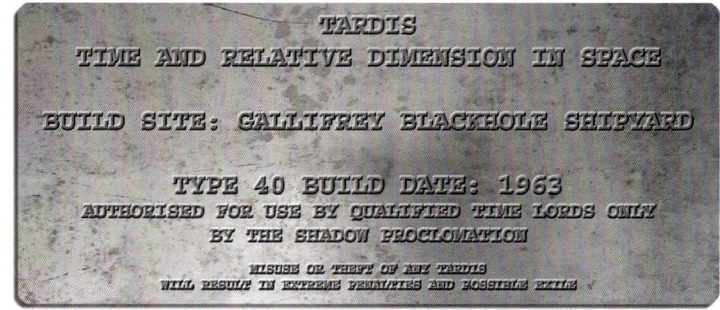

TARDIS CORRIDOR

It had always bothered me that, in the new series of the show, the TARDIS interior beyond the control room was left a mystery (although the wardrobe area had appeared briefly in *The Christmas Invasion* (2005)). As a kid watching the classic series, I'd loved catching glimpses of other spaces: the Zero Room, the Cloister Room, even the swimming pool.

Despite discussions in the art department, the chance to create a doorway leading from the console room had failed to materialise. The most successful version blends elements of both past and present TARDIS designs, with remnants of the old coral structure forming a swirling spiral along the length of the corridor, as if the TARDIS wasn't quite ready to let go of her previous self. Sadly, it was decided – with regret – that a corridor was a luxury rather than a requirement, and plans did not proceed at that time.

THE HUNGRY EARTH / COLD BLOOD

SILURIAN WARRIOR COSTUME

The Silurians seen in this story are revealed to be a different caste of the species, which explains their appearance differing from those in the classic series. My goal with these images wasn't to reinvent the Silurian; that was the job of Millennium FX, who were in charge of creating and applying the prosthetic pieces. My design work focused more on the costume. I included neck rings – stiff jewellery worn around an individual's neck – as used by various cultures throughout history.

LOCKKED
16/9/9

TASER

While it's fun to let your imagination go wild, for certain props the aim was to ground the item in the real world, such as this taser.

LASER SCAPLEL

This finely tuned implement could be used medically or for torture! It needed to look capable of precision work while also appearing to be of non-human origin.

SILURIAN TECH: MEDBAY, LAB, CONSOLE, DISC CONTROL

Ed suggested that the look of the Silurians' subterranean civilisation should be influenced by the work of architect and designer Antoni Gaudí. His use of organic forms and geological textures was incorporated into the story's design to evoke a society that is both ancient and highly advanced. By adapting Gaudí's fluid, nature-inspired aesthetics, the design suggests a civilisation that has evolved in harmony with its environment, blending advanced technology with the natural world in ways beyond human comprehension.

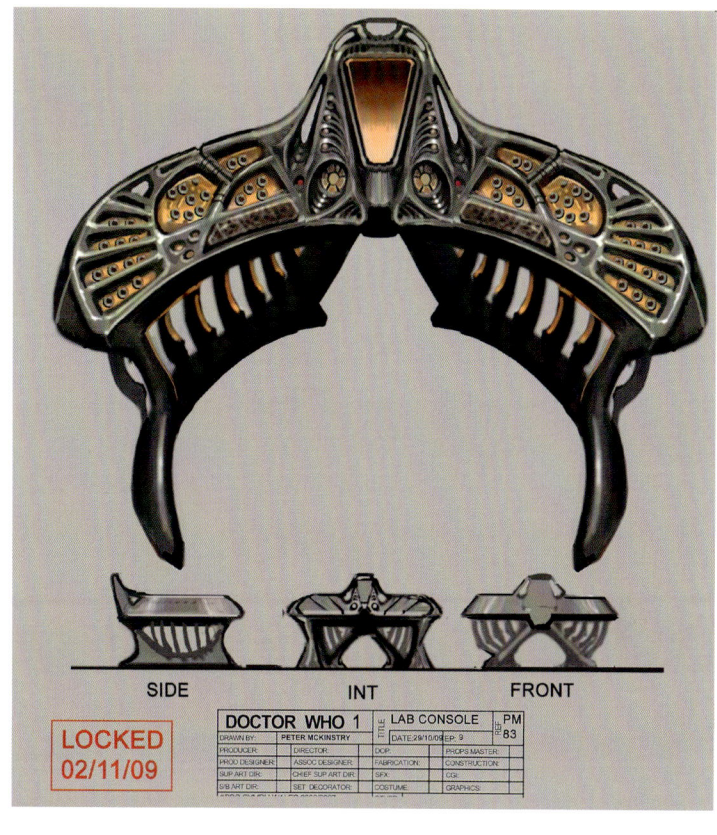

SEISMIC NEEDLE

Another piece of 'heightened' real-world tech, this seismograph was designed to look interesting but clearly recognisable.

VINCENT AND THE DOCTOR

VINCENT'S MONSTER

These designs show ideas I had for the look of Vincent's monster, the final design of which was arrived at during post-production.

The episode writer, Richard Curtis, and his wife, Emma Freud, dropped in on a particularly cold and gloomy day. They both joked that the art department would be nice and cosy – if only the heating worked. Despite the chill, Richard spent time with me, looking over the work-in-progress monster designs and the Visual Recognition Harness.

If I'd known beforehand that I was going to be chatting about *Doctor Who* with the leading writer of British comedy, I probably would have clammed up! Instead, his easy-going manner made it a very enjoyable chat and brought a much-needed burst of energy to the room.

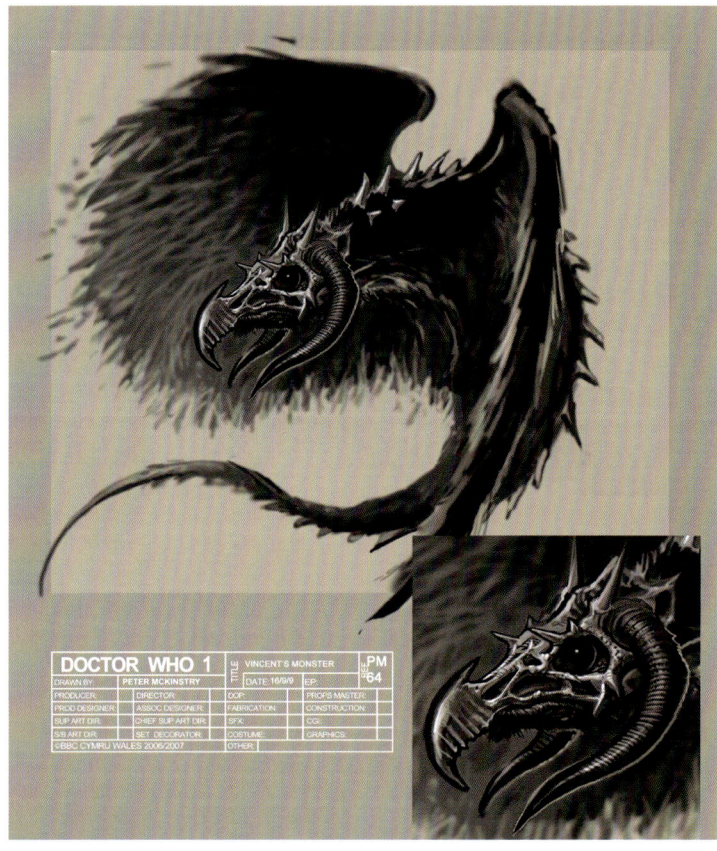

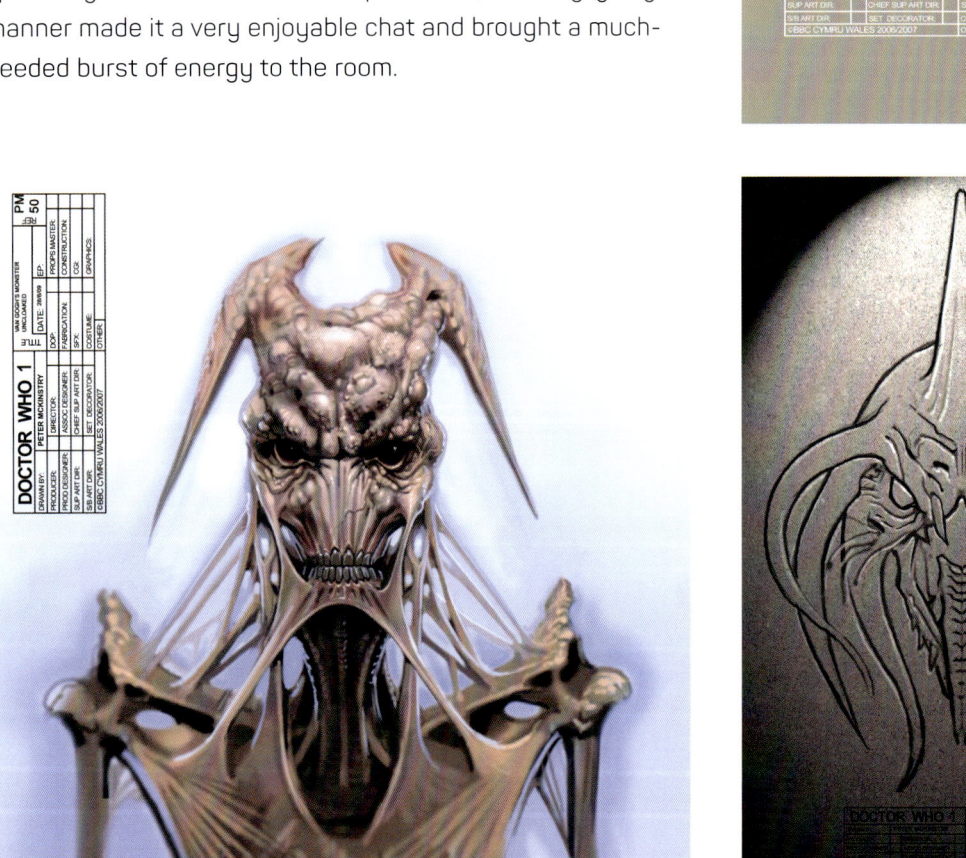

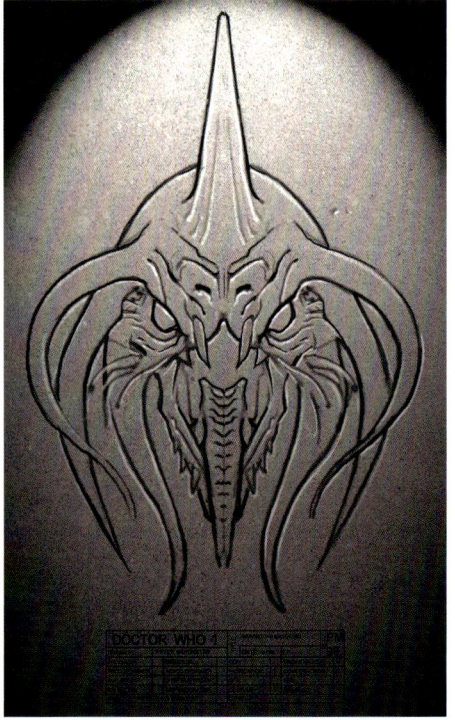

GRAVESTONE

The Krafayis was to be given its own gravestone to mark its passing. However, as the script developed, the idea was dropped and this concept design was no longer needed.

VISUAL RECOGNITION HARNESS

The Doctor's knack for repurposing bits and pieces of existing technology to make something greater than the sum of its parts is what inspired this design; it's not just a generic sci-fi prop, but something that reflects the Doctor's boisterously quirky nature. The goal was to bring a smile of recognition – 'That's so Doctorish!' – and the harness itself is key to the episode, as it allows the Doctor to interact with the creature that only Vincent could hitherto see, the Krafayis.

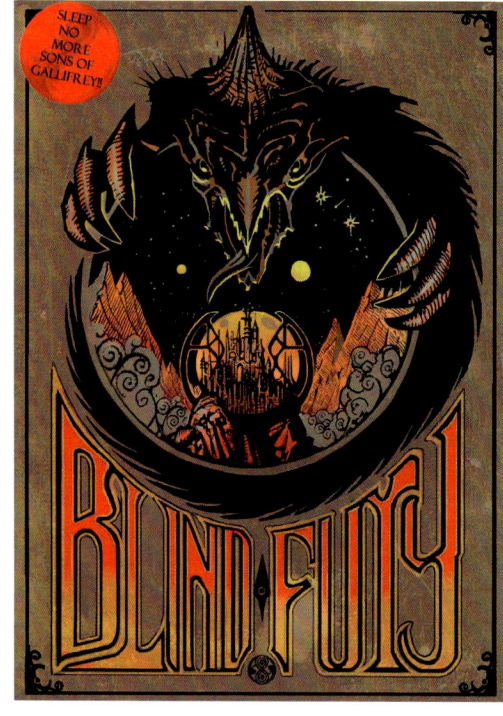

BLIND FURY BOOK COVER

At one point in the script's development, the Krafayis was going to get a little backstory as a scary folk tale told to young Gallifreyans. The Doctor was going to show Amy this book in the TARDIS to explain the creature further.

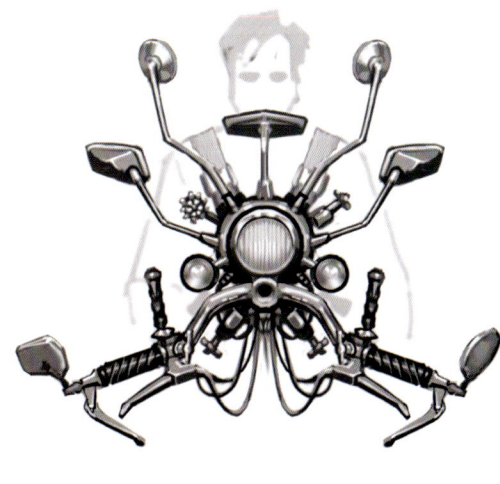

DOCTOR WHO 1		VISUAL RECOGNITION DEVICE		PM	
				96	
DRAWN BY:	PETER MCKINSTRY	DATE: 9/11/9	EP: 6		
PRODUCER:		DIRECTOR:	DOP:	PROPS MASTER:	
PROD DESIGNER:		ASSOC DESIGNER:	FABRICATION:	CONSTRUCTION:	
SUP ART DIR:		CHIEF SUP ART DIR:	SFX:	CGI:	
S/B ART DIR:		SET DECORATOR:	COSTUME:	GRAPHICS:	
©BBC CYMRU WALES 2006/2007			OTHER:		

LOCKED
10/9/9

THE LODGER

TIME ENGINE

Since the Time Engine is someone's attempt to build a TARDIS, I felt it needed to share some visual connections with the Doctor's craft, even if only subtly. The design incorporates a control unit divided into separate panels, echoing the multi-panel TARDIS console, along with a central column reminiscent of the Time Rotor. There are even some roundels. However, to align with the story's tone, the space also needed to feel darker and more unsettling.

The plot revolves around the Time Engine's emergency hologram luring passersby inside for use as potential pilots, only for each candidate to perish. This immediately brought to mind a line from Mary Howitt's famous poem: *'Will you walk into my parlour?' said a spider to a fly.* That inspired the idea of the surrounding columns loosely resembling spider legs, with the great Time Engine looming above like a dangling predator. This design was approved almost instantly, before I had even finished the concept sketch. From there, I refined the design, adding more detail and defining the control panels more clearly.

I'm particularly fond of this design because, throughout my time on the show, I never had the chance to design the TARDIS console room. In a way, this malevolent version makes up for that.

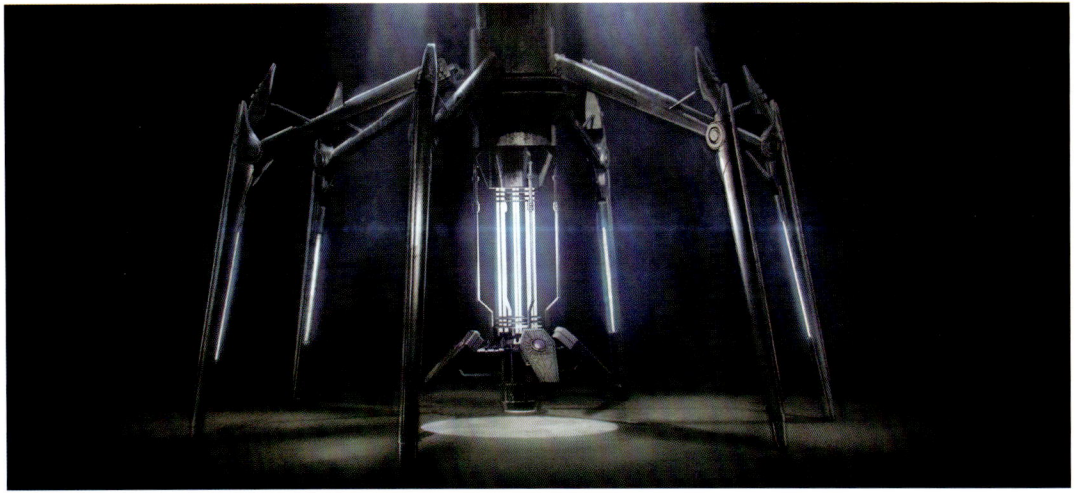

SHIP EXTERIOR

The exterior design of this ship was dictated by its position above Craig's home. The first three sketches were completed before a filming location had been chosen. Once the location was finalised, I was able to refine the design, extending the lower legs to appear as if they had settled into place on Craig's flat. The name *Time Engine* suggested a slightly industrial aesthetic, which influenced the overall look and feel of the ship.

THE DOCTOR'S EARPIECE

The earpiece used by the Doctor to communicate with Amy, who's still on board the TARDIS, is a perfect example of his knack for improvisation. As ever, it's made up of various mundane parts – including the back of the arm from a pair of National Health spectacles, a hi-fi jack, and an earpod – all hastily wired together.

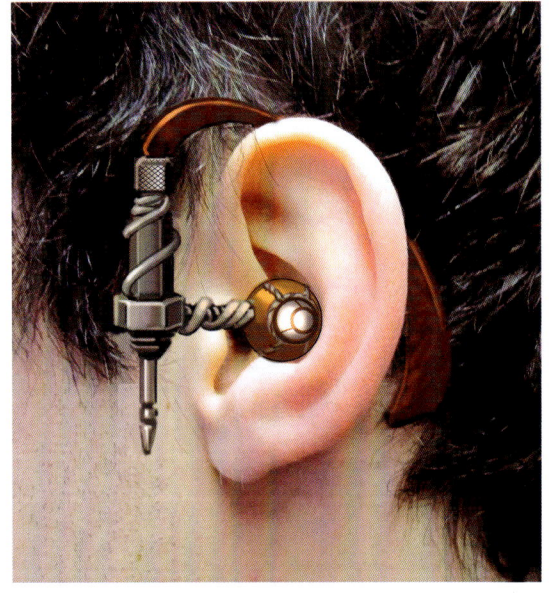

THE DOCTOR'S SCANNER CONTRAPTION

Created using the non-technological technology of Lammasteen, this sophisticated invention was made entirely of objects that the Doctor wheels home in a shopping trolley.

It reminded me of my first day at art school. I had expected to start learning the finer techniques of the old masters. Instead we were sent out to collect junk from the streets, bring it back to class, and create something new. Looking back, it was a strangely accurate precursor to this sort of design brief!

When I saw the finished contraption on set, I was amazed at how closely the props department had followed the original drawings.

A quick note on the sketchiness of these images. The props department didn't need a fully rendered, textured, and beautifully lit image, simply a clear visual guide as to the overall design so they could get on with building it.

AMY SKETCH

This doesn't appear on screen but at one point the Doctor was to be seen doodling this picture of 'Amy Pond – TARDIS Pilot' in Craig's flat.

THE PANDORICA OPENS / THE BIG BANG

RIVER'S GUN

This time around, River used a repainted version of the gun from *Gridlock* (2007). Renamed the alpha-meson blaster, River used it first to destroy a wooden cabinet, then – slightly more impressively – a Dalek made of stone.

CYBER DART

Fired at Amy from an opened Cyberman head, this projectile was the cyborg's last line of defence. I imagined it as capable of incapacitating intruders, tracking them, or even initiating the early stages of cyber-conversion and so incorporated a capsule into the design which could house the necessary technology for those functions.

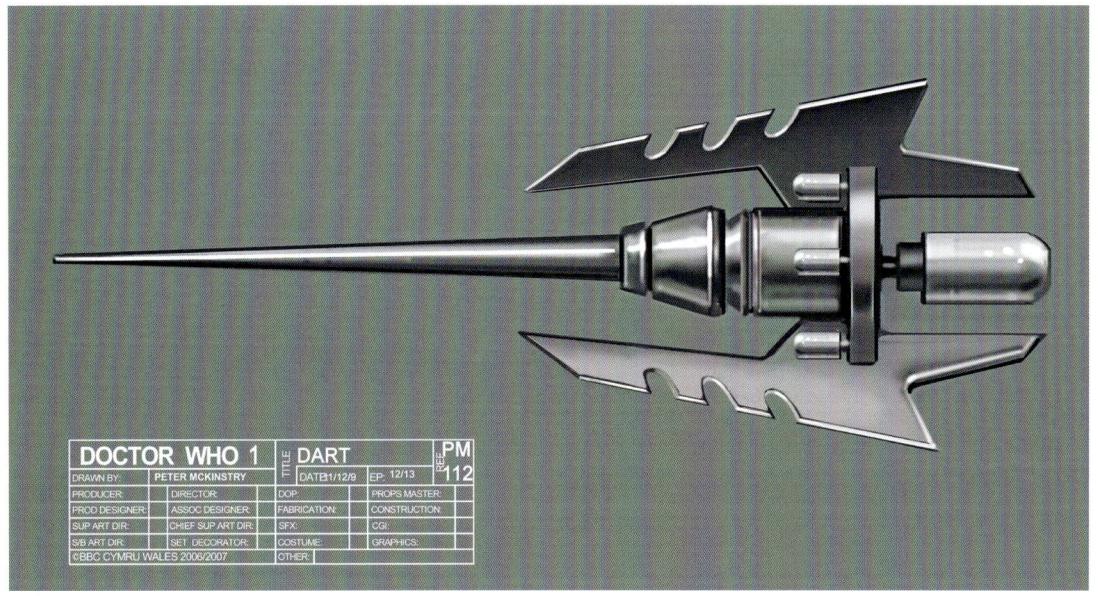

GRAVITY CLAMP

These particular gravity clamps, supplied by River, are used to move one of the giant monoliths at Stonehenge – revealing the stairway down to the sinister Underhenge.

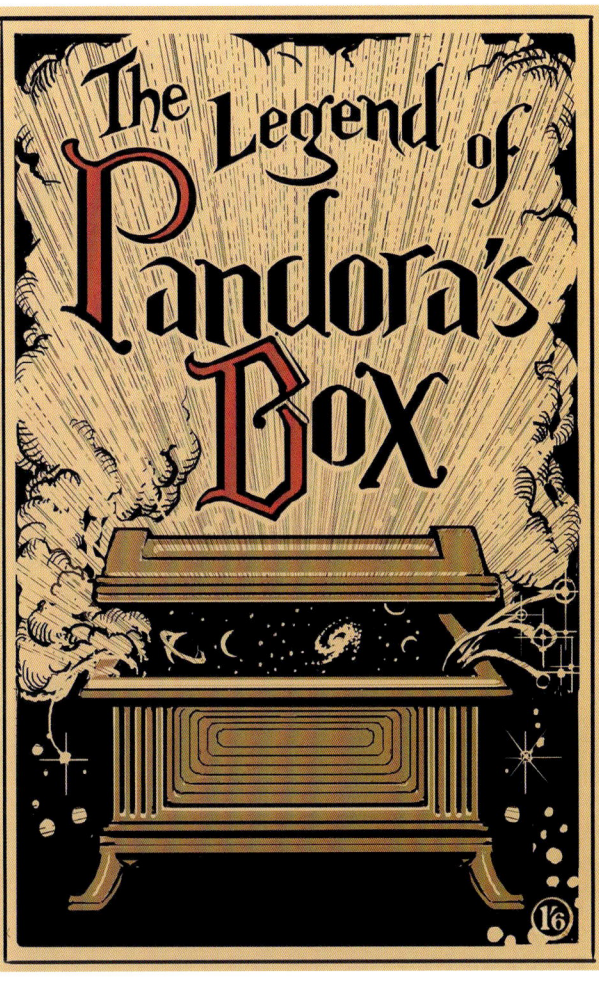

PANDORA'S BOX BOOK COVER

The cover for Amy's childhood copy of *Pandora's Box* was designed in the style of the old Ladybird children's books.

THE PANDORICA AND PANDORICA INTERIOR

I was really excited by the idea of designing a large-scale prop vital to the story. The script described it as:

a gleaming black cube, [each side] about ten feet square... its surfaces are covered in intricate, inlaid patterns. It looks like a black-varnished puzzle-box.

My first version perhaps took the puzzle-box idea a little too far, so I reworked the design, creating a series of concentric circular locks on each face of the cube. That way, I was able to keep the rest of the cube blank, giving it a more monolithic feel. In 'sleep mode' the Pandorica is dark and inert, only to light up and come to life when the Doctor touches it.

Watching the Pandorica design transition from concept art to screen-ready prop excited me just as much as when my telescope from *Tooth and Claw* (2006) had undergone the same process, back at the very beginning of my time on the show. All the details came together exactly as I'd envisioned. Considering this would be my final design to feature in the series, it felt like a fitting, full-circle moment on which to bow out. I'm grateful to have crowned my work on *Doctor Who* with such a memorable element of the show. And an appropriate one too. After all, the Pandorica is used to reboot the universe – the end of one era, and the start of another.

CYBERMEN VARIATIONS

This illustration, in the style of the much-pasticched movie poster for *The Usual Suspects* (1995), presents a line-up of different types of Cybermen from both eras of the show.

(Source: *Doctor Who: The Secret Lives of Monsters* by Justin Richards, BBC Books)

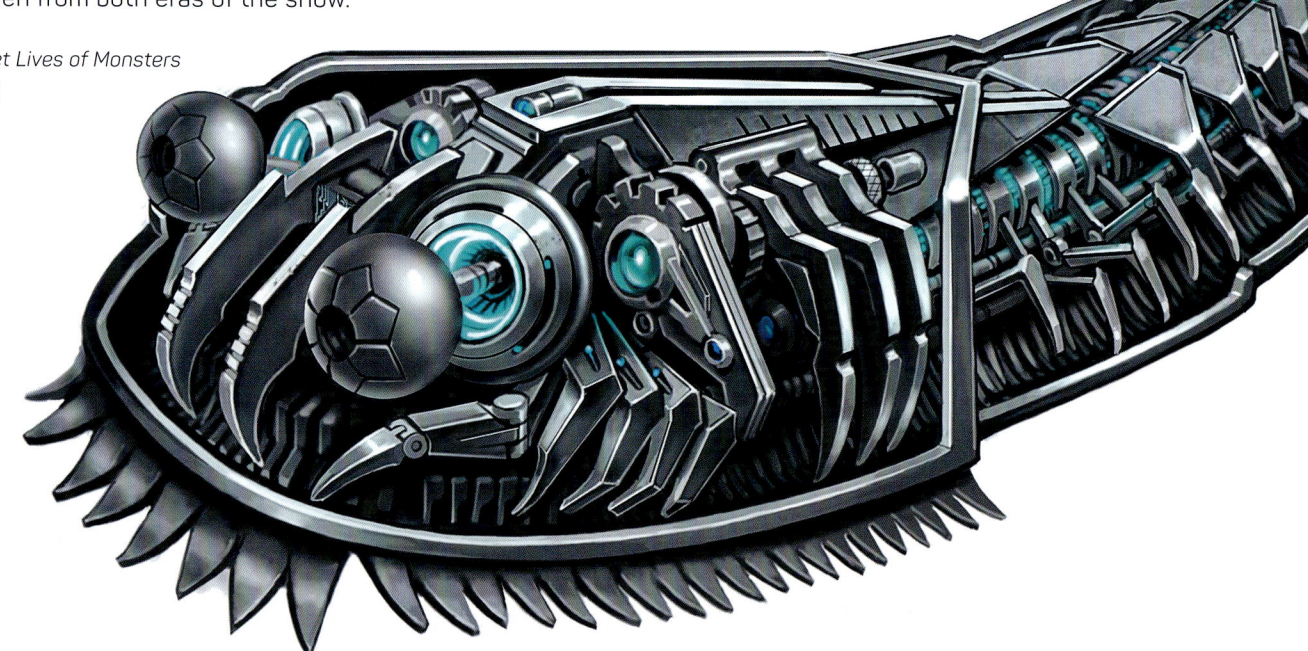

CLASSIC SERIES CYBERMAN – CUTAWAY

The Cybermen are terrifying because they represent the gradual erosion of humanity through technological augmentation. So I wanted to emphasise that while the Cyberman is now mostly machine, there are still traces of the original human form lingering underneath the metal. Vital organs and limbs have been systematically replaced during the Cyber conversion process, leaving only traces of the original subject. Its pose is a nod to a panel from *Junkyard Demon*, a Fourth Doctor comic strip first published in 1981, drawn by the legendary British comic artist Mike McMahon.

(Source: *Doctor Who: The DVD Files* magazine, GE Fabbri)

CYBERMAT – CUTAWAY

Debuting in *The Tomb of the Cybermen* (1967), the Cybermats were robotic critters in the silent-but-deadly vein. By the time they made it into colour in *Revenge of the Cybermen* (1975), the design had been altered – they retained the segmented bodies but the googly eyes had been binned.

(Source: *Doctor Who: The DVD Files* magazine, GE Fabbri)

CYBER-SCOUT – CUTAWAY

Attack of the Cybermen (1985) gave the relentless cyborgs an even more ruthless streak than usual, and overall the production has a harder, edgier tone. The Sixth Doctor's era in general came under fire for its portrayal of violence, and this story – with its brutal executions, torture, and graphic body horror – became notorious in that regard. Still, that raw intensity made the story gritty and impactful, and that's exactly why *Attack of the Cybermen* stands out in my memory.

It also features the only on-screen appearance of the Cyber-Scout. Traditionally, the Cybermen are known for their uniform, metallic look, but this black-suited variant – with special training in reconnaissance or assassination,

perhaps? – indicated that there are specialised roles within the Cyber-ranks. Most importantly, it was a striking image, almost symbolically darker, which fit with the more mature, grim tone of the story itself.

When I came to create this cutaway illustration of the Cyber-Scout, I wanted to reflect its sinister tone, and so I opted for a low angle, with the Cyber-Scout looming over us as if it's just woken from a cryo-nap. Building everything new from scratch in 3D, I made sure to represent various aspects seen on screen, including the metal hand and the chin brace.

(Source: *Doctor Who: The Gold Archive* by Mike Tucker and Steve Cole, BBC Books)

'The greatest thing about both time travel
and creativity isn't where you've been.
It's where you're going next.'

AFTERWORD

Perhaps many people who worked on the show would say the same thing, but I really feel like I had the *best* job on *Doctor Who*.

I didn't carry the weight of responsibility that the 'grown-ups' did: the heads of department with their budget meetings and location recces, or the people at the very top – Russell and Steven and the other execs – bringing the whole thing to life. My job was simple: I got to create, to imagine, and to help bring the Doctor's world to life with every drawing and every design. Teams evolved, ideas came and went, and eventually, it was time to move on. But what we made still exists and is constantly being rewatched and reappraised by new audiences.

As I write this, it's hard to believe that almost 20 years have passed since I first started work on *Doctor Who*. Back then, in the thick of it, I *knew* my future self would look back and relive those years. It's funny how time shifts your perspective. Back then, I knew how special those days were. Now, I see that even the moments that felt ordinary at the time were actually *extra*ordinary, shaping not just the stories we told but the people we became.

When I left, I knew no job could ever match the satisfaction and joy I found working on *Doctor Who*. Whether it was designing a spaceship, creating an alien language or even spray-painting graffiti on set, I embraced every opportunity. That's why I'm always happy to return to the world of *Doctor Who* whenever I'm asked. I grew up a fan, I was a fan while working on the show, and I'm still a fan today.

But as wonderful as it is to look back, *Doctor Who* taught me something important: the future is where the next adventure lies. Because the greatest thing about both time travel and creativity isn't where you've been. It's where you're going next.

Creating this book has been an adventure in itself; another TARDIS trip I've been grateful to take. Perhaps *that's* the art of time travel – not just moving through time but leaving something behind… preferably without creating a paradox or getting trapped in a time loop with a Dalek!

ACKNOWLEDGEMENTS

This book wouldn't have materialised without the following people.

A TARDIS full of gratitude to Russell T Davies for giving this book the green light, providing the foreword, and generously allowing me to include our working emails.

To Mike Tucker, who was the first to see my initial pitch and encouraged me to go for it, and to Albert DePetrillo at BBC Books, for setting it all in motion. Special thanks to Katie Fisher, my editor, and to designer Bobby Birchall – both of whom went above and beyond to help turn a mountain of words and pictures into something beautiful. Thanks also to Steve Cole for his sharp eye and thoughtful edits.

I'm doubly grateful to two key figures of the *Doctor Who* art department, Arwel Jones and Matt Savage – not only for capturing so many great photos back in the day, but also for their kind permission to include them here.

To Eithne and James – Mum and Dad – and my sisters Karen, Maria, Julie, Clare, and Fiona – for cheering me on all the way. And to my sister Kate, the first Whovian in our house, whose shelf of *Doctor Who* Target novels fascinated me as a boy. Kate called me on the evening of my first day on the show and said, 'Keep a diary!' Well, I didn't manage a diary, Kate – but I hope this will do instead.

And finally, to Chris – who I would never have met if I hadn't followed the blue box to Cardiff. Thank you for everything. Always.

BBC BOOKS

UK | USA | Canada | Ireland | Australia
India | New Zealand | South Africa

BBC Books is part of the Penguin Random House group of companies whose addresses can be found at
global.penguinrandomhouse.com

Penguin Random House UK
One Embassy Gardens, 8 Viaduct Gardens, London SW11 7BW

penguin.co.uk
global.penguinrandomhouse.com

First published by BBC Books in 2025
1

Copyright © Peter Mckinstry 2025
Illustrations © Peter Mckinstry 2025

Picture credits: p8, 9, 10 James Mckinstry, p11 Kate Mckinstry, p13, 14, 17 Matt Savage,
p35, 123 Arwel Jones, p185 Maria Kilby

The moral right of the author has been asserted.

Publishing Director: Albert DePetrillo
Editor: Katie Fisher
Production Controller: Percie Bridgwater
Designer: Bobby Birchall, Bobby&Co

Colour origination by Altaimage Ltd
Printed and bound in China by C&C Offset Printing Co., Ltd.

The authorised representative in the EEA is Penguin Random House Ireland, Morrison Chambers,
32 Nassau Street, Dublin D02 YH68.

A CIP catalogue record for this book is available from the British Library

ISBN 9781785949692

Penguin Random House is committed to a sustainable future for our business, our readers and our planet.
This book is made from Forest Stewardship Council® certified paper.